Shakespeare and Ovid

Shakespeare and Ovid

JONATHAN BATE

CLARENDON PRESS · OXFORD

Oxford University Press, Walton Street, Oxford OX2 6DP

Oxford New York
Athens Auckland Bangkok Bombay
Calcutta Cape Town Dar es Salaam Delhi
Florence Hong Kong Istanbul Karachi
Kuala Lumpur Madras Madrid Melbourne
Mexico City Nairobi Paris Singapore
Taipei Tokyo Toronto

and associated companies in
Berlin Ibadan

Oxford is a trade mark of Oxford University Press

Published in the United States
by Oxford University Press Inc., New York

British Library Cataloguing in Publication Data
Data available

Library of Congress Cataloging in Publication Data
Bate, Jonathan.
Shakespeare and Ovid/Jonathan Bate.
Includes bibliographical references and index.
1. Shakespeare, William, 1564–1616—Knowledge—Literature.
2. Ovid, 43 B.C.–17 or 18 A.D. Metamorphoses. 3. Ovid, 43 B.C.–17
or 18 A.D.—Influence. 4. English literature—Roman influences.
5. Mythology, Classical, in literature. 6. Metamorphosis in
literature. 7. Rome in literature. I. Title.
PR2955.086B38 1993
822.3'3—dc20 92–39574
ISBN 0–19–818324–0

Printed in Great Britain
on acid-free paper by
Biddles Ltd.,
Guildford and King's Lynn

For
John Adams, Jonathan Campbell, Alan Hurd
magistri

Preface

People who are interested in Shakespeare are likely at some point to ask themselves about his reading. If you admire a writer, it is natural to wonder which writers that writer admired. For a long time it has been widely agreed that Shakespeare's favourite classical author, probably his favourite author in any language, was Publius Ovidius Naso. Readers who wish to pursue the relationship can consult a large number of specialized studies of particular aspects of it, but no single book which explores it in a variety of ways and across a broad range of works. That is the gap which this study aims to fill.

As will be clear from the length of my bibliography, a single book could never exhaust the subject. By its nature it invites many different approaches, ranging from the minutely linguistic to the broadly conceptual, from consideration of little words which Shakespeare snapped up from Arthur Golding's translation of the *Metamorphoses* to reflection upon such large matters as the representation of sexuality and the function of myth. This book is deliberately eclectic in its approach—sometimes it dwells on particular verbal details, while at other times it proposes less tangible infusions; sometimes it unweaves complex intertextual entanglements, while at others it simply helps the student or theatre-goer to see what Shakespeare is getting at when he alludes to Actaeon or Proserpina. It must, however, be stressed that the aims of the book are more ambitious than those of positivistic 'source-study' often are: what we read does much to make us what we are (or so Renaissance educational theorists believed), so by reading Shakespeare's reading of Ovid we may come to a remarkably full—though not, of course, complete—picture of the sort of artist that Shakespeare was.

Chapter 1 is an introduction to Shakespeare's Ovid and the sixteenth-century Ovid more generally; after what in the Renaissance would have been called an exordium, it surveys Shakespeare's classical education and then the Ovidianism of his immediate forebears in the theatre, John Lyly and Christopher Marlowe. Chapter 2 reads Shakespeare's most directly Ovidian works, his narrative poems, in relation to their sources in the *Metamorphoses* and the *Fasti*.

Chapter 3 considers the Sonnets in the light of Renaissance theories of imitation; it then demonstrates how Shakespeare's first tragedy, *Titus Andronicus*, is explicitly 'patterned' upon Ovid. Chapters 4 and 5 explore the processes of metamorphosis and the uses of mythological allusion in comedy and tragedy respectively. Chapter 4 examines *The Taming of the Shrew*, *A Midsummer Night's Dream*, *Twelfth Night*, and *The Merchant of Venice* in some detail, while treating *As You Like It* and *The Merry Wives of Windsor* more selectively and mentioning the other comedies only in passing (I have written less about the Ovidianism of the comedies than I might have done because others have written about it more); the broad argument of the chapter is supported by a reading of Ben Jonson's *Poetaster*, a play in which Ovid actually appears as a major character. Chapter 5 concentrates on five tragedies which I take to be Ovidian to varying degrees and in a range of ways, *Richard II*, *Romeo and Juliet*, *Othello*, *King Lear*, and *Antony and Cleopatra*. Finally, Chapter 6 argues that the 'late romances' may be considered as dramatic transformations of mythical matter derived from Ovid; after summary discussions of *Cymbeline* and *Pericles*, there are fuller readings of *The Winter's Tale* and *The Tempest*, which I take to be two of the most subtly Ovidian works in the English language. The chapter, and with it the book, ends with a brief discussion of Ovidianism in Shakespeare's collaborations with Fletcher, *The Two Noble Kinsmen* and *Henry VIII*.

In recent years, the possibility of disinterested scholarship has been called into question and it has become customary for critics to stake out a position within or between the competing discourses into which literary studies have disintegrated. So: my orientation is broadly historical, in that the book is an attempt to reconstruct an aspect of the mentality of Shakespeare and his contemporaries. Recent critical developments have helped me to see what I did not see when I began work on the project twelve years ago, that the subject has a political dimension. The so-called New Historicism in Renaissance studies is interested above all in power; for the Renaissance, Ovid was an exemplar of poetic power, a narrator of sexual power, and a victim of political power, so he would seem to be fertile ground for a New Historicist reading. However, it seems to me that the problem with the New Historicism is that it collapses these three different kinds of power into one; Ovid and Shakespeare sometimes do this, but more often they keep them apart and I have followed them in this. Indeed, one of the arguments of the book is that Shakespeare sometimes viewed

Ovidianism as a means to transcend contemporaneity, and in this his Ovidianism is different from that of Spenser and Jonson.

With regard to its own hermeneutical procedures, the book is pluralistic but not radically sceptical, in so far as it follows the Renaissance commentator on Ovid, George Sandys, in the direction of multiplicity—'But why may not this fable receave a double construction? Those being the best that admit of most senses'—but also wants interpretation to be historically grounded. Thus I accept that my interpretations come from me as a reader, but by making a leap of faith and bringing forward a body of evidence I believe that they could also have been Shakespeare's interpretations or those of certain members of his original audience and readership. I like to think of the book as a kind of conversation between Shakespeare and Ovid. It doubles as a conversation between myself and certain current trends in Shakespearian criticism. The first of these conversations is much the more interesting, so the second one takes place between the lines. I have therefore avoided the temptation to translate the shared language of Ovid and Shakespeare ('the myth of Actaeon') into the jargon of the modern academy ('Cixous's feminist revision of Lacan's theory of the gaze').

Among other things, the book is an attempt to salvage a tradition that is rapidly disappearing. I recently encountered a roomful of first-year university students none of whom had heard of Narcissus; nearly all teachers of the humanities in both Britain and America will have had similar experiences. Does that matter? Who cares about old stories in dead languages? In reply to such questions, I want simply to say that it is a fact that not so many centuries ago there was a series of revivals of classical learning in Europe, which for convenience we call the Renaissance, and that those revivals made a major contribution to the spread of literacy, scientific advancement, and political change (in England, these three developments are exemplified by the founding of grammar schools, the method of Bacon, and the seventeenth-century experiment with republicanism, which would not have been possible without the example of Rome). It is modish for criticism to dwell on the barbarisms committed in the name of high culture during the Renaissance, but it seems to me that such an emphasis runs the risk of being counter-productive at a time when the institutional survival of the humanities is something that has to be struggled for. It is no longer easy to make the old high moral claims for the humanities, but I hope to show that Shakespeare's and Ovid's representations of myth, metamorphosis, and sexuality can still work the traditional magic of poetry by moving us—to tears, to laughter, and to thought—and by awakening our wonder.

Acknowledgements

A synoptic treatment such as this will inevitably draw heavily on the work of the many previous scholars who have addressed various aspects of it: my bibliography should accordingly be considered as, among other things, a list of acknowledgements. There has seemed little point in recording specifically which editor or commentator first noted each individual correspondence; but when I am especially indebted to another scholar or I wish to suggest where the reader might go for further development of a particular argument, I have included footnotes. My greatest scholarly debt is to T. W. Baldwin's monumental *William Shakspere's Small Latine and Lesse Greeke*; my critical thinking has been especially stimulated by four books, Leonard Barkan's *The Gods Made Flesh : Metamorphosis and the Pursuit of Paganism*, William Carroll's *The Metamorphoses of Shakespearian Comedy*, Thomas M. Greene's *The Light in Troy : Imitation and Discovery in Renaissance Poetry*, and William Keach's *Elizabethan Erotic Narratives : Irony and Pathos in the Ovidian Poetry of Shakespeare, Marlowe and their Contemporaries*.

For permission to use revised and expanded versions of previously published material, I am grateful to Cambridge University Press (for articles on *Othello*, *King Lear*, and the Sonnets in *Shakespeare Survey*, vols. 41 and 42 (1989, 1990)) and to Andrew Gurr (for an article on *Venus and Adonis* in the *Yearbook of English Studies*, vol. 23 (1993)). The most extensive revisions are those from the article 'Ovid and the Sonnets; or, Did Shakespeare Feel the Anxiety of Influence?' (*Shakespeare Survey*, vol. 42) to the first part of Chapter 3: explicit reference to Harold Bloom's ahistorical theory of 'The Anxiety of Influence' is dropped and the historical argument is bolstered.

For their comments on all or part of the typescript, I am deeply indebted to Leonard Barkan, Catherine Belsey, Warren Boutcher, Edward Burns, Tom Craik, Richard Gaskin, Peter Holland, John Kerrigan, and Tony Taylor. I would also like to thank Christopher Ridgway for more general critical advice and Hilary Gaskin for constancy in change. This book is partly about Shakespeare's debt to his grammar-school education, so the dedication reflects my debt to mine. Oscar Wilde said in *The Critic as Artist* that criticism is the only civilized form of autobiography, so I shall record that my father was a teacher of the classics and that of all my books this is the one that I wish he could have lived to read.

Contents

Abbreviations

Aen.	Virgil, *Aeneid*
Ars Am.	Ovid, *Ars Amatoria*
CL	*Comparative Literature*
ELH	*ELH: Journal of English Literary History*
ELN	*English Language Notes*
ELR	*English Literary Renaissance*
Her.	Ovid, *Heroides*
HLQ	*Huntington Library Quarterly*
JEGP	*Journal of English and Germanic Philology*
JMRS	*Journal of Medieval and Renaissance Studies*
Met.	Ovid, *Metamorphoses*
MLN	*Modern Language Notes*
MLQ	*Modern Language Quarterly*
MLR	*Modern Language Review*
MP	*Modern Philology*
N&Q	*Notes and Queries*
NS	new series
PQ	*Philological Quarterly*
RenQ	*Renaissance Quarterly*
RES	*Review of English Studies*
SEL	*Studies in English Literature, 1500–1900*
ShS	*Shakespeare Survey*
SP	*Studies in Philology*
SQ	*Shakespeare Quarterly*
TAPA	*Transactions of the American Philological Association*
Trist.	Ovid, *Tristia*
TSLL	*Texas Studies in Literature and Language*

Abbreviation of titles of Shakespearian works follows standard practice.

A Note on References

Quotations from Shakespeare are followed by line reference to the Oxford *Complete Works* of Stanley Wells and Gary Taylor (1986; quoted from Compact Edition, 1988), though occasionally, when I disagree with their editorial decisions, I have silently emended. So, for example, the Oxford edition's 'seamews' revert to the 'scamels' given to Caliban in the First Folio. In particular, it should be noted that I use the names Iachimo and Imogen rather than Giacomo and Innogen, since even if the Oxford renamings are true in the first case to the principle of modernization of spelling and in the second to the first performance of *Cymbeline* (and I have doubts on both these fronts), the received names have entered so deeply into English culture that it seems to me fruitless to undo them now. Having said this, I would wish to add that I find the Oxford edition especially valuable precisely because it forces the attentive reader to rethink detail after detail in Shakespeare's text. Readers using other texts will find that the Oxford scene divisions sometimes vary from the customary practice of earlier editions; *King Lear* is quoted from the Folio version unless otherwise stated.

Quotations from Ovid are also followed by line reference; I have used the Loeb texts. Arthur Golding's translation of the *Metamorphoses* is quoted from the edition of W. H. D. Rouse, which went under the title of *Shakespeare's Ovid* (1904, repr. 1961); Golding's touch is sometimes heavy, so on some occasions when Ovid's lightness is important to my argument I have quoted from A. D. Melville's splendid Oxford World's Classics translation (1987). One aim of my book is to convince those who enjoy Shakespeare that they will also enjoy Ovid; fascinating as it is to read the translation which Shakespeare read, the Latinless may well find Melville's the most accessible version. Translations into prose are my own, though they frequently make use of the Loeb.

Quotations from Shakespeare's other sources are followed by reference to Geoffrey Bullough's *Narrative and Dramatic Sources of Shakespeare* (8 vols., 1957–75).

—Lucius, what book is that she tosseth so?
—Grandsire, 'tis Ovid's *Metamorphoses*;
My mother gave it me.

(*Titus Andronicus*, IV. i. 41–3)

Everything existed of old, everything happens again,
And only the moment of recognition is sweet.

(Osip Mandelstam, 'Tristia')

I

Shakespeare and the Renaissance Ovid

Ovidius, surnamed *Naso*, Borne in *Sulmo*, brought up in Rome, and dylygentlye instructed in latyne letters from his tender age, he gave most dylygente studye to the makynge of verses, from the whiche he was withdrawen by his father, and put to learne Rhetorike, wherein a while he much profyted and was in the numbre of the best oratours of that tyme, and was advaunced to sundrye authorities, and made a Senatour. Not withstandynge he chiefely dedicated himselfe to poetrie, wherein by nature he was excellent in facilitie and abundance of sentences. He was in good favour with the emperour Augustus, of whom at the laste he was exiled into Pontus, where he spente the reste of his lyfe in a towne called *Tomos*, among people most barbarous, who not withstandynge lamented his death, for his courtesie and gentle maners. The cause of his exile is uncertaine, savynge some suppose it was for abusynge Julia, daughter of the emperour Augustus, although the pretence of the emperour was for the makynge of the booke of the crafte of love, wherby yonge myndes myght be styred to wantonnes. He lyved at the tyme when Christ our saviour was conversaunt with us here on earth.[1]

I

We need stories to help us make sense of the world. Things change. Men and women are driven, powerfully if not exclusively, by sexual desire (men in more aggressive ways). Myth, metamorphosis, sexuality: doubtless Shakespeare knew something about them by instinct; as a young man who got an older woman pregnant and then

---

[1] Thomas Cooper, *Thesaurus Linguae Romanae et Britannicae . . . Accessit dictionarium historicum et poëticum propria vocabula* (London, 1565), sig. N2^v–N3^r. Cooper is correct that Ovid held some minor administrative positions in his early adult life, but in fact the poet withdrew from politics shortly before he would have been due to attain senatorial rank. Technically, Ovid was relegated rather than exiled: this meant that he retained his property and his civic rights but he was banished from Rome itself—but banishment to Tomis on the Black Sea, at the distant edge of the Empire, was an unusually severe form of relegation.

married her, he must have known a good deal about one of them from experience; but much of his most profound and characteristic thinking about them was derived from his reading of Ovid.

The enchantment which the law student from Sulmona exercised over the grammar-school boy from Stratford-upon-Avon was a matter of style as well as substance. Through the mouth of Holofernes the schoolmaster, the dramatist wittily apostrophized his own favourite classical poet: 'for the elegancy, facility, and golden cadence of poesy . . . Ovidius Naso was the man: and why indeed "Naso" but for smelling out the odoriferous flowers of fancy, the jerks of invention?'[2] 'Naso' is, of course, from the Latin for 'nose'; the poet's very name is made to embody the gift for verbal play which Shakespeare inherited from him and which is exhibited to supreme effect in the drama in which Holofernes appears, *Love's Labour's Lost.* Ovid was the epitome of poetic stylishness: what better model for the ambitious young Elizabethan writer? The title-page of *Venus and Adonis,* the first work which Shakespeare saw into print, was adorned with an epigraph from the *Amores,* a proclamation of the poem's affiliation: 'Vilia miretur vulgus; mihi flavus Apollo | Pocula Castalia plena ministret aqua'—'Let what is cheap excite the marvel of the crowd; for me may golden Apollo minister full cups from the Castalian fount' (*Amores,* I. xv. 35–6). Ovid is claimed as Shakespeare's route to the Castalian spring on the side of Parnassus, which is to say as his source of inspiration and his guarantor of high cultural status, his way of rising above the 'vulgus'. The poem from which the epigraph is quoted ends with the claim that poetry is a way of cheating death— the claim which is also that of Shakespeare's Sonnets and which is borne out every time Shakespeare reanimates Ovid and every time we reanimate either of them in the act of reading.

Ovid's inspiriting of Shakespeare seems to have been recognized ever since 1598, when Francis Meres undertook an exercise in the art of simile entitled 'A Comparative Discourse of our English Poets with the Greeke, Latine, and Italian Poets'. Not all of Meres's comparisons have been borne out by literary history—William Warner is no longer thought of as 'our English Homer'—but one of them is justly famous: 'As the soule of Euphorbus was thought to live in Pythagoras: so the sweete wittie soule of Ovid lives in mellifluous and hony-tongued Shakespeare, witness his *Venus and Adonis,* his *Lucrece,* his sugred

---

[2] *Love's Labour's Lost,* IV. ii. 122–5.

Sonnets among his private friends, &c.' Meres went on to assert that 'As Plautus and Seneca are accounted the best for Comedy and Tragedy among the Latines: so Shakespeare among the English is the most excellent in both kinds for the stage'.[3] But this was not to say that Ovid's influence was restricted to Shakespeare's non-dramatic works, for the comparison with Plautus and Seneca is simply made in terms of shared excellence, whereas that with Ovid is phrased in such a way as to imply both stylistic and spiritual resemblance. The soul that has been metamorphosed into Shakespeare is that of Ovid, the poet of metamorphosis. Pythagorean metempsychosis, as expounded in the fifteenth book of the *Metamorphoses*, becomes a figure for the translation of one poet into another.[4]

In support of Meres, one could list many points of similarity: a method of composition which involves shaping inherited stories in such a way that they are wrought completely anew; a refusal to submit to the decorums of genre, a delight in the juxtaposition of contrasting tones—the tragic and the grotesque, the comic and the pathetic, the cynical and the magnanimous; an interest above all else in human psychology, particularly the psychology of desire in its many varieties; an exploration of the transformations wrought by extremes of emotion; a delight in rhetorical ingenuity, verbal fertility, linguistic play; variety and flexibility as fundamental habits of mind and forms of expression. The Ovidian and the Shakespearian self is always in motion, always in pursuit or flight. And, bewilderingly, one can never be sure whether one is running towards what one desires or running away from it: no myth is more emblematic of the worlds of the two writers than that of Actaeon, the hunter who in punishment for his gaze upon the naked Diana becomes the hunted. When you think you've seen what you most desire, it destroys you.[5]

Recent criticism has been much concerned with 'the flexibility of the self in Renaissance literature'.[6] Such criticism has not always recognized that the flexible self has a prime classical exemplar in

[3] Meres, *Palladis Tamia*, in *Elizabethan Critical Essays*, ed. G. Gregory Smith, 2 vols. (Oxford, 1904), ii. 317–18.

[4] Dryden uses the figure in this way in the Preface to his *Fables*: 'Spenser more than once insinuates that the soul of Chaucer was transfused into his body'—*Of Dramatic Poesy and other Critical Essays*, ed. George Watson, 2 vols. (London, 1962), ii. 270.

[5] For the centrality of the Actaeon myth to the poetics of desire in the Renaissance from Petrarch onwards, see Nancy Vickers, 'Diana Described: Scattered Woman and Scattered Rhyme', *Critical Inquiry*, viii (1981–2), 265–79.

[6] The quotation is of the title of Thomas M. Greene's seminal essay, in *The Disciplines of Criticism: Essays in Literary Theory, Interpretation, and History*, ed. Peter Demetz,

Ovid.[7] There could be no better motto for the Renaissance self-fashioner than some lines in the *Ars Amatoria*, which Shakespeare's fellow-dramatist Thomas Heywood translated as follows:

> He that is apt will in himself devise
> Innumerable shapes of fit disguise,
> To shift and change like *Proteus*, whom we see,
> A Lyon first, a Boar, and then a Tree.[8]

The *Ars* is about how you fashion yourself as a lover; it recognizes that the well-fashioned lover is dextrous in the assumption of poses (you may even have to fake orgasm) and the handling of masks (Ovid also wrote a verse treatise on facial cosmetics). It also recognizes that the fashioning of the self is limited by the constraints of social convention and ultimately of state power; ironically for Ovid himself, this point was proved drastically when Augustus exiled him from Rome, partly because the poem appeared to be advocating sexual licence in general and female adultery in particular at a time when the Emperor was pursuing a programme of domestic moral reform. The specific impulse for the banishment of the poet in AD 8, a decade after the writing of the *Ars*, seems to have been connected with the adultery of the Emperor's granddaughter, Julia, who was also exiled that year. Nine years earlier, Augustus' daughter, Julia's mother, also called Julia, had committed the same offence—Renaissance commentators confused the two Julias: hence Thomas Cooper's phrase, 'for abusynge Julia, daughter of the emperour Augustus', in the biography of Ovid cited at the beginning of this chapter. The confusion between the two Julias, and the identification of them with the 'Corinna' of Ovid's *Amores*, goes back at least as far as Sidonius Apollinaris in the fifth century.[9]

What the *Ars* argues in its mock-didactics, the *Amores* exemplify in their nimble practice; the flexible self in these love elegies is the poet himself, working through a repertoire of attitudes and voices, writing as both subject and object, both poet and lover, in anticipation of the manner of Elizabethan love-poets like Sidney and Shakespeare in their sonnet sequences. Though theirs is a poetry of frustration and his of

Thomas Greene, and Lowry Nelson, Jr. (New Haven, Conn., 1968), 241–64. The definitive treatment of the subject is Stephen Greenblatt's *Renaissance Self-Fashioning: From More to Shakespeare* (Chicago, 1980).

[7] A notable exception is Richard A. Lanham, in his splendid study *The Motives of Eloquence: Literary Rhetoric in the Renaissance* (New Haven, Conn., 1976).

[8] *Ovid De Arte Amandi, And the Remedy of Love Englished*, trans. Heywood, quoted from edn. of 1682, p. 32 (from bk. 1, ll. 759–62).

[9] See Ronald Syme, *History in Ovid* (Oxford, 1978), 215.

consummation, Petrarch could not have created Laura or Sidney Stella without the example of Ovid's Corinna.[10] But Ovid is not only a self-dramatizer: in the *Heroides* and the *Metamorphoses*, he dramatizes others, most notably victims of desire, many of them women. The females who speak the *Heroides* and a variety of related figures in the *Metamorphoses*, for instance Myrrha and Medea, are among the models for the soliloquizing that is the distinctive activity of Shakespeare's most admired characters. The Ovidian dramatic monologue and the Shakespearian soliloquy create the illusion that a fictional being has an interior life. This illusion is achieved principally by the arts of language. The character's 'self' is both created and transformed by the very process of verbal articulation; her or his 'being' is invented rhetorically. In Shakespeare, of course, the verbal rhetoric inherited from Ovid and other classical exemplars is accompanied by a new visual rhetoric of stage gestures and actions.

To think of Shakespeare as an Elizabethan Ovid is to see him as a typical, if exceptionally gifted, product of his age. Renaissance thinkers believed passionately that the present could learn from the past; the belief was the starting-point of education and a formative influence upon writing in the period. It was the essence of what we now call Renaissance humanism. The great Spanish humanist Juan Luis Vives acknowledged that 'It is true there are those men who persuade themselves that a knowledge of antiquity is useless, because the method of living all over the world is changed, as for example in the erection of elegant dwellings, the manner of waging war, of governing people and states'. But he went on to claim that such an opinion was 'opposed to the judgement of wise men' and therefore against reason. 'To be sure,' he wrote,

no one can deny that everything has changed, and continues to change, every day, because these changes spring from our volition and industry. But similar changes do not ever take place in the essential nature of human beings, that is in the foundations of the affections of the human mind, and the results which they produce on actions and volitions. This fact has far more significance than the raising of such questions as to how the ancients built their houses or how they clothed themselves. For what greater practical wisdom is there than to know how and what the human passions are: how they are roused, how quelled?[11]

---

[10] For Sidney's Ovid, via Petrarch, see Paul Allen Miller, 'Sidney, Petrarch, and Ovid, or Imitation as Subversion', *ELH* lviii (1991), 499–522.

[11] *Vives on Education: A Translation of the De tradendis disciplinis of Juan Luis Vives*, trans. Foster Watson (Cambridge, 1913), 232.

The passage occurs in Vives' treatise of 1531, *De tradendis disciplinis*, 'on the transmission of knowledge'. There is no more vital humanist activity than the translation of the classics with the aim of transmitting knowledge, making the wisdom of the past available in the vernacular. Shakespeare was a product of the educational revolution in which Vives played a part: he was trained to value the classics and he was glad to use the new translations of them, such as Sir Thomas North's version of Plutarch's *Lives of the Noble Grecians and Romanes*. As a dramatist and hence a student of what Vives calls the 'human passions', he was especially interested in the classical texts in which the extremes of emotion were explored. Among these, none was more congenial to him than Ovid's *Metamorphoses*. This, I suspect, was partly because his sceptical, dynamic temperament would have had a certain resistance to the humanist implication that 'the essential nature of human beings' does not change; what Ovid taught him was that everything changes—'In all the world there is not that that standeth at a stay', as the character of Pythagoras sums it up in Book Fifteen[12]—and this accorded with his desire as a dramatist to examine human beings at key moments of change in their lives, such as when they fall in love or make a renunciation or, most drastically, decide to kill themselves. Ovid's philosophy of instability modified the 'essentialist' premiss of humanism even as his exemplary force sustained it.

I use the word 'essentialism' to mean 'the belief that we possess some given, unalterable essence or nature in virtue of which we are human'.[13] The passage from Vives is a magisterial statement of this belief, though elsewhere, for example in his *Fabula de homine* of 1518, the same writer posits a more protean, Ovidian view of human nature: he imagines Jupiter sitting in an auditorium and watching man on a stage demonstrating his capability to become 'all things', one moment lion, wolf, boar, fox, and donkey (emblematic of the passions), the next a prudent and just civic being.[14] One reason why

---

[12] Golding's trans. xv. 197.

[13] Jonathan Dollimore, *Radical Tragedy: Religion, Ideology and Power in the Drama of Shakespeare and his Contemporaries* (Brighton, 1984), 18.

[14] 'A Fable about Man', trans. Nancy Lenkeith, in *The Renaissance Philosophy of Man*, ed. Ernst Cassirer, Paul Oskar Kristeller, John Herman Randall, Jr. (Chicago, 1948), 385–93. Proteus is also cited in Pico della Mirandola's discussion of man's self-fashioning power in the great 'Oration on the Dignity of Man', repr. in the same collection (p. 225).

Ovid was so valuable to sceptical humanists like Vives, Montaigne, and Shakespeare was that the fifteenth book of the *Metamorphoses* provided a beautiful solution to the problem of instability and change. Change itself becomes constancy, instability a fixed principle: the humanist is thus able to retain his faith that there is an essence in both human and non-human nature, whilst acknowledging the infinite variety of human passions and actions.

Readers who have inherited John Milton's image of Shakespeare in the poem 'L'Allegro' as 'Fancy's child', 'warbling his native wood-notes wild', will be puzzled by claims that he can be read in the context of Renaissance humanism and that his plays have an especially close relationship with the work of a classical author. Didn't Ben Jonson write in his elegy 'To the Memory of My Beloved, the Author Mr William Shakespeare', 'thou hadst small Latine, and lesse Greeke'? What about John Dryden's claim in the essay *Of Dramatic Poesy* that Shakespeare 'needed not the spectacles of books to read nature'? These are, however, relative statements: Shakespeare may have been unlearned by the standards of the Jonson who furnished his play *Sejanus* with marginal notes written in Latin or the Dryden who translated the complete works of Virgil, yet the classical accomplishments of the average Elizabethan grammar-school boy were considerable indeed by the standard of most of us today. And if 'lesse Greeke' really means 'less' rather than 'no', Shakespeare would have been above average, for Greek was only studied in the upper forms of the better schools, and it was not begun until Latin had been thoroughly mastered.

In his *Essay on the Learning of Shakespeare*, published in 1767, Richard Farmer, whose standards were those of the Master of a Cambridge college, showed that Shakespeare used Sir Thomas North's translation of Plutarch, and Arthur Golding's of Ovid, and furthermore that Plautus' *Menaechmi*, the principal source for *The Comedy of Errors*, his most formally classical play, had been done into English (albeit unpublished) by Warner. Dr Johnson was impressed: 'Dr Farmer,' he said, 'you have done that which never was done before; that is, you have completely finished a controversy beyond all further doubt.'[15] But the scholarship of the subsequent two centuries has decided the question in the opposite direction: although Shakespeare used translations when he could, presumably for speed

[15] Quoted, James Northcote, *Memoirs of Sir Joshua Reynolds* (London, 1813), 90.

and convenience, he did read sources in Latin and French—in the
case of Ovid he did not rely solely on Golding's Englished *Metamorphoses* of 1567.

His use of both the Latin original and the early Elizabethan
translation may be demonstrated from his most powerful imitation of
Ovid, Prospero's renunciation of his rough magic. The relevant
passage in Ovid begins 'auraeque et venti montesque amnesque
lacusque, | dique omnes nemorum, dique omnes noctis adeste', of
which a literal translation might be 'ye breezes and winds and
mountains and rivers and lakes, and all ye gods of groves and of night,
draw near' (*Met.* vii. 197–8). Golding translated this as 'Ye Ayres and
windes: ye Elves of Hilles, of Brookes, of Woods alone, | Of standing
Lakes, and of the Night approche ye everychone' (Golding, vii.
265–6). The first line of Prospero's speech is 'Ye elves of hills, brooks,
standing lakes, and groves' (*Tempest*, v. i. 33). Shakespeare got his
elves from Golding (in Ovid they are 'gods' and are not associated with
the hills) and he also followed the translator in amplifying 'lacus' into
'*standing* lakes'. But later in the speech, where Ovid had 'convulsaque
robora' ('and rooted up oaks'), Golding did not specify the kind of tree
('and trees doe drawe'), so Shakespeare must have gone to the Latin
for his 'and rifted Jove's stout oak'. Again, Golding lacks an
equivalent for the ghosts actually coming out of their tombs:
Prospero's 'Graves at my command | Have waked their sleepers,
oped, *and let 'em forth*' is a version of Ovid's 'manesque *exire* sepulcris'.
Medea in Ovid says that she has made the sun go pale by means of her
song ('carmine nostro'); Golding has 'Our Sorcerie dimmes the
Morning faire'; Shakespeare neatly combines the song and the
sorcery with Prospero's climactic 'By my so potent art', the art being
that of both the sorcerer and the poet-singer. Medea's use of the noun
'carmen' allies her with Ovid himself, for he began the *Metamorphoses*
with a reference to his own unbroken song, 'perpetuum carmen'
(i. 4); in a similar way, the phrase 'my so potent art', spoken by a
character who has a little earlier put on a play, cannot but ally
Prospero's magic with the magic of Shakespeare's verbal and
theatrical arts. This is not, however, to say that Prospero's
renunciation of his magic is Shakespeare's farewell to the stage.[16]

[16] On Shakespeare's use of both Golding and Ovid's Latin as an example of
Renaissance imitative practice, see Marion Trousdale's important article, 'Recurrence
and Renaissance: Rhetorical Imitation in Ascham and Sturm', *ELR* vi (1976), 156–79
(pp. 172–4).

The fact of Shakespeare's imitation of Ovid is beyond dispute; it is much more difficult to be sure of its implications. Were Jacobean audiences of *The Tempest* supposed to recognize the imitation and, if so, were they then supposed to reflect upon Prospero's art in relation to that of Ovid's Medea? Charles and Michelle Martindale, in their book on *Shakespeare and the Uses of Antiquity*, think that the answer to the first part of the question is probably 'yes', to the second part, definitely 'no':

In this instance it should be plain that the use Shakespeare is making of Ovid is imitative, not allusive; educated members of the audience would recognize the presence of Ovid, but there is no question of any such complex interplay between the divergent meanings of the two texts as our more ingenious critics so often suppose.[17]

I believe that the Martindales are wrong about this. The distinction between stylistic imitation and purposeful allusion would not have been made in this way in the Renaissance. Sixteenth-century models of reading were always purposeful: texts from the past were valued for their applicability to present endeavour.[18] Hence the widespread habit of extracting wise passages from their sources and transcribing them in 'commonplace' books which built up a composite model of ideal behaviour. In writing Prospero's speech, Shakespeare is following a standard humanist procedure: he needed a formal invocation of magical powers, so he imitated a famous classical example of one. To imitate it was to assert its continuing relevance; humanist imitation was based on the premiss that classical texts were appropriate patterns or models because they embodied fundamental, enduring truths. This was the point that Vives made. The act of imitation here implies that all invocations of magical power are in some sense the same—just as a Renaissance imitation of an Ovidian *locus amoenus* implies that all *loci amoeni* are in some sense the same—and therefore that Prospero and Medea are in some sense the same. This has important critical implications for the play, as will be shown in Chapter 6. In that chapter, further evidence will be brought forward to suggest that the imitation is an allusion and is supposed to be

---

[17] *Shakespeare and the Uses of Antiquity* (London, 1990), 23.

[18] See Anthony Grafton, 'Renaissance Readers and Ancient Texts: Comments on some Commentaries', *RenQ* xxviii (1985), 615–49, and Lisa Jardine and Anthony Grafton, ' "Studied for Action": How Gabriel Harvey Read his Livy', *Past and Present*, no. 129 (Nov. 1990), 30–78.

recognized as such. What I mean by allusion is that the source text is *brought into play* (from Latin *al-ludo*, to play with); its presence does significant aesthetic work of a sort which cannot be performed by a submerged source.

It should also be pointed out that the Martindales' sneer at 'our more ingenious critics' is oddly patronizing to the Renaissance. It implies that Shakespeare and his audience were simple souls who never got beyond stylistic elegance, who lacked the ingenuity to make associations between dramatic characters and mythical archetypes. But Renaissance mythography was as inventive as anything in modern critical theory. Despite the reservations of humanists such as Erasmus, for whom myth was a repository of moral wisdom rather than a system of mystical correspondences,[19] the tradition of multiple interpretation, inherited and adapted from the Middle Ages, was still very much alive. Edmund Spenser, say, or George Sandys, author of *Ovid's Metamorphosis Englished, Mythologiz'd, and Represented in Figures*, would have had no difficulty in finding historical, moral, and allegorical meanings in a single story. Sir John Harington's reading, published in 1591, of the slaying of the Gorgon Medusa by Perseus is worth quoting at length as an example of this interpretative technique:

Perseus sonne of Jupiter is fained by the Poets to have slaine *Gorgon*, and, after that conquest atchieved, to have flown up to heaven. The Historicall sence is this, *Perseus* the sonne of *Jupiter*, by the participation of *Jupiters* vertues which were in him, or rather comming of the stock of one of the kings of Creet, or Athens so called, slew *Gorgon*, a tyrant in that countrey (*Gorgon* in Greeke signifieth earth), and was for his vertuous parts exalted by men up unto heaven. Morally it signifieth this much: *Perseus* a wise man, sonne of Jupiter, endewed with vertue from above, slayeth sinne and vice, a thing base & earthly signified by Gorgon, and so mounteth up to the skie of vertue. It signifies in one kind of Allegorie thus much: the mind of man being gotten by God, and so the childe of God killing and vanquishing the earthlinesse of this Gorgonicall nature, ascendeth up to the understanding of heavenly things, of high things, of eternal things, in which contemplacion consisteth the perfection of man: this is the naturall allegory, because man [is] one of the chiefe works of nature. It hath also a more high and heavenly Allegorie, that the heavenly nature, daughter of *Jupiter*, procuring with her continuall

---

[19] For humanist opposition to the reading of pagan myths as Christian allegories, see Erasmus' letter of 7 May 1518 to Maarten Lips, no. 843 in *The Correspondence of Erasmus: Letters 842 to 992, 1518 to 1519*, trans. R. A. B. Mynors and D. F. S. Thomson, vol. vi of the *Collected Works of Erasmus* (Toronto, 1982), 23–4.

motion corruption and mortality in the inferiour bodies, severed it selfe at last from these earthly bodies, and flew up on high, and there remaineth for ever. It hath also another Theological Allegorie: that the angelicall nature, daughter of the most high God the creator of all things, killing & overcomming all bodily substance, signified by *Gorgon*, ascended into heaven. The like infinite Allegories I could pike out of other Poeticall fictions, save that I would avoid tediousnes.[20]

Readers who are inclined to accuse modern critics of over-ingeniousness should keep an analysis such as this beside them as a touchstone of Renaissance ingenuity. As will be shown, even Shakespeare, whose hermeneutics were much less formal than Harington's are in this passage, frequently invoked myths as patterns within the plays, and when invoking myths sometimes also assumed knowledge of the received moral interpretation of them. When Cleopatra says that Antony is 'painted one way like a Gorgon', it is left to the audience to supply the interpretation of the simile.

Harington's interpretative strategy is premissed on the conviction that allegory shadows forth a universal interconnectedness; this enables him to pull together pagan narrative and divine revelation, and thus to defend poetry from the strictures of puritans.[21] Ultimately, both the practice of humanist imitation and Renaissance hermeneutics more generally draw strength from a belief in the readability of the world: myths, classical texts, nature itself, are books in which moral truths may be read. Thus not only are all *loci amoeni* alike, they may all be read as vestiges of the classical Golden Age, which, according to the syncretic way of thinking so much favoured in the Renaissance, is itself equivalent to Eden before the Fall.

Mythological allusion pervades Elizabethan and Jacobean writing, as I will demonstrate later in this chapter from the examples of Lyly and Marlowe. For it to have been worth its place in the drama, dramatists must have presumed that at least a proportion of their

---

[20] 'A Preface, or rather a Briefe Apologie of Poetrie', prefixed to Harington's 1591 trans. of Ariosto's *Orlando Furioso*, quoted from *Elizabethan Critical Essays*, ii. 202–3.

[21] I follow Jonas Barish, *The Anti-Theatrical Prejudice* (Berkeley, Los Angeles, and London, 1981) in using 'puritan' as a convenient term for all those who attacked the English Renaissance stage on moral grounds. Stephen Gosson, the most influential anti-stage polemicist of the late 16th cent., was not in fact in sympathy with Elizabethan puritanism; he was almost certainly commissioned by the city fathers to attack the stage because of concern over 'absenteeism, law and order, public decency, infection and the danger of sedition'—Margot Heinemann, *Puritanism and Theatre* (Cambridge, 1980), 30.

auditory was capable of 'reading' it. Having described the different ways of interpreting the story of Perseus and the Gorgon, Harington anatomized Renaissance readers into three kinds: 'the weaker capacities will feede themselves with the pleasantnes of the historie and sweetnes of the verse, some that have stronger stomackes will as it were take a further taste of the Morall sence, a third sort, more high conceited then they, will digest the Allegorie' (p. 203). Ben Jonson made a similar, though twofold, distinction with regard to the audience for theatrical shows: he contrasted those with 'grounded judgements' who merely used their 'gaze' to enjoy the spectacle, and 'the sharpe and learned' who had the wit to comprehend his allegories.[22] Shakespeare's colleagues, John Heminges and Henry Condell, addressed the First Folio of 1623 'To the great Variety of Readers', who, they said, were numbered 'From the most able, to him that can but spell'. The great variety of playgoers who frequented the Rose, the Globe, and the Blackfriars in Shakespeare's lifetime covered a similar spectrum; the most able—the university and Inns of Court men—would have been intimately versed in both classical texts and the art of allegorical interpretation, while even those who had read but little would have had a rudimentary working knowledge of ancient mythology. And for Elizabethan culture, Ovid's *Metamorphoses* constituted the richest storehouse of that mythology.[23]

Shakespeare's ideal spectator would have shared the dramatist's own grammar-school education. The comic but affectionate portrayals of pedantic schoolmasters in *Love's Labour's Lost* and *The Merry Wives of Windsor* suggest that Shakespeare may often have been bored at school, but they leave no room for doubt that he did go to school. John Aubrey, on the not wholly unreliable testimony of the son of a member of Shakespeare's acting company, established a tradition that in the so-called 'lost years' of the 1580s Shakespeare was himself a schoolmaster; E. A. J. Honigmann has recently proposed that those years were spent as tutor to a Catholic family in Lancashire, and that the recommendation for this post may have come from a Stratford schoolmaster with a high opinion of

[22] *Ben Jonson*, ed. C. H. Herford, Percy and Evelyn Simpson, 11 vols. (Oxford, 1925–52), vii. 91. All quotations from Jonson are from this ed.; those from the plays are followed in my text by line references.

[23] Its only possible rival was Boccaccio's *De Genealogia Deorum*, which was frequently reprinted in the period—but it was not studied in schools as Ovid was, and it did not have the 'elegancy, facility, and golden cadence of poesy' which was so highly valued by the Elizabethans.

Shakespeare's accomplishments.[24] Even if we discount these scholastic possibilities, we cannot question the competence of Shakespeare's Latin, small as it may have been by Ben Jonson's prodigious standards. Latin was the substance of the grammar-school curriculum (it is to Latin that the epithet 'grammar' applies); and within that curriculum, Ovid occupied a very special place, as will be shown in the next section of this chapter. Shakespeare got a good enough education for him to be able to base his *Lucrece* on a story in Ovid's *Fasti*, which was not published in an English translation until well after his death.

I do not suppose for a moment that any individual seventeenth-century reader of Shakespeare, still less a playgoer, would have consciously recognized, let alone reflected upon the significance of, all the Ovidian associations which I discuss in this book. Where professional critical readers pursue their theme with relentless single-mindedness, readers for pleasure and, to an even greater degree, playgoers—both Renaissance and modern—attend to many different facets of the Shakespearian text and cannot always be expected to attend to it at all (in the Elizabethan theatre there would have been a lot of distractions, what with nut-cracking neighbours and prostitutes plying their trade). A literary-historical book of this sort by its nature regularizes and gives apparent unity to connections that an ordinary reading or viewing will only make fragmentarily and spasmodically. But by picking out the figure in the carpet it becomes possible to discern that Shakespeare was an extremely intelligent and sympathetic reader of Ovid and that his readings are embedded in his own works. And I am convinced that every individual connection I make could have been perceived by an educated Elizabethan: it must be stressed again that the method of reading which this book adopts is a Renaissance method. For the Renaissance, reading meant reading with a consciousness of the classics. The author of the *Gesta Grayorum*, an account of the revels at Gray's Inn during the winter of 1594–5, considered *The Comedy of Errors* to be 'like to *Plautus* his *Menechmus*'.[25] This book imagines other educated Elizabethan playgoers returning to Shakespeare's works and again and again finding them, despite the differences of genre, like to Ovid his *Metamorphoses*.

[24] Honigmann, *Shakespeare: The 'Lost Years'* (Manchester, 1985).
[25] See the relevant extract from *Gesta Grayorum*, repr. as app. 2 of R. A. Foakes's Arden edn. of *The Comedy of Errors* (London, 1962), 116.

As I affirmed in my preface, one compelling reason for writing a study of Shakespeare and Ovid at this time is the simple fact that fewer and fewer students and playgoers are now versed in the classics as their Renaissance forebears were. Dramatists like Shakespeare and Thomas Heywood did not want the classics to be what they have now become, the preserve of a tiny intellectual élite. They took Ovid out of the academy and put him on the popular stage; in his *Golden Age*, *Silver Age*, *Brazen Age*, and *Iron Age* plays, Heywood actually dramatized a whole collection of stories from the *Metamorphoses* for the audience of the Red Bull, the most notoriously 'lowbrow' of the London theatres.[26] In the prologue to *The Silver Age*, he made a distinction regarding his audience that was similar to Jonson's: the 'learned' come to the theatre with their 'judging wits', while the 'ruder' respond only with their 'eyes'.[27] The prologue continues, 'Since what we do, we for their use compile': 'their' refers to both segments of the audience, which is to say that Heywood is compiling his mythological material for the 'use' of all kinds of theatregoer. In the epilogue to *The Brazen Age*, he addressed the 'unlettered' in the audience, asking them 'Rather to attend than judge; for more than sight | We seeke to please'.[28] Heywood was writing at a time when the morality of the theatre was under attack from puritan polemicists: there could be no better riposte than the claim that the drama could traverse 'The ground of ancient Poems' and bring edification of the kind that was the rationale of humanist educational theory.[29] Indeed, performance could evoke the substance (*res*) of ancient poems,

---

[26] Heywood used a copybook Renaissance method of composition: first he wrote *Troia Britanica*, a Spenserian romance epic, based on William Caxton's prose translation of Raoul Lefevre's *Recuyell of the Historyes of Troye*, the influential medieval repository of classical matter, much of it transmitted via Ovid; then he dramatized his own poem, but in so doing made extensive use of Ovid, in both the Latin original and Golding's translation. As well as producing the *Age* plays and translating the *Ars Amatoria*, Heywood wrote an Ovidian erotic narrative, *Oenone and Paris*, and dramatized the story of the rape of Lucrece. The shared Ovidianism of Heywood and Shakespeare is symbolically demonstrated by the implicit attribution to Shakespeare on the title-page of the third (1612) edn. of *The Passionate Pilgrim* of Heywood's imitations of the Paris and Helen letters of the *Heroides*, which were lifted from the *Troia Britanica* and included in that volume.

[27] Heywood, *The Dramatic Works*, 6 vols. (London, 1874), iii. 85–6. Subsequent references from this edn.

[28] *Dramatic Works*, iii. 256.

[29] Quotation from the closing sequence of *The Golden Age*, *Dramatic Works*, iii. 78. In his *Apology for Actors* (London, 1612), Heywood defended the drama by citing the positive and negative moral examples afforded by the classical narratives which he staged in the *Age* plays (sig. F4^v–G1^v).

whereas education was locked into analysis of their grammar, syntax, and rhetoric (*verba*); the drama brought the classics to life, whereas the techniques of the schoolroom killed them stone dead. In his own way, Shakespeare had anticipated Heywood in this project: my third chapter will suggest that in *Titus Andronicus* he undertook both a critique of a schoolroom education and a defence of a theatrical one. Shakespeare's Ovidianism proposes that the classics need not be only a matter of rote-learning and beatings, of Sir Hugh Evans's 'hig, hag, hog' and 'If you forget your *quis*, your *ques*, and your *quods*, you must be preeches'.[30] Elizabethan theatrical Ovidianism constitutes an exceptionally fruitful embrace between 'high' and 'low' culture; it proves that the classics can reach a popular audience, can give pleasure even as they edify, can be a source of profound vitality.

Shakespeare enjoyed Ovid hugely, but also found in him a source of disturbance. The coexistence of vitality, enjoyment, and disturbance is apparent above all in the matter for which Ovid was best known in the Renaissance, that of human desire and sexuality. Sexual behaviour is of course determined by culture as well as nature, but culture has its continuities: in the *Ars Amatoria*, Ovid associates theatregoing with sex, noting that the theatre is a good place to take a prospective lover, since 'the rows compel closeness, like it or not, and by the conditions of space your girl must be touched' (*Ars Am.* i. 141–2). This is as good a piece of advice for the young man about town in Shakespeare's time or in ours as for Ovid's implied reader. Whether Ovid is advising on such preliminaries or on the art of achieving simultaneous orgasm (*Ars Am.* ii. 719–28), he has a modernity which may be seen as testimony to literature's power to continue to work beyond its moment of production. Using the *Ars Amatoria* as a sex manual may not be quite what the learned humanists had in mind when they recommended the study of the classics, but the efficacy of doing so proves their point that we can learn from the literature of the past. Roman marriage, Elizabethan marriage, and modern marriage are very different things, but to read Ovid and Shakespeare today is to see that neither the lightness nor the darkness of sexual desire has changed so very much over two millenniums.

This continuity might seem to offer support for Vives' claim about 'the essential nature of human beings'. His grand phrase 'the

[30] *Merry Wives of Windsor*, IV. i. 38, 71–2.

foundations of the affections of the human mind, and the results
which they produce on actions and volitions' could be translated into
Sigmund Freud's single word, *libido*. Freud himself viewed both
classical myth and Shakespearian drama as anticipations, and hence
proofs, of his own 'essentialist' account of human sexuality. There
has accordingly been a steady stream of books and articles translating
the language of Shakespeare's plays into that of psychoanalysis—
every student knows about Hamlet's Oedipus complex. I am,
however, sceptical of this procedure and I have done everything I can
to avoid such translation, on the grounds that it is tendentious
enough to move between the languages of texts composed for
particular purposes in Rome around the beginning of the Christian
era and in London around the beginning of the seventeenth century
without also introducing that of texts which Freud composed for
particular purposes in Vienna around the beginning of the twentieth.
Shakespeare's representations of sexuality may be Freudian—or
Kleinian or Lacanian—but my concern is to show that they are
Ovidian.

Freud notwithstanding, the fact that these representations still
elicit a nod of recognition does not necessarily mean that the
dynamics of sexual desire are universally constant. Their endurance
may instead be a demonstration of the way in which life imitates art.
That sexuality is learnt from poets as much as it is determined by
biology would seem to be the view of Montaigne in the sixteenth
century's wisest and most playful essay on the subject, 'Upon some
Verses of Virgil': there it is argued that the 'power and might' of erotic
desire 'are found more quick and lively in the shadowe of the Poesie,
th[a]n in their owne essence'. For Montaigne, literature serves to
educate the reader in sexual language: 'It is high time indeed for us to
go studie the phrases of *Amadis*, the metaphors of *Aretine*, and
eloquence of *Boccace*'—that is to say, to study erotic texts—'thereby
to become more skilfull, more ready and more sufficient to confront
them: surely we bestow our time wel'.[31] As one recent commentator
on the mythological tradition in the French Renaissance puts it,
'When Montaigne turns to himself he finds that it is not in searching
his own memory that he recovers most fully the experience of love,

[31] *The Essayes or Morall, Politike, and Millitarie Discourses of Lo. Michaell de Montaigne*,
trans. John Florio (1603), iii. 5, quoted from Modern Library edn. (New York, 1933),
introd. J. I. M. Stewart, pp. 764, 771.

but in reading the stylised formulations of poetic fiction.'[32] In Shakespearian comedy, love is among other things an art learnt from Ovid.

Ovid was not of course the first poet to make sex full of both fun and anguish, but for Western culture he has been the one in whom the joy of sex has found its foremost apologist and the pain of desire one of its most skilled analysts. This is due in considerable measure to the hazards of manuscript transmission in pre-print culture: had more of Sappho survived, she might have taken the credit. Indeed, Ovid would have been the first to acknowledge the supremacy of Sappho. In the *Tristia* (ii. 365) she is cited as his precedent as a teacher of the art of love, and in the fifteenth of the *Heroides* he writes in her voice and so celebrates her poetry even as he ironically twists her lesbianism by making her the victim of heterosexual desire:

> But once I seemed beautiful enough, when I read my poems to you.
> > You swore that, alone among women, I took grace always from the words I spoke.
> I would sing, I remember—lovers remember it all—
> > As I sang, you returned me my kisses, kisses stolen while I sang.[33]

Whilst listening to Ovid's reanimation of Sappho, we should take the opportunity to acknowledge that his writing can be charged with a sexual intensity which Shakespeare was wholly incapable of reproducing (in the Elizabethan age only Donne comes near it).[34] Here, for instance, is a translation of what must be Western poetry's most stirring account of a woman's wet dream:

> My dreams bring you back to me:
> > dreams more intense and dazzling than radiant day.
> I find you in those dreams, although you are worlds away.
> > But sleep offers pleasures too brief to satisfy.
> Often it seems that your arms are holding the weight of my neck,
> > often I seem to be holding your head in my arms;

---

[32] Ann Moss, *Poetry and Fable: Studies in Mythological Narrative in Sixteenth-Century France* (Cambridge, 1984), 4.

[33] *Heroides*, xv. 41–4, in the lovely trans. of Florence Verducci, in her study of the *Heroides*, *Ovid's Toyshop of the Heart* (Princeton, NJ, 1985). The authorship of this epistle has been contested, but it is hard to doubt it in view of Ovid's claim in the *Amores* (ii. xviii. 26) that he has spoken for Sappho.

[34] Donne's elegies are masterly exercises in the tradition of the *Amores* (Elegy xix, for instance, takes off from *Amores*, i. v) and his 'Sapho to Philaenis' is a revision of *Heroides* xv which restores Sappho to a lesbian partner.

the kisses are familiar, those kisses, tongue to tongue, I recognize them,
    the kisses you used to take and give back to me.
Sometimes I caress you, and say words that seem utterly real,
    and my lips are awake, responsive to all that I feel.
I hesitate to say what happens next, but it all happens,
    there's no choice, just joy, and I'm inundated with it.[35]

In the arena of sexuality, Ovid was both an original and an
inheritor of Sappho and others; in that of myth, he was equally both
an innovator and a rewriter of material from a vast range of earlier
writers, most notably Euripides and Callimachus. He did not invent
his stories, he just happened to have codified them and told them in an
artful and memorable way at an unusually stable moment in early
Western culture. The idea of myth presents as many theoretical
problems as that of sexuality. Again, my aim has been to present the
material in the terms of Ovid and his Renaissance readers, not to
translate it into those of some later theorist. There may be a book to be
written on Shakespeare and the *Metamorphoses* in relation to Claude
Lévi-Strauss's theory that myths encode the deep binary structures of
all cultures, but this is not it. Jacques Derrida's essay on Lévi-Strauss,
'Structure, Sign and Play in the Discourse of the Human Sciences', is
one of the foundation texts of deconstruction, but my aim is to
reconstruct, not deconstruct Renaissance mythography. There is a
certain smack of Derridean hermeneutic play about Sir John
Harington's multiplication of readings of the Gorgon myth, but with a
crucial difference: for a Renaissance reader multiple readings offer
many roads to truth, whereas for Derrida reading is a circular road
going to nowhere but itself. In order to understand the work that
myth does for Shakespeare—and to try out for ourselves whether it
can do any work for us—we have to suspend our disbelief in the
possibility of words and stories referring to a reality beyond
themselves. We certainly do not have to believe that Shakespeare's
sonnets were written out of personal desire for the Earl of
Southampton or whoever, but we do have to believe that even if desire
may be read as a textual phenomenon, as Montaigne seems to imply,
love-poetry can be made to serve extra-textual ends. We do not have
to believe in gods; we do not even have to believe that Shakespeare
and Ovid believed in them. But we do have to believe in the reality of

---

[35] *Heroides*, xv. 123–34, trans. Verducci. 'Inundated' for the orgasm in the final line
does not quite catch Ovid's witty use of a negative: 'et siccae non licet esse mihi' ('and I
am unable to remain dry').

the human conditions and aspirations that are storied in myth—negatively, that desire is often blind (Cupid) or self-consuming (Narcissus, Actaeon); positively, that a marriage might be blessed (Hymen), a harvest might be good (Ceres), or society a fairer place (the Golden Age). In its assumption that one of the values of literary and dramatic creations is their capacity to speak of such conditions and aspirations, this book is unapologetically a work of reconstructed humanism.

II

Shakespeare was fortunate in his place of birth. In 1553 the King's New School at Stratford-upon-Avon was chartered as a free grammar school that would employ one master who was to be comparatively well remunerated with twenty pounds a year and housing.[36] Shakespeare probably entered the grammar school at the age of seven in 1571, having already spent two or three years at an attached petty school where, under the auspices of an usher, he would have learnt reading, writing, and the catechism. The grammar-school master from 1571 to 1575 was one Simon Hunt, and for the next four years the post was held by Thomas Jenkins. They both seem to have been able men, with Oxford degrees; Jenkins had for some years been a fellow of St John's College. A measure of the quality of the Stratford education is that Richard Field, a near contemporary of Shakespeare, began an apprenticeship in London after leaving school and rapidly became one of England's best printers of classical texts—his work included an important annotated edition of the *Metamorphoses* published in 1589. It was to Field that Shakespeare turned a few years after this for the printing of his *Venus and Adonis* and *Lucrece*.

The grammar-school curriculum was limited but intense. It depended on learning by rote: Shakespeare and his contemporaries had Latin words and structures ingrained upon their memories in such a way that classical influences would inevitably shape their verbal forms in later life. The principal aim of an Elizabethan education was for the student to learn not merely to read Latin with

[36] The following account makes considerable use of T. W. Baldwin, *William Shakspere's Small Latine and Lesse Greeke*, 2 vols. (Urbana, Ill., 1944), which remains the most comprehensive guide to the Elizabethan grammar-school curriculum and its influence on Shakespeare.

facility, but also to write and speak it. He (girls did not attend the grammar school) would begin with William Lily's *A Shorte Introduction of Grammar* and complete his accidence and syntax in the same author's *Brevissima Institutio*, which was illustrated with examples from various Latin authors, such as the line from Horace that Chiron in *Titus Andronicus* remembers from reading in his grammar. At this early stage, he would also be required to construe and translate from collections of maxims such as Leonhardus Culmannus' *Sententiae Pueriles* and the *Disticha Moralia* (ascribed to Cato, with scholia by Erasmus). These collections provided the origin of many of the tags and *sententiae* that are found so frequently in Elizabethan and Jacobean drama. It was a favourite Renaissance practice to extract moral wisdom from the classics in the form of adages and apophthegms; the educated members of Shakespeare's audience would accordingly have been adept in the art of recognizing classical allusions, whether they were highly self-conscious, as in some of the early works, or woven more subtly into the text, as in the later plays.

At a later stage, the *sententiae* in Culmannus and Cato would provide the basis for rhetorical exercises in amplification. Thus not only the pithiness, but also the prolixity and rhetorical inventiveness of Elizabethan writers have their roots in the educational system. One of the major rhetorical texts used in schools was Erasmus' *De Copia*, which instructed in the art of using tropes and schemes to imitate classical copiousness; Ovid was seen here as the most copious of authors, his description of Hecuba in the thirteenth book of the *Metamorphoses* as the exemplary illustration of the use of extreme 'copia' to create emotion. Dramatic laments in plays from *Gorboduc* onwards make Hecuba into 'a mirror' of woefulness.[37] The player's speech in *Hamlet*, with its accumulation of figures designed to elicit sympathy for the passion of Hecuba, is a standard rhetorical set-piece. But although any grammar-school boy would have been given the training to have a stab at the exercise, few could have undertaken it with the facility of Shakespeare. His contemporaries recognized and appreciated this, praising his distinctive qualities with such epithets as 'sweet', 'honie-tong'd', 'hony-flowing Vaine', 'fine filed phrase', 'happy and copious', 'mellifluous'. These were the terms in which the

---

[37] 'Happy was Hecuba, the woefull'st wretch | That ever liv'd to make a mirror of': *Gorboduc*, III. i. 14–15, in *Minor Elizabethan Tragedies*, ed. T. W. Craik (London, 1974). See further, Wolfgang Clemen, *English Tragedy Before Shakespeare*, trans. T. S. Dorsch (London, 1961), 230–2.

Elizabethans also praised Ovid. Gabriel Harvey spoke of 'conceited' Ovid, Thomas Lodge of his 'promptnes' in versification; to Thomas Nashe, he was 'silver-tong'd' and 'well-tun'd' in his style.[38] The two writers offered respective Latin and English exemplars of facility, copiousness, mellifluous rhetoric, and verbal wit. In the mid-seventeenth century, Thomas Fuller would associate Shakespeare with 'Ovid, the most naturall and witty of all Poets'.[39]

Rigorous rhetorical training was undergone in the upper school, where boys were drilled in the writing of epistles, themes, and orations. The textbook for themes was Aphthonius' *Progymnasmata*, in which Shakespeare would have found Ovid's story of Venus and Adonis discussed as an example of *narratio* (and immediately followed by citation of Pyramus and Thisbe). The upper school would also have provided Shakespeare with his first exposure to the major Roman poets in themselves, rather than in extract. Ovid, being perhaps the easiest to read and to imitate in verse-writing exercises, occupied the foremost place. Extensive reading and memorizing of the *Metamorphoses* was almost universally required in sixteenth-century grammar schools. In addition, at most schools selections from one or more of Ovid's other works were studied, most frequently the *Fasti*, his poem on Roman festivals and ceremonies, the *Heroides*, his elegies in the form of imaginary letters from legendary heroines to their lovers or husbands, and *Tristia*, his laments written in exile.

Exercises in imitation were usually based on passages from collections of elegant extracts, such as Mirandula's *Illustrium Flores Poetarum*, in which Ovid was heavily represented. Little changed in the grammar-school curriculum between the late sixteenth and the early seventeenth centuries, so Shakespeare was in all probability taught in a manner similar to that recommended by John Brinsley a generation later (Brinsley explicitly based his system on the *Scholemaster* of Roger Ascham, Queen Elizabeth's tutor):

[38] The epithets commending Shakespeare are by William Covell (1595), John Weever (1595), Richard Barnfield (1598), John Webster (1612), and Thomas Heywood (1635), all cited in E. K. Chambers, *William Shakespeare: A Study of Facts and Problems*, 2 vols. (Oxford, 1930); for the characterization of Ovid's style, see Harvey, *Marginalia*, ed. G. C. Moore Smith (Stratford-upon-Avon, 1913), 231; Lodge (1579), cited in *Elizabethan Critical Essays*, i. 70; Nashe, *Works*, ed. R. B. McKerrow, 5 vols. (1904–10; repr. Oxford, 1958), i. 193.

[39] Fuller further suggested that Shakespeare compounded this Ovidian nature with Plautine skills in comedy and a warlike-sounding surname to compare with Martial's— *The History of the Worthies of England: Warwickshire* (London, 1662), 126.

Take *Flores Poetarum*, and in every Common place make choise of Ovids verses, or if you find any other which be pleasant and easie: and making sure, that your schollars know not the verses aforehand, use to dictate unto them as you did in prose. Cause also so many as you would have to learne together, to set downe the English as you dictate. . . . having just the same words, let them trie which of them can soonest turne them into the order of a verse . . . And then lastly, read them over the verse of Ovid, that they may see that themselves have made the very same; or wherin they missed: this shall much incourage and assure them.[40]

Thus the boys would be expected not merely to translate back into Latin, but to produce a rhetorical arrangement that corresponded to Ovid's original; the exercise is analogous to that in the training of a musician, whereby the student is given a melody and asked to harmonize it in the style of a particular composer. It is not an exaggeration to say that Shakespeare's first lessons in poetry were lessons in the imitation of Ovid. Brinsley describes the method of double translation as the pupil's 'first entrance into versifying':

By the translations of the Poets, as of Ovid, and Virgil, to have a most plain way into the first entrance into versifying, to turne the prose of the Poets into the Poets owne verse, with delight, certainty and speed, without any bodging; and so by continuall practice to grow in this facilitie, for getting the phrase and veine of the Poet.[41]

Another common exercise was to write letters in the style of the *Heroides*: in so doing, the student had to find a rhetoric appropriate to a fictional character's circumstances and passions. The dramatist's art begins here. Even as a mature playwright Shakespeare would continue to base his composition on inherited texts; in *Antony and Cleopatra* and *Coriolanus*, for example, Sir Thomas North's prose originals are transformed into elegant verse, sometimes word for word, but always with a distinctive rhetorical arrangement.

The exclusive study of Latin, learning by rote, writing according to rhetorical formulas, reproducing the *sententiae* and the beauties of classical authors, the work of imitation: these fundamentals of Elizabethan education exercised a profound influence on Shakespeare's writings and the ways in which his audiences read them, whether on stage or page. It is only by an effort of historical reconstruction that we can learn to share the educated Elizabethan's *frisson* of pleasure in the recognition of a familiar sentiment, an

---

[40] *Ludus Literarius: or, The Grammar Schoole* (London, 1612), 193.
[41] Ibid. 107.

elegantly turned phrase, a delicate rhetorical manœuvre, a full-scale imitation.

We have no record of Shakespeare's early reading habits outside the classroom, but it is not fanciful to suppose that his experience was similar to Montaigne's (though one suspects that Shakespeare would not have been such a precocious developer, since his father would not have educated him in Latin from his very early years, as Montaigne's did): 'The first taste or feeling I had of bookes, was of the pleasure I tooke in reading the fables of *Ovids* Metamorphosies; for being but seven or eight yeares old, I would steale and sequester my selfe from all other delights, only to reade them.'[42] From his grammar-school training and his reading of Golding's translation, Shakespeare grew to know the fables extremely well. All fifteen books of the *Metamorphoses* make themselves felt in his works in the form of mythological allusions and borrowings of phrase. His range of reference may be seen from a list of the stories which we will find were of particular significance to his work: the Golden Age (Book One); Phaëthon (Book Two); Actaeon, Narcissus and Echo (Book Three); Pyramus and Thisbe, Salmacis and Hermaphroditus (Book Four); Ceres and Proserpina (Book Five); Arachne's tapestries depicting the Olympian gods as rapists and seducers, Tereus and Philomel (Book Six); Medea (Book Seven); the Calydonian boar, Baucis and Philemon (Book Eight); Hercules and the shirt of Nessus (Book Nine); Orpheus, Pygmalion, Venus and Adonis (Book Ten); Ceyx and Alcyone (Book Eleven); Ajax and Ulysses, Hecuba (Book Thirteen); the philosophy of Pythagoras, Julius Caesar (Book Fifteen). Books Twelve and Fourteen may have been the least used, but Shakespeare seems to have derived from them his knowledge of the battle of the Centaurs and Lapithae (Book Twelve, alluded to in *Titus Andronicus* and *A Midsummer Night's Dream*) and Circe's enchantments (Book Fourteen, importantly alluded to in *The Comedy of Errors*).

Many mythological references are of a vague character that makes it impossible to pin down a precise source for them, but the great majority of them—approximately 90 per cent—could come from Ovid, and would usually have been thought of by mythologically literate playgoers as Ovidian.[43] Where Ovid is an obvious source,

[42] 'Of the Institution and Education of Children', *Essayes*, i. 25, p. 138. For Montaigne and Ovid, see François Rigolot, *Les Métamorphoses de Montaigne* (Paris, 1988).

[43] For a comprehensive listing of Shakespeare's mythological allusions, see R. K. Root, *Classical Mythology in Shakespeare* (New York, 1903).

there is little point in making claims for more obscure sources (Pyramus and Thisbe is a classic instance: the play in *A Midsummer Night's Dream* is supposed to be Quince's translation of Ovid, yet critics have insisted on relating it to such obscure works as Thomas Mouffet's poem *Of the Silkewormes, and their Flies*, which was not published and may not even have been written when the *Dream* was first performed). Since we know from his direct borrowings, both narrative and verbal, that Shakespeare was well versed in Ovid, we may assume that the bulk of his incidental mythological allusions derive from the *Metamorphoses*, unless there is proof positive of a debt to another source; the only exception to this rule is that the primary source for a particular work must take precedence, though in these cases the audience, not all of whom would have been familiar with such sources as, say, Greene's *Pandosto*, might still have thought of Ovid. A much smaller number of references derive from Virgil, who would have been the second most widely read author at school. The most celebrated Virgilian story is that of Dido and Aeneas, yet the image in *The Merchant of Venice* of 'Dido with a willow in her hand' (v. i. 10) is Ovidian rather than Virgilian—it is an adaptation of Ariadne's parting from Theseus in the tenth epistle of the *Heroides*, possibly mediated via Chaucer's version of this tale in his *Legend of Good Women*. Furthermore, as will be shown, Shakespeare's reading of *The Aeneid*, important as it was for *Antony and Cleopatra* and *The Tempest*, was contaminated by Ovid's reading of it in the *Metamorphoses* and the letter of Dido in the *Heroides*. In addition to the *Metamorphoses* and the *Heroides*, Shakespeare knew the *Fasti*—his principal direct source for *Lucrece*—and at least parts of the *Amores*, *Ars Amatoria*, and *Tristia*. As has been noted, the *Fasti* was not published in an English translation until 1640, so this was one work which Shakespeare could only read by making use of his 'small Latine'.

Texts such as the notoriously licentious *Ars Amatoria*, denounced by Stephen Gosson as 'that trumpet of Baudrie',[44] were not of course studied in school. In the sixteenth century Ovid was condemned for his 'wantonness' as frequently as he was praised for his verbal sweetness—a mark of Shakespeare's Ovidianism is William Covell's

[44] Gosson, *The Schoole of Abuse, Conteining a plesaunt invective against Poets, Pipers, Plaiers, Jesters and such like Caterpillers of a Commonwelth* (1579), ed. Edward Arber (London, 1906), 20.

juxtaposition, 'All praiseworthy. Lucrecia Sweet Shakspeare . . . Wanton Adonis.'[45] Shakespeare lived during a period in which ways of reading Ovid underwent radical transformation, as a newly unapologetic delight in the poetic and erotic qualities of the *Metamorphoses* came to compete with the predominant medieval practice of moralizing and even Christianizing them. This broad shift does not, however, mean either that moral and allegorical readings disappeared in the Elizabethan period—witness Harington on Perseus and the Gorgon—or that moralization was the only medieval approach to Ovid: Chaucer provides the principal example of what might be thought of as a playful Elizabethan-style reading two hundred years before its time.[46]

The allegorizing and moralizing of Ovid's often explicitly erotic tales was an interpretative device that enabled his poetry to retain currency and escape suppression in an age when all education and most art was dominated by the precepts of Christianity. The fourth-century Latin poet Prudentius used Ovidian allusion in his poems on Christian dogma and tales of the martyrs; his *Contra Symmachum* drew together the transformation of Lot's wife into a pillar of salt and the metamorphosis of Niobe into stone, thus foreshadowing a strategy that would become common a thousand years later. Similarly, a sixth-century bishop, Venantius Fortunatus, moralized Ovid's amorous poetry by applying it to a nun's love for Christ. When John Milton in the seventeenth century converted one of Ovid's cries of post-coital bliss into the climax of a vision of Lancelot Andrewes, the late Bishop of Winchester, entering into heaven, he was doing something very traditional.[47]

There was, then, a millennium-long tradition of reading Ovid's poems as if they were allegorical and as if their sentiments were morally elevated rather than erotically charged.[48] The tradition was

---

[45] Marginalia by Covell, cited in Chambers, *Facts and Problems*, ii. 193.

[46] J. M. Fyler's *Chaucer and Ovid* (New Haven, Conn., 1979) is a useful starting-point. Ovid is to be found throughout Chaucer, but the relationship between the *Heroides* and the *Legend of Good Women* is especially close; the *Heroides* (the letter of Helen to Paris in particular) also gave Chaucer much for the psychology of Criseyde. For the creative use of Ovid in the Middle Ages, see also the chapter on Dante in Leonard Barkan's *The Gods Made Flesh: Metamorphosis and the Pursuit of Paganism* (New Haven, Conn., 1986) and the reading of the *Roman de la Rose* in the context of the Narcissus myth in Kenneth J. Knoespel, *Narcissus and the Invention of Personal History* (New York, 1985).

[47] 'Elegia tertia: In Obitum Praesulis Wintoniensis' ('Elegy III: On the Death of the Bishop of Winchester'), l. 68, adapting the last line of *Amores*, 1. v.

[48] The best introduction to the history of the allegorical interpretation of classical

formalized and codified by the French writers of the fourteenth century who produced detailed theological elucidations of the *Metamorphoses*. The anonymous *Ovide moralisé*, a translation which introduced commentary that swelled the length of the poem to some seventy thousand lines, was the most influential work of this sort. Ovid's account of the creation was yoked to that in Genesis, Deucalion's flood to Noah's, and so on. Allegorical and biblical interpretations were set beside moral ones; thus the revolt of the giants against the Olympian gods was made to represent the building of the tower of Babel, but also the pride of any worldly human who rebels against the authority of God. Some of the interpretations of individual stories are ingenious, to say the least: Lycaon, who plotted to make Zeus eat human flesh and was turned into a wolf for his pains, is read as Herod, and his plot as the attempt on the life of the infant Jesus; his destruction of sheep is made to represent the massacre of the innocents, and his metamorphosis into a wolf, Herod's dethronement and damnation. It was this kind of reading which went into decline, though not desuetude, in the sixteenth century. In accordance with the secularization of literary texts which is one of the great characteristics of the Renaissance, allegorical translation of Ovid into biblical terms gradually became less prominent, save in the case of such powerful correspondences as the creation and the flood. George Schuler, Melanchthon's son-in-law, whose edition of 1555 (published under the name of Georgius Sabinus) was one of the most widely used, viewed *allegoresis* as a hermeneutical discipline of some value, but argued that sacred truth should not be mixed with pagan fable save when both agreed on historical fact.[49] The moral interpretation, in which Lycaon represents all oppressive and cruel men, was more readily sustainable, and indeed gained new strength from the humanist emphasis on the moral wisdom of pagan culture.

Through the *Ovide moralisé* and such commentaries as the *Metamorphosis Ovidiana moraliter . . . explanata*, ascribed to 'Thomas Walleys' but in fact by Pierre Bersuire, the medieval conception of Ovid reached the Renaissance mythological handbooks, of which the

mythology remains Jean Seznec's magisterial *The Survival of the Pagan Gods: The Mythological Tradition and its Place in Renaissance Humanism and Art* (Princeton, NJ, 1953), trans. by Barbara F. Sessions from the original French of 1940.

[49] See the preface to Sabinus' edn. and the discussion in Ann Moss, *Ovid in Renaissance France: A Survey of the Latin Editions of Ovid and Commentaries printed in France before 1660* (London, 1982), 48–53.

most notable were the *Mythologiae* (1551) of Natalis Comes (otherwise known as Natale Conti) and *Le Imagini, con la Spositione de i Dei degli Antichi* (1556) of Vincenzo Cartari. Their interpretations were condensed and rendered into the vernacular in Shakespeare's lifetime, first in Thomas Cooper's comprehensive *Thesaurus* (1565, frequently reprinted), then in such texts as Stephen Batman's *Golden Booke of the Leaden Goddes* (1577) and Abraham Fraunce's *Third part of the Countesse of Pembrokes Ivychurch* (1592), which contained sixteen Ovidian tales in verse and the fullest English commentary of the sixteenth century.[50] In 1632 George Sandys published his magnificent *Ovid's Metamorphosis Englished, Mythologiz'd, and Represented in Figures*, a compendium of the previous hundred years' interpretative work.[51] Although Sandys's book was published after Shakespeare's death, it may, since it is a synthesis of earlier interpretations with many passages translated or developed from commentators such as Sabinus and Comes, be used to suggest some of the meanings which sophisticated readers and playgoers of the late sixteenth and early seventeenth centuries would have found in Shakespeare's mythological allusions.

The plundering of the handbooks by Elizabethan writers in search of mythological elaboration is suggested by John Marston in one of his satirical poems:

> Reach me some Poets Index that will show.
> *Imagines Deorum*. Booke of Epithetes,
> *Natales Comes*, thou I know recites,
> And mak'st Anatomie of Poesie.[52]

Shakespeare, however, went directly to Ovid rather than to the mythographies. It was the more self-consciously learned and allegorical poets, George Chapman especially, who plundered Comes. Indeed, one sense in which Chapman stood in a rival tradition to that

---

[50] Batman was an Anglican cleric who sought to Christianize the pagan tradition; he made considerable use of Cartari. Fraunce compiled his allegorical interpretations from Cartari, Comes, Leo Hebraeus, and an annotated Ovid printed in Cambridge in 1584. For this material, see further Douglas Bush, *Mythology and the Renaissance Tradition in English Poetry* (1932; rev. edn. New York, 1963), ch. 2, and Don Cameron Allen, *Mysteriously Meant: The Rediscovery of Pagan Symbolism and Allegorical Interpretation in the Renaissance* (Baltimore, 1970), chs. 7–8.

[51] Sandys published his translation of the first five books of the poem in 1621 and the full text in 1626, but the commentary did not appear until 1632.

[52] *The Poems of John Marston*, ed. Arnold Davenport (Liverpool, 1961), 72, quoted in Bush, *Mythology and the Renaissance Tradition*, 29, and Seznec, *Survival of the Pagan Gods*, 313–14.

of Shakespeare is that his Ovidianism was far more allegorical. The way in which readings of Ovid were contested in late Elizabethan literature is a matter which I will discuss further at the end of Chapter 4.

Annotated editions, most of them deriving from one which first appeared in 1492 with a commentary by the great textual scholar Raphael Regius, contributed to the sixteenth-century knowledge of Ovid in England. There is in the Bodleian Library in Oxford a copy of the Aldine edition of 1502, bearing the signature 'Wm She' and a note by one 'T N' dated 1682, 'This little Booke of Ovid was given to me by W. Hall who sayd it was once Will. Shakesperes'. The testimony is questionable—'Hall' presumably refers to Shakespeare's son-in-law, but his name was John, and he died in 1635—but plausible, given the comparatively early date (Shakespearian forgery did not become a vogue until the mid-eighteenth century). With the exception of a Montaigne in the British Library, no other surviving book can plausibly be said to have belonged to Shakespeare; it is perhaps a little too convenient that the two which survive are copies of two of his favourite texts, the *Metamorphoses* and the *Essais*. The Aldine Ovid includes a life of the poet and an index of tales,[53] as well as a good text; even if this is not Shakespeare's, he must have owned a similar edition. It is significant for the nature of Ovid's influence on Shakespeare that sixteenth-century editions tended to eschew the more elaborately allegorical form of interpretation; Sabinus was representative in suggesting that the transformation of men into beasts should be viewed metaphorically as an image of monstrous human behaviour. This implicit internalizing, which reads metamorphosis as psychological and metaphorical instead of physical and literal, is one key to Shakespeare's use of Ovid.

As important a part of the Renaissance as the multiplication of editions was the translation, the 'Englishing', of the classics. In 1560 one Thomas Howell published *The Fable of Ovid treting of Narcissus, translated out of Latin into Englysh Mytre, with a Moral ther unto*, an accurate translation of just under two hundred lines of Book Three of the *Metamorphoses*, together with nearly seven hundred lines of moralizing on Narcissus as an emblem of pride and vanity. Also in the tradition of the *Ovide moralisé* was Thomas Peend's *The pleasant Fable*

---

[53] *Ovidii Metamorphoseon libri quindecim* (Aldus, 1502), including 'Vita Ovidii ex ipsius operib.' (mainly based on autobiographical material in the *Tristia*; includes a mention of Ovid's lost play, *Medea*) and 'Index fabularum et caeterorum'.

of Hermaphroditus and Salmacis, published five years later; here
Hermaphroditus represents youth and purity and Salmacis the
allurements of the world. Peend intended to translate more of the
Metamorphoses, but Arthur Golding beat him to it: his version of the
first four books was published in 1565 and the whole poem two years
later.

The fourteener couplet, Golding's verse form, has none of the
crispness that is one of Ovid's glories. Ezra Pound exaggerated
typically when he claimed that the translation is 'the most beautiful
book in the language', but it was undoubtedly prized by the
Elizabethans.[54] It is best when Ovid is most down to earth, as J. F.
Nims implies when he writes, justly if patronizingly, of Golding
'turning the sophisticated Roman into a ruddy country gentleman
with tremendous gusto, a sharp eye on the life around him, an ear for
racy speech, and a gift for energetic doggerel'.[55] Mythological figures
are tricked out in sixteenth-century dress, rather as they are in the
tapestries of the period—when Atalanta runs in Ovid she has bare feet
and ribbons fluttering at her knees, whereas Golding gives her socks
and 'embroydred garters that were tyde beneathe her ham' (Golding,
x. 692). The process of 'Englishing' not just the words but also the
atmosphere of Ovid is an important precedent for Shakespeare's own
combinations of the native and the classical. The introduction of
'elves' in the Medea passage cited earlier is typical. Golding is
characterized by his robust vernacular vocabulary—he finds no
indecorum in words like 'queaches', 'plash', 'skapes', 'collup', and
'codds'[56]—and his bustling narration of the stories, which was
probably the main reason for the popularity of his translation (it was
reprinted in 1575, 1584, 1587, twice in 1593, 1603, and 1612). If
Shakespeare and his contemporaries owed their intimacy with
Ovidian rhetoric to the grammar schools, their easy familiarity with
Ovidian narrative was as much due to Golding.

In 1586 William Webbe, in his *Discourse of English Poetrie*,
commended

[54] For Pound's encomium, see his *ABC of Reading* (London, 1934), 127; for
Golding's style, see Gordon Braden, *The Classics and English Renaissance Poetry: Three
Case Studies* (New Haven, Conn., 1978), 16–54; for the influence on subsequent
Elizabethans—Marlowe and Spenser as well as Shakespeare—see the articles by
Anthony Brian Taylor, cited in my bibliography.

[55] Nims, introd. to *Ovid's 'Metamorphoses': The Arthur Golding Translation* (New
York, 1965), p. xxxi.

[56] i. 138, i. 381, iii. 327, v. 651, x. 839. The last of these words is slang for testicles,

Master *Arthur Golding,* for hys labour in englishing *Ovids Metamorphosis,* for which Gentleman surely our Country hath for many respects greatly to gyve God thankes: as for him which hath taken infinite paynes without ceasing, travelleth as yet indefatigably, and is addicted without society by his continuall laboure to profit this nation and speeche in all kind of good learning.[57]

Webbe's emphasis on Golding's service to his country reminds us that the Elizabethan translation movement in which Golding was prominent was a significant part of a post-Reformation project to establish England as a Protestant nation with its own high culture.[58] Golding's patron was a key figure in this early Elizabethan endeavour, the Earl of Leicester.[59] The dedication to *The Fyrst Fower Bookes,* dated December 1564, praises Leicester for his encouragement of translators 'in their paynfull exercises attempted of a zeale and desyre too enryche their native language with thinges not heretoofore published in the same'.[60] The transformation of Ovid into an English country gentleman is not just a quaint aesthetic move, as J. F. Nims implies—it fulfils the humanist requirement that 'the general end' of literary creation should be 'to fashion a gentleman or noble person in vertuous and gentle discipline'.[61]

Golding stressed the morality and civic worth of his project in the prose dedication to Leicester. The complete translation of 1567 had a fuller verse epistle, also addressed to Leicester, which expounded Ovid's 'dark Philosophie of turned shapes' in a manner which goes back to the *Ovide moralisé.* A number of traditional interpretations are followed, as Ovid is reconciled with the Bible: 'Not only in effect he dooth with Genesis agree, | But also in the order of creation, save that hee | Makes no distinction of the dayes' (Epistle, 344–6). Golding does not commit himself as to whether Ovid is 'following of the [biblical] text aright' or unconsciously recognizing 'that there are no

used by Golding to translate Ovid's 'inguine' (x. 715, 'groin') with reference to the anatomical part where the boar gores Adonis.

[57] *Elizabethan Critical Essays,* i. 243.

[58] See C. H. Conley, *The First English Translators of the Classics* (New Haven, Conn., 1927).

[59] See Eleanor Rosenberg, *Leicester: Patron of Letters* (New York, 1955), and L. T. Golding, *An Elizabethan Puritan: Arthur Golding the Translator of Ovid's Metamorphoses and also of John Calvin's Sermons* (New York, 1937).

[60] *Shakespeare's Ovid,* ed. Rouse, p. iii.

[61] Spenser's 'A letter of the Author[']s expounding his whole intention in the course of this worke . . . To the Right noble and Valorous, Sir Walter Raleigh knight', prefixed to *The Faerie Queene* (1590).

Gods but one' (393–4). The Golden Age is compared to 'Adams tyme in Paradyse' (470) and Deucalion's flood to Noah's, but once Golding's exposition gets beyond the first book, interpretations of this kind give way to moral ones, in accordance with common sixteenth-century practice. Medieval *allegoresis* is replaced by a humanist emphasis on the ethical exemplariness of the classic text. Thus, much of the Epistle consists of select moralizations of tales from the second book onwards: Daphne is 'A myrror of virginitie' (68), Phaëthon 'ambition blynd, and youthfull wilfulnesse' (72), Narcissus 'scornful-nesse and pryde' (105), Pyramus and Thisbe 'The headie force of frentick love whose end is wo and payne' (110), and so forth.

Golding's Epistle probably constituted Shakespeare's only sus-tained direct confrontation with the moralizing tradition—that is, if he bothered to read it and did not skip straight to the English text of his admired Ovid. The Epistle may certainly be said to have provided a convenient embodiment of the interpretations of major myths that Shakespeare and his audience would have shared. The interpretative tradition should not, however, be over-stressed: in the second half of the sixteenth century the *Metamorphoses* was being read as much for its wit as its wisdom. Golding himself spoke in his 'Preface too the Reader' of Ovid's 'lyvely Image[s]' and 'pleasant style' (152, 179). The poem had an energetic life as a linguistic resource that could not be contained by the work of moralization.

The momentum of the translation movement was such that the Elizabethans soon tried their hand at Englishing Ovid's other works: George Turbervile's *The Heroycall Epistles of the Learned Poet P. Ovidius Naso Translated into English Verse* appeared in the same year as Golding's complete *Metamorphoses*, Thomas Underdowne translated the *Invective against Ibis* two years later, together with notes that formed a compendium of mythological reference, and in 1572 Thomas Churchyard produced a version of the first three books of the *Tristia*. Turbervile's *Heroides*, an attempt to make 'A Romaine borne to speake with English jawes',[62] went through four editions before the end of the century. It brought a further series of mythological love-stories into the vernacular, strengthened the link between the Ovidian tradition and the medieval convention of the despairing lover's 'complaint', and eventually inspired an extremely popular

---

[62] *The heroycall epistles of Publius Ovidius Naso, in Englishe verse : tr. G. Turbervile with A. Sabinus aunsweres* (London, 1567), 'The Translator to the captious sort of Sycophants', sig.)(ii^v.

English imitation, Michael Drayton's *England's Heroicall Epistles* of 1597, which took the form of exchanges of letters between famous couples from English history. By the time Drayton was writing, another translation, Marlowe's version of the *Amores*, was circulating in manuscript and being produced in surreptitious editions. By the 1590s then, Ovid had become for many writers, readers, and playgoers a source of poetic and even licentious delight rather than moral edification. The apogee of the new Ovidianism was constituted by the genre which modern critics call epyllion, the erotic narrative poetry, influenced by both the *Heroides* and parts of the *Metamorphoses*, that flourished in the 1590s and of which Marlowe's *Hero and Leander* and Shakespeare's *Venus and Adonis*, discussed in my next chapter, are the pre-eminent examples. In this erotic tradition, Ovid became once again what he described himself as in the *Ars Amatoria* (ii. 497), 'lascivi praeceptor amoris', the preceptor of wanton love. And with this development, the wheel turned full circle to Augustus' proscription of the poet: in 1599 Marlowe's *Amores* were banned and burned by episcopal order. Late-Elizabethan Ovidian eroticism was distinctly difficult to reconcile with the humanist conviction that the classics should be translated because of their moral worth.

III

The theory of early sixteenth-century humanists like Erasmus and John Colet (founder of St Paul's, the model grammar school) was that the dissemination of the wisdom of the classics would produce new generations of worthy public servants. By the end of the century, the practice looked more complicated. The rigorously rhetorical basis of the educational system made its products gifted in the writing and speaking of polished Latin and English, but a stylish man was not necessarily an embodiment of civic virtue. The case of Ovid was especially acute: no education in style would have been complete without him, but his 'wanton' matter could not be tamed, despite the efforts of moralizers like Golding. Linguistic profligacy became associated with other forms of potential licentiousness. Roger Ascham saw the problem when he remarked in his *Scholemaster* that quick-wittedness—the facility associated with Ovid—was not necessarily the best preparation for public duties: 'the quickest wits commonly may prove the best poets, but not the wisest orators; ready of tongue to speak boldly, not deep of judgment, either for good council or wise writing'.[63] It is a short step from this insight to the career of John Lyly, grandson of Lily the grammarian, in whose work verbal 'wit' is split apart from moral 'wisdom'.

Lyly's much-imitated *Euphues. The Anatomy of Wyt* (1578) is the key Elizabethan text for a consideration of the dichotomy between stylistic and moral education. Here, facility in the classics becomes a mark of *sprezzatura*, not a path to virtue. Ovid is associated with the worldliness of Naples, not the wisdom of Athens; he is set up as a counter-example to Aristotle (who stands here for education in ethics and politics, not for medieval scholasticism): 'There was all things necessary and in redinesse that myght eyther allure the minde to luste, or entice the hearte to follye, a courte more meete for an *Atheyst*, th[a]n for one of *Athens*, for *Ovid* th[a]n for *Aristotle*, for a gracelesse lover th[a]n for a godly lyver: more fitter for *Paris* th[a]n *Hector*, and meeter for *Flora* th[a]n *Diana*.'[64] We will find the opposition between Ovid and Aristotle reiterated in *The Taming of the Shrew*. *Euphues* is structured as a moral fable, in that the young man has to learn to reject erotic desire and return to the academy (*Love's Labour's Lost* is a brilliant reversal of this movement), but the book's stylistic prodigality is such that austerity doesn't really stand a chance.[65]

It was above all from Ovid that Lyly derived his technique of putting verbal wit in the service of love. Though Shakespeare did not hesitate to parody Euphuism's endless generation of phrases, he could not have written his own witty love-debates—those between Rosaline and Berowne, then Beatrice and Benedick—without the example of Lyly. *Euphues*, like Shakespeare's *Two Gentlemen of Verona*, is constructed on a principle of pairings: the friendship of Euphues and Philautus is threatened by their rivalry in love for Lucilla but briefly re-established when she rejects them both. The book consists principally of exchanges, often in the form of letters; this 'rhetoric of the divided mind'[66] is in a tradition that goes back to the *Heroides*. Indeed, Lucilla's reply to Euphues' proposal of marriage consists in

---

[63] Ascham, *The Scholemaster* (written in the 1560s), ed. R. J. Schoeck (Don Mills, Ontario, 1966), 25.

[64] Lyly's *Complete Works*, ed. R. W. Bond, 3 vols. (Oxford, 1902), i. 185.

[65] On Lyly and 'prodigality', see the ch. on him in Richard Helgerson's *The Elizabethan Prodigals* (Berkeley and Los Angeles, 1976).

[66] G. K. Hunter's phrase, in *John Lyly: The Humanist as Courtier* (Cambridge, Mass., 1962), 51.

large measure of a paraphrase of Helen's epistle to Paris, elaborated from Turbervile's translation.[67] Again, the climax of the first part of *Euphues* is the protagonist's pamphlet of worldly-wise advice, 'A cooling Carde for Philautus and all fond lovers', much of which is adapted and expanded from Ovid's *Remedia Amoris*. It was almost certainly Lyly whom Thomas Nashe had in mind when he jibed in the preface to Greene's *Menaphon* at writers who 'in disguised array vaunt Ovids and Plutarchs plumes as their owne'.[68]

Here, for example, are three lines from the first book of the *Remedia*: 'Ad mea, decepti iuvenes, praecepta venite, | Quos suus ex omni parte fefellit amor. | Discite sanari, per quem didicistis amare' (41–3). A literal translation might be 'Come to my precepts, deceived youths, you whom your own love has cheated in every way. Learn healing from him through whom you learnt to love'; Lyly's elaboration is 'Come therefore to me all ye lovers that have bene deceived by fancie, the glasse of pestilence, or deluded by woemen the gate to perdition: be as earnest to seeke a medicine, as you wer eager to runne into a mischiefe'.[69] The insertion of additional epithets—'the glasse of pestilence', 'the gate to perdition'—is the key to the expansion. It is exactly the linguistic move that is mimicked when Holofernes and Don Armado dip into the alms-basket of words at the great feast of language in *Love's Labour's Lost*.[70]

Lyly also owed his mythological facility to Ovid. Take a typical metamorphic catalogue, which occurs a little earlier in *Euphues*:

Love knoweth no lawes: Did not Jupiter transforme himselfe into the shape of Amphitrio to imbrace Alcmoena? Into the forme of a Swan to enjoye Loeda? Into a Bull to beguyle Io? Into a showre of golde to winne Danae? Did not Neptune chaunge himselfe into a Heyfer, a Ramme, a Floude, a Dolphin, onelye for the love of those he lusted after? Did not Apollo converte himselfe into a Shepheard, into a Birde, into a Lyon, for the desire he had to heale hys disease? If the Gods thoughte no scorne to become beastes, to obtayne their best beloved, shall Euphues be so nyce in chaunging his coppie to gayne his Lady? No, no: he that cannot dissemble in love, is not worthy to live.   (Lyly, i. 236)

The specific source of this is Arachne's weaving in Book Six of the

---

[67] See Lyly's *Complete Works*, i. 220–2, and the discussion in M. P. Tilley, '*Euphues* and *Ovid's Heroical Epistles*', *MLN* xlv (1930), 301–8.

[68] *Works*, ed. McKerrow, iii. 312.

[69] *Complete Works*, i. 247.

[70] See e.g. Don Armado's letter, read at I. i. 216–67, and Holofernes in the dialogue at the beginning of IV. ii.

Metamorphoses, in which all the transformations listed by Euphues are depicted (except that Jupiter becomes a bull to deceive Europa, not Io); more generally, Ovid is the *locus classicus* for the motif of dissembling in sexual pursuit. As will be seen in later chapters, Arachne's woof also attracted Shakespeare on a variety of occasions. Lyly's version of the list of divine rapes found its way, in compressed form, into Robert Greene's Euphuistic romance, *Pandosto*: 'And yet Dorastus, shame not at thy shepheards weede: the heavenly Godes have sometime earthly thoughtes: Neptune became a ram, Jupiter a Bul, Apollo a shepheard: they, Gods, and yet in love: and thou a man appointed to love' (Bullough, viii. 184). From here, it reached *The Winter's Tale*:

> The gods themselves,
> Humbling their deities to love, have taken
> The shapes of beasts upon them. Jupiter
> Became a bull, and bellowed; the green Neptune
> A ram, and bleated; and the fire-robed god,
> Golden Apollo, a poor humble swain,
> As I seem now.

> (IV. iv. 25–31)

This is a good example of how Shakespeare is often Ovidian even when his direct source is not Ovid: his introduction of details such as 'bellowed' and 'bleated' may be said to 'reovidianize' the passage. While the letter is that of *Pandosto*, the spirit is that of the *Metamorphoses*, where local colour is always vivid and animal forms spring to life.

Lyly did not follow Euphues back to the academic cloister; his literary style served not as a cooling card, but as a calling card with which he sought to gain entrance at court. He took his alms-basket of allusions along with him, so once he gained the opportunity to write entertainments for the Queen he became the first to introduce sustained Ovidianism into English drama.[71] He plucked from his Roman exemplar not just verbal plumes but whole plots. The fifteenth epistle of the *Heroides*, tactfully emptied of its lesbian connotations, is the principal source for *Sapho and Phao* (published in 1584). The first three acts of *Midas* (composed in 1589) closely follow the eleventh book of the *Metamorphoses*, while also satirizing Philip II of Spain by reading his colonialism in the context of Midas-like love of gold. *Love's*

---

[71] The other notable early mythological drama, George Peele's *The Arraignment of Paris* (performed *c.*1583), was also a court play.

Metamorphosis (not published till 1601, but probably acted in the 1580s) skilfully weaves together the story of Erysichthon, who in the eighth book of the *Metamorphoses* is condemned to hunger after axing a tree in which a nymph of Ceres was confined, and a number of other transformations involving three nymphs and some amorous foresters. As so frequently in Ovid and Shakespearian comedy, metamorphosis takes place in a pastoral landscape.[72] Lyly's plays also rely on Ovid for a host of incidental mythological allusions, and there is the occasional passage of sustained imitation similar to that in the 'cooling Carde'; in *Sapho and Phao*, for instance, the sybil discourses to Phao on the art of love—rather as 'Ganymede' does to Orlando in *As You Like It*—and in so doing makes extensive use of the precepts in Ovid's *Ars Amatoria*.

Gallathea, entered in the Stationers' Register in 1585, is probably Lyly's best play; it certainly gives the best sense of his creative, transformational use of Ovid. It is not an overt dramatization of a single Ovidian story, as some of the other plays are; instead, it is stuffed with a rich variety of Ovidian matter. The main plot turns on Gallathea and Phillida, two girls who are disguised as boys by their shepherd fathers so that they will not be chosen as the virgin who has to be sacrificed to Neptune (the boys playing the girls on stage thus become boys again). The two girl-boys meet in the woods and fall in love; their dilemma is finally resolved when Venus agrees to change one of them into a boy, pointing out that she has already done 'the like to Iphis and Ianthes' (v. iii. 143). The allusion is to the ninth book of the *Metamorphoses*, where a Cretan called Ligdus insists that he wants a boy, girls being less strong and more trouble—if his wife has a girl, it will be put to death. The wife is delivered of a girl but she tells her husband it's a boy, gives it the unisex name Iphis, and dresses it like a boy. At the age of thirteen, Iphis and another lovely girl, Ianthe, fall mutually in love. Iphis laments at what she takes to be the unnaturalness of her own desire: 'interque animalia cuncta | femina femineo conrepta cupidine nulla est' (ix. 733–4)—'But never man could shew | That female yit was tane in love with female kynd' (Golding, ix. 861–2). The story ends happily when Isis metamor-

---

[72] On the whole question of landscape in the *Metamorphoses*, see Charles Segal, *Landscape in Ovid's Metamorphoses: A Study in the Transformation of a Literary Symbol* (Wiesbaden, 1969), and Hugh Parry, 'Ovid's Metamorphoses: Violence in a Pastoral Landscape', *TAPA* xcv (1964), 268–82.

phoses Iphis into a real boy. A patterning myth is thus explicitly invoked as a precedent for the resolution of *Gallathea*, and an Ovidian sex-change takes place within the drama. Here an important difference between Lyly and Shakespeare is apparent: the latter always resolves the apparent need for a sex-change naturalistically, he does not resort to direct divine intervention in the Ovidian manner. Shakespearian metamorphoses take place within the mind: even when they are imposed from without, as with the love-juice in *A Midsummer Night's Dream*, the change is psychologically purposeful.

Lyly's court drama, like the masque in its Jacobean development, actually embodies and develops divinities as characters on stage; the classical gods are brought to the banks of the Humber in a fusion of ancient and native elements which anticipates *A Midsummer Night's Dream*.[73] In the second act, Neptune speaks of his capacity to metamorphose himself in order to deceive men, just as men themselves try to deceive through the more mundane metamorphosis of disguise:

Doe sillie Sheepeheards goe about to deceive great Neptune, in putting on mans attire uppon women: and Cupid to make sport deceive them all, by using a womans apparell upon a God? then Neptune that hast taken sundrie shapes to obtaine love, stick not to practise some deceipt to shew thy deitie, and having often thrust thy self into shape of beastes to deceive men, be not coy to use the shape of a Sheepehearde, to shew thy selfe a God. (II. ii. 15–21)

The link here between divine metamorphosis and mortal *dressing up* hints towards a move that will be vital in Shakespeare, namely a shift from the register of myth into that of self-conscious theatricality.

Although he is writing for the Queen, Lyly's is a boy's own world (the company for whom he wrote had no adult actors). The device of cross-dressing the female characters in the first scene enables him to confront head-on the drama's battle with puritanism over the matter of transvestism.[74] Tyterus argues that though it is

[73] The combination of fractious deities, youthful lovers, a mischievous Cupid, and apprentice artisans in a confused forest-world makes the likelihood of direct influence considerable—see further, Leah Scragg, 'Shakespeare, Lyly and Ovid: The influence of *Gallathea* on *A Midsummer Night's Dream*', *ShS* xxx (1977), 125–34, and *The Metamorphoses of Gallathea: A Study in Creative Adaptation* (Washington DC, 1982).

[74] The scene is discussed in this context by Lisa Jardine, *Still Harping on Daughters: Women and Drama in the Age of Shakespeare* (Brighton, 1983), 21. She then cites the examples of Ganymede and Gaveston, as I do, but does not mention that Ovid is the common factor.

'an unlawfull meanes' to cross-dress his daughter, it is a necessary one in view of the threat to her life. He then appeals to divine precedent:

TYTERUS. To gaine love, the Gods have taken shape of beastes, and to save life art thou coy to take the attire of men?
GALLATHEA. They were beastly gods, that lust could make them seeme as beastes.

(I. i. 88–91)

The puritan accusation that cross-dressed boys on stage are incitements to bestiality (sodomy) is neatly displaced on to the pagan gods. But at the same time the standard sixteenth-century moralization of Ovid is written into the exchange: metamorphosis to a beast emblematizes the bestiality of sexual desire. Having established this idea by means of mythological reference, Lyly subsequently reiterates it in the form of a direct association that does not require the underpinning of allusion: 'I have heard of such a beast called love' (III. i. 39). Like so many of Ovid's tales and Shakespeare's comedies, *Gallathea* explores the ambivalences of love in terms of its shifting orientation—the homoerotic is never far away—and its double aspect as both creative and destructive, both divine and bestial.

Christopher Marlowe, the seminal figure for the translation of Ovid on to the public stage, was not afraid to depict the gods as beastly. The shining crystal pavement in *Hero and Leander* shows 'the gods in sundry shapes, | Committing heady riots, incest, rapes'.[75] 'Riots' suggests a link between political and sexual transgression, an association that is especially significant in *Edward II*, in which the barons' disdain for—and fear of—Piers Gaveston is as much to do with rank as sexuality. When Gaveston plans the wantonness, poetry, and masquing with which he will delight and thus manipulate his King and lover, the show he elaborates at greatest length is a vision of Actaeon and Diana:

> Sometime a lovely boy in Dian's shape,
> With hair that gilds the water as it glides,
> Crownets of pearl about his naked arms,
> And in his sportful hands an olive tree
> To hide those parts which men delight to see,

[75] 'Hero and Leander', i. 143–4, in Marlowe, *Complete Plays and Poems*, ed. E. D. Pendry and J. C. Maxwell (London, 1976). All subsequent Marlowe quotations are from this edn., followed in my text by line references.

> Shall bathe him in a spring; and there hard by,
> One like Actaeon peeping through the grove,
> Shall by the angry goddess be transform'd,
> And running in the likeness of an hart,
> By yelping hounds pull'd down, and seem to die.
>
> (I. i. 60–9)

The economy of Marlowe's lines here is that they achieve at least three effects simultaneously: they evoke the opulence and decadence of a court which has Gaveston as favourite; they make explicit the homoeroticism which is latent in any reference to a boy actor; and through the image of the hunted Actaeon, they foreshadow Gaveston's own nemesis. Later, he will be pursued like Actaeon and the audience may then remember the Renaissance reading of the myth as an emblem of the fate of those who peer into the secret cabinets of princes. The *frisson* of homoeroticism also anticipates Shakespeare: in *Twelfth Night*, a lovely boy, Cesario, will be compared to Diana in a manner just as sensuous; the same play will also allude to Actaeon being hunted down by the hounds of his own desires. Gaveston has in fact begun with an image of 'surfeit', also reiterated by Orsino, behind which is an interpretation of Ovidian metamorphosis as a consequence of excess appetite.

Marlowe's iconoclasm is also exhibited in *Dido Queen of Carthage*.[76] The play is based primarily on Virgil, but it begins by denying the title's promise of epic grandeur in the style of *The Aeneid*, and displaying instead an Ovidianly randy Jupiter dandling the lovely boy Ganymede on his knee. *Dido* contaminates Virgil with Ovid in the area of female suffering as well as homoerotic passion. In Aeneas' narrative of the fate of Hecuba, such lines as 'At which the frantic queen leap'd on his face, | And in his eyelids hanging by the nails, | A little while prolong'd her husband's life' are imitations of Ovid's thirteenth book (compare Golding's phrase 'Did in the traytors face bestowe her nayles').[77] The account of Polyxena's slaughter at the hands of the rugged Pyrrhus is also an *imitatio* of Ovid, an especially interesting association in that the Player's grandiose speech on the same subject in *Hamlet* seems to be a parody of, or at least an allusion to, the Marlovian *Dido* play. If Shakespeare is playing out a contest with his deceased contemporary, he is doing so in the context of a shared Ovidianism.

---

[76] According to its title-page, written in collaboration with Nashe.
[77] *Dido Queen of Carthage*, II. i. 244–6; Golding, xiii. 673.

Marlowe's Ovidianism is a style as well as a passion. Brian Gibbons has shown how Golding's Englished Ovid foreshadows the dramatist in the way that he 'is lyrical and heroic, yet indulges the wilful exuberance and playful indecorous spirit in the language: he wittily elicits latent—and often unexpected—energies'.[78] Golding's version of the story of Phaëthon is characterized by imagery of the sort which Marlowe made his own a generation later:

> The Princely Pallace of the Sunne stood gorgeous to beholde
> On stately Pillars builded high of yellow burnisht golde,
> Beset with sparckling Carbuncles that like to fire did shine.
>
> .   .   .   .
>
> Phaëton both yong in yeares and wit,
> Into the Chariot lightly lept, and vauncing him in it
> Was not a little proud that he the brydle gotten had.
>
> (ii. 1–3, 197–9)

The language is marked by a 'precipitation'—Coleridge applied the term to *Romeo and Juliet*, the play in which Shakespeare comes closest to this manner[79]—that corresponds to its subject-matter. The verse itself lightly leaps and vaunces with not a little pride, tumbles from line to line as Phaëthon eventually does from his chariot.

For Marlowe, the bold but foolish Phaëthon, who drives the horses of the sun to disaster, was a powerfully emblematic figure. Whether or not the brazen handling of the mighty verse line can be said to make Marlowe himself into a Phaëthon, there is no doubt that the characteristic Marlovian hero is one. Phaëthon was one of those mythical personae who continued to be moralized in the same way from the Middle Ages, through Golding, and well into the seventeenth century. He is the embodiment of ambition and pride. George Sandys interprets crisply: 'This fable to the life presents a rash and ambitious Prince, inflamed with desire of glory and dominion: who in that too powerfull, attempts what so ever is above his power; and gives no limit to his ruining ambition.'[80] As late as 1655, Thomas Hall published *Phaetons folly, or, the downfall of pride : being a translation of the second book of Ovids Metamorphosis . . . where is lively set forth the danger of pride and rashness*. Hall's title and to an even greater extent

---

[78] Gibbons, '"Unstable Proteus": Marlowe's "The Tragedy of Dido Queen of Carthage"', in *Christopher Marlowe*, ed. Brian Morris, Mermaid Critical Commentaries (London, 1968), 25–46 (p. 29).

[79] See *The Romantics on Shakespeare*, ed. Jonathan Bate (London, 1992), 517.

[80] Sandys, *Ovid's Metamorphosis Englished*, 66.

Sandys's summary interpretation are readily applicable to Marlowe's two plays that follow Tamburlaine the Great as he is transformed from Scythian shepherd to mighty emperor and scourge of God, then brought down through his pride when he presumptuously burns the holy book. Indeed, the sight on stage of Tamburlaine in his chariot could have summoned up the image of Phaëthon, as a visual mythological allusion to parallel the verbal ones with which the text is littered.[81]

The most famous moment in *Tamburlaine* is that in Part 2 when the protagonist enters in his chariot drawn by two kings with bits in their mouths. His cry, 'Holla, ye pampered jades of Asia! | What, can ye draw but twenty miles a day[?]',[82] is parodied by Ancient Pistol in *2 Henry IV*—'hollow pamper'd jades of Asia, | Which cannot go but thirty mile a day' (II. iv. 164–5)—principally because it is magniloquent almost to the point of bombast. It is linguistically *hollow*. But it is also a target for Pistol since it is an image that had been knocking around in Elizabethan fourteeners for thirty years. Like all Pistol's quotations, it is poetic old hat. Marlowe is, as Nashe would have said, vaunting one of Golding's plumes as his own: the phrase is snatched from 'the pampred Jades of Thrace' in the latter's translation of the story of Hercules (ix. 238—'pampred' is Golding's ingenious translation of Ovid's 'pingues'). The theft may be apt in that Tamburlaine is a Herculean hero, but the phrase had become a cliché by the 1590s since it had already been appropriated by George Gascoigne in his satire of 1576, *The Steele Glas*, and by John Studley in his translation of Seneca's *Hercules Oetaeus*.[83]

Pistol's parody of the image draws attention to a kind of linguistic transmission that is habitual to Renaissance literary composition. Shakespeare himself frequently lined his own poetic nest with Golding's plumes; one of the things that he may be doing in the 'tedious brief scene of young Pyramus | And his love Thisbe' is parodying his own habit. But in the absence of parody or some other signalling device, such as the striking change of style which occurs when the Player delivers his Hecuba speech in *Hamlet*, an audience is not likely to register the intersection between text and source when

---

[81] Such allusions often occur in groups: in pt. I, IV. iii. 3–4, for example, the Calydonian boar is juxtaposed to Cephalus.

[82] *Tamburlaine the Great*, pt. 2, IV. iii. 1–2.

[83] Gascoigne, *The Steele Glas*, ed. Edward Arber (London, 1869), l. 366; *Seneca, His Tenne Tragedies* (London, 1581), fo. 215ʳ.

it is merely a matter of a local verbal appropriation. Sometimes, however, Marlowe alludes to a detail in Ovid that he manifestly expects his audience to recognize. And on some of these occasions, text clashes dramatically with source.

In his valuable book *The Light in Troy*, Thomas M. Greene anatomizes Renaissance imitation into four kinds.[84] Marlowe's dramatic recastings of Ovid provide good examples. Most rudimentary is 'reproductive' or 'sacramental' imitation, in which a classical original is followed with religious fidelity: thus in *The Jew of Malta*, Marlowe merely reproduces Ovid's image of Morpheus, the god of sleep.[85] More sophisticated is 'eclectic' or 'exploitative' imitation, in which heterogeneous allusions are mingled: the contamination of Virgil with Ovid makes *Dido Queen of Carthage* sustainedly eclectic. Most sophisticated is 'dialectical' imitation, in which the later text actively conflicts with and dissociates itself from its classical pre-text. There is a striking instance in *The Jew of Malta*, when Don Mathias sees Abigail dressed as a nun and alludes to the rape of Proserpine:

> The sweetest flower in Cytherea's field,
> Cropp'd from the pleasures of the fruitful earth,
> And strangely metamorphis'd nun.[86]

The image thrives on the contextual incongruity of the allusion, which adds to the incongruity of the Jewish girl wearing the nun's habit: where Proserpina's association with the earth is linked to her chastity, Abigail's is described in terms of 'pleasures', doubtless sexual; then in the second half of the image, in a twist wholly characteristic of Marlowe's seamy Malta, the nunnery is implicitly made synonymous not with heaven but with the underworld to which Proserpina was abducted.

In this instance, there is a double signal alerting the audience to the Ovidian character of the image: a mythological allusion is yoked to the word 'metamorphis'd'. Elizabethan drama is full of transformations; indeed, for an actor to assume a costume is to undergo a kind of metamorphosis, a process highlighted when—as here, and so often in Shakespeare—a character within the play becomes an actor and

---

[84] Greene, *The Light in Troy: Imitation and Discovery in Renaissance Poetry* (New Haven, Conn., 1982), 39 ff.

[85] Compare *Jew* II. i. 35–7 with *Met.* xi. 635 ff.

[86] I. ii. 376–8. Shakespeare uses an analogous image in a very different context in his Marlovian-Ovidian tragedy *Romeo and Juliet*: the apparently dead Juliet is described as 'the sweetest flower of all the field' (IV. iv. 56).

assumes a new disguise or role. But a theatre audience would not consider all such changes Ovidian. A flag is needed if Ovid is to be brought into play: this might be an actual quotation, a reference to a story of which he provides the standard version, or simply the word 'metamorphosis' (or one of its cognates). Whilst the term 'metamorphosis' existed in early sixteenth-century English, its cognates first appeared after the publication of Golding's translation, and seem to originate in writers strongly influenced by Ovidian mythology. The earliest recorded user of the verb 'metamorphose' and the noun 'metamorphoser' is George Gascoigne in his *Delicate Diet for daintie mouthde Droonkards* of 1576; the verb occurs in a highly Ovidian context, 'They feigned that Medea, Circe, and such other coulde Metamorphose and transforme men into Beastes, Byrdes, Plantes, and Flowres'. The *Oxford English Dictionary* gives *The Two Gentlemen of Verona* (I. i. 66 and II. i. 30) as the earliest use of the form 'metamorphis'd', but if, as seems probable, *The Jew of Malta* antedates that play, then Shakespeare may have picked up the word from Marlowe.

William Adlington's Englishing of *The xi Bookes of the Golden Asse, conteininge the Metamorphosie of Lucius Apuleius* appeared the year before Golding published his complete translation of the *Metamorphoses*,[87] but throughout the Elizabethan period the word 'metamorphosis' was effectively synonymous with Ovid's work. This may be seen from a joke in the academic play, *The Return from Parnassus*, Part 2, when Will Kemp, the clown in Shakespeare's company, is given the lines, 'Few of the university men pen plaies well, they smell too much of that writer Ovid, and that writer Metamorphosis, and talke too much of Proserpina and Juppiter'.[88] The accusation here is that the university-educated dramatists are profligate in their love of mythological embroidery; our Shakespeare, Kemp claims, can put them down with his native wit. But the joke does not have literary historical validity: as I will show in Chapters 2 and 3, Shakespeare established his credentials as a dramatist, and a rival to the university wits, precisely by smelling of that writer Ovid (as in Holofernes' joke on 'Naso') and that writer Metamorphosis. Even at the very end of his career he would go on talking of Jupiter (in *Cymbeline*) and Proserpina (in *The Winter's Tale*).

[87] For the possibility that Shakespeare read Apuleius, see J. J. M. Tobin, *Shakespeare's Favourite Novel: A Study of The Golden Asse as Prime Source* (Lanham, Md., 1984).

[88] ll. 1766 ff., in *The Three Parnassus Plays (1598–1601)*, ed. J. B. Leishman (London, 1949).

Marlowe was the epitome of the university man. *Tamburlaine* glitters with the kind of mythological allusiveness which Kemp mocks, while *Edward II* sometimes seems to require an extremely detailed recall of Ovid's Latin. As Shakespeare would in *Antony and Cleopatra*, Marlowe makes a dramatic point by playing on the court's preoccupation with precedence, as it is manifested in the question of who sits where or who sits first.[89] Edward sits Gaveston by his side in the second Chair Royal, which would normally have been occupied by the queen; Mortimer senior is outraged, 'What man of noble birth can brook this sight? | *Quam male conveniunt!*' (I. iv. 12–13). He is quoting, or rather slightly misquoting, Ovid, 'non bene conveniunt nec in una sede morantur | maiestas et amor' (*Met.* ii. 846–7). A literal translation of this would be 'majesty and love do not go well together and cannot last long in one seat'; Golding's translation neatly incorporates the Elizabethan sense of 'state' as 'Chair of State', 'Betweene the state of Majestie and love is set such oddes, | As that they can not dwell in one' (ii. 1057–8). The listener to Marlowe's line is supposed to reconstruct the full sentence from Mortimer's three words: only then can the punning reference to the throne be understood and the opposition between majesty and love perceived. That opposition is, of course, the play's central topos. Marlowe may even be asking his ideal spectator to recall the context in the *Metamorphoses*: it refers to an undignified union between high and low, Jupiter's descent to the form of a bull in pursuit of his desire for Europa.[90]

When a writer's mind goes to an earlier writer's work, it will often remain there for a moment and undertake a second appropriation. Thus, three lines later in *Edward II*, Warwick introduces a favourite Marlovian simile, 'Ignoble vassal that like Phaeton | Aspir'st unto the guidance of the sun' (I. iv. 16–17). Both images—the king as the sun, the ambitious aspirant as Phaëthon—are conventional, but when combined in this context they are given fresh life. Mortimer replies, 'Their downfall is at hand': once the audience recognizes that Gaveston is Phaëthon-like in his ambition, they know that he will fall. Again, this is a model for the kind of dramatically economic mythological allusion at which Shakespeare subsequently becomes

---

[89] See the spat between Octavius and Antony at *Antony and Cleopatra*, II. ii. 27–30.

[90] Contextual recollection also undercuts Mortimer's quotation from Niobe: '*Maior sum quam cui possit fortuna nocere*' (V. iv. 69, quoting *Met.* vi. 198, 'I am too great for fortune to harm')—the pride of each character is swiftly followed by a fall.

adept. The horses of the sun recur, but without Phaëthon, after Gaveston's death. In the language of precipitation which anticipates that of *Romeo and Juliet*, Edward wills time forward to the moment of reckoning in battle, 'Gallop apace, bright Phoebus, through the sky, | And dusky night, in rusty iron car . . .' (IV. iii. 44–5—'rusty iron' is Golding's idiom). Since Phaëthon has already been brought into the consciousness of the listener, he does not have to be explicitly invoked for it to be seen that Edward is hurrying towards his own downfall.

A variant on the image of the celestial chariot constitutes perhaps the most extraordinary Ovidian allusion in Elizabethan drama. Dr Faustus in his final hour cries,

> *O lente, lente, currite noctis equi!*
> The stars move still, time runs, the clock will strike,
> The devil will come, and Faustus must be damn'd.
>
> (V. ii. 143–5)

The Latin-knowing and literary-minded member of the audience will recall the famous aubade in Ovid's *Amores*, where the lover calls on the horses of the night to slow down so that he may remain in his lover's arms, ' "lente currite, noctis equi!" ' (I. xiii. 40—in his *Ovids Elegies*, Marlowe translates, 'Stay night, and run not thus', omitting the image of the horses, as if he is saving it up for the drama). Faustus would no doubt have repeated the line had he been allowed a night in the arms of Helen of Troy; the final irony of his fate is that he speaks it in the face of damnation instead of love. The introduction of this pagan and erotic line in a sequence of the play in which one would expect attention to be wholly focused on Christian matter—the possibility of last-minute salvation, the descent into hell—is one of Marlowe's boldest strokes. The juxtaposition renders the relationship with both Christianity and Ovidian eroticism 'dialectical'.

Later in his final soliloquy, Faustus recognizes that he will not be allowed the release of metamorphosis,

> Ah, Pythagoras' *metempsychosis*, were that true,
> This soul should fly from me, and I be chang'd
> Unto some brutish beast.
>
> (V. ii. 175–7)

Although in the scene at the German Emperor's court there is a plan to use Faustus' magic to enact the myth of Actaeon, *Dr Faustus* is in important respects un-Ovidian—the play's transformations are associated primarily with necromancy rather than classical metamorphosis. Faustus' recognition that Pythagorean metempsychosis does not apply, that he will not change but must be damned perpetually, dramatizes the difference between the Ovidian, where all things change but nothing is destroyed, and the Christian, where there is a judgement and an ending. Many major Elizabethan writers combine Ovidian allusions and analogies with a marked sense, usually determined by the Christian tradition, of difference and distance from their classical forebear. This is Thomas Greene's remaining category, 'heuristic' imitation, which in its own processes dramatizes the historical difference between the poet and his precursor—sameness is combined with difference, continuity with change. The text acknowledges its predecessor, but in so doing finds its own distinctive voice; it 'acts out its own coming into being' and in so doing 'creates a bridge' which heals the sense of estrangement from the past which was the melancholy downside of the humanist project of cultural renovation.[91]

Greene recognizes that it is not always possible to distinguish between heuristic and dialectical imitation: the difference is essentially tonal in that heuristic imitation seeks to hold together past and present, whereas dialectical imitation is a more aggressive attempt to reject the past. Edmund Spenser provides a case in point. Book 3 of *The Faerie Queene*, as originally published in 1590, offers a dazzling etiology of love that is both Ovidian and non-Ovidian. Ovid is a source when the narcissistic origins of desire are acknowledged as Britomart falls in love with an image in a glass, but thanks to her Chastity the heroine is able to rescue Love in the person of Amoret from the power of rapacious Ovidian enchantment (Busyrane's castle, with its tapestries of the Arachnean rapes of the gods), yet then the closing consummation is a return to Ovid as Amoret and Scudamore fuse in the manner of Salmacis and Hermaphroditus. The book's pervasive sexual charge is Ovidian, but what makes it different from the world of the *Metamorphoses* is that most Christian and least Ovidian virtue, Chastity. Similarly, the 'Mutabilitie' cantos begin with an Ovidian sense of 'Change, the which all mortall things doth sway',[92] but in the Faunus episode the story of Diana and Actaeon is updated and

[91] *The Light in Troy*, 41.
[92] 'Two Cantos of Mutabilitie', VI. i. 2, in Spenser, *The Faerie Queene*, ed. A. C. Hamilton (London, 1977). All subsequent quotations from this edn.

reworked in such a way that what is metamorphosed is the landscape of Ireland rather than the body of the voyeur—as punishment for seeing Diana bathing, Faunus is clad in a deer-skin and pursued, but he does not actually become a deer; Diana, however, abandons her stream and the fair forests around Arlo hill, thus transforming Ireland into a wilderness ravaged by wolves and thieves. This is heuristic in that the force of Ovidian transformation is acknowledged, yet held together with a 'modern' concern—the Irish problem. The heuristic slides into the dialectical when the cantos break off with a more resounding rejection of the metamorphic spirit, as Spenser alludes to 'that great Sabbaoth God' and the time

> when no more Change shall be,
> But stedfast rest of all things firmely stayd
> Upon the pillours of Eternity,
> That is the contrayr to *Mutabilitie*.
>
> (VIII. ii. 2–5)

Ovidian fluidity is replaced by the stability of Christian faith.

Spenser's relationship with Ovid, like Milton's a generation later, was self-consciously problematic. The wit, metamorphic power, and mythological range of the Roman poet, besides being profoundly admired in themselves, were vital poetic resources; yet Ovid was both a pagan poet and an erotic one. Spenser's task was to metamorphose Ovid's poem itself, simultaneously to replicate its art and to rewrite it in Christian or at least moral terms.[93] Difference was as important as imitation. Difference, particularly of literary medium, also became increasingly important for Shakespeare in his dealings with Ovid. But before fully developing an art which dispersed the *Metamorphoses*, transposing aspects of them into dramatic form, the young poet disciplined himself as an imitator in the brilliant apprentice-works in which he modelled himself on his Roman exemplar as consciously as did any other writer of the age.

---

[93] Recent critical work on Spenser and Ovid, as well as Milton and Ovid, has addressed this issue in relation to theoretical questions of poetic authority and revisionary reading: see in particular John Guillory, *Poetic Authority: Spenser, Milton, and Literary History* (New York, 1983) and Richard J. DuRocher, *Milton and Ovid* (Ithaca, NY, 1985). The best treatment of Ovid and the 'Mutabilitie' cantos is M. N. Holahan, '"Iamque opus exegi": Ovid's Changes and Spenser's Brief Epic of Mutability', *ELR* vi (1976), 244–70.

2

Sexual Poetry

Vertues or vices theame to thee all one is:
Who loves chaste life, there's *Lucrece* for a Teacher:
Who list read lust there's *Venus* and *Adonis*,
True modell of a most lascivious leatcher.[1]

I

Late in 1589, Thomas Lodge published his poem *Scillaes Metamorphosis: Enterlaced with the unfortunate love of Glaucus*. In so doing, he established a new poetic genre, the witty mythological love-poem dressed in the manner of Ovid but translated into an English setting (Glaucus complains from the river Isis near Oxford). Following in Lodge's wake, Marlowe wrote *Hero and Leander* and Shakespeare *Venus and Adonis*—to judge by frequency of allusions to the former and reprintings of the latter, two of the most popular poems of the age. *Hero and Leander* is based more on the late Alexandrian poet Musaeus than on the exchange of letters between these two famous lovers in the *Heroides*, but in technique the poem is pure Ovid, with its rhetorical persuasions to love and its embedded narratives of gods whose sexual appetites are ample and polymorphous (Neptune entwines himself around Leander, Mercury tumbles a country maid). Hero is (oxymoronically) Venus' nun and Leander meets her at a festival of Adonis; Shakespeare picks up from this and retells the metamorphic narrative of the goddess and her mortal boy—a story which serves to explain the perverse nature of sexual love.

In the prose dedication to the first edition of his translation, Arthur Golding wrote that the myths of the *Metamorphoses* were 'outwardly moste pleasant tales and delectable histories', but that they were

---

[1] Thomas Freeman, *Runne and a Great Cast*, the second part of *Rubbe, and a Great Cast* (London, 1614), epigram 92.

'fraughted inwardlye with most piththie instructions and wholsome examples'.[2] As was shown in the last chapter, Golding, with not inconsiderable ingenuity, peeled off the narrative skin and found hidden 'inner' moral meanings in the text. He thus contrived to make Ovid sound at least a little like the other major author whom he translated into English: John Calvin. Lodge's poem, by contrast, sets out to enjoy Ovid's poetry of passion, as the Roman poet did himself. Lessons may be learnt from this world of desire and metamorphosis, but they are lessons about the games and the anguish of love. The examples are *not* wholesome, the instruction is not moralistic. Lodge and his successors show how love is; they don't moralize about how behaviour should be. Golding's argument is that if you give in to passion, you will suffer, whereas the argument of late Elizabethan Ovidianism often seems to be that however you behave, whether you rein in your passion or not, love will make you suffer. Hero and Leander embrace love and end up dead. Adonis rejects love and ends up dead. In Lodge's poem, first Glaucus woos a reluctant Scilla, then Cupid fires an arrow that stops up his wound and cures him of his love; but Cupid also fires at Scilla, so she is in turn afflicted and tries to seduce a now reluctant Glaucus. Cupid, the blind, diminutive, and illegitimate child of Venus, is very literally a contrary little bastard, as Shakespeare's Rosalind knows—'that same wicked bastard of Venus, that was begot of thought, conceived of spleen, and born of madness, that blind rascally boy that abuses everyone's eyes because his own are out'.[3]

But these poems cannot be described as tragedies of love. That is partly because, as in Ovid, metamorphosis lets the characters off the hook: they are arrested in the moment of intense emotion and released into a vital, vibrant, colourful world of anthropomorphic nature. And it is also, pre-eminently, because the poet is ultimately more interested in the beginnings than the ends of love. Marlowe's poem breaks off at the consummation and does not bother with the death. The primary focus is upon the psychological causes of love—what is it that the lover desires?—and the linguistic arts with which the love-object is pursued. Lodge in *Scillaes Metamorphosis*, Marlowe in *Hero and Leander*, and Shakespeare in *Venus and Adonis*, devote most

---

[2] *The Fyrst Fower Bookes of P Ovidius Nasos Worke, intitled Metamorphosis, translated oute of Latin into Englishe meter by Arthur Golding Gent.* (London, 1565), dedication to Leicester, dated Dec. 1564.

[3] *As You Like It*, IV. i. 201–4.

of their attention to the arguments of the characters, in particular to the topos of the persuasion to love. The pleasure for the Elizabethan reader resides in the cunning rhetoric; Shakespeare was above all known as a sweet, witty, mellifluous, honey-tongued writer.

The skill of the writers of erotic narrative poetry manifested itself in their way of combining two Ovids: the witty preceptor of love, the poet of arguing one's way into bed, as in the *Amores* and the *Ars Amatoria*, is brought together with the weaver of 'interlaced' mythological tales of metamorphosis. Thus Leander makes use of an argument from the *Amores* about how a woman's sexual treasure (her virginity) should, like all wealth, be used instead of hoarded, and Venus follows the speaker of the *Ars Amatoria* in pointing to a randy horse as an example of how natural it is to accept love.[4] In the terms of William Keach, the best modern reader of the genre, Ovid's irony is combined with his pathos—his witty detachment and his emotional intensity are fused.[5] Love is acknowledged to be confusing and painful, but desire is also revealed to be comic and undignified. 'Perverse it shall be where it shows most toward', says Venus in her curse on love (1157): contrariness is the key.

It is easy to share the cultivated Elizabethan reader's delight in the conceits of the genre. The resourceful Venus has many a memorable example:

> I'll be a park, and thou shalt be my deer.
> Feed where thou wilt, on mountains or in dale;
>   Graze on my lips, and if those hills be dry,
>   Stray lower, where the pleasant fountains lie.
>
>   (231–4)

Ovid tells the story of Venus and Adonis in less than a hundred lines, Shakespeare in more than a thousand: the classical text provides a narrative framework into which the Elizabethan writer inserts elaborate arguments, thus demonstrating his own rhetorical skills. Because the persuasions given to the characters are the major interpolations into the source, critical readings tend to concentrate on

---

[4] *Hero and Leander*, i. 231–40 is a translation and expansion of *Amores*, I. viii. 51–3 (also trans. by Marlowe in his *Ovid's Elegies*). Venus on the palfrey (385–96) borrows from *Ars Am.* i. 277–80. The topos from the *Amores* of using, not hoarding, beauty is also adapted by Shakespeare in the third quatrain of Sonnet 9.

[5] See Keach, *Elizabethan Erotic Narratives: Irony and Pathos in the Ovidian Poetry of Shakespeare, Marlowe, and their Contemporaries* (New Brunswick, NJ, and Hassocks, 1977).

them.[6] But it will be the contention of the first half of this chapter that within Shakespeare's poem there are signals that we must consider the Ovidian source-text to be much broader than the seventy or so lines of direct material. Golding's outward/inward distinction works differently in Shakespeare's reading of Ovid: whilst the moral translator claimed to find meaning 'inwardlye' but in fact imposed it from outside the text, the creative imitator interprets his source narrative partly by means of other narratives that lie both outside and inside, around and within, it. Surrounding the text is a distinctly unwholesome context.

When Shakespeare read Book Ten of the *Metamorphoses*, the first thing he was told about Adonis was that he was the 'misbegotten chyld' of the union between Myrrha and her father, Cinyras (Golding, x. 577). At the same time, he would have learnt that the lovely boy was born not from his mother's womb, but by the splitting open through Lucina's agency of the tree into which his mother had been metamorphosed.[7] Incest and a kind of posthumous caesarean section—a bizarre birth like that of Marvell's 'Unfortunate Lover'—initiate the reader into a world of unorthodox swervings of gender and generation.

Ovid's story of Venus and Adonis is narrated by Orpheus as part of his long lament to the trees and wild animals after his loss of Eurydice. The Orphic section of the *Metamorphoses* begins with a series of tales of homosexual love. Orpheus says that after losing his Eurydice he shunned all love of woman and turned to boys instead:

> And *Orphye* . . . did utterly eschew
> The womankynd. . . .
>
> .   .   .   .
>
> He also taught the *Thracian* folke a stewes of Males too make
> And of the flowring pryme of boayes the pleasure for too take.
>
> (x. 87–92)

Orpheus is the patron saint of homosexuality, or, more specifically, of pederasty. Among the trees to which he sings is the cypress, etiologized as the metamorphosed form of a boy loved by Apollo, Cyparissus, who erroneously killed a tame stag whom he loved and

---

[6] See e.g. the rhetorically oriented reading of the poem by Heather Dubrow in her fine *Captive Victors: Shakespeare's Narrative Poems and Sonnets* (Ithaca, NY, 1987).

[7] Should we think forward to Ariel's rebirth from a tree through Prospero's agency in *The Tempest* and thence to the other strange rebirths of that play, such as Prospero's extraordinary image of his own labour on the sea-voyage?

consequently resolved to die himself, asking as a last boon that he should be allowed to mourn for ever. He is thus 'sad cypress'—there is a resonance forward in Shakespeare's career, to the figuration of love's sorrows in *Twelfth Night*, where, as with Ovid's Orphic narration, the context is homoerotic, Orsino's desire for Cesario echoing Apollo's for Cyparissus. More locally, there is a prefiguration of and variation on Adonis: both boys are loved by gods, while one slays and the other is slain by accident.

Cyparissus homoeroticizes the audience of Orpheus. The singer himself then picks up the motif: he tells of Ganymede, loved by Jove (and impersonated, we may add, by the gender-bending Rosalind of Lodge and Shakespeare), then of Hyacinth, loved by Apollo. The latter is a second prefiguration of Adonis, in that he loves hunting. He is inadvertently killed by Apollo's discus while sporting with him; the flower that grows from his blood has Apollo's lament ('AI AI') inscribed upon it—as with Venus and Adonis, the story ends with the creation from the beloved boy's blood of a plant that is also a signifier of grief. George Sandys's commentary speaks of 'an afflicted ingemination, charactred in the leaves', a phrase nicely catching the two key elements which the story shares with that of Adonis: floral inscription and repetition (the story is retold with each year's new growth).[8]

Orpheus' argument that homoerotic desire is licensed by the precedent of the gods is of considerable importance for Elizabethan poetry, which is so frequently polymorphous in its sexual orientation. Heterosexuality and homosexuality are anachronistic concepts here: Marlowe and Shakespeare, the latter most notably but by no means exclusively in the Sonnets, take delight in lovely boys one moment and females the next. In the theatre, the embrace between a male and a female character may bring with it a *frisson* of the homoerotic, in that it is an embrace between two male actors—this was of course one reason for 'puritan' hostility to the stage. Despite the astringent laws against sodomy in Elizabethan England, the poetry of the age is unapologetic in its celebration of the charms of teenage boys.[9]

For Ovid's Orpheus, 'unnatural' desire is to be found elsewhere, not in homosexuality but in the examples cited in the next section of Book

---

[8] Sandys, *Ovid's Metamorphosis Englished*, 359.

[9] On this whole area, see Bruce Smith, *Homosexual Desire in Shakespeare's England* (Chicago, 1991), esp. its treatment (ch. 6) of Elizabethan versions of the Ganymede/minion.

Ten: the Propoetides, the first prostitutes; Pygmalion, who makes love to his statue; and Myrrha, who falls in love with her father. Elizabethan and Jacobean interest in sexual 'beastliness' found a focus in these stories, as may be seen from the titles of Marston's *Metamorphosis of Pigmalions Image* (1598) and William Barksted's *Myrrha, the Mother of Adonis; or Lustes Prodegies* (1607). The final act of the *The Winter's Tale* is exceptional in its way of reworking the Pygmalion story without any implication of beastliness or, in Paulina's term, unlawfulness. The traditional moralization of Book Ten is summarized by Golding in the epistle prefixed to his 1567 translation:

> The tenth booke cheefly dooth containe one kynd of argument,
> Reproving most prodigious lusts of such as have bene bent
> Too incest most unnaturall.
>
> (Epistle, 213–15)

But the intentions of Ovid's Orpheus are not quite this simple: he sings with a lighter touch ('leviore lyra')[10] of the delights as well as the dire consequences of sexuality. And in so far as Orpheus' songs are an apology for homoeroticism, the moralizing Golding is forced to read the text against the grain.

Even in the case of incest, Ovid is more interested in exploring the lover's mental state than condemning her. Myrrha may resort to a bestial comparison ('animals commit incest, so why shouldn't humans?'), but she is revealed to be a tortured victim of desire, as she lies restlessly at night:

> Shee wisshes and shee wotes not what too doo, nor how too gin.
> And like as when a mightye tree with axes heawed rownd,
> Now reedye with a strype or twaine to lye uppon the grownd,
> Uncerteine is which way to fall and tottreth every way:
> Even so her mynd with dowtfull wound effeebled then did stray
> Now heere now there uncerteinely, and tooke of bothe encreace.
>
> (x. 419–24)

This kind of representation of the mind under the stress of conflicting emotions is Ovid's prime gift to the Elizabethan narrative poets. Like their master, Marlowe and Shakespeare as poets are psychopathologists rather than moralists. Where the moral interpreter Golding assumes that metamorphosis is a punishment for sexual unnatural-

---

[10] *Metamorphoses*, x. 152.

ness, the poets are more interested in causes than effects, in explanations than judgements.

As so often in the *Metamorphoses*, a festival in honour of a god provides the occasion for resolution of the Myrrha story; rather as the 'holiday' moment in Shakespearian comedy precipitates transformative action, the festival's interruption of the quotidian provides the impulse which causes the tottering tree to fall. With characteristic Ovidian irony, the festival in question is that of Ceres, goddess of fertility—in these circumstances, foison is the last thing Myrrha needs. Sandys's commentary reminds the Renaissance reader of the distance between Myrrha and Ceres, to whose worship 'none were admitted that were either uncleane, or whose consciences accused them of any secret crime'.[11] Cinyras' wife goes off to celebrate this distinctively female festival, leaving him alone in his bed for nine nights; a nurse offers to provide him with comfort in the form of a girl who loves him. She gives a false name, but says that the 'pretye lasse' is Myrrha's age; she escorts her to the bedroom in the dark and father makes love to daughter, ignorant of her identity. Ovid observes the behaviour of the lovers with his usual perspicuity and irony: 'by chaunce as in respect of yeeres | He daughter did hir call, and shee him father' (x. 536–7). An older man and a young girl in bed together are always at some level father and daughter; here Cinyras describes the relationship metonymically when it is in fact biological. The encounter ends with his 'cursed seede in [her] wicked womb' (538). Adonis is the fruit of that seed.

The Venus and Adonis story must be seen in the broader context of the Orphic series of narratives concerning destructive passion, female desire—Book Ten teems with aggressive female wooers—and homoerotic charm. Venus the lover is also Venus the mother: 'Hot, faint, and weary with her hard embracing . . . like the froward infant stilled with dandling, | He now obeys' (559–63); 'Like a milch doe whose dwelling dugs do ache, | Hasting to feed her fawn hid in some brake' (875–6). Such juxtapositions of sexuality and parenting suggest that Adonis is forced to re-enact, with gender and generational roles reversed, his mother's incestuous affair.

The contextual pressure of Myrrha is signalled by Shakespeare's two explicit allusions to Adonis' mother. As part of her argument that the lovely boy should accept love, Venus says:

[11] *Ovid's Metamorphosis Englished*, 363.

Art thou obdurate, flinty, hard as steel?
Nay, more than flint, for stone at rain relenteth.
Art thou a woman's son, and canst not feel
What 'tis to love, how want of love tormenteth?
  O, had thy mother borne so hard a mind,
  She had not brought forth thee, but died unkind.
                                                    (199–204)

She suggests that he somehow owes it to his mother's experience of love to experience love himself. In the light of Book Ten, it is a richly ironic suggestion: Myrrha found that love 'tormented' as much as— more than—'want of love' did. The 'mind' that she bore was not exactly a seemly model; the child 'brought forth' by her, the fruit of incest, would have been better unborn. She would have 'died unkind' if she hadn't loved a man and thus borne a child, says Venus—but it would have been better if she had died untouched by her own kind, her kin. In the incestuous bed she was a little more than kin and more than kind. As for Venus' phrase 'died unkind', ironically it was only in death that Myrrha achieved a kind of kindness or softness. She is metamorphosed into the 'weeping' myrrh tree, oozing drops that signify her repentance.

Later, Venus addresses the sun: 'There lives a son [i.e. Adonis] that sucked an earthly mother | May lend thee light, as thou dost lend to other' (863–4). The sun/son pun invokes Adonis' mother for a second time. Again the irony rebounds on Venus: Myrrha never did suckle Adonis, since he was born from the tree after her death. Instead, Venus herself eventually becomes a surrogate mother, suckling Adonis—she ends the poem with his flower in her breast, imaged as the 'cradle' in which she 'rock[s]' him (1185–6). Adonis' life begins with a father and daughter in bed together, and ends with sexual desire for him being sublimated into an image of a mother by the bed of her baby son. For Ovid, Venus' love for Adonis is the direct consequence of Myrrha's illicit desire: 'Dame *Venus* fell in love with him: wherby | He did revenge the outrage of his mothers villanye' (x. 604–5). Venus is held responsible for Myrrha's love, since she is the goddess of love, even in its illicit forms, and she is punished by being smitten with unrequited love herself.

The Myrrha story, then, provides an ironic, darkening pre-text for the tale of Venus and Adonis, which points to the perverse origins of desire. A second parallel narrative occupies a position as what might be called an *in-text*. When Ovid's Venus advises Adonis not to hunt the boar, she tells a story to support her case. Embedded within Orpheus' tale of Venus and Adonis is Venus' tale of Atalanta, a girl who has been told by an oracle that if she takes a husband she will die. Being a fast runner, she repels her suitors by saying that they must race her: if they win she will be the prize, if they lose they will die. Like Adonis, Atalanta is an image of the self in flight: 'nec tamen effugies teque ipsa viva carebis'—'you will be separated from your self and yet be alive' (x. 566). The youthful Hippomenes initially scorns men who are willing to risk their lives in a race for a girl, but when Atalanta strips off to run, he is won over by her beauty—'the which was like too myne, | Or rather (if that thou wert made a woman) like too thyne' (x. 674–5) explains Venus, taking the opportunity to dwell on Adonis' female charm, which is further echoed in Hippomenes' 'maydens countenance' (742). Atalanta promptly falls in love herself: suddenly she is uncertain whether she wants to win or lose this race. Golding's translation is flat-footed at this point; a modern version catches more concisely Ovid's exquisite account of Atalanta's attempt to rationalize her faltering:

> It's not his beauty
> That touches me (though that could touch me too);
> But he is still a boy; it's not himself
> That moves me but his tender years, his youth.
> Think of his courage, unafraid of death.[12]

The parenthesis is a wonderfully revealing moment. His beauty has of course touched her. As with Myrrha, the mind is pulled in conflicting directions, love induces weakness, and then a disastrous mistake is made—the oracle is disregarded.

Hippomenes, being in love, invokes the assistance of the love-god Venus. She assists him by throwing three golden apples at strategic moments during the race, causing Atalanta to go off course and pick them up. Hippomenes thus wins both the race and her. Venus points the moral:

> Thinkst thou I was not woorthy thanks, *Adonis*, thinkest thow
> I earned not that he too mee should frankincence allow?
> But he forgetfull, neyther thanks nor frankincence did give.
> By meanes where of too sooden wrath he justly did me drive.
>
> (x. 798–801)

[12] A. D. Melville's World's Classics trans. (Oxford, 1987) of *Metamorphoses*, x. 614–16.

She accordingly turns against the young lovers, determining to have her revenge and make an example of them. She inflames them to sexual desire while they are in the temple of Cybele; they defile it by making love there, and Cybele transforms them into lions.

Ostensibly, Venus tells Adonis this story in order to persuade him not to go hunting dangerous beasts like lions and boars. But it's not really a tale warning against wild animals; it is Venus saying 'don't rile me', 'do as I say, I'm a powerful woman'. The key moment is the one where she addresses Adonis directly, demanding that he assent to her claim that she deserved a thank-offering and was justified in taking revenge when not given one. She tells the story to demonstrate her power. But the song is still that of Orpheus—it is a narrative within a narrative, creating the kind of multiple perspective allowed for by the Shakespearian play within a play. For Orpheus, the story is another warning against love: Atalanta submitted to desire and no good came of it. So Venus is saying to Adonis 'do not resist love', while simultaneously Orpheus is saying to his audience 'resist love'. The Orphic context undercuts Venus' rhetoric. The story is being *used* by both characters; narratives about love, Ovid seems to be saying, are never disinterested. The narrator always has ulterior motives, is always driven by his or her own desires.

I have described the embedded Atalanta narrative at some length because of a striking fact about the structure of Ovid's Venus and Adonis. Forty lines are devoted to Venus falling in love with Adonis, then one hundred and forty-seven lines to Venus telling her admonitory tale, and finally thirty-two to Venus' departure and Adonis' being gored by the boar and metamorphosed. The discourse of Venus thus occupies twice as much space as the story's action. It may thus be seen that the narrative of Atalanta fulfils the role in Ovid that Venus' rhetorical persuasions to love do in Shakespeare. Shakespeare's Venusian discourse—the traditional *carpe diem* arguments of the male lover put into the mouth of the aggressive female wooer—is engendered by Adonis' active resistance to love, a resistance which is the major alteration to the source. Ovid's Adonis likes hunting, but does not object to love on principle as Shakespeare's does. Like all good imitators, Shakespeare enters into the same arena as his model, but does his own turn there. His version is very much his own, as Ovid's is his, in that the *Metamorphoses* do not lean particularly on the older versions of the Venus and Adonis story, such as that of Theocritus. In Ovid, Atalanta goes against the advice of the

oracle in falling for Hippomenes; in Shakespeare, Adonis goes against
the advice of Venus in hunting the boar. Atalanta's death results from
the way that she does not resist love, Adonis' from the way that he
does resist it. Put the two stories together and one reaches the
irresistible conclusion that whichever way you turn love will destroy
you. It is essentially something out of your control, a force that drives
you rather than vice versa.

In both Ovid and Shakespeare the story ends with the death of
Adonis, described as a pattern which will be repeated perpetually.
This sense of inevitable future repetition is what gives the story its
mythic, archetypal quality. One tradition of interpretation thus comes
to read the story as a vegetation myth: Abraham Fraunce, in a
mythography published the year before *Venus and Adonis*, interpreted
Adonis as the sun, Venus as the upper hemisphere of the earth, and
the boar as winter.[13] Ovid and Shakespeare do not take their
interpretations in this direction; they are not interested in external
nature so much as the nature of sexual desire. In Ovid, Venus creates
the anemone from Adonis' blood as a 'remembrance' (Golding,
x. 848) of her suffering. The passing of the seasons will be a figuration
of love's sorrows; the flower symbolizes the transience of beauty and
the vulnerability of desire. *Venus and Adonis* moves towards an
etiology of love's anguish: 'Since thou art dead, lo, here I
prophesy | Sorrow on love hereafter shall attend' (1135–6). Ovid
closes Book Ten with an image of the flower blasted by the wind and
shed all too soon; so too, according to Shakespeare's Venus, love will
'Bud, and be blasted, in a breathing-while' (1142). Adonis' flower is
the purple of the blood from which it springs, the colour a reminder of
the violence and death that will attend on love. Shakespeare's Venus
then plucks it: 'She crops the stalk, and in the breach
appears | Green-dropping sap, which she compares to tears'
(1175–6). This comparison between liquid drops falling from
vegetable matter and tears reintroduces Myrrha, whose guilt and
sorrow are symbolized by the gum that drops from the Arabian tree
into which she is metamorphosed. ' "Poor flower," quoth [Venus],
"this was thy father's guise— | Sweet issue of a more sweet-smelling
sire" ' (1177–8). It is an adroit variation: where Ovid begins his tale
with Adonis as a son issuing from a tree, Shakespeare ends his with a

    [13] Fraunce, *The Third part of the Countesse of Pembrokes Yvychurch* (London, 1592),
p. 45[v].

flower issuing from Adonis, who thus becomes a father. Shakespeare's Venus acts out an extraordinary family romance. By imaging her lover as a father, she makes herself into the mother and the flower into the fruit of their union. But the logic of the imagery dictates that the flower is her sexual partner as well as her child, for it clearly substitutes for Adonis himself—she comforts herself with the thought that it is a love-token, which she can continually kiss. The fusion of lover and mother in the context of vegetative imagery makes Venus into Myrrha once again. It is as if, having slept with her father, the girl is now sleeping with her son.

In the next and last stanza, Venus flies off to Paphos, the site of her principal temple on Cyprus. The naming of the place takes the mythologically literate reader back to Orpheus' narrative in Book Ten, for Cyprus is the location of the stories of the Propoetides, Pygmalion, and Myrrha, the figures associated with Venus and with the rapacious female sexuality that Orpheus uses to justify his misogyny. Ovid explicitly states that the name Paphos derives from the child of the union between Pygmalion and his statue; Paphos in turn produces Cinyras, who, thanks to the incestuous union with Myrrha, is both father and grandfather of Adonis. Golding and Sandys took Paphos to be a boy ('a Sun that *Paphus* hyght'—Golding, x. 323), presumably because most Greek words ending in -os become in Latin the masculine -us. Sixteenth-century editions tended to follow the manuscript variant 'quo' (masculine) for 'qua' (feminine) in Ovid's line 'Illa Paphon genuit, de qua tenet insula nomen' (x. 297—'she [the statue] bore Paphos, from whom the island takes its name'), despite the fact that the next line makes the child feminine: 'Editus hac ille est' ('he [Cinyras] was borne by *her*'). Ovid *could* be deliberately confusing the gender—that would be in accordance with the sexual ambiguity of Book Ten—but it is more likely that 'qua' is the correct reading and a girl is intended. The Renaissance, however, stuck to the masculinized name Paphus: Marston ends his *Metamorphosis of Pigmalions Image* with the lines 'Paphus was got: of whom in after age | Cyprus was Paphos call'd, and evermore | Those Ilandars do Venus name adore.'[14] Whatever the gender, the identification of Venus with Paphos further embroils her in the incest plot.

If we are alert to the signals in *Venus and Adonis* that activate the

---

[14] Stanza 39, text from *Elizabethan Minor Epics*, ed. Elizabeth Story Donno (New York and London, 1963).

other parts of Book Ten of the *Metamorphoses*, it becomes quite clear that this is a poem about transgressive sexuality. And since it is supposed to be an etiology of sexual love—the goddess of love's own experience of desire sets the tone for everybody else's—there is a strong implication that sexual love is always at some level transgressive of the norms laid down by Church and State. The broader Ovidian context reveals two persistent characteristics of sexual desire: it is bound up first with the polymorphous perversity of family romance and second with a dissolution of the conventional barriers of gender, for in these stories women take the active role usually given to men and young men always look like girls. The first characteristic is an essentially destructive one, associated above all with the Myrrha pre-text. The second, which is partly a function of Orpheus' conversion to homosexuality, is also potentially destructive—as may be seen from the fate of the singer at the beginning of Book Eleven. Orpheus' narratives may charm rocks and trees and birds, but they cut no ice with a horde of Thracian women who descend on him in bacchic fury and tear him to pieces in punishment for his attitude to their sex.

The girlish-boy motif also takes the reader to other parts of the *Metamorphoses*. Adonis is one of Ovid's many beautiful young men on the threshold of sexual maturity; like the sixteen-year-old Narcissus, 'he seemde to stande beetwene the state of man and Lad' (iii. 438). Shakespeare's Venus herself makes the link, first in her persuasion to love—'Is thine own heart to thine own face affected? . . . Narcissus so himself himself forsook, | And died to kiss his shadow in the brook' (157–62)—and again in her final lament to the flower, 'To grow unto himself was his desire' (1180). Coppélia Kahn sees this association as the key to the poem: 'In Adonis, Shakespeare depicts not only a narcissistic character for whom eros is a threat to the self, but also a boy who regards women as a threat to his masculinity. But the real threat is internal, and comes from his very urge to defend against eros.'[15] Narcissism, then, is another aspect of destructive sexuality in *Venus and Adonis*. What is it that the lover desires? If not her parent, like Myrrha, then himself, like Narcissus—it is not a happy prognosis.

But Echo never gets near Narcissus; the physical interplay between a desiring female and a resistant male, the poem's body-contact,

[15] *Man's Estate: Masculine Identity in Shakespeare* (Berkeley, Los Angeles, and London, 1981), 33.

derives from neither the tale of Adonis nor that of Narcissus but another Ovidian narrative, that of Salmacis and Hermaphroditus.[16] Golding moralized the fate of Hermaphroditus as a warning against effeminacy (Epistle, 116), but Shakespeare, I would suggest, read it very differently. If the quasi-incestuous aspects of *Venus and Adonis* are derived primarily from Book Ten of the *Metamorphoses* and the self-consuming absorption of Adonis from Narcissus, the poem's playfulness and delicate eroticism, its enjoyment of sexuality and the dissolution of gender barriers, owe much to the Hermaphroditus tale in Book Four.

The nymph Salmacis' wooing of the coy youth Hermaphroditus is a bravura performance, in which the norms of seduction poetry are systematically reversed. It is the boy who blushes and looks more sexually desirable as a result, the boy who has a perfectly formed body resembling a work of art (swimming in the translucent water, he looks like an ivory figure encased in glass), the girl who hides in a bush and watches the object of desire undress to bathe. In both Ovid and the Elizabethans the prurient gaze usually rests on the female, on the gradual stripping of Diana, Arethusa, and the rest; but here the tease is for the benefit of the reader (female or male) who likes fresh-limbed boys:

> and by and by amid
> The flattring waves he dippes his feete, no more but first the sole
> And to the ancles afterward both feete he plungeth whole.
> And for to make the matter short, he tooke so great delight
> In cooleness of the pleasant spring, that streight he stripped quight
> His garments from his tender skin.
>
> (iv. 421–6)

And in the scene of aquatic love-making, it is the male breast that is reached for ('And willde he nillde he with hir handes she toucht his naked brest'—446), the female who presses down 'with all hir weight' (458). Salmacis ultimately achieves total intercourse with

---

[16] This story has long been recognized as a supplementary source for *Venus and Adonis*: see e.g. Bullough, i. 161–3. Most interestingly, sonnets 4 and 6 of *The Passionate Pilgrim*, possibly attributable to Shakespeare, also fuse Venus' wooing of Adonis with Salmacis' spying on the bathing Hermaphroditus. In the last line of sonnet 4, Adonis is described as 'froward', Golding's epithet for Hermaphroditus (iv. 459). Compare the Actaeon/Adonis fusion in the induction to *The Taming of the Shrew*, cited in Ch. 4, below.

her object of desire (notice how the force which effects the union is 'hir
hugging and hir grasping'):

> The bodies of them twaine
> Were mixt and joyned both in one. To both them did remaine
> One countnance. Like as if a man should in one barke beholde
> Two twigges both growing into one and still togither holde:
> Even so when through hir hugging and hir grasping of the tother
> The members of them mingled were and fastned both togither,
> They were not any lenger two: but (as it were) a toy
> Of double shape: Ye could not say it was a perfect boy,
> Nor perfect wench: it seemed both and none of both to beene.

(iv. 462–70)

At one level the story is meant as an etiology of the Hermaphrodite.
Hermaphroditus gets the last word—just as he, not Salmacis, gets to
keep his name—and the final image is of enfeeblement, of the waters
in which the union took place having the power to convert a man into
a half-man ('semivir'—iv. 386). This is the basis of Golding's
moralization in terms of effeminacy. The description of interpenetration, however, with its wonder-filled sense of total coition, suggests
not halving of strength but doubling of perfection. As so frequently in
Ovid, the moment of wild passion paradoxically seems to outlast the
subsequent stasis. This, we feel, is an image of how sex should be.

So it was that the Renaissance did not always read the
hermaphrodite as a transgressive abomination. An alternative
interpretation made it into an image of the complete union and
interpenetration that Donne strives for in 'The Extasie'; as one
modern commentator puts it, 'the *form* of the hermaphrodite was
uniquely that of perfect love because it alone imaged that mystical
union wherein the two sexes became one self-sufficient sex that
contains both'.[17] He/she represents the re-creation of the original
unitary gender imagined by Aristophanes in his account of the origins
of love in Plato's *Symposium*. The paradox of the hermaphrodite is
even more condensed than Stephen Greenblatt supposes: in his essay

[17] A. R. Cirillo, 'The Fair Hermaphrodite: Love-Union in the Poetry of Donne and
Spenser', *SEL* ix (1969), 81–95 (p. 94). Cirillo here cites the *Lezzioni* of Benedetto
Varchi (Venice, 1561). For a more complex and less affirmative reading of the
hermaphrodite in *The Faerie Queene*, see Lauren Silberman, 'The Hermaphrodite and
the Metamorphosis of Spenserian Allegory', *ELR* xvii (1987), 207–23. See also Gayle
Whittier, 'The Sublime Androgyne Motif in Three Shakespearean Works', *JMRS* xix
(1989), 185–210, esp. on the youth as 'master-mistress' in Sonnet 20.

'Fiction and Friction', he argues that the discourses of hermaphrodi-
tism and 'normal sexuality' are 'the same discourse, for the
knowledge that enables one to understand the monstrous conjunction in one individual of the male and female sexes is the identical
knowledge that enables one to understand the normal experience of
sexual pleasure';[18] Greenblatt's 'the identical knowledge' depends on
Michel Foucault's notion of discourses containing their own oppo-
sites, whereas in the positive Renaissance reading of Ovid the figure of
the hermaphrodite is more directly an image of the normal experience
of sexual pleasure. Spenser used the figure thus when describing the
passionate union of Amoret and Scudamour in the 1590 ending of
The Faerie Queene:

> No word they spake, nor earthly thing they felt,
> But like two senceles stocks in long embracement dwelt.

(This is Ovid's image of the two twigs growing into one.)

> Had ye them seene, ye would have surely thought,
> That they had beene that faire *Hermaphrodite*.[19]

The story which provides the ideal image of union between a man and
a woman is one in which the initial desire for that union stems from
the woman. Women in both Ovidian and Elizabethan poetry usually
have to be seduced and hence to some degree coerced—the dividing-
line between the verbal coercion of rhetoric and the physical one of
rape is thin, as Shakespeare shows in *The Rape of Lucrece* and the
Countess of Salisbury scenes in *Edward III*. Salmacis and Hermaphroditus is a rare example of a union that is not tainted by the exercising
of male power. It might be described as the nearest thing available in a
patriarchal culture to a myth of sexual equality.

All this may seem at some remove from *Venus and Adonis*: surely the
point there is that coitus is not achieved. Granted, Shakespeare
derives the style of Adonis' behaviour from Hermaphroditus and the
'woman on top' position from Salmacis, but there the resemblance
ends. The nymph's love for her boy is never aggressive to the point of
grotesquerie, as the goddess's is in, for example, the stanza
concerning her kisses:

[18] Greenblatt, *Shakespearean Negotiations* (Oxford, 1988), 77.
[19] *The Faerie Queene*, bk. 3, canto xii, stanzas 45–6, in the 1590 edn., quoted from
the edn. of A. C. Hamilton (London, 1977).

> Even as an empty eagle, sharp by fast,
> Tires with her beak on feathers, flesh, and bone,
> Shaking her wings, devouring all in haste
> Till either gorge be stuffed or prey be gone,
> > Even so she kissed his brow, his cheek, his chin,
> > And where she ends she doth anew begin.
>
> (55–60)

But perhaps the difference is the point. The resemblance of Adonis to Hermaphroditus is denoted by his beauty, his blushing, and his petulance. The reader who recognizes those marks will perceive Adonis' *potential* to participate in an ideal Salmacian/Hermaphroditic union. But such a union never takes place—coitus only occurs in the form of parodic variations, as Adonis is nuzzled by the boar[20] and Venus cradles the flower—because the partners are not equals. An oppressive power-relation has to exist: after all, this is a goddess dealing with a mortal. Shakespeare has some fun inverting the traditional power structure—Venus' problem is that she can't actually rape Adonis, as Jove rapes Danaë, Neptune Theophane, and Apollo Isse—but in the end the poem shows that a sexual relationship based on coercion is doomed. The inequality is highlighted by the difference in age of the two characters; one function of the allusions to Adonis' mother is to suggest that the sexual dealings of partners of greatly unequal age are bound at some level to replicate the archetypal relationship based on an unequal power-structure, incest between a parent and a child.

Venus and Adonis is a disturbing poem in that violent death takes the place of the unfulfilled Salmacian/Hermaphroditic potential. But stylistically it is a poem that bubbles along in the manner more of the story it's not telling than of the one that it is. Of the later poems in the genre, the one that is closest to it is not Barksted's prurient *Myrrha, the Mother of Adonis; or Lustes Prodegies*, but Beaumont's scintillating *Salmacis and Hermaphroditus*, a narrative full of youthful energy and unabashed sexuality, of 'lovers sweet delight'.[21] In the address which prefaces the poem, Beaumont expresses the hope that it will enable

---

[20] The image of the boar kissing Adonis (1114) is traditional to the story (it is to be found in Theocritus, a Latin epigram by Minturno, and elsewhere—see Bush, *Mythology and the Renaissance Tradition*, 140 n.), but in Shakespeare it adds to the flavour of bestial, violent sexuality. Ovid's Calydonian boar (Golding, viii. 376–82, esp. the bristles) lies behind the description of the beast.

[21] *Salmacis and Hermaphroditus* (1602, attributed to Beaumont in edn. of 1640), l. 254, quoted from *Elizabethan Minor Epics*.

the male reader to dissolve his sexual identity and himself 'turne halfe-mayd'. Salmacis and Hermaphroditus achieve oneness because they are of the same age and the same kind (a naiad and a boy who has been nursed by naiads), as well as because the girl has attributes that are traditionally seen as male and the boy ones that are traditionally female. Their union is an enduring reminder of the creative potential of sexuality. By incorporating the tone of their tale, its lightness of touch and its delight in the charm of androgyny, Shakespeare makes his poem into a celebration of sexuality even as it is a disturbing exposure of the dark underside of desire. As Bruce Smith perceives, the effect is a kind of polymorphous liberation:

In their androgyny, finally, figures like Leander, Adonis, and Hermaphroditus embody, quite literally, the ambiguities of sexual desire in English Renaissance culture and the ambivalences of homosexual desire in particular. They represent, not an exclusive sexual taste, but an *inclusive* one. To use the categories of our own day, these poems are bi-sexual fantasies. The temporary freedom they grant to sexual desire allows it to flow out in all directions, towards all the sexual objects that beckon in the romantic landscape.[22]

This inclusiveness, extending even to the sexualization of the landscape, is one of Ovid's prime gifts to late Elizabethan culture.

II

Venus doesn't metamorphose herself into the boar in the manner of Jupiter becoming an animal in order to rape a mortal girl. The story is about frustration rather than violation because a woman can't rape a man. The tone is set not by the spilling of blood towards the end, but by the earlier sequences in which the violence is playful and nobody really gets hurt: 'Backward she pushed him, as she would be thrust' (41). For much of *Venus and Adonis*, sexual desire is a source of comedy, whereas Shakespeare's second narrative poem is unquestionably tragic because Tarquin does rape Lucrece. The story of sexual pursuit is replayed in a darker key; having made a comic spectacle of the rapacious goddess, Shakespeare makes a tragic spectacle of the

---

[22] Smith, *Homosexual Desire in Shakespeare's England*, 136. Leander's androgynous charm is manifested in the way in which he is fondled by Neptune, who mistakes him for Ganymede, as he swims the Hellespont on his way to Hero's bedroom.

raped emblem of chastity. The two poems are opposite sides of the same coin, as may be seen from their structural resemblance: in each, an ardent suitor attempts to gain the reluctant object of her/his sexual desire by means of rhetorical persuasion, fails, and indirectly or directly precipitates the death of the object of desire. The difference between the two works is that Adonis dies with his chastity intact— he is only metaphorically raped by the boar—while Lucrece stabs herself because she has been ravished. But both poems are centrally interested in the way in which, as in Ovid's *Amores* and *Ars Amatoria*, linguistic art is instrumental in the pursuit of sexual satisfaction. *The Rape of Lucrece* is not only Shakespeare's most sustained imitation, it is also a supreme example of Renaissance *copia*.

As Shakespeare followed the prescription for *copia* by expanding Ovid's seventy-odd lines of Venus and Adonis narrative into a poem of just under twelve hundred lines, so he expanded the seventy-three lines of the Lucrece story into nearly two thousand. As with *Venus and Adonis*, the most significant expansions are those that invest the characters with linguistic arts: in particular, three extended discourses are introduced, namely Tarquin's inward disquisition as to whether he should carry through his desire, the disputation between the two characters in the bedroom, and Lucrece's formal complaint after the rape. The complaint gave Shakespeare the opportunity to fuse his classical material with a popular vernacular form, the lyrical lament of the (frequently female) victim who has been deserted by a lover or otherwise abused. This genre, which reaches back to the *Heroides* and the *Tristia*, had a rich medieval pedigree and a storehouse of examples in the *Mirror for Magistrates*.[23] It was probably from Samuel Daniel's 1592 'Complaint of Rosamond' that Shakespeare derived the seven-line 'rime-royal' stanza form which makes the movement of his second narrative poem so conspicuously more rounded and less crisp than that of the hexameters of the *Metamorphoses* or the elegiac couplets of Ovid's other works. The complaint seeks to give a voice to the women who are the victims of history: it is the mode of Queen Margaret in her *Heroides*-like farewell

[23] For the tradition of complaint, see John Kerrigan's *Motives of Woe : Shakespeare and 'Female Complaint' : A Critical Anthology* (Oxford, 1991). I cite the *Tristia* as well as the *Heroides*, which are traditionally thought of as the Ur-Complaints, because of the process whereby the lamenting voices which Ovid gives to the deserted heroines in the epistles he wrote early in his career are reiterated in his own voice in the poems of exile. Thus one of the strongest precedents for Lucrece's extended anaphoric complaint to Time is *Tristia*, IV. vi. 1–18.

to the Duke of Suffolk in *2 Henry VI* ('even now be gone! | O, go not yet'—III. ii. 356–7). It is also the voice of the team of lamenting women in *Richard III*.

A further mark of Shakespeare's copiousness in *Lucrece* is his use of material from other versions of the Lucrece story: thus, while he closely followed the line of the action as it unfolded in Ovid's *Fasti*, he incorporated a number of details from Livy's *History of Rome*. It was easy for him to do this, since sixteenth-century editions of the *Fasti* included commentaries with cross-references; in a magisterial analysis, T. W. Baldwin has shown that all the details in the poem which are derived from Livy and not Ovid would have been available in the commentary by Paulus Marsus in Shakespeare's copy of Ovid.[24] But the fact that Shakespeare's main source was the poet's rather than the historian's version is a first indication that he was not primarily interested in the political significance of the story.

As in *Venus and Adonis*, Shakespeare's principal interest is the psychology of desire. The moment in Ovid from which he begins is that when Tarquin catches sexual fire. A longish quotation from the Latin is needed here in order to show how Shakespeare built on not merely a narrative and a psychology, but also a rhetoric:

> interea iuvenis furiales regius ignis
>   concipit et caeco raptus amore fuit.
> forma placet niveusque color flavique capilli,
>   quique aderat nulla factus ab arte decor;
> verba placent et vox, et quod corrumpere non est,
>   quoque minor spes est, hoc magis ille cupit.
> iam dederat cantus lucis praenuntius ales,
>   cum referunt iuvenes in sua castra pedem.
> carpitur adtonitos absentis imagine sensus
>   ille. recordanti plura magisque placent:
> 'sic sedit, sic culta fuit, sic stamina nevit,

---

[24] See Baldwin, *On the Literary Genetics of Shakspere's Poems and Sonnets* (Urbana, Ill., 1950), 97–153. My account of Shakespeare's compositional process in *Lucrece* builds on Baldwin's invaluable groundwork; his contention that Shakespeare used an annotated edn. of the *Fasti*, perhaps that published in Basle in 1550, is wholly persuasive. According to Baldwin, although the poem could have been written with Ovid and Marsus' notes alone, the argument prefixed to it seems to make use of Livy's original text, Painter's translation of it in *The Pallace of Pleasure* (1566), and Cooper's standard Latin *Thesaurus*. The argument thus appears to differ from the poem in its use of source-material as well as in its content (the argument includes but the poem omits the visit to Rome by all the principal men of the army, in which Lucrece is discovered virtuously spinning among her maids while all the other wives are out revelling and disporting).

neglectae collo sic iacuere comae,
hos habuit voltus, haec illi verba fuerunt,
  hic color, haec facies, hic decor oris erat.'
ut solet a magno fluctus languescere flatu,
  sed tamen a vento, qui fuit, unda tumet,
sic, quamvis aberat placitae praesentia formae,
  quem dederat praesens forma, manebat amor.
ardet et iniusti stimulis agitatus amoris
  comparat indigno vimque dolumque toro.
'exitus in dubio est: audebimus ultima!' dixit,
  'viderit! audentes forsque deusque iuvat.
cepimus audendo Gabios quoque.'

Meantime the royal youth caught fire and fury, and transported by blind love he raved. Her figure pleased him, and that snowy hue, that yellow hair, and artless grace; pleasing, too, her words and voice and virtue incorruptible; and the less hope he had, the hotter his desire. Now had the bird, the herald of the dawn, uttered his chant, when the young men retraced their steps to camp. Meantime the image of his absent love preyed on his senses crazed. In memory's light more fair and fair she grew. '"Twas thus she sat, 'twas thus she dressed, 'twas thus she spun the threads, 'twas thus her tresses careless lay upon her neck; that was her look, these were her words, that was her colour, that her form, and that her lovely face.' As after a great gale the surge subsides, and yet the billow heaves, lashed by the wind now fallen, so, though absent now that winsome form and far away, the love which by its presence it had struck into his heart remained. He burned, and, goaded by the pricks of an unrighteous love, he plotted violence and guile against an innocent bed. 'The issue is in doubt. We'll dare the utmost,' said he. 'Let her look to it! God and fortune help the daring. By daring we captured Gabii too.'[25]

This passage is like Shakespeare's poem—or rather the first half of Shakespeare's poem—in miniature. It is driven by ardour. As 'ignis' ('fire') and 'ardet' ('he burned') are key words here, so Shakespeare from his first stanza onward plays persistently on Tarquin's heat:

From the besieged Ardea all in post,
Borne by the trustless wings of false desire,
Lust-breathèd Tarquin leaves the Roman host
And to Collatium bears the lightless fire
Which, in pale embers hid, lurks to aspire
  And girdle with embracing flames the waist
  Of Collatine's fair love, Lucrece the chaste.

(1–7)

[25] *Fasti*, ii. 761–83, with J. G. Frazer's Loeb trans., adapted.

The first line seems to introduce a pun that Ovid could well have made but didn't: the city which the Romans happen to be besieging is *Ard*ea and its name prepares the reader for Tarquin's sexual *ard*our.

Shakespeare further complicates Ovid on the matter of colour. Red is of course the colour of Tarquin's hot desire. In the Latin, white is the colour of Lucrece's purity ('niveusque color', 'and her snowy complexion'), but in Shakespeare that white mingles with the red of beauty's blushes, so that the two colours wage heraldic war in Lucrece's face ('Argued by beauty's red and virtue's white'—65), somehow contaminating Lucrece with Tarquin's colour. What Shakespeare has found here is a physical emblem for Ovid's sense that nothing provokes desire more than antithesis. The more artless Lucrece is ('aderat nulla factus ab arte decor'), the more Tarquin wishes to exercise the arts of love upon her; the very fact that she has not dressed her hair seductively, that it falls carelessly ('neglectae') on her neck, makes him all the more hot to seduce her. In Shakespeare, 'Her hair like golden threads played with her breath— | O modest wantons, wanton modesty!' (400–1): the oxymoron in the second line of this comes to the core of the poem's depiction of Tarquin's antithetical desire. Shakespeare learnt his oxymoronic rhetoric from Ovid: the Latin text frequently plays on words, as when Tarquin enters Collatinus' house 'hostis ut hospes' (787), 'an enemy as a guest'; *Lucrece* in turn is full of puns like 'for his prey to pray he doth begin' (342).

But the play of linguistic contraries is not just ornament, for it figures the psychology of contrariness. In the long passage quoted above, Tarquin's desire increases in proportion to Lucrece's unattainability; the point is embodied in the antithetical structure of the line 'quoque *minor* spes est, hoc *magis* ille cupit'—the less the hope, the more the desire. This is one of the many respects in which Shakespeare follows Ovid even as he differs from him. In the passage quoted, Ovid's Tarquin is taking fire at the sight and then the memory of Lucrece's beauty. Shakespeare omits this first visit to Rome, in which Tarquin, Collatinus, and their comrades travel together; he proceeds straight from Collatine's indiscreet verbal 'unlocking' or 'publishing' of Lucrece's beauty to Tarquin's solitary lust-breathing rush to Rome. Tarquin is smitten before he has actually seen Lucrece. In effect, Shakespeare has transformed the line 'quoque minor spes est, hoc magis ille cupit' into the main source of Tarquin's desire. He is turned on and driven to Lucrece's bed not so much by the report of her beauty as by the very thing which gives him no hope of obtaining her, the image of her exemplary chastity. The word itself is enough to fire him up: 'Haply that name of chaste unhapp'ly set │ This bateless edge on his keen appetite' (8–9). His lust is also bound up with the dynamics of power: the idea of her loyalty to her husband provokes envy and the thought that 'meaner men' should not be entitled to possess anything which he, the king's son, lacks (39–42). Tarquin is an image of the same thing as Angelo in *Measure for Measure*: a man who is made very excited by the thought of purity and whose dominant social position gives him (he thinks) a freedom to satisfy his desires without paying a price.

Shakespeare's extended exploration of Tarquin's state of mind is developed from a few brief hints in Ovid. Sometimes the imitation is of a fairly routine nature. For example, the technique of comparing desire to a force of nature (the image of the storm and its aftermath in the passage quoted above) is merely used in passing ('No cloudy show of stormy blust'ring weather │ Doth yet in his fair welkin once appear │ Till sable night . . .'—115–17). Again, Ovid's stock image of Tarquin as wolf and Lucrece as lamb (800) is improvised upon in equally stock figures of wolf, lamb, and foreboding owl (165–7).[26] But more often, there is an injection of verbal energy of the sort that delighted Elizabethan readers. Ovid's 'surgit' (793, 'he rises'), for Tarquin getting up in the middle of the night, becomes a lively, alliterative 'And now this lustful lord leapt from his bed' (169). And the sword ('et aurata vagina liberat ensem'—'and from the gilded scabbard he draws his sword', 793) is wittily made into both a source of physical light and a pretext for mental darkness in that the wielding of it anticipates the rape:

> His falchion on a flint he softly smiteth,
> That from the cold stone sparks of fire do fly,
> Whereat a waxen torch forthwith he lighteth,
> Which must be lodestar to his lustful eye,
> And to the flame thus speaks advisedly:

---

[26] These images occur in the stanza 'Now stole upon the time the dead of night . . .' (162–8) which is a formal *chronographia* expanded from Ovid's 'Nox erat et tota lumina nulla domo' (792, 'it was night and there was no light in the whole house') and incorporating details from the textbook *chronographia* of the moment when Virgil's Dido resolves on suicide ('Nox erat, et placidum carpebant fessa soporem │ corpora per terras . . .', *Aeneid*, iv. 522 ff., 'It was night, and over the earth weary creatures were tasting peaceful slumber').

'As from this cold flint I enforced this fire,
So Lucrece must I force to my desire.'
(176–82)

There is a certain labour about Tarquin's spelling out of the 'As . . . so'
formulation; Ovid invests his single line with a sexual charge in much
more economic fashion ('surgit' has phallic overtones and 'vagina'
does not only suggest a scabbard).[27] The sharper part of Shakespeare's
expansion is the lighting of the torch; in a correlative image a little
later, this same torch will be almost extinguished by the wind which
tries to stay Tarquin's steps and then reignited by his own hot breath
(314–15). Such attention to the mundane matter of the means by
which the rapist sees his way through the dark house is a mark of
Shakespeare the dramatist: it is no coincidence that he reimagined
this stealthy pacing to the bedroom in his great theatrical night-
pieces, Macbeth as withered murder *en route* to Duncan's chamber
'With Tarquin's ravishing strides' (II. i. 55) and Iachimo emerging
from the trunk in Imogen's bedroom with the words, 'Our Tarquin
thus | Did softly press the rushes ere he wakened | The chastity he
wounded' (*Cymb.* II. ii. 12–14, superbly written lines which will be
discussed in Chapter 6).

Lucrece is not a dramatic poem in the dynamic sense—it is interested
in the action of language, not a language of action—but it shares with
the Shakespearian drama a taste for interior monologue. Ovid's
Tarquin hesitates for a moment before resolving to go forward: 'exitus
in dubio est' ('the issue is in doubt'). Shakespeare's stops in his tracks
'And in his inward mind he doth debate' (185) for twelve whole
stanzas. Although this has the effect of retarding the action, it opens up
the character of Tarquin, allowing the reader to get inside his mind, to
see the 'disputation | 'Tween frozen conscience and hot-burning will'
(246–7). This is a dry run for the soliloquies of Angelo and Macbeth.

Once in the bedroom, Shakespeare continues in his mode of *copia*.
When Ovid's Tarquin recollected Lucrece's beauty, he accumulated
images of her in a pattern of repetition: 'sic sedit, sic culta fuit, sic
stamina nevit . . . hic color, haec facies, hic decor oris erat' (771–4,
quoted above). For Ovid's brief phrases, Shakespeare substitutes
whole descriptive stanzas in the manner of the blazon: 'Her lily hand

---

[27] John Kerrigan would defend the 'labour' of Tarquin's 'spelling out' in
Shakespeare on the grounds that the work of interpretation—of spelling out—is very
much the matter of the poem: see his article, 'Keats and *Lucrece*', *ShS* xli (1989),
103–18, esp. pp. 106–7, 115.

. . . Her hair like golden threads . . . Her breasts like ivory globes . . .
Her azure veins, her alabaster skin, | Her coral lips, her snow-white
dimpled chin' (386–420).

The stanza on the breasts is the most striking expansion. Ovid has a
single and painfully tactile couplet: 'effugiat? positis urgentur pectora
palmis, | tunc primum externa pectora tacta manu' (803–4, 'could
she flee? [No,] his hands pressed heavily on her breasts, her breasts
which then for the first time felt the touch of a strange hand'). A lot of
work is done by a very few words here. A sense of suffocation is
established by the way that the pressure on the breasts prevents
Lucrece from moving; there is a parallel with the horrible moment in
Shakespeare when Tarquin silences his victim by stuffing her 'nightly
linen' in her mouth (680–1). 'Urgentur' powerfully catches the
rapist's frenzied pressure, and the second line suggests something of
how the rape is a double violation because it is like a second loss of
virginity—it is not strictly true that Tarquin is the first stranger to
touch Lucrece's breasts, for presumably Collatinus did so when he
first made love to his wife, but the point here is that because his was a
lover's touch his hand did not seem external and invasive as
Tarquin's does. Shakespeare sacrifices the economy for the sake of a
more explicit reference to Collatine and his prior possession of his
wife's body:

> Her breasts like ivory globes circled with blue,
> A pair of maiden worlds unconquerèd,
> Save of their lord no bearing yoke they knew,
> And him by oath they truly honourèd.
> These worlds in Tarquin new ambition bred,
>   Who like a foul usurper went about
>   From this fair throne to heave the owner out.
>   (407–13)

The conceit of the breasts as globes may be borrowed from Marlowe's
Hero and Leander,[28] but the twist in the couplet has a powerful
resonance in the context of *Lucrece* as a whole. A blazon is a mapping
of the woman's body and mapping is a means of control; Tarquin is
like an ambitious Elizabethan adventurer setting out to conquer the
virgin land of the New World, so that it can be mapped and appear on

---

[28] 'For though the rising iv'ry mount he scal'd, | Which is with azure circling lines
empal'd, | Much like a globe (a globe may I term this, | By which love sails to regions full
of bliss)' (ii. 273–6).

the globe emblazoned with a name denoting the queen (Virginia). But he has no intention of giving his conquest over to a higher power in the manner of, say, Ralegh returning from Guiana; he wants the 'maiden worlds' for himself and that entails displacing the rightful owner (there is no proto-feminist questioning of Collatine's right of possession: Lucrece is yoked to him by the oath of marriage). Ironically, the man of royal blood usurps the throne of the commoner; this inversion prepares the way for the end of the poem, where the final consequence of the rape is played through as the Tarquins are heaved off their throne and the Roman republic is established.

It is because loss of empire is the ultimate cost which Tarquin pays for his conquest—the military metaphors are all-pervasive—that the victory is a defeat. Ovid states this in another of his highly economic couplets, immediately after the rape and before the dawn: 'quid, victor, gaudes? haec te victoria perdet. | heu quanto regnis nox stetit una tuis!' (811–12, 'why, victor, do you rejoice? this victory will ruin you. Alas [for you], how much one night has cost you—your kingdom!'). 'Haec te victoria perdet' brings the oxymoronic structure to a climax. Tarquin's gain is his family's loss; Lucrece's loss is Rome's gain—she is the sacrificial victim required for the bringing of a new political order. But Shakespeare does not give prominence to this idea of Lucrece as a republican martyr, which is what she so often became when the story was retold.[29]

The *Fasti* is Ovid's most 'official' poem; it tells the public story of Rome's civic traditions and the calendrical rites which commemorate key events in the city's history. The story of Tarquin and Lucrece is entered on 24 February, the date on which the city celebrated the *Regifugium* ('flight of the king'). Shakespeare's poem, on the other hand, is more interested in desire than in politics; it implicitly endorses Sir Philip Sidney's argument that poetry can transcend the particularities of history. In accordance with his innovative emphasis on Tarquin's psychology, Shakespeare withholds the political conse-

[29] For a feminist argument that rape is made the price for the establishment of a republic, pursued in relation to both classical Rome and Italian Renaissance humanism, see Stephanie H. Jed, *Chaste Thinking: The Rape of Lucretia and the Birth of Humanism* (Bloomington, Ind., 1989). But it seems to me that the argument will not work for Shakespeare's less obviously republican version of the story. Indeed, Ian Donaldson argues that certain images in the poem, far from being republican, suggest a 'discreet political counter-attack': the simile of Tarquin as 'a foul usurper' is an irony at his expense—it makes him into a deposer of himself—but the irony depends on a deep respect for kingship and a sense of the heinousness of the very notion of rebellion. See Donaldson, *The Rapes of Lucretia: A Myth and its Transformations* (Oxford, 1982), 117.

quences until the very final stanza of the poem and in the immediate aftermath of the rape concentrates instead on the rapist's mental state: 'haec te victoria perdet' becomes 'A captive victor that hath lost in gain' (730), but the loss is articulated as 'the burden of a guilty mind' (735) rather than banishment from Rome. Tarquin's departure from the bedchamber is not even recorded in the *Fasti*, whereas in *Lucrece* he creeps away 'like a thievish dog' and sweats 'with guilty fear' (736, 740). We half expect him actually to become a dog, as a character in the *Metamorphoses* would. He has been transformed from a historical character into a mythic one: he is an archetypal figure, standing for all who are unable to curb their own will. As in Sonnet 129, the sexual will is ultimately self-consuming: 'His taste delicious, in digestion souring, | Devours his will that lived by foul devouring' (699–700). Here Tarquin undergoes an inward transformation that is the inevitable consequence of the desire that drives him. It is at the same time the kind of fitting punishment that is externalized in such figures as Ovid's Erysichthon, who pays for his wilfulness with perpetual hunger, and Spenser's Malbecco, who is so jealous that he eventually 'woxen so deform'd, that he has quight | Forgot he was a man, and Gelosy is hight' (*Faerie Queene*, III. x. 60). The souring of Tarquin's desire and the welling up of his guilt constitute early examples of a manœuvre that Shakespeare continued to practise in his mature tragedies: the rewriting of Ovid's physical changes in the form of mental transformations.

For the rest of the poem—more than a thousand further lines—the focus is on the raped Lucrece. At times the imitation of the *Fasti* remains quite close, as when Shakespeare copies Ovid's line about Lucrece being thrice unable to open her mouth to tell her husband and father what has happened, so unspeakable is the crime, so intense her shame. Thus Ovid's 'ter conata loqui ter destitit, ausaque quarto . . .' (823, 'three times she tried to speak, three times she gave over speaking, and daring on the fourth attempt . . .') becomes Shakespeare's 'Three times with sighs she gives her sorrow fire | Ere once she can discharge one word of woe' (1604–5); in a typical Renaissance amplification, Shakespeare combines the figure of three silences to one speech with a new figure that is not in Ovid, a military image ('gives fire', 'discharge') that harks back to the metaphors of siege warfare in the bedroom scene. But the second half of the poem also includes some much more substantial amplifications. These travel some distance from the source: where Tarquin after the rape is taken from the *Fasti* and rewritten in the mode of a moralized reading of the *Metamorphoses*, Lucrece is rewritten as an emblem of the power of art to relieve suffering. She too seems to enter the *Metamorphoses*, but she does so not as one of Ovid's victims, but as one of his artists, a weaver of narrative like the daughters of Minyas, who reject the wild sexual rites of Bacchus and stay indoors to narrate the matter of Book Four, including the contrasting love-stories of Pyramus and Thisbe and Salmacis and Hermaphroditus. As they spin and weave, so Lucrece artfully constructs a visual set-piece, an *ekphrasis*.

First, however, she tries to sublimate her anguish through the traditional mode of the female complaint, with its highly formalized expressions of woe. But this tradition is moribund: the rhetoric simply does not work for her.[30] She endlessly reduplicates verbal figures without achieving any emotional advance. Formal complaint offers no remedy: it is a 'helpless smoke of words' that does Lucrece 'no right' (1027). Only when exemplary *narratives* are made available to her does the poem move forward. Her accusing apostrophe to night, opportunity, and time is finally exhausted at dawn. Cessation of the nightingale's song effects the temporal punctuation: 'By this, lamenting Philomel had ended | The well-tuned warble of her nightly sorrow' (1079–80). The end of the night and of the nightingale's song is also the textual marker for the end of Lucrece's complaint; Lucrece and Philomel are thus identified with each other. Since they are both archetypal rape victims, it is an obvious enough identification (Shakespeare might have been drawn to it by the fact that the brief entry in the *Fasti* for the day after 24 February concerns the swallow who is both the harbinger of spring and the metamorphosed form of Procne, Philomel's sister). Lucrece then goes on to complain to the day for revealing her shame and to the daytime birds for singing merrily. This leads her to invoke Philomel as a more appropriate songster:

> 'Come, Philomel, that sing'st of ravishment,
> Make thy sad grove in my dishevelled hair.

[30] 'Shakespeare is writing not merely within the complaint tradition but also against it: he is rendering many of its assumptions very prominent and very problematical. If Lucrece delivers a complaint against Tarquin, in a sense Shakespeare delivers one against his genre': Heather Dubrow, 'A Mirror for Complaints: Shakespeare's *Lucrece* and Generic Tradition', in *Renaissance Genres*, ed. Barbara Kiefer Lewalski (Cambridge, Mass., 1986), 399–417 (p. 400); the substance of the essay is incorporated in Dubrow's *Captive Victors*.

As the dank earth weeps at thy languishment,
So I at each sad strain will strain a tear,
And with deep groans the diapason bear;
    For burden-wise I'll hum on Tarquin still,
    While thou on Tereus descants better skill.

'And whiles against a thorn thou bear'st thy part
To keep thy sharp woes waking, wretched I,
To imitate thee well, against my heart
Will fix a sharp knife to affright mine eye,
Who if it wink shall thereon fall and die.
    These means, as frets upon an instrument,
    Shall tune our heart-strings to true languishment.

'And for, poor bird, thou sing'st not in the day,
As shaming any eye should thee behold,
Some dark deep desert seated from the way,
That knows not parching heat nor freezing cold,
Will we find out, and there we will unfold
    To creatures stern sad tunes to change their kinds.
    Since men prove beasts, let beasts bear gentle minds.'
                                                (1128–48)

Dialogue with the nightingale provides a way out which is not
available to the isolated complainer; this is the first moment of shared
emotion in the poem. It is achieved by imagining two female voices
harmonized musically—'strain', 'diapason', 'descants', 'means',[31]
and 'frets' are all technical terms. Instruments of pain become the
means of making music: Shakespeare is moving towards a classical
definition of tragedy, the traditional work of which is to transform
knives to frets and thus to tune the cracked heart-strings. Lucrece
proposes that she and Philomel will team up to play the part of
Orpheus singing to the beasts. Within the allusion there is a
sophisticated interpretation of the place of Orphic song in the
Metamorphoses as a whole: Lucrece implicitly argues that it inverts
the normative pattern of the poem, in which 'men prove beasts', by
using music to make 'beasts bear gentle minds'. Before the rape, her
verbal art is compared to that of Orpheus in an earlier part of the
myth, the moment when the singer descends into the underworld and
plays his lyre so sweetly that Pluto sleeps and Eurydice is able to
escape: 'So his unhallowed haste her words delays, | And moody
Pluto winks while Orpheus plays' (552–3). In the previous stanza to

---

[31] A technical term for the middle register between bass and treble.

this, Tarquin is explicitly described as a 'rough beast' (545). But, as Eurydice's escape was short-lived, so is Lucrece's: Tarquin's bestial desire only 'winks' for a moment and soon he silences her with her linen. The second Orphic allusion, in the address to Philomel, undoes this silence and offers a glimpse into an alternative world of gentleness, created by the female voice.

Lucrece begins to help herself through her attempt to help Philomel, as she holds a knife against her breast in imitation of the thorn against which the nightingale presses her breast. The thorn's pricking is what causes the metamorphosed Philomel to cry 'tereu, tereu', the name of her rapist, Tereus; Lucrece's long and painful performance comes to a corresponding climax when she finally brings herself to say the name of Tarquin. Like Philomel's, hers is a stifled, half-inarticulate cry:

> Here with a sigh as if her heart would break
> She throws forth Tarquin's name. 'He, he,' she says—
> But more than he her poor tongue could not speak.
>
> (1716–18)

At this moment, it is as if the two women are speaking together. A kind of sisterhood is achieved, but it has no meaning in the male world of Rome, and in the next instant Lucrece kills herself. Nancy Vickers points out that the poem then ends as it began with the woman absent and the men 'rhetorically compet[ing] with each other over Lucrece's body'.[32]

But before the climax is reached Lucrece progresses from music to painting and from speech to action. Her contemplation of 'a piece | of skilful painting made for Priam's Troy' (1366 ff.) gives Shakespeare and his reader the opportunity to enjoy some highly colourful descriptive writing in the manner of Ovid's intricate account of Arachne's tapestries at the beginning of Book Six of the *Metamorphoses* or Spenser's imitation of those tapestries in the House of Busyrane in Book 3 of *The Faerie Queene*. In Book 1 of the *Aeneid*, Aeneas sees a painting of the Trojan war in a temple in Dido's Carthage; this may be the model for the inclusion of an *ekphrasis* in *Lucrece*, but the descriptions themselves—of the contention of Ajax and Ulysses, the venerable Nestor, the grieving Hecuba—are derived

---

[32] Nancy J. Vickers, ' "The blazon of sweet beauty's best": Shakespeare's *Lucrece*', in *Shakespeare and the Question of Theory*, ed. Patricia Parker and Geoffrey Hartman (New York, 1985), 95–115 (p. 108).

from Ovid's account of the Trojan war in Book Thirteen of the *Metamorphoses*. As in *Troilus and Cressida* and *The Tempest*, Shakespeare contaminates high Virgilian matter with its Ovidian revision. Ovid switches the emphasis from the march towards the establishment of empire to the expression of female suffering. He sidesteps rather than plods in the master's tracks, he weaves a dance around the unbending line of the Virgilian text. His improvisation on Virgil prefigures Shakespeare's on him: again, Shakespeare is drawn to the emotions rather than the politics of the story. He dwells not on the public and specifically republican consequences of the rape, but on the private and distinctively female space in which suffering can be voiced and the silence to which a woman must submit in public can be temporarily broken—Lucrece in fact gets to speak more lines than any other female persona in any other individual work of Shakespeare.[33]

Having identified with the suffering Philomel, Lucrece finds more woe, yet also more companionship, in the suffering Hecuba (her maid weeps in sympathy with her, but it is only in the mythological *exempla* that Lucrece can confide):

> So Lucrece, set a-work, sad tales doth tell
>   To pencilled pensiveness and coloured sorrow:
>   She lends them words, and she their looks doth borrow.
>   (1496–8)

There is a creative reciprocity at work here, an artful exchange. Lucrece goes to the painting in search of 'a face where all distress is stelled' (1444)—'stelled' is a coruscating multiple pun, suggesting 'stalled', penned up, 'stiled', penned with a stylus, 'steeled', engraved, and 'stelled', fixed. She finds the face she is looking for in the despairing Hecuba. The latter is the exemplary picture of grief—'Time's ruin, beauty's wreck, and grim care's reign' are 'anatomized' in her (1450–1)—but, being painted, she has no tongue. Lucrece therefore says that she will sing for her, perform her grief: ' "Poor instrument," quoth she, "without a sound, | I'll tune thy woes with my lamenting tongue" ' (1464–5). It is a performance intended to elicit from the Elizabethan reader a response akin to Hamlet's when the Player once more expresses and beautifies the grief of Hecuba.

---

[33] She speaks 645 lines (more than a third of the text). Her only possible competitor is Rosalind (who has about 635, but a strict line-count is hard, since she speaks so much prose). I agree with Philippa Berry's sense that this part of the poem allows a female

With the painting of Hecuba, as with the address to Philomel, a 'sympathy of woe' (to use a phrase that belongs to the Andronicus family)[34] is established between two female figures. It is a pattern which Shakespeare reiterates in the opening lines of 'A Lover's Complaint': 'From off a hill whose concave womb re-worded | A plaintful story from a sist'ring vale.' The echo effect here creates a sister for the deserted woman who is voicing the complaint: that sister is Echo, herself a despairing lover. We learn a few lines later that the lover is tearing up letters. Initially we assume that these are epistles to or from the man who has deserted her, as they would be in the *Heroides*; we discover later that they are in fact letters to the man from his previous lovers, which he has tactlessly passed on to her as tokens of his desirability. The tearing of them may then be seen as a revision of the *Heroides*. Ovid's women write to their lovers in a tone of anger mixed with grief; the letters veer between threats of suicide and pleadings for a second chance, for the man to return. The pathos of the collection is the reader's knowledge that the end will usually be suicide, not reunion. The tearing of letters in 'A Lover's Complaint' is a recognition that the attempt to get a fickle man back by writing to him is doomed; the lover rejects the written appeal to the man and finds instead a feminine *locus*—a hill with a womb, a vale that is a sister—in which her voice can be doubled with that of Echo and the plaint can offer some relief.

But the male will always intrude. In 'A Lover's Complaint' the double female voice is overheard by the narrator of the poem, the 'I' who in the first stanza 'laid to list the sad-tuned tale'. In *Lucrece*, male eyes watch the woeful women. At the climax of the viewing of the painting, a face stares back at Lucrece. It is that of false Sinon, who insinuated the fatal Horse into Troy. In Lucrece's mind, Sinon's face is metamorphosed into that of Tarquin. Shakespeare has taken Sinon from Virgil's second book (*Aen.* ii. 77 ff.) and grafted him on to an Ovidian image of Tarquin as the same kind of deceiver. In the passage of the *Fasti* quoted earlier, Tarquin cites a personal precedent for his decision to take Lucrece by cunning followed up with force: 'cepimus

voice to be heard and that this voice makes Lucrece more than 'a sign used to mediate and define men's relationships to men' (which is what she is in readings such as those of Nancy Vickers, cited in my previous n., and Coppélia Kahn, in 'The Rape in Shakespeare's *Lucrece*', *Shakespeare Studies*, ix (1976), 45–72)—Berry, 'Woman, Language, and History in *The Rape of Lucrece*', *ShS* xliv (1992), 33–9 (p. 33).

[34] *Titus*, III. i. 148.

audendo Gabios quoque', 'by daring we captured Gabii too'. The allusion is to the incident narrated in the first half of the *Fasti* for 24 February, in which Sextus Tarquinius gained entry to Gabii by pretending to have been cast out from Rome, then betrayed the city from within. In his annotated edition of the *Fasti*, Shakespeare would have found a note by Marsus that made the Trojan parallel explicit: 'Ut Sinon apud Virg.' ('as Sinon in Virgil').[35] Shakespeare thus maps Tarquin on to Sinon and triangulates the destruction of Troy, of Gabii, and of Lucrece: the intertextual weave is artful in the extreme. But just as the educated reader is finding a way through it, Lucrece scratches Sinon out of the painting in her most vigorous action prior to her suicide. Self-reflexive art by itself—what I have called 'the intertextual weave'—can only do so much: it must lead to action. The whole sequence exemplifies the difficulty the human mind has in forgetting; rape is mental as well as physical spoliation in that the image of the rapist enters his victim's mind. She then tries to erase him, but cannot: you can't undo a rape, you can't undo history. Sinon and Tarquin will never be unwritten. Lucrece herself recognizes this, but her action, built upon her reading, has afforded her a limited catharsis: 'At last she smilingly with this gives o'er: | "Fool, fool," quoth she, "his wounds will not be sore"' (1567–8). That wry smile—her first—is a boldly Ovidian change of tone. It affords Lucrece a kind of satisfaction. For a moment, there seems to be an indecorum in a smile at such a moment, but then the reader perceives its psychological truth and sees Lucrece as the opposite of Tarquin, as at least momentarily a victor in defeat.

The intrusive eyes are also those of the male reader, who earlier in the poem has been made complicit with the rape: the artfully rhetorical twist of referring to the golden threads of Lucrece's hair as 'Modest wantons, wanton modesty' unavoidably endorses Tarquin's own wantonness. So too, the blazon that describes Lucrece's body, relishing the ivory globes of her breast, elides the reader's gaze with Tarquin's: like the rapist, the reader of the blazon has 'mightily noted' the woman's passive, sleeping form—and 'What did he note but strongly he desired?' (414–15). Once this is perceived, one realizes why Lucrece's artful rhetoric is needed in the second half of the poem: it must compensate for Tarquin's duplicitous art. Language must be shown to have sympathetic capabilities as well as coercive and

---

[35] *Fasti* (Basle, 1550), 141, cited in Baldwin, *Literary Genetics of Poems*, 145.

voyeuristic ones. The rape of Helen led to the fall of Troy; the rape of Lucrece leads to the rise of the Roman republic. That is the immediate relevance of the passage concerning Lucrece and the painting. But its profounder relevance is aesthetic more than historical. Shakespeare concentrates on the art of the painter, the 'imaginary work', the 'Conceit deceitful, so compact' (1422-3), in order to suggest that art may be a lie which outdoes the truth of nature—not a malicious lie, but a comforting one. The comfort has ultimately to be ours, not Lucrece's. To be true to history—and the historical plot does finally enter in the poem's last stanza—she must commit suicide. And even in the sections of the poem when we are to imagine her gaining comfort through her communion with Philomel and Hecuba, a moment's reflection reveals that the emotions are ours, not hers. 'Lucrece' has no more reality than the two female mythological figures whom she addresses; but then she also has no less reality than them, in that all three of them have the truth of exemplarity. To put her in front of a picture is to remind us that we are in front of an artwork ourselves, a verbal picture, an exemplary rather than a particular truth. But that is how rhetoric works: it creates emotion *in the listener*. The narrative of her works for us as the image of Hecuba works for her.

Nevertheless, Shakespeare did, I think, recognize that there is potentially something tasteless about giving so much rhetorical copiousness to a persona who is supposed to have been raped. The *ekphrasis* is introduced as a way of getting beyond the flat rhetoric of the complaint tradition. But it still depends on Lucrece's speech, on an eloquence that may well appear indecorous in the mouth of the violated. Her linguistic art is displayed for the pleasure of the predominantly male readership. The male reader stares in upon the suffering Lucrece as Sinon intrudes upon the female space of Hecuba; the scratching out of Sinon is a marvellous move, but the reader cannot be similarly erased unless the poem is to be torn up like the letters in 'A Lover's Complaint'. Shakespeare overcame this problem quite remarkably in *Titus Andronicus*. There Lavinia is permanently silenced at the time of her rape: the way in which she is deprived of the musical art that was previously a mark of her grace is an emblem of the pathos of her loss. Despite the innovative *ekphrasis*, *The Rape of Lucrece* remains 'The Complaint of Lucrece'; in a bolder revision—one might even call it a deconstruction—of the genre of complaint, Shakespeare invents in the character of Lavinia a 'Speechless complainer' (III. ii. 39).[36] The musical voice of complaint, loaded in every rift with Ovidian poetic ore, is given over to Marcus. Where Lucrece is a poet even as she is a sufferer, in *Titus* there is a stark disjunction between rhetorically measured language and the woman's mutilated body. Lavinia is not vouchsafed Philomel's release into song; her rape is never sublimated. She is not even allowed an artful suicide, as Lucrece is—her father can only expiate her shame by killing her.

[36] I believe that *Titus* really was a 'new' play when Philip Henslowe recorded it as such at the Rose Theatre on 23 Jan. 1594 and that it was therefore composed in very close proximity to *Lucrece*, which must belong to this period—Shakespeare presumably had his second narrative poem in mind when he referred to 'some graver labour' in the dedication to *Venus and Adonis* (entered 18 Apr. 1593); it was itself entered on the Stationers' Register on 9 May 1594. My date for *Titus* is later than that given by most scholars; I shall argue my case for it in the introd. to my forthcoming Arden edn. of the play. It should, however, be noted here that there is particular emphasis on Lavinia as a 'speechless complainer' in the fly-killing scene, which was a late addition to the play (it does not appear in the quarto that was entered on 6 Feb. 1594) and therefore almost certain to have post-dated *Lucrece*.

3

The Art of Precedent

There is nothing in man of all the potential parts of his mind
(reason and will except) more noble or more necessary to the
active life th[an] memory: because it maketh most to a sound
judgement and perfect worldly wisedome, examining and
comparing the times past with the present, and by them both
considering the time to come . . . Right so no kinde of argument
in all the Oratorie craft, doth better perswade and more
universally satisfie than example, which is but the representation of old memories.[1]

I

Venus and Adonis and *The Rape of Lucrece* are dazzling proofs of
Shakespeare's art, self-conscious Renaissance exercises in the imitation and amplification of Ovid. They demand to be read side by side
with the narratives upon which they improvise. They set themselves
up as variations upon Ovidian themes, and thus give support to the
idea that the culture in which they are produced is a renovation of an
admired earlier culture. It was with this in mind that Francis Meres
wrote of the infusion of the sweet witty soul of Ovid into mellifluous
and honey-tongued Mr Shakespeare.

But for Meres the idea that contemporary texts were renovations of
classical ones went far beyond works of overt imitation like
Shakespeare's two narrative poems. He read the civil war poems of
Daniel and Drayton as revisions of Lucan's *Pharsalia*, proclaimed
Ausonius to be the precursor of William Warner, and so on.[2] What

[1] George Puttenham, *The Arte of English Poesie* (1589), bk. I, ch. xix, ed. G. D.
Willcock and Alice Walker (Cambridge, 1936), 39.

[2] Meres, 'A Comparative Discourse of our English Poets with the Greeke, Latine, and
Italian Poets', in his *Palladis Tamia, Elizabethan Critical Essays*, ed. Smith, ii. 316–17.
Meres may not in fact have read all the authors whom he cites. He derived most of
his classical allusions from a popular handbook, the *Officina* of J. Ravisius Textor—see
Don Cameron Allen, *Francis Meres's Treatise 'Poetrie': A Critical Edition* (Urbana, Ill.,

are being proposed here are *precedents*, not *sources*—the *Fasti* of Ausonius is a conceptual exemplar, not a reservoir of raw material, for Warner's *Albion's Englande*. The trope used by Meres is that which Puttenham in his *Arte of English Poesie* denominated '*Paradigma*, or a resemblance by example':

if in matter of counsell or perswasion we will seeme to liken one case to another . . . and doe compare the past with the present, gathering probabilitie of like successe to come in the things wee have presently in hand: or if ye will draw the judgements precedent and authorized by antiquitie as veritable, and peradventure fayned and imagined for some purpose, into similitude or dissimilitude with our present actions and affaires, it is called resemblance by example: as if one should say thus, *Alexander* the great in his expedition to Asia did thus, so did *Hanniball* comming into Spaine, so did *Caesar* in Egypt, therfore all great Captains & Generals ought to doe it.[3]

Antiquity, then, offers a paradigm or an example which, by serving as a precedent, authorizes 'the things wee have presently in hand'. Puttenham, in his oratorical handbook for courtiers, had an eye on public affairs; Meres used the trope to bolster a sense of the literary achievements of the English nation. The purpose of his 'Comparative Discourse of our English Poets with the Greeke, Latine, and Italian Poets' was to dignify the poetry that was presently in hand in Elizabethan England by bringing paradigms to bear upon it. The structure with which he worked was Puttenham's 'as . . . so . . .' formulation: 'As Virgil doth imitate Catullus in the like matter of *Ariadne* for his story of Queene *Dido*: so Michael Drayton doth imitate Ovid in his *England's Heroical Epistles*'; 'As the soule of Euphorbus was thought to live in Pythagoras: so the sweete wittie soule of Ovid lives in mellifluous and hony-tongued Shakespeare'. Inverting the process whereby Castiglione applied a traditional image of literary imi-tation—the bee flitting from flower to flower—to the courtier's imitation of worthy models of behaviour,[4] Meres turned Puttenham's trope for humanist action to literary account by making *paradigma* into both a figure of speech and a design for the construction of literary history.

1933). Allen castigates Meres for lack of originality, failing to see that his value lies precisely in his status as a purveyor of Elizabethan *commonplaces*.

[3] Puttenham, *The Arte of English Poesie*, bk. 3, ch. xix, p. 245.

[4] Castiglione, *The Courtier*, trans. Hoby (Everyman edn., London, 1966), 45. The standard source for the image of the bee is Seneca, *Ad Lucilium Epistulae Morales*, lxxxiv. 3–4.

Meres implicitly proposes two different kinds of relationship between English poets and their forebears, the specifically imitative and the grandly paradigmatic. *Imitatio* is a symptom of *paradigma*, but *paradigma* is not dependent on recognizable *imitatio* (Caesar's Egyptian expedition cannot really be described as an *imitation* of Alexander's Asian one). Thus *Englands Heroicall Epistles* is an imitation of Ovid's *Heroides*, as *The Shepheardes Calender* is of Theocritus' *Idylls* and Virgil's *Eclogues*, whereas the affiliation of Shakespeare to Ovid is more broadly paradigmatic. Meres cites not only *Venus and Adonis* and *Lucrece*, which may be seen as imitations of parts of the *Metamorphoses* and the *Fasti*, but also the sonnets, which, being in a genre unknown to Ovid, cannot be so directly imitative. The metaphor used for this relationship is suggestively self-performing: the metamorphosis of Ovid into Shakespeare is imaged in an allusion to the fifteenth book of the *Metamorphoses*, where Pythagoras supports his theory of metempsychosis by claiming that he is a reincarnation of the soul of Euphorbus (*Met.* xv. 161). Meres's comparison is an inspired one, for the fifteenth book of the *Metamorphoses* is the prime *paradigma* for the sonnets. The principle of metempsychosis which Book Fifteen articulates is enacted in the metempsychosis of Book Fifteen into the sonnets.[5]

At this juncture one needs a bridge between the theory and the poetry. It must be demonstrated that Elizabethan sonnets did invite their readers to think about imitation and paradigm. One does not have to look very far to find such a bridge, for Thomas Watson actually built one into the first Elizabethan sonnet-cycle, the *Hekatompathia* of 1582. Probably working under the influence of E.K.'s marginal glosses to *The Shepheardes Calender*, he prefaced each poem with a brief critical account of its own imitative practices. In the headnote to 'Harke you that list to heare what sainte I serve', the blazon of which 'My mistress' eyes are nothing like the sun' is a direct or indirect parody, he proclaims that he is proud to be a parasite:

This passion of love is lively expressed by the Authour, in that he lavishlie

---

[5] The aim of my analysis here is to reread the relationship between Ovid and the sonnets in the light of 16th-cent. imitation theory. It is not to enumerate Shakespeare's 'debt' in detail: there are accounts of Ovid as a 'source' for the sonnets in Sidney Lee, 'Ovid and Shakespeare's Sonnets', *The Quarterly Review*, ccx (1909), 455–76, repr. in his *Elizabethan and other Essays* (Oxford, 1929), 116–39; T. W. Baldwin, *On the Literary Genetics of Shakspere's Poems and Sonnets* (Urbana, Ill., 1950); J. W. Lever, *The Elizabethan Love Sonnet* (London, 1956), 248–72; and the commentary and app. 2 of Stephen Booth's edn. of *Shakespeare's Sonnets* (New Haven, Conn., and London, 1977).

praiseth the person and beautifull ornamentes of his love, one after an other as they lie in order. He partly imitateth herein *Aeneas Silvius*, who setteth downe the like in describing *Lucretia* the love of *Euryalus*; & partly he followeth *Ariosto cant. 7.* where he describeth *Alcina*: & partly borroweth from some others where they describe the famous *Helen* of *Greece*: you may therefore, if you please aptlie call this sonnet as a Scholler of good judgement hath already Christened it *ainē parasitikē*.[6]

Further assistance is provided for the reader in the form of learned marginal references along the lines of 'Vide Chiliad. I. cent. 5 adag. 74. vbi. Erasm. ex Philostrati ad uxorem epistola mutuatur'. Like some student anxious to impress his tutor, Watson brazenly displays his classical credentials.

One of his reasons for doing so is suggested by the headnote to the sonnet in *Hekatompathia* which immediately follows 'Harke you that list to heare what sainte I serve'. It includes a quotation from Ovid's *Tristia* (ii. 103–6) and an explication which reveals whom the poet is really anxious to impress: 'The Author alluding in al this Passion unto the fault of *Actaeon*, and to the hurte, which hee susteined, setteth downe his owne amorous infelicitie; as *Ovid* did after his banishmente, when in an other sense hee applied this fiction unto himselfe, being exiled (as it should seeme) for having at unawares taken *Caesar* in some great fault.' Whether the 'error' (*Tristia*, ii. 207) for which Ovid was exiled was something he saw in the imperial household or an actual involvement with the emperor's grand-daughter, the figure of Actaeon was a perfect image in which to convey it. Watson's verses set down the poet's own infelicity through the same allusion:

> Actaeon lost in middle of his sport
> Both shape and life, for looking but a wry,
> Diana was afraid he would report
> What secretes he had seene in passing by:
> > To tell but trueth, the selfe same hurt have I
> > By viewing her, for whome I dayly die.
> > > (*Hekatompathia*, viii, p. 22)

What this is implicitly about is fear of loss of patronage. By referring to

---

[6] Thomas Watson, *The Hekatompathia or Passionate Centurie of Love* (London, 1582), sonnet vii, p. 21. Greek transliterated in both title and quotation. The poem is discussed by John Kerrigan in the introd. to his edn. of *The Sonnets and A Lover's Complaint* (Harmondsworth, 1986), 19–20.

Ovid's comparison of himself to Actaeon after he fell out of favour with the emperor, Watson acknowledges his own need for the protection of Edward de Vere, the Earl of Oxford, to whom his 'Passionate Centurie of Love' is dedicated.

Shakespeare was subtler in his pursuit of admiration and hence patronage. He did not parade the imitativeness of his sonnets in the Watsonian manner, but on one occasion he did write a piece of literary criticism of his own work which suggests, as Meres did, that Ovid was the sonneteer's paradigm. The sonnet 'If love make me forsworn, how shall I swear to love?', originally composed for Berowne in *Love's Labour's Lost* but published as Shakespeare's by William Jaggard in *The Passionate Pilgrim*, is subjected to the astringent scrutiny of Holofernes: 'Here are only numbers ratified, but for the elegancy, facility, and golden cadence of poesy—*caret* ['it is lacking']. Ovidius Naso was the man. And why indeed "Naso" but for smelling out the odoriferous flowers of fancy, the jerks of invention? *Imitari* is nothing. So doth the hound his master, the ape his keeper, the tired horse his rider' (*Love's Labour's*, IV. ii. 121–7). Holofernes may be a pedant, but he is not a fool: he sees that Berowne's sonnet is a catalogue of commonplaces without novel application. Holofernes also knows his imitation theory. He has been reading in the tenth book of Quintilian: 'imitatio per se ipsa non sufficit'; 'invenire primum fuit estque praecipuum'—imitation by itself is not sufficient; invention came first and is all-important.[7] Contained within Holofernes' analysis is Quintilian's celebrated distinction between imitation and emulation: the business of poesy is not ape-like imitation but the emulation of Ovid's elegance and facility. Like Puttenham's figure of *paradigma*, emulation leaves room for dissimilitude as well as similitude; it ultimately comes down to matter, not mere words.

That good imitation involves difference as well as similarity is a cardinal principle of Renaissance poetics. Again and again, sixteenth-century theorists make the point which was first made by Petrarch in his letter to Boccaccio written from Pavia on 28 October 1366. The 'proper imitator should take care that what he writes resembles the original without reproducing it'; the resemblance should be that 'of a son to his father', not that of a portrait to the sitter; individual features will diverge, but the whole will, through some mysterious power, have the feel of the original. Petrarch continues,

---

[7] Quintilian, *Institutiones Oratoriae*, x. ii. 4, x. ii. 1.

Thus we writers must look to it that with a basis of similarity there should be many dissimilarities. And the similarity should be planted so deep that it can only be extricated by quiet meditation. The quality is to be felt rather than defined. Thus we may use another man's conceptions and the colour of his style, but not use his words. In the first case the resemblance is hidden deep; in the second it is glaring. The first procedure makes poets, the second makes apes. This is the substance of Seneca's counsel, and Horace's before him, that we should write as the bees make sweetness, not storing up the flowers but turning them into honey, thus making one thing of many various ones, but different and better.[8]

Shakespeare's Ovidianism answers to Petrarch's ideal: there are dissimilarities as well as resemblances; the relationship is often more easily felt than analysed; it is sometimes 'planted so deep that it can only be extricated by quiet meditation'.

The distinction between poet-son and ape may be made by contrasting the handling of Ovidian mythology in a routine allusion and a Shakespearian sonnet. Sonnet 63 of Barnabe Barnes's *Parthenophil and Parthenophe* begins as follows:

> JOVE for EUROPA's love, took shape of Bull;
> And for CALISTO, played DIANA's part:
> And in a golden shower, he filled full
> The lap of DANAE, with celestial art.
> Would I were changed but to my Mistress' gloves,
> That those white lovely fingers I might hide!
> That I might kiss those hands, which mine heart loves![9]

Thereafter the poet expresses the desire to be metamorphosed into his mistress's necklace or belt, or the wine that she is drinking. In an Ovidian conceit—indeed, an Ovidian indecency—he imagines being the wine that kisses her lips, trickles down her throat, runs through her veins, and finally 'pass[es] by Pleasure's part'.[10] Ovidian metamorphic mythology has furnished Barnes with images through which to convey his desire for a metamorphosis in his own standing

---

[8] *Le familiari*, xxiii. 19, in *Letters from Petrarch*, selected and trans. Morris Bishop (Bloomington, Ind., 1966), 198–9. See further the magisterial treatment of Petrarch in Greene's *The Light in Troy*.

[9] Barnes, *Parthenophil and Parthenophe* (London, 1593), quoted from Sidney Lee's anthology of *Elizabethan Sonnets*, 2 vols. (London, 1904), i. 207.

[10] The fountainhead for this kind of poem is *Amores*, II. xv, in which the poet imagines himself as the ring on his mistress's finger, touching various other parts of her body.

with regard to his lover.[11] Ovidian wit has furnished the sonnet with its tail. But the opening quatrain is formulaically dependent on Ovid and the final couplet crude in comparison with him. Barnes in no way advances on Ovid, in no way sublimates him.

But consider Shakespeare's Sonnet 53:

> What is your substance, whereof are you made,
> That millions of strange shadows on you tend?
> Since every one hath, every one, one shade,
> And you, but one, can every shadow lend.
> Describe Adonis, and the counterfeit
> Is poorly imitated after you.
> On Helen's cheek all art of beauty set,
> And you in Grecian tires are painted new.
> Speak of the spring and foison of the year:
> The one doth shadow of your beauty show,
> The other as your bounty doth appear,
> And you in every blessèd shape we know.

In Barnes the Ovidian mythological figures are fixed points, ideal substances which are shadowed in his own love. In Shakespeare the opposite is the case: the lovely boy is the substance, the mythological figure the shadow. 'Describe Adonis, and the counterfeit | Is poorly imitated after you': where Barnes offers counterfeits, poor imitations of Ovidian originals, Shakespeare makes the lovely boy into the ideal figure of beauty and Adonis into the counterfeit. The third quatrain performs a similar trumping, in this instance an overgoing of those figures of natural plenty who are so central to Ovid's world: 'Speak of the spring and foison of the year', and one would usually speak of Proserpina and Ceres, but here nature is a shadow of the youth's beauty. The sonnet's innovation is in its appropriation of the term 'imitate'. Where a poet like Giles Fletcher announces on the title-page of his sonnet-sequence *Licia* (1593) that he is writing in 'imitation of the best Latin Poets, and others', Shakespeare claims within his poem that classical figures are imitations of his own beloved. 'Figure' is an analogous term: *paradigma* is a figure of speech whereby classical

---

[11] This is a much-used topos which may be traced back to Ronsard's 'Je vouldroy bien richement jaunissant . . .' (*Amours*, 20), a lyric translated closely as sonnet 34 of Thomas Lodge's *Phillis* (1593) and more freely as 'Would I were chaung'd into that golden showre', a poem in *The Phoenix Nest* (1593) attributable to Ralegh. Sidney, who so often detaches himself from the literariness of other sonneteers, mocks the topos in *Astrophil*, 6: 'Some one his song in Jove, and Jove's strange tales, attires, | Broidered with bulls and swans, powdered with golden rain.'

figures serve as authorities, but Sonnet 106 goes so far as to make the claim that all praises of past beauties 'are but prophecies | Of this our time, all you prefiguring'. The ideal figures are but prefigurings of the poet's present love.

When Shakespeare deploys this effect of inverted *paradigma*, he exercises a turn on the concept of metamorphosis. The paradigmatic function of myth is to provide poet and reader with a stock of archetypes. But where it is customary to suggest the force of a present change by comparing it to a traditional mythological metamorphosis that is known to be forceful, Shakespeare makes the myths into the shadow, the present change into the archetype or true substance. In Ovid, extreme emotion precipitates the metamorphosis of a person into an object of nature, whereas in Sonnet 113, extreme emotion precipitates the metamorphosis of the objects of nature into a person:

> [Mine eye] no form delivers to the heart
> Of bird, of flower, or shape which it doth latch.
> Of his quick objects hath the mind no part,
> Nor his own vision holds what it doth catch;
> For if it see the rud'st or gentlest sight,
> The most sweet favour or deformèd'st creature,
> The mountain or the sea, the day or night,
> The crow or dove, it shapes them to your feature.

The sympathetic eye of Ovid looks at the natural world and reads out of it an array of mythic lovers and objects of desire; the possessed eye/I of the Sonnets sees in all the forms of nature its own love, its single object of desire.

But Shakespeare does not always seem so readily able to overturn his prototypes. Sonnet 59 opens with a troubled expression of poetic belatedness:

> If there be nothing new, but that which is
> Hath been before, how are our brains beguiled,
> Which, labouring for invention, bear amiss
> The second burden of a former child!

The darkness of this is manifest if we recollect Holofernes' distinction between *imitari*, which is nothing, and 'the jerks of invention' to which the poet should aspire. Whereas Shakespeare proved his inventiveness in Sonnet 53 by appropriating the idea of imitation, now he laments that the labour for originality is fruitless since nothing is new, what one writes will be already written, and what one imagines to be the child of one's invention will turn out to be the child of one's poetic father. 'Burden' is a key word: together with 'labouring' it establishes an image of writing as giving birth, but at the same time it suggests the burden of the past, the oppressive weight of 'the wits of former days'. The notion of eternal repetition on which the sonnet rests carries the melancholy implication that all writing is mere imitation of previous writing. Line 8, 'Since mind at first in character was done', evokes an originary act of writing that can never be recovered. The sense of loss derives from the contrast between that 'at *first*' and the poet's own '*second* burden'.

Sonnet 59 exemplifies its own contention that there is nothing new by means of its own nature as something that is not new. For what is its argument about repetition other than a repetition of Pythagoras' argument in *Metamorphoses* Fifteen? The image of birth as rebirth of something that has been before is itself the second birth of Ovid's 'nascique vocatur | incipere esse aliud, quam quod fuit ante' (*Met.* xv. 255–6), or as Arthur Golding has it, 'For that which wee | Doo terme by name of being borne, is for too gin too bee | Another thing than that it was' (Golding, xv. 279–81). Ovid's technique in the *Metamorphoses* is to slide from one story to the next in a process of repetition and variation that embodies the neo-Pythagorean theory of constancy and change. The structure of the sonnets is the same: 60 picks up from 59.[12] In particular, it picks up on the language of Pythagoras' discourse. As every educated Elizabethan reader would have recognized,

> Like as the waves make towards the pebbled shore,
> So do our minutes hasten to their end,
> Each changing place with that which goes before;
> In sequent toil all forwards to contend.

is a version of

> But looke
> As every wave dryves other foorth, and that that commes behynd
> Bothe thrusteth and is thrust itself: Even so the tymes by kynd
> Doo fly and follow bothe at once, and evermore renew.
>
> (Golding, xv. 200–3)

---

[12] I follow Katherine Duncan-Jones, 'Was the 1609 *Shake-speares Sonnets* Really Unauthorized?', *RES* NS xxxiv (1983), 151–71, and John Kerrigan, ed., *The Sonnets and A Lover's Complaint*, in ascribing authority to the 1609 order.

Here Shakespeare is imitating closely: his 'sequent' derives from Ovid's 'sequuntur' (xv. 183) and 'in the main of light' in the following line translates 'editus in lucem' (xv. 221). He pursues a similar *imitatio* with the image of sea encroaching on land and land on sea in Sonnet 64.[13]

But in Sonnet 60 he is also revising, for he undertakes an elision that is thoroughly Ovidian but which is never actually explicitly articulated by Ovid. In this sense, Shakespeare is, in Petrarch's terms, using his model's conceptions and the colour of his style, but not his exact words. The elision consists of a movement from past to future. Where Sonnet 59 looks back, and ends with the rather half-hearted couplet, 'O, sure I am the wits of former days | To subjects worse have given admiring praise', Sonnet 60 frees itself from eternal repetition by claiming that the verse itself will endure. A few sonnets earlier, in 55, Shakespeare had reiterated the great envoi of the *Metamorphoses*: 'Iamque opus exegi, quod nec Iovis ira nec ignis | nec poterit ferrum nec edax abolere vetustas' (xv. 871–2); 'Nor Mars his sword nor war's quick fire shall burn | The living record of your memory'. Now in the couplet of 60 this idea of triumphing through writing recurs and offers itself as the overcoming of time's inexorability: 'And yet to times in hope my verse shall stand, | Praising thy worth despite his cruel hand.' In *Metamorphoses* Fifteen, the envoi stands alone, not as a reply to Pythagoras. It is Shakespeare who makes the connection and thus uses one part of Ovid to unwrite or rewrite another.

Shakespeare has thus both cleared a space for himself, enabled himself to say something new, and at the same time remained responsive to his paradigm. In the very act of asserting his own immortality, he asserts Ovid's. There is a kind of mutuality whereby imagining the past and imagining the future are one and the same; Ovid's paradigmatic status proves his immortality and implicitly opens the way for Shakespeare to achieve similar immortality through becoming paradigmatic to eyes not yet created and when rehearsed on tongues to be. As Puttenham put it in his account of *paradigma*, the example of the past gathers probability of like success for the present.

The idea that Ovid has been reborn in sonnets such as 60 effects a curious effacement of the poetic 'I'. The conceit of Shakespeare writing Ovid will not do here. Meres's image of 'the sweete wittie soule

---

[13] An image reiterated dramatically in King Henry IV's night scene: *2 Henry IV*, III. ii. 47–9.

of Ovid liv[ing] in mellifluous and hony-tongued Shakespeare' carries the converse implication that it is Ovid who is writing Shakespeare. If it is Ovid who 'lives', Shakespeare has disappeared in the very moment of asserting his own enduring life. Consider the 'I' of Sonnet 64:

> When I have seen the hungry ocean gain
> Advantage on the kingdom of the shore,
> And the firm soil win of the wat'ry main,
> Increasing store with loss and loss with store;
> When I have seen such interchange of state . . .

and so on. Who is this 'I'? Is it the speaker of the sonnets, or is it Ovid's speaker, Pythagoras—or the speaker of the Englished Ovid, Arthur Golding?

> Even so have places oftentymes exchaunged theyr estate.
> For I have seene it sea which was substanciall ground alate,
> Ageine where sea was, I have seene the same become dry lond . . .
>
> (Golding, xv. 287–9)

Or could it be a version of the later Ovid, exiled from Rome and complaining about a friend who has now forgotten about him, as Timon is forgotten by his supposed friends once he is exiled:

> The freshe floudes shall from Seas retyre, againe their springs unto,
> So shall the Sunne wyth horses tourn'de, his course revoke also.
> The earth shal eke the bright starre beare, and ayre the plough shal cleve,
> The water shall bringe forth the flames, and fyre shall water geve.
> All thinges shall come to passe which I, denyed afore could bee,
> For nothinge is so straung to heare, but we may hope to see.
> It shall be so I gesse because, of him I was rejecte,
> Whose helpe I hoped now that should my wofull cause protecte.
> O faythlesse frende how came so great, forgetfulnes of mee,
> Why were thou then so sore afrayd, my carefull corpes to see?[14]

The use of anaphora to render the perpetual process of change is replicated by Shakespeare, even as the situation is different (he hasn't yet lost his friend, but he senses that one day he will).

---

[14] *The Three first Bookes of Ovids de Tristibus*, trans. Thomas Churchyard (London, 1572), I. vii [I. viii in modern edns.], sig. A7ᵛ. Churchyard gives the poems of the *Tristia* titles that are similar to those which are given to Shakespeare's Sonnets in Benson's 1640 edn. (this one is called 'To his frende that breake his promise'; proximate titles include 'To his constant frende', 'To his frendes that Ware his Image ingravde', and 'To his frende that the common people followeth fortune').

The 'I' who speaks the poem has been transformed into a polyphony of voices. According to one view, this dissolution is a source of anxiety. One might apply to Sonnet 64 Terence Cave's general conclusion regarding Renaissance imitation theory: 'it recognizes the extent to which the production of any discourse is conditioned by pre-existing instances of discourse; the writer is always a rewriter, the problem then being to differentiate and authenticate the rewriting. . . . Rewriting betrays its own anxiety by personifying itself as the product of an author; it imprints on itself— one might even say *forges*—an identity.'[15] But the polyphonic 'I' can equally well be seen as an expansion rather than a dissolution, a product of generosity rather than anxiety. There is a modesty about Shakespeare's self-effacement which is the counterpart to the arrogance of his inverted *paradigma*. Again, there is a process of repetition and variation in the movement from sonnet to sonnet: 60 overcomes the anxiety of 59, then 64 assuages the potential egotism of 60.

John Kerrigan sees modesty at work in Sonnet 55, and differentiates Shakespeare's claims for immortality from Ovid's. The final word of the *Metamorphoses* is in the egotistic first-person future: 'vivam', 'I shall live'. Golding renders the poem's last line 'My lyfe shall everlastingly bee lengthened still by fame' (Golding, xv. 995). 'Strikingly, though,' says Kerrigan, 'Shakespeare promises to preserve the young man in verse, not himself.' Kerrigan notes that this difference has led to the citation of a third possible 'source' for 55, an elegy of Propertius (III. ii) where immortality is bestowed on the person praised, not the poet himself; he is rightly dismissive of this possibility, since Propertius was barely read in the 1590s. 'It seems more likely', Kerrigan concludes, 'that Shakespeare adapted Ovid and Horace in Sonnet 55, and virtually certain that early readers would have understood the lines that way.'[16] Early readers might also have remembered the later Ovid. Images of the text outliving sword and fire

---

[15] Terence Cave, *The Cornucopian Text: Problems of Writing in the French Renaissance* (Oxford, 1979), 76–7.

[16] *The Sonnets and A Lover's Complaint*, 241; see also p. 21. For the citation of Propertius, see J. B. Leishman, *Themes and Variations in Shakespeare's Sonnets* (London, 1961), 42. For Horace's self-immortalizations, see the closing poems of bks. 2 and 3 of his *Odes* (II. xx, III. xxx)—the latter begins with the famous 'Exegi monumentum aere perennius'. The first and third books of Ovid's *Amores* follow Horace in ending with the claim that the poet will live on ('vivam': I. xv) through his work, that it will endure after his death ('post mea mansurum fata superstes opus!': III. xv).

derive from the end of the *Metamorphoses*, but the modesty of '*You* live in this' suggests the end of the *Tristia*:

> Quanta tibi dederim nostris monumenta libellis,
>   o mihi me coniunx carior, ipsa vides.
> detrahat auctori multum fortuna licebit,
>   tu tamen ingenio clara ferere meo;
> dumque legar, mecum pariter tua fama legetur.

What a monument I have raised to thee in my books, O my wife, dearer to me than myself, thou seest. Though fate may take much from their author, thou at least shall be made illustrious by my powers. As long as I am read, thy fame shall be read along with me.[17]

It is, I think, from the tender 'tibi' and 'tu' of this passage that Shakespeare works his immortalization of the beloved, just as it is from the structure of repetition in the last line of this—'As long as I am read, thy fame shall be read along with me'—that he creates the couplet of Sonnet 18, 'So long as men can breathe or eyes can see, | So long lives this, and this gives life to thee'.[18] The trope of the joint immortalization of poet and lover may also be traced back to the *Amores*: 'So likewise we will through the world be rung, | And with my name shall thine be always sung'.[19] The transformation of the mistress of the *Amores* and the wife of the *Tristia* into Shakespeare's fair youth is another suggestive revision: between the antique and the modern pen there is a constancy in love but a change in the object of love.

In these patterns of reiteration and variation, there is a rapid interchange between *verba* and *res*. The language of such sonnets as 18 and 19, 60 and 64, is for ever shifting as it interlocks with and then extricates itself from the words, *verba*, of Ovid. Textual transforma-

---

[17] *Tristia*, v. xiv. 1–5, with Loeb trans., adapted.

[18] It is strange that scholars (e.g. Baldwin, *Literary Genetics of Poems and Sonnets*, 215; Lever, *Elizabethan Love Sonnet*, 201) have derived the first line of Sonnet 19, 'Devouring Time, blunt thou the lion's paws', from *Tristia*, IV. vi. 5, but not the couplet of 18 from *Tristia*, v. xiv. 5. An earlier poem in the *Tristia* also gives immortality to the poet's wife: 'quantumcumque tamen praeconia nostra valebunt, | carminibus vives tempus in omne meis'—'Yet so far as my praise has power, thou shalt live for all time in my song' (I. vi. 35–6). The *Tristia* also includes many iterations of the topos of the poet's own work as enduring monument to himself: e.g. 'On Tombe these shal suffice: but yet, my bookes that longer byde, | As monumentes of mee, which that, no tract of tyme shall hyde' (III. iii. 77–8, trans. Churchyard). The topos of Time as enemy has a history as long as poetry itself, but there are particularly close links between Shakespeare's treatment of it and that of Ovid in the *Tristia*.

[19] Marlowe's trans. of the final couplet of *Amores*, I. iii.

tions furnish the alert reader with a reminder of the metamorphic substance, *res*, which Ovid and Shakespeare share. And in responding to the *res*, Shakespeare is going beyond the imitative poet like Watson who is stuck with the *verba* of his models. The Pythagoras of Book Fifteen has a figure which comes to the quintessence of the *res*, the matter, of both the *Metamorphoses* and the Sonnets:

> And even as supple wax with ease receyveth fygures straunge,
> And keepes not ay one shape, ne bydes assured ay from chaunge,
> And yit continueth alwayes wax in substaunce: So I say
> The soule is ay the selfsame thing it was, and yit astray
> It fleeteth intoo sundry shapes.
>
> (Golding, xv. 188–92)

That the soul, the self, is like wax is an idea which possessed Shakespeare deeply. One thinks of Theseus addressing Hermia,

> you are but as a form in wax,
> By him imprinted, and within his power
> To leave the figure or disfigure it.
> (*A Midsummer Night's Dream*, i. i. 49–51)

and of related images of 'impression' and 'imprint' in the sonnets.[20] It is an idea that takes us beyond intertextuality.

In his frequent references to antique books, and especially in Sonnet 59, Shakespeare focuses his anxieties about time and endurance by means of unobtrusive classical citations. In most of his Ovidian sonnets, and especially 60, he overcomes the burden of time by means of a process of reiteration and variation that is itself a form of Pythagorean metempsychosis. But what the sonnets cannot escape is the burden of love. The real melancholy of the sequence comes from the way in which the poet is *impressed*, not by Ovid, not by the 'rival poet', but by the fair youth himself. The sense in which Ovid, and indeed the whole panegyric tradition, begets the sonnets is far less troubling than that in which the youth himself begets them and can reject them:

> Farewell—thou art too dear for my possessing,
> And like enough thou know'st thy estimate.
> The charter of thy worth gives thee releasing;
> My bonds in thee are all determinate.
> For how do I hold thee but by thy granting,
> And for that riches where is my deserving?

[20] e.g. Sonnet 112, l. 1, and Sonnet 77, l. 3.

The cause of this fair gift in me is wanting,
And so my patent back again is swerving.
Thyself thou gav'st, thy own worth then not knowing,
Or me to whom thou gav'st it else mistaking;
So thy great gift, upon misprision growing,
Comes home again, on better judgement making.
   Thus have I had thee as a dream doth flatter:
   In sleep a king, but waking no such matter.

                                    (87)

This sonnet is troubled not about the poetic tradition but about the whims of the beloved. Like Hermia's father, the youth has power to mould another person's self; he is able to shape the poet, 'To leave the figure or disfigure it'. Anxiety is wrought by the fear of losing the beloved; the truly terrifying thought is that he has only been possessed in a dream. Images of literary textuality are replaced by those of legal and commercial textuality. The instability of both desire and patronage are central concerns here. The speaker of the sonnet shares Actaeon's discovery that the person you desire has the greatest power to destroy you. The 'swerving' is not between the text and its aesthetic paradigm, but of the 'patent' back to the 'I' who has registered it; the 'misprision' is of the 'gift' of love which in this poem sounds suspiciously like a cipher for that of patronage. If the sonnet is to be granted its force, extra-textual reality must be allowed to intrude in some such terms as these.

It is possible that the Sonnets' Ovidian topoi ask to be read in connection with Shakespeare's clientage. The so-called 'breeding' sequence which opens the collection (numbers 1 to 17) invokes the figure of Narcissus. The most frequently cited words of that lovely boy, 'inopem me copia fecit', 'my plentie makes me poore',[21] are improvised upon in the very first sonnet:

> But thou, contracted to thine own bright eyes,
> Feed'st thy light's flame with self-substantial fuel,
> Making a famine where abundance lies,
> Thyself thy foe, to thy sweet self too cruel.

Not only is famine in abundance a version of poverty in plenty, the image of the self-regarding eye is also a sure sign of Narcissus, and the

[21] *Met.* iii. 466; Golding, iii. 587; quoted on innumerable occasions in the Renaissance, often in contexts of unrequited love, as when Spenser writes of the desiring lover's eyes 'in their amazement lyke *Narcissus* vaine | whose eyes him starv'd: so plenty makes me poore' (*Amoretti*, 35). 'Vaine' is a much-used pun in this context.

self-consuming flame is based on Ovid's densely packed line, 'uror amore mei: flammas moveoque feroque' (iv. 464, 'I burn with love of my own self: I both kindle the flames and suffer them'). Sonnet 3 begins with the narcissistic gaze ('Look in thy glass') and proceeds to 'self-love'. Line 10 of Sonnet 5, 'A liquid prisoner pent in walls of glass', refers metonymically to the youth and in so doing elicits the watery fate of Narcissus. And so on. When the 'only begetter' read these first sonnets in manuscript, he could not have failed to see the face of Narcissus mirrored in Shakespeare's lines. If he was the teenage Earl of Southampton it would have been a familiar identification: in 1591 one of Burghley's secretaries, John Clapham, had dedicated to that youth a Latin poem entitled *Narcissus*—an unsubtle hint on the occasion of his refusal to marry his guardian's granddaughter.[22]

If exhortation to marriage is also the true purpose of Shakespeare's first group of sonnets, the reading is obvious enough: 'Consider the fate of Narcissus and act to prevent it being yours'. But other possibilities suggest themselves. The fable of Narcissus 'presents the condition of those, who adorned by the bounty of nature, or inriched by the industry of others, without merit, or honour of their owne acquisition, are transported with selfe-love'. The sonnets could accordingly be read as a plea to the fair youth to share his bounty in material ways, not least by reciprocally 'inriching' the industrious sonneteer who is celebrating the adornments. Alternatively or additionally, the exhortation to marriage may be a cipher for an exhortation to public service, as suggested by another interpretation of Narcissus, namely his figuration of those 'Who likely sequester themselves from publique converse and civill affaires, as subject to neglects and disgraces, which might too much trouble and deject them: admitting but of a few to accompany their solitarinesse; those being such as only applaud and admire them, assenting to what they say, like as many *Ecchos*'. When the sonnet sequence exfoliates from its original occasion and explores the selves and souls of its desiring and desired personae in diverse ways, the reader versed in mythography might also bring into play the reading of the Narcissus story as an examination of the distinction between physical and spiritual beauty, in which the youth embodies someone who

[22] See 'Clapham's *Narcissus*: A Pre-Text for Shakespeare's *Venus and Adonis?* (text, translation, and commentary)', ed. Charles Martindale and Colin Burrow, *ELR* 22 (1992), 147–76.

considers only his bodily appearance (physical beauty being but the 'shadow of the soule'), who neglects 'his proper essence of virtue', and who is thus a representation of the soul 'alienated from it selfe'.[23]

In an analysis of Elizabethan sonnet sequences as social transactions, Arthur Marotti argues that Shakespeare gave up on the prospect of persuading the youth out of his narcissism:

Recognizing that the young man is really uneducable, morally obtuse, and generally unworthy of anything more sincere than the kind of praise rendered in encomiastic formulae, the poet discovers he is engaging in self-praise finally, celebrating a love whose constancy, growth, and worth exist in himself rather than in a beloved friend who is actually abandoned to his imperious narcissism. He discovers also in his resources as a poet the means both for enacting a kind of revenge and for establishing an authority and status better than the benefits of clientage. Shakespeare uses the eternizing conceit, among other purposes, for asserting a power that reverses the roles of inferior and superior; he also projects onto the recurrent figure of time-as-destroyer the hostility and resentment implicit in his disadvantageous position as a client.[24]

In this account, it is Shakespeare who becomes the Narcissus or even one of Actaeon's avenging dogs. What is omitted by Marotti is the distinctive twist on 'the eternizing conceit' away from the self-assertion of Ovid's 'vivam' and Horace's 'Exegi monumentum aere perennius', towards the immortalization of the beloved. If the beloved is also the patron, then the sequence's rapid development from the Narcissus topos to the immortalizing one is an intensification, not an ironic reversal, of clientage. Shakespeare is doing the oldest work of the laureate: singing for his supper by eternizing his master.[25]

As far as Renaissance theorists of imitation were concerned, bad imitators were concerned only with the *verba* of their paradigms, good ones with the *res*. For all writers in the period, formal literary *imitatio* was co-ordinate with, not in opposition to, literature's traditional mimetic function with regard to nature. *Paradigma* in Puttenham is both a trope and a means to action. Shakespeare makes new senses

[23] All quotations in this paragraph are from the synthesis of interpretations of Narcissus in Sandys, *Ovid's Metamorphosis Englished*, 106.

[24] Arthur F. Marotti, ' "Love is not love": Elizabethan Sonnet Sequences and the Social Order', *ELH* xlix (1982), 396–428 (p. 412).

[25] The point is made in strong, if vulgar, fashion by John Barrell when he suggests that the pathos of Sonnet 29 'is that the narrator can find no words to assert the transcendent power of true love, which cannot be interpreted as making a request for a couple of quid'—*Poetry, Language and Politics* (Manchester, 1988), 42.

out of Ovid as a way of making sense out of love more than as an assertion of his own hopes for literary immortality (to judge from his lack of interest in publication, the latter was not consciously a prime concern). And he tried to make sense of love in his writing not just because mimesis is, as Aristotle recognized, a primary pleasure, but also because it was a way of making himself known. Whether the sonnets were an attempt to gain or maintain the patronage of the Earl of Southampton, as were the Ovidian narrative poems, or whether they were directed at the Earl of Pembroke or some unknown WH, they did their required work: by 1598, together with *Venus and Adonis* and *Lucrece*, they had won Shakespeare a place in the English pantheon outlined in Meres's commonplace book—they had made their author into a modern reincarnation of Ovid, someone who would have been an addition to any sophisticated and ostentatious nobleman's coterie.

II

Shakespeare's ambitions do not, however, seem to have been those of Puttenham's courtier or of Lyly hanging around the Revels office. Having proved his literary credentials with the narrative poems, he chose to return to the theatre in 1594 and became a shareholder in the new Chamberlain's Men. It was for his company, not himself, that he subsequently sought patronage. But some of his methods of doing so were the same as in the non-dramatic works: *paradigma* could also be a mode of dramatic composition. *The Comedy of Errors*, performed at one of the Inns of Court in 1594, is a textbook case: the *Menaechmi* of Plautus is its paradigm, but, as in the Sonnets, Shakespeare seeks to outdo rather than merely reproduce his model. Thus he squares the main plot-feature by adding to the twin brothers of *Menaechmi* the doubled servant from another Plautine comedy, *Amphitruo*.[26] He also demonstrates his artful eclecticism by contaminating the hard-edged farce of Plautus with a framework of romance—shipwrecks, strangers, magic, losses and reunions—that anticipates his own later plays. The Duke's baffled exclamation when the confusions of the plot are at their height, 'I think you all have drunk of Circe's cup' (v. i. 270), evokes the most beguiling but sinister of the enchantments

---

[26] For a detailed study of *The Comedy of Errors* as humanist *imitatio*, see Wolfgang Riehle, *Shakespeare, Plautus and the Humanist Tradition* (Woodbridge, 1991).

encountered during the sea-wandering of the romance-style later books of the *Metamorphoses*.

In pursuing the matter beyond the clear-cut case of *The Comedy of Errors*, I want to begin with a remark of Richard Farmer, the eighteenth-century Master of Emmanuel College, Cambridge. He was dismissive not only about Shakespeare's classical capacities, but also about the scholarship of Edward Capell, who was something of an outsider in the world of eighteenth-century Shakespearian editing: 'Capell thought *Edward III* was Shakspeare's because *nobody* could write so, and *Titus Andronicus* because *every body* could! Well fare his heart, for he is a jewel of a reasoner!'[27]

Modern scholarship has moved towards the endorsement of Capell's once idiosyncratic view on the canonicity of these two plays. It is now widely agreed that Shakespeare wrote at least the Countess of Salisbury scenes in *Edward III*. I think it is highly probable that he did so between 1592 and 1594, not least because that was a period when he was experimenting with ways of writing about and representing rape and seduction. When the Countess's constancy to her husband finally persuades the libidinous King to call off the hunt, he says,

> Arise, true English Ladie, whom our Ile
> May better boast of th[a]n ever Romaine might
> Of her, whose ransackt treasurie hath taskt
> The vaine indevor of so many pens.[28]

That 'her' is, of course, Lucrece, and I would wager that one of the pens was the author's own. Whether Shakespeare had Lucrece in mind, in hand, or in print at this time, the lines are wryly self-referential. As for *Titus Andronicus*, given the vogue for blood-and-guts revenge drama in the later 1580s and early 1590s, how could an aspiring young dramatist like Shakespeare have made his mark without contributing to the genre? If Shakespeare did not write *Titus*, we had better quickly find another revenge drama to attribute to him.

This was Capell's point in making the seemingly perverse claim that *Titus Andronicus* must be by Shakespeare because everybody at the time wrote thus: Shakespeare wrote for money and was eminently capable of adapting himself to the most popular style of the

---

[27] Farmer, quoted from James Boswell Jr.'s revision of Edmond Malone's 1790 Variorum edn. of Shakespeare, 21 vols. (London, 1821), xxi. 381.

[28] *The Raigne of King Edward the Third* (publ. 1596), ii. ii. 194–7, quoted from *The Shakespeare Apocrypha*, ed. C. F. Tucker Brooke (Oxford, 1908).

day. There is, however, more to it than this. There is much to be said
for Edmond Malone's opinion that *Titus* was 'coined in the same mint'
as plays like *The Battle of Alcazar*, *Selimus Emperor of the Turks*,
Jeronimo, and *Locrine*.[29] But if we then consider one of the identifying
marks of this currency, its self-authentication as true classical gold,
one notices something rather remarkable: where a 'learned' writer
like Thomas Kyd, educated by no less a classicist than Richard
Mulcaster at Merchant Taylors', merely spices his revenge drama
with classical tags along the lines of 'Enter Hieronimo *with a book in his
hand. Vindicta mihi! . . . Per scelus semper tutum est sceleribus iter*',[30] the
provincial grammar-school boy Shakespeare shapes his effort with a
far more thoroughgoing classicism. Even if the Titus Andronicus
chapbook was Shakespeare's narrative source—and I follow the
minority of scholars who believe that it was not[31]—the play's main
structural model is the Ovidian tale of Philomel, Tereus, and Procne.
As will be shown, that structural patterning is proclaimed much more
loudly by the text than is usually the case in the genre. Thomas
Lodge's *Wounds of Civil War* is a Roman play which skilfully conflates
two classical sources (Plutarch and Appian), but it does not tell its
audience that it is doing so, as *Titus* reminds the audience of its own
Ovidianism.

Muriel Bradbrook has convincingly argued that Shakespeare wrote
Venus and Adonis partly in response to Greene's 'upstart crow' quip—
the Stratford lad decided to show that he could outdo the Oxbridge
men in that most sophisticated of genres, the Ovidian erotic
narrative.[32] *Titus* is also beautified with the feathers of classicism—
and with a vengeance. If we posit an early date for the play we may
consider it as a provocation of Greene; if a later one, as a response to
him. This, then, is the additional force of Capell's point: precisely
because Shakespeare had less formal education than certain other
dramatists, his play has more display of learning. He trumps his
contemporaries in their own suit.

[29] Malone, in the commentary to his 1790 edn., quoted from 1821 edn., xxi. 259.

[30] *The Spanish Tragedy*, ed. Philip Edwards (London, 1959), III. xiii. 1–6, citing
Seneca (*Agamemnon*, l. 115).

[31] Marco Mincoff, 'The Source of *Titus Andronicus*', *N&Q*, ccxvi (1971), 131–4; G. K.
Hunter, 'Sources and Meanings in *Titus Andronicus*', in *The Mirror up to Shakespeare*, ed.
J. C. Gray (Toronto, 1983), 171–88, and 'The "Sources" of *Titus Andronicus*—Once
Again', *N&Q*, xxx (1983), 114–16; MacDonald P. Jackson, 'The Year's Contribution
to Shakespearian Study: Editions and Textual Studies', *ShS* xxxviii (1985), 249–50.

[32] Bradbrook, 'Beasts and Gods: Greene's *Groats-Worth of Witte* and the Social
Purpose of *Venus and Adonis*', *ShS* xv (1962), 62–72.

From the outset, the characters in *Titus* establish mythical and historical patternings for the action. The first of them is already familiar from *Edward III*: 'Take this of me: Lucrece was not more chaste | Than this Lavinia, Bassianus' love' (II. i. 109–10). The parallel between Lavinia and Lucrece recurs at the end of Act III, scene i, where rape becomes the pretext for the expulsion of an emperor:

> If Lucius live, he will requite your wrongs
> And make proud Saturnine and his empress
> Beg at the gates like Tarquin and his queen.
> (III. i. 295–7)

The important parallel, implicit here, between Lucius and Lucius Junius Brutus, who revenged his kinswoman's rape by persuading the people to expel the Tarquins, is made explicit in Act IV, scene i; as the early Roman republic was established at the cost of Lucrece's chastity, so the fictionalized late Roman empire is renewed at the cost of Lavinia's.

The play's classical allusiveness is deep, not wide. It relies on sustained involvement with a few sources—Ovid and a little Livy, the most famous part of Virgil, some Plutarch and the odd tag from Seneca that might well be derived at second hand—not on deployment of a Jonsonian range of learning.[33] In what is perhaps the most self-consciously literary moment in all Shakespeare, the play's most significant source is actually brought on stage:

TITUS. Lucius, what book is that she tosseth so?
BOY. Grandsire, 'tis Ovid's *Metamorphoses*;
My mother gave it me.
(IV. i. 41–3)

---

[33] For an ingenious argument about the play as a destabilization—a 'dismemberment'—of Virgil, see Heather James, 'Cultural Disintegration in *Titus Andronicus*: Mutilating Titus, Vergil and Rome', in *Violence in Drama, Themes in Drama*, xiii (1991), 123–40. The argument coheres with my sense of Ovid being used to destabilize a Virgilian, imperial idiom in *Antony and Cleopatra* and *The Tempest*, discussed in Chs. 5 and 6, below. Early 20th-cent. critics took the *Thyestes* of Seneca to be the main source for the play's bloody banquet, but their argument was effectively disposed of in Howard Baker's *Induction to Tragedy* (Baton Rouge, La., 1939), a book which remains methodologically salutary in its way of attending solidly to what the text says about its own filiations, not imposing on it connections which satisfy the modern academician's desire to draw together the great classical drama and that of the Renaissance. The story of Hecuba is an important secondary strand in the patterning of the play, but I am not convinced by Emrys Jones's argument in his otherwise excellent *The Origins of*

(This passing allusion to an absent mother is one of the many features that *Titus* shares with *King Lear*.) Lavinia then 'quotes' the leaves of the *Metamorphoses* in order to tell her own tragic tale. Later, Titus himself is explicit about the patterning of the action in a pair of lines which are constructed every bit as formally as the whole play is:

> For worse than Philomel you used my daughter,
> And worse than Procne I will be revenged.
>
> (v. ii. 193–4)

The switch from rape to revenge is modelled on the narrative of Philomel, to whom Lavinia is repeatedly compared, and Procne, in whose revenge, as George Steevens said of Shakespeare's play, '*justice* and *cookery* go hand in hand'.[34]

Titus Andronicus is a prime exhibit in the case for Shakespeare's artfulness: to put it simply, the play is an archetypal Renaissance humanist text in that it is patterned on the classics. It is to Ovid's Philomel story what *Venus and Adonis* is to Ovid's Venus and Adonis, what *Lucrece* is to Ovid's *Fasti*, and what *The Comedy of Errors* is to Plautine comedy. The 'quoting' of the leaves of Ovid's book by Lavinia tells the audience that this is the case. Her reading signals that the play is itself both a revisionary reading of the Ovidian text and an examination of the efficacy of humanist education.

By virtue of their reading and imitation of Ovid and other classical authors, the characters in the play come to resemble students in grammar school and university. The language of the schoolroom suffuses the play—characters keep coming up with remarks like 'Handle not the theme', 'I'll teach thee', 'I was their tutor to instruct them', and 'well has thou lessoned us'; they also refer to key educational texts such as Tully's *Orator*.[35] In one of his most powerful images, Titus seeks to fix, to memorialize, the most terrible truth that he has learnt. Like a schoolchild, Lavinia reads from her Ovid and then writes her text: '*Stuprum*—Chiron—Demetrius' (IV. i. 77). But she has written on sand, so the text may be erased, as from a pupil's writing slate ('the angry northern wind | Will blow these sands like Sibyl's leaves abroad, | And where's our lesson then?'—IV. i. 103–5).

Shakespeare (Oxford, 1977) that Shakespeare read that story in a Latin translation of Euripides' *Hecuba* as well as in the *Metamorphoses*.

[34] Steevens, commentary on revised Johnson edn.: see Malone's Variorum, 1821 edn. xxi. 378.

[35] III. ii. 29, IV. i. 119, V. i. 98, V. ii. 110, IV. i. 14.

So it is that Titus asks to inscribe the lesson in a more permanent form; steel and brass replace the humbler writing tools of the sixteenth-century schoolroom: 'I will go get a leaf of brass | And with a gad of steel will write these words, | And lay it by' (IV. i. 101–3). The image furnishes an extraordinarily physical twist on the pedagogic routine of etching the words of the classics on the memories of students.

An imitation is not a slavish copy and, as we will see, there are important differences between *Titus* and the tale of Philomel which is read out from the *Metamorphoses* and into the action of the play. *Dissimilitudo* and *contrarium* are as important to *imitatio* as are *similitudo* and *collatio*. And *imitatio* does not restrict the imitator to one model. The good imitator is eclectic to the point of promiscuity, which is why *Titus* invokes Hecuba, Lucrece, Livy's Virginius, Coriolanus, Dido and Aeneas, and a host of other *exempla*. Here, Shakespeare is following the Erasmian prescription for *copia*: 'Most powerful for proof, and therefore for *copia*, is the force of *exempla*'. If you want an example of, say, inconstancy, Erasmus says, you have Mercury and Proteus and Circe, and many, many more:

From the tragedies I will borrow Phaedra, with her varying moods . . . likewise Medea, before the slaying of her sons, tormented by various emotions; Byblis and Narcissus from Ovid; from Virgil, Dido, when Aeneas is already preparing his departure. And scattered through the works of the poets there are innumerable characters of this type.[36]

In stressing the importance of *exempla* (Puttenham's *paradigma*), Erasmus is following Quintilian:

Above all, our orator should be equipped with a rich store of examples both old and new: and he ought not merely to know those which are recorded in history or transmitted by oral tradition or occur from day to day, but should not neglect even those fictitious examples invented by the great poets. For while the former have the authority of evidence or even of legal decisions, the latter also either have the warrant of antiquity or are regarded as having been invented by great men to serve as lessons to the world.[37]

Fables, so the argument goes, have all the rhetorical power of histories. 'You shall perceive', wrote Puttenham, 'that histories were

---

[36] Erasmus, *On Copia of Words and Ideas (De utraque verborum ac rerum copia)*, trans. D. B. King and H. D. Rix (Milwaukee, 1963), 95. Testimony to the enormous influence of the *De Copia* in the 16th cent. is the fact that it went through 150 edns. between 1512 and 1572.

[37] *Institutio Oratoria*, XII. iv. 1–2.

of three sortes, wholly true and wholly false, and a third holding part of either, but for honest re-creation, and good example they were all of them.'[38] The ingenuity of *Titus* is that it is a feigned history—in contrast to Shakespeare's later Roman plays, the plot is fictional—based on a series of fabulous and historical exemplars.

Those exemplars are reflected upon with bold critical self-consciousness. *The Wounds of Civil War* again serves as a contrast: Lodge alludes incidentally to the Tarquin myth in order to achieve local copiousness, whereas *Titus* proposes that its whole *inventio* is generated out of its *exempla*. Like good humanists, the characters model their behaviour on the classical figures they learnt about in school. Should Mutius be given a proper burial despite the fact that he disobeyed his father? He should, argues Marcus, citing the precedent of Ajax: 'The Greeks upon advice did bury Ajax, | That slew himself' (I. i. 376–7). 'My lord the Emperor, resolve me this', begins Titus in the final scene, sounding every bit like a schoolmaster exercising his pupil,

> Was it well done of rash Virginius
> To slay his daughter with his own right hand,
> Because she was enforced, stained, and deflowered?
>
> (v. iii. 36–8)

'It was, Andronicus', replies the Emperor, submitting to the role of the schoolboy. 'Your reason, mighty lord?', continues Magister Titus. 'Because the girl should not survive her shame, | And by her presence still renew his sorrows', says the well-rehearsed pupil. 'A reason mighty, strong, and effectual', answers Titus, concluding the exercise. The next step is to make the humanist move from precept to practice, from literary *exemplum* to noble action. At the centre of humanism was 'the belief in the importance of the active life and the conviction that we are best persuaded to ethical praxis by the rhetorical practice of literature'.[39] This is the context in which we must read Titus' justification for the slaying of his daughter:

> A pattern, precedent, and lively warrant
> For me, most wretched, to perform the like.
> Die, die, Lavinia, and thy shame with thee,

---

[38] *The Arte of English Poesie*, 41.
[39] Victoria Kahn, *Rhetoric, Prudence, and Skepticism in the Renaissance* (Ithaca, NY, 1985), 9.

And with thy shame thy father's sorrow die.
He kills her.

(v. iii. 42–6)

But is this a 'good example', leading to what Puttenham calls 'honest re-creation'? If the metaphor may be allowed in the context of Titus' cookery, I would say that Shakespeare has his cake and eats it too. He displays his own learning ('do *you* remember Virginius in Livy?' he seems to ask his audience); he maintains his copious generation of *exempla*. But he also implicitly offers a critique of the very humanism he is embodying. What kind of education by example is it, he seems to ask, that leads you to murder your daughter? Quintilian linked the rhetoric of example to 'the authority of evidence or even of legal decisions'; Titus uses the terminology which that rhetoric shares with the law—'pattern, precedent, and lively warrant'—to justify the most heinous transgression of the law.

The process recurs throughout the play. What kind of exemplary pattern is it that fits a place for murder and rape? When Lavinia 'quotes the leaves' of the *Metamorphoses* in the reading scene, Titus finds in the text 'such a place' as the one in which Act II was located:

O, had we never, never hunted there!—
Patterned by that the poet here describes,
By nature made for murders and for rapes.

(iv. i. 55–7)

It is as if the Ovidian text has licensed the violent action. Lavinia's quotation at first seems to be a constructive use of the classical text, but it turns out to be another violent, destructive one, in that it patterns the bloody revenge.

Again, consider what Chiron and Demetrius have learnt from their classical education. Titus sends them a bundle of weapons inscribed with a hortatory text from Horace, 'Integer vitae, scelerisque purus, | Non eget Mauri iaculis, nec arcu' ('The man of upright life and free from crime does not need the javelins or bow of the Moor'). 'O,' says Chiron, ''tis a verse in Horace, I know it well. | I read it in the grammar long ago' (iv. ii. 20–3). He remembers the text, but does not see its application to himself. The case of Chiron exposes the stupidity of the idea that rote learning of the classics is preparation for a noble life. Worse than this, such applications of education to life as there are turn out to be sinister in the extreme. What Chiron and Demetrius have learnt from their reading of the classics at school is not *integer*

vitae, but some handy information about how a rape victim was able
to reveal the identity of her attacker even though he had removed her
tongue because he had left her with her hands. As Marcus puts it,

> Fair Philomel, why she but lost her tongue,
> And in a tedious sampler sewed her mind;
> But, lovely niece, that mean is cut from thee.
> A craftier Tereus, cousin, hast thou met,
> And he hath cut those pretty fingers off,
> That could have better sewed than Philomel.
>
> (II. iv. 38–43)

What is the point of a humanist education if, instead of instilling in
you *integer vitae,* it makes you into a craftier Tereus? The word that is
etched upon the memory, as with a gad of steel, is not *integer* but
Stuprum, not integrity but rape. It is one of Shakespeare's darkest
thoughts. One is irresistibly reminded of *Julius Caesar,* where the
linguistic art of Mark Antony works its effect and brings about—the
tearing to pieces of a practitioner of the linguistic art, a poet, Cinna.

In *From Humanism to the Humanities,* Anthony Grafton and Lisa
Jardine note that the great Italian humanist educator Guarino was 'at
pains to remind any friend or alumnus who had passed through his
hands that his literary, political and military triumphs were owed
directly to the lessons he had learned in his Ferrara classroom'.[40] That
intriguing off-stage character, Chiron and Demetrius' Gothic schoolmaster, may be seen as a kind of perverted Guarino. The triumphs
which these alumni owe to the lessons of his classroom back north or
out east are in the arena of rape and mutilation. What they learnt at his
hands was the value of chopping off hands. The ideal of Renaissance
humanism assumed a correspondence between the study of classical
texts and the cultivation of civic virtue. The idea was to imitate Rome,
which was viewed as both the supremely civilized culture and the
exemplum for the study of classical literature (for the Romans, of course,
this meant the Greeks). Shakespeare stands this idea on its head in
Titus: here, Rome is not civilized but the very thing it set itself up in
opposition to—barbaric. The scheming of Saturninus and the
sacrifice of Alarbus break down the distinction between Romans and
barbarians; Rome itself becomes 'but a wilderness of tigers' (III. i. 53).
And furthermore, civic virtue breaks down not because the classic
texts are neglected, but for the very reason that they are studied and

---

[40] Grafton and Jardine, *From Humanism to the Humanities* (London, 1986), 2.

applied selectively. They are evacuated of their wholesomeness and become instead manuals for barbarians. Horace's ode, 'Integer vitae' (1. xxii), claims that if one is armed with integrity one can roam in the Sabine wood and the wolf will flee from you. *Titus Andronicus* inverts this: Bassianus and Lavinia are anything but safe in the wood, while Chiron and Demetrius, readers of the ode, are the wolves. What Shakespeare is doing is comparable to some inconceivable scenario in which Cicero claims that Athens was the home of barbarism and that such barbarism was inculcated by the canonical Greek texts such as Homer.

Seen from this perspective, *Titus Andronicus* becomes a forerunner to *Troilus and Cressida*, Shakespeare's most thoroughgoing critique of the ancient world. It is significant in this respect that Ovid, the model for *Titus*, is used in *Troilus and Cressida* to destabilize the epic idiom associated with Homer and Chapman's Englished *Iliads*: the contention between Ajax and Ulysses for the arms of Achilles in Book Thirteen of the *Metamorphoses* reduces the stature of these two heroes almost to the point of parody—Ajax is a boasting 'dolt and grossehead', 'slye Ulysses' a slippery wordsmith 'who dooth all his matters in the dark'.[41] Ovid thus provides a precedent for Shakespeare's debunking representation of them. Reuben Brower's description of Ovid's revision of Homer serves equally well as a summary account of *Troilus and Cressida*:

the effect of [Ajax's] windy eloquence is to undermine any respect for his claim to glory. The great words of the Roman and Elizabethan heroic style are there: *virtus, nobilitas, heros, gloria*, but they grow less and less convincing the more Ajax talks, and his demonstration that he has indeed acted valiantly only waits for Odysseus' demolition. With Ovidian cunning, Odysseus, not Ajax, is introduced as 'hero', *Laertius heros*, and in a great ridiculing oration he scores point after point against the heroism of brute force, as he harps constantly on the superiority of 'both thought and deed', *consilio manuque*, over deeds alone.[42]

Ulysses' manipulation of Ajax in *Troilus and Cressida* offers a clinical demonstration of how rhetorical skill leads not to principled heroic action but to pragmatic machiavellian efficacy, just as the play as a

[41] Golding, xiii. 168, 115, 129.

[42] Brower, *Hero and Saint : Shakespeare and the Graeco-Roman Heroic Tradition* (Oxford, 1971), 123. The standard moral interpretation of the contention between Ajax and Ulysses endured well into the 17th cent.: in his *Wisdoms Conquest* of 1651, Thomas Hall affirmed that 'The scope and drift of this Fable and fiction is, to shew the folly of those who preferred Strength before Policy, Warriours before Scholars, and Weapons before Wisdome'.

whole destabilizes the entire humanist project of learning from the exemplars of the past.[43]

Between *Titus* and *Troilus* comes the figure of Richard III, who, unable to metamorphose himself out of a deformed body, makes language his means to power instead. When he lays out his project in *3 Henry VI*, he prefigures the deconstruction of Nestor and Ulysses effected by *Troilus and Cressida*, whilst also casting himself Tarquin-like as Sinon:

> I'll play the orator as well as Nestor,
> Deceive more slily than Ulysses could,
> And, like a Sinon, take another Troy.
> I can add colours to the chameleon,
> Change shapes with Proteus for advantages,
> And set the murderous Machiavel to school.
>   (*3 Henry VI*, III. ii. 188–93)

The conjunction of Proteus and Machiavelli suggests how the ideal of humanism may be inverted so that a character's modelling himself on a paradigm from the repertoire of the classics may be a way to villainy instead of virtue.

Where rhetoric is murderously clinical in *Richard III* and sordidly debased in *Troilus and Cressida*, in *Julius Caesar* it is exposed as potentially self-destructive. The orator precipitates the death of the poet. The archetype for Cinna, the artist torn apart by the mob who have been intoxicated by art, is Orpheus ripped to pieces by Dionysiac bacchants.[44] Orpheus is always a figure of the poet, as Proteus reminds the Duke in a strangely self-destructive image in *The Two Gentlemen of Verona*: 'For Orpheus' lute was strung with poets' sinews' (III. ii. 77): Orpheus only gets strings for his lute if sinews are torn from the poet's body. Shakespeare was fascinated by the extremes of harmony and violence in the Orpheus story; the successive stages of the narrative betoken the civilizing power of poetry but also its destructive power. The dismemberment of Orpheus is a reminder that the poet's own position is always precarious, whilst

---

[43] On Shakespeare's 'refashioning, decomposing, vulgarizing, declassicizing' of his precursor texts in *Troilus and Cressida*, see Elizabeth Freund, '"Ariachne's broken woof": The Rhetoric of Citation in *Troilus and Cressida*', in *Shakespeare and the Question of Theory*, ed. Patricia Parker and Geoffrey Hartman (New York and London, 1985), 19–36. The title cites Troilus' fusion of Ariadne and Arachne at v. ii. 155.

[44] On Cinna as Orpheus, see Gary Taylor, 'Bardicide', *London Review of Books*, xiv, no. 1 (9 Jan. 1992), 7.

his art can also lead to the abuses of poetic privilege—Proteus cites his example in the context of coercive sexual advances. So too in *Cymbeline*, another play which alludes to the Philomel story, Cloten— whose head, like Orpheus', floats out to sea still speaking—is both a bringer of music and a potential rapist. In Marcus' speech in *Titus*, Lavinia's Orphic music has been silenced; in a typical piece of Shakespearian syncretism, the Thracian tyrant (Tereus, figuring Demetrius and Chiron) has mutilated the 'Thracian poet' (Orpheus, figuring Lavinia):

> O, had the monster seen those lily hands
> Tremble like aspen leaves upon a lute
> And make the silken strings delight to kiss them,
> He would not then have touched them for his life.
> Or, had he heard the heavenly harmony
> Which that sweet tongue hath made,
> He would have dropped his knife and fell asleep,
> As Cerberus at the Thracian poet's feet.
>
> (II. iv. 44–51)

The silencing of Lavinia's musical art is at the heart of the *dissimilitudo* between 'the tragic tale of Philomel', as Titus calls it (IV. i. 47), and Shakespeare's play. That *dissimilitudo* lies in the very sense in which Ovid's tale is *not* tragic. Philomel is released *into* song; she becomes a nightingale, archetypal songster and poet. That song may be wrung out of her by pain—the breast against the thorn, as in *Lucrece* and the twentieth poem of *The Passionate Pilgrim*—but at least it is song, not the terrible combination of silence and shame to which Lavinia must submit. To stick with the Orphic image that Marcus introduces: Ovidian metamorphosis is a release into Orphic song, whilst tragedy witnesses the dismemberment of Orpheus. Paradoxically, however, tragedy makes a song out of that dismemberment: Lavinia may be silenced, but Marcus sings like a poet of her dismemberment. In that song a recovery is enacted. The poet, Orpheus, is the one figure who can—though fleetingly—unravel the thread of fate and bring back that which has been lost: 'Eurydices, oro, properata retexite fata'.[45]

Marcus' elaborate set speech is not to everyone's taste. In an influential article, 'The Metamorphosis of Violence in *Titus*

---

[45] Orpheus to Pluto at *Met.* x. 30: 'I | Beseech yee of *Eurydicee* unreele the destinye | That was so swiftly reeled up' (Golding, x. 31–3).

Andronicus',[46] Eugene Waith argued that it was a prime example of incompatibility between gorgeous Ovidian language and violent stage-action: it is all very well for Pyramus' blood to 'spin on hie | As when a Conduite pipe is crackt, the water bursting out' on the page of the *Metamorphoses* (Golding, iv. 147–8), but on the stage it is indecorous for Marcus to speak of Lavinia losing blood 'As from a conduit with three issuing spouts' (II. iv. 30) when we are at the same time confronting the victim herself. There may be ethical as well as aesthetic objections: the linguistic display might be considered to be a public humiliation, an insult added to Lavinia's injuries. Read in terms of the critique of humanism, the speech could be said to show that having all the rhetorical tropes at your fingertips doesn't actually help you to *do* anything. It is only after the highly rhetorical language of lament has broken down into incoherent laughter that the Andronicus family get around to *action*.

In defence of the speech, I want to say that in a good production—I am thinking here of Deborah Warner's definitive version of 1987–8—there is none of the dislocation or indecorum that Waith finds. As audience members, we need Marcus' formalization just as much as he does himself in order to be able to confront the mutilated Lavinia. The presence of the audience is crucial: a critique of humanism is built into the action, but the audience is capable of discriminating between right and wrong uses of learning. Co-ordinate with the implicit attack on a theoretical education is a defence of a theatrical one. The characters put their knowledge of the classics to destructive use; the play in the theatre gives the audience a creative knowledge in that it teaches them how to respond sympathetically to suffering. In this sense, the play is Shakespeare's 'Defence of Poesie'. Thus one might say: if Chiron and Demetrius had seen a dramatization of the Philomel story, instead of read it cold-bloodedly in the classroom, they would have wept for her instead of re-enacted her rape. Remember the story of the tyrant Alexander of Pherae, recounted in Plutarch's *Life of Pelopidas*:

he made some men to be buried alive, and others to be put in the skins of Bears and wild Bores, and then to set Hounds upon them to tear them in pieces, or else himself for his pastime would kill them. . . . And another time being in a Theatre, where the Tragedy of *Troades* in *Euripides* was played, he went out of the Theatre . . . ashamed his People should see him weep, to see the miseries

[46] *ShS* x (1957), 39–49.

of *Hecuba* and *Andromacha* played; and that they never saw him pity the death of any one man, or of so many of the Citizens as he had caused to be slain.[47]

Alexander has not been reformed by the drama, but he has been moved and shamed by it. Sir Philip Sidney used the story to defend the stage against puritan attacks on its immorality: 'a Tragedy, wel made and represented, drewe aboundance of teares' from the eyes of a tyrant 'who, without all pitty, had murthered infinite nombers, and some of his owne blood. So, as he, that was not ashamed to make matters for Tragedies, yet coulde not resist the sweet violence of a Tragedie.'[48] Sidney's term 'sweet violence' captures beautifully not only the complex of ideas evoked by the Orpheus myth but also the tone of the scene where Marcus is brought face to face with Lavinia.

Also apposite here is Edward III's address to the poet Lodowick concerning the power of the poet's pen to 'rayse drops in a Tarter's eye, | And make a flyntheart Sythian pytifull'. It is a speech which ends with language remarkably similar to that of Marcus:

> For, if the touch of sweet concordant strings
> Could force attendance in the eares of hell,
> How much more shall the straines of poets wit
> Beguile and ravish soft and humane myndes?
>   (II. i. 71–2, 76–9)

As in *Titus*, the context is sexual coercion and hence there is a conjunction between Orpheus and Philomel—a few lines later the king compares the Countess's voice 'to musicke or the nightingale' and then asks himself, 'why should I speake of the nightingale? | The nightingale singes of adulterate wrong' (II. i. 106, 109–10). For Shakespeare, as for Rilke, but more troublingly because Philomel displaces Eurydice, 'Ein für alle Male, | ists Orpheus, wenn es singt', 'Once and for all, it's Orpheus whenever there is song'.[49]

The fusion of Philomel and Orpheus is symptomatic of the revisionary nature of Shakespeare's reading and rewriting of Ovid. The combination of *similitudo* and *dissimilitudo* in the treatment of the Philomel pattern in *Titus* must now be examined in more detail. The Ovidian narrative is as follows: the story begins with a wedding in inauspicious circumstances; the husband is the Thracian tyrant,

---

[47] Plutarch, 'Life of Pelopidas', in Sir Thomas North's 1579 trans. (repr. London, 1676), 251.

[48] *Apologie for Poetrie*, in *Elizabethan Critical Essays*, i. 178.

[49] Rilke, *Sonette an Orpheus* (Leipzig, 1923), 1st part, 5th sonnet.

Tereus, his wife, Procne, daughter of Pandion. After a length of time
(the events do not have the compression of a dramatic work), Procne
asks her husband if her sister, Philomel, may visit. Tereus goes to
Pandion to fetch her and when he sees her he is smitten with the most
ardent desire. Like a kind of perverted Viola, he pleads his own desire
under the guise of Procne's request. She eagerly agrees to go, despite
her father's forebodings. When they land on Tereus' own shore,
instead of taking Philomel home he drags her to a hut deep in the old
woods, 'silvis obscura vetustis', or, as Golding has it in his usual vivid
but uneconomic fashion, 'a pelting graunge that peakishly did
stand | In woods forgrowen' (vi. 663–4). There he rapes her. Like
Lavinia, she says what women are traditionally forced into saying in
the literature of rape, that she would rather he had killed her. When
she threatens to proclaim his villainy, his response is not that of an
Angelo ('Who will believe thee, Isabel?'[50]—possibly the most chilling
line in Shakespeare), but something more physical:

> And with a paire of pinsons fast did catch hir by the tung,
> And with his sword did cut it off. The stumpe whereon it hung
> Did patter still. The tip fell downe, and quivering on the ground
> As though that it had murmured it made a certaine sound,
> And as an Adders tayle cast off doth skip a while: even so
> The tip of *Philomelaas* tongue did wriggle to and fro,
> And nearer to hir mistresseward in dying still did go.
>
> (Golding, vi. 709–15)

Tereus then rapes his maimed victim many more times. For twelve
months she is unable to communicate—'os mutum facti caret indice'
(vi. 574, 'speechless lips can give no index of what has happened').
But then she weaves her story and sends the web to Procne, whose
response is first speechlessness, then a denial of tears and a dedication
to revenge. A literal translation renders the economy of this
progression more effectively than Golding does: 'Grief chokes the
words that rise to her lips, and her questing tongue can find no words
strong enough to express her outraged feelings. Here is no room for
tears, but she hurries on to confound right and wrong, her whole soul
bent on the thought of vengeance' (vi. 583–6). Since it is the time
when the Thracian women are celebrating the festival of Bacchus,
Procne dresses the part, feigns frenzy, and, with Bacchic women in
attendance, carries Philomel off. She vows revenge but, in Lear-like

---

[50] *Measure for Measure*, II. iv. 154.

fashion—'I am prepared for some great deed; but what it shall be I am still in doubt' (vi. 618–19)—cannot initially decide on a method. When her son comes in, however, she makes up her mind (how can she continue a normal family life when her husband has raped her sister?) and drags him away, 'as a tigress drags a suckling fawn through the dark woods on Ganges' bank' (vi. 636–7). She cuts the boy's throat, Philomel assisting, and then dishes him up in a stew at her husband's dinner table. Tereus calls for his son and Procne cries in elation that he is there already: ' "intus habes, quem poscis" ' (vi. 655, 'What you're asking for, you have inside you'). Philomel then thrusts the head in Tereus' face. He pursues the two women and all three are metamorphosed into birds. Pandion dies of grief.

It is easy to see the elements that Shakespeare dramatizes. An ill-fated marriage at the outset, a rape in the woods, the severing of the tongue, a revelation of the deed in a form which can be read, a response so intense that utterance is impeded, a move from tears to revenge (it is from here that the bipartite structure of *Titus* is derived), a confounding of right and wrong in the act of revenge ('fasque nefasque confusura' might be the motto of revenge drama), the mutilated victim's assistance in the retributive murder, the revenger killing his or her own child, the climactic banquet. A number of linguistic relations are also apparent: Tereus is 'barbarus'; Philomel 'tremit' (compare Marcus' 'Tremble, like aspen leaves' in his description of the mutilated Lavinia); then there is the language of the dark woods, the tigress and the stricken deer, and the centrality of 'pudor', shame. The grand climax is identical: the summoning of offspring, the revenger's triumphant announcement of said offspring's presence. 'Why, there they are, both bakèd in this pie' (v. iii. 59).

But Shakespeare's variations on his theme are more illustrative of his inventive *copia*. Precisely because the 'pattern' of Philomel is available in the text, the recourse to sewing is foreclosed and a new method of revealing the rapists has to be introduced. In his usual syncretic manner, Shakespeare turns to a detail elsewhere in Ovid's book—Lavinia's writing on the ground is an *imitatio* of the transformed Io's hoof-scratchings after Jupiter has raped her. Then there is considerable difference in the role of the fathers. Unlike Titus, Pandion stands aloof. He expresses foreboding at the outset and grief at the end; his role is more that of spectator and commentator, a function which Shakespeare gives over to uncle Marcus. As well as varying, Shakespeare leaves alone certain facets of Ovid's narrative. He does not explore the psychology of the rapist, as Ovid does with his vivid account of how Tereus is inflamed by the sight of Philomel kissing her father. Shakespeare reserves such explorations for *Lucrece* and *Measure for Measure*, making this rape not so much a pure act of lust as part of a multiple revenge pattern that has already been instigated. The killing of Alarbus—and, for that matter, Mutius— means that the premiss of the revenge is different. And, as I have already said, the conclusion also varies in so far as the Ovidian release into metamorphosis is a relief that tragedy does not offer.

There is also a striking variation in the banquet. Where Procne stews Tereus' son's body but keeps the severed head whole so that Philomel can confront the tyrant with it, Titus prepares a pastry rather than an entrée. His kitchenware includes a pestle and mortar to grind the bones to powder small. Shakespeare perhaps decided not to produce two severed heads in the banquet scene because he had already dished up a pair in Act III, when, during the action to which the bloody banquet is a reaction, he had introduced his grisliest stage direction '*Enter messenger with two heads and a hand*'. A little earlier in the scene, Titus has for the first time been brought to the sight of his mutilated daughter; now, confronted with the heads of his sons, all he can do is laugh. After his extraordinary, cathartic line, 'Ha, ha, ha', he asks the way to Revenge's cave and the counter-action is initiated. Lavinia's response to the entrance of the severed heads is an attempted kiss, eliciting Marcus' line, 'Alas, poor heart, that kiss is comfortless | As frozen water to a starvèd snake' (III. i. 249–50). The proximity of the tongueless Lavinia to the image of the snake echoes that moment after Tereus has been to work with his pincers. To quote the lines again, this time translating them more literally than Golding, 'as the severed tail of a mangled snake is wont to writhe, [the tongue] twitches convulsively, and with its last dying movement it seeks its mistress's feet'. The key word in the Latin, reiterated in successive lines at the prominent line-ending position, is 'lingua', which of course means both tongue and language. Philomel is severed from her language; language struggles to be reunited to her, it seeks its mistress's feet. In a moment utterly characteristic of the *Metamorphoses*, Ovid literalizes a metaphor: the separation of character and language (*lingua*) is enacted through the independent life of the tongue (*lingua*).

And it is here that *Titus Andronicus* owes its essence not just to the letter but to the spirit of Ovid. For it is a play replete with literalized metaphors. Where Lear will cry his imprecations to the heavens, Titus writes his down, sticks them on arrows, and shoots them into the air. Furthermore, it is a play that is deeply concerned with the idea of giving language back to the silenced woman. As that tongue in Ovid struggles to return to its mistress, so Marcus reaches out linguistically to Lavinia in his lyric monologue. There is a deep dramatic irony in his first address to his mutilated niece, spoken before he has seen that she is tongueless: 'Cousin, a word' (II. iv. 12). In the rest of the speech Marcus needs so many words, so much poetry, in order to compensate for the fact that Lavinia has none. 'Shall I speak for thee?', he asks: it is the question, always present but rarely voiced so explicitly, that every tragedy asks. Shakespeare returned to this idea in his later addition to the play, the fly-killing scene. There Titus describes Lavinia, in a phrase cited in my previous chapter, as a 'Speechless complainer'—compare the 'os mutum' of Philomel—who can only produce dumb shows. His role, he says, is to translate her gestures into language, to read, interpret, and transform into speech the 'map of woe' that is her body: 'But I of these will wrest an alphabet, | And by still practice learn to know thy meaning' (III. ii. 44–5). Where Tarquin wanted to subjugate the 'maiden worlds' of Lucrece's body, Titus wants desperately to empathize with his daughter's pain, to try to understand its cause. Titus here, and Marcus in his monologue, figure forth the process that is at the very core of tragedy. Their words mark out this play, crude as it may sometimes be, as Shakespeare's paradigmatic tragedy. For what is tragedy but the restitution of *lingua* to suffering, the wresting of an alphabet out of woe?

4
Comedy and Metamorphosis

This interpenetration of gods, men, and nature does not imply
an unequivocal hierarchical order, but an intricate system of
interrelations in which each level can influence the others,
though to differing extents. Myth, in Ovid, is the field of tension
in which these forces clash and balance. Everything depends on
the spirit in which the myth is related. Sometimes the gods
themselves recount the myths in which they are involved, as
moral examples intended as warnings to mortals; at other times
mortals use the same myths to challenge or argue with the gods,
as do the daughters of Pierus or Arachne. Or it may be that there
are some myths that the gods love to hear told, and others they
prefer to have silenced.[1]

I

The Taming of the Shrew is one of Shakespeare's earliest comedies,
possibly his first. Its opening scenes may be read as an induction not
only to this play but to the whole phenomenon of Shakespearian
comedy. An artisan is taken in by a lord who patronizes a company of
players; a dramatic performance is staged for his delight and
instruction. Christopher Sly watches from above, the London
groundlings from below, he watches for free, they have to pay a
penny, but he still functions as their representative. The theatre offers
the audience what the lord offers Sly: a fantasy of entry into a world of
gentle birth, sophistication, wealth (fine clothes and good food are the
norm in the Padua of the play, which is why Kate's deprivation of
them is so cruel), and sexual ambiguity (a lovely boy dressed as a
desirable wife: Bartholomew the page is an induction to the
succession of cross-dressed heroines, Julia, Portia, Rosalind, Viola,
Imogen). The gaze will be allowed to rest on an exotic, erotic, poetic

---

[1] Italo Calvino, 'Ovid and Universal Contiguity', in *The Literature Machine: Essays*,
trans. Patrick Creagh (London, 1987), 150.

world, on strange transformations and experiences far removed from
the audience's quotidian experience. The lord will offer the artisan a
glimpse of 'wanton pictures' (supposed wantonness was a great
provoker of anti-stage polemic on the part of Elizabethan 'puritans');
his servants (and it may be remembered here that the theatre
companies were known as the 'servants' or 'men' of the lord who was
their patron) will assist in describing the sight:

> 2ND SERVINGMAN. Dost thou love pictures? We will fetch thee straight
>   Adonis painted by a running brook,
>   And Cytherea all in sedges hid,
>   Which seem to move and wanton with her breath
>   Even as the waving sedges play wi'th' wind.
> LORD. We'll show thee Io as she was a maid,
>   And how she was beguilèd and surprised,
>   As lively painted as the deed was done.
> 3RD SERVINGMAN. Or Daphne roaming through a thorny wood,
>   Scratching her legs that one shall swear she bleeds,
>   And at that sight shall sad Apollo weep,
>   So workmanly the blood and tears are drawn.
>
>   (*Shrew*, Ind. ii. 48–59)

What is laid out here is almost a programme for Shakespeare's
subsequent Ovidianism. Adonis, whose story was soon to be told in
the form of Shakespeare's non-dramatic comedy, is placed in the
voyeuristic position of Actaeon, whose story will be vital to *The Merry
Wives of Windsor*. Io is on the brink of being raped; her fate and her
means of communicating it will be Lavinia's. Daphne runs through
the wood, scratched with briars, as Helena will in *A Midsummer
Night's Dream*. As in the *ekphrasis* in *Lucrece*, the emphasis is on the
skill of the workmanship: the *trompe-l'œil* is such that the figures
really seem to be alive and to move. We are on the road to
Shakespeare's most astonishing Ovidian coup, Hermione's statue, so
'lively painted' that it comes to life.

There is, however, a difference between the endings of the Ovidian
stories described here and those of Shakespearian comedy. Adonis is
gored, Actaeon dismembered, Io raped, Daphne saved from rape only
by being dehumanized. In the previous chapter I showed how
Shakespeare reversed Ovid in tragedy: the Philomel story has the
release of metamorphosis whereas the Lavinia one offers no such
consolation. In comedy, it is the other way round: Shakespeare is the
one who lets his characters off the hook. He does so a stage sooner

than Ovid, in whom release tends to come after extreme violence. Orlando is only nipped by the lioness, not killed as Adonis is by the boar. Falstaff is only pricked and pinched, not torn to pieces as Actaeon is. Julia is saved by Valentine from Proteus' attempt to rape her in the forest. It is the third servingman's narrative that most accurately predicts the course of Shakespearian comedy: true love does not run smooth, but drastic violence is always forestalled and those who intend it are converted or expelled. In the third servingman's picture, Apollo stops pursuing and starts empathizing; in *The Two Gentlemen of Verona*, Proteus stops making advances upon Silvia and is reunited with Julia.

But the resolutions are always fragile, and in this sense the Ovidian allusions, with their violent ends, remain to remind the audience that we can never be sure that all will end well. When she is playing the role of a boy, Julia pretends to remember a pentecost pageant in which (s)he wore Julia's gown and played a woman's 'lamentable part', that of 'Ariadne, passioning | For Theseus' perjury and unjust flight'. The effect of her (his) 'lively' acting is the same as that of the lifelike painting described by the third servingman:

> Which I so lively acted with my tears
> That my poor mistress, movèd therewithal,
> Wept bitterly.
> (*Two Gentlemen*, IV. iv. 164–8)

The allusion here is to *Heroides* x, the passionate, lamenting letter of Ariadne to Theseus after he has left her on Naxos.[2] Its function is to evoke the pain of a deserted lover; that pain cannot be made to go away by the brisk reunion with the changing Proteus a few scenes later (his conversion is even less convincing than that of Bertram in *All's Well*). As will be seen, Shakespeare alludes to the desertion of Ariadne again in *A Midsummer Night's Dream* and, indirectly, in *The Merchant of Venice*, in contexts which undermine the illusion that these are just happy comedies of fulfilled love.

But what about *The Taming of the Shrew*? Can it any way be construed as a happy comedy of fulfilled love? Petruchio never hits Kate, but surely real violence is done in this play—to the woman's mind. Is this not a drama in which women are subjugated, as Jupiter subjugates Io?

---

[2] The passion is so excessive that the poem may plausibly be read as a parody of its ante-type, Catullus 64—see ch. 6 of Florence Verducci's *Ovid's Toyshop of the Heart*—but that is not how it was read in the Renaissance.

As the only release for Daphne was to become a tree, is not the only release for Kate to become a branch of Petruchio, bent to his will?

In answering these questions, one faces the problem that the text as we have it may not represent the play as Shakespeare wrote it. Current scholarship suggests—though the textual problem in question is extremely difficult and conclusions must be tentative—that in its original form it maintained the Christopher Sly business throughout the action by means of a series of brief interludes and an epilogue. The content of these, it is suggested, may be reconstructed from the play *The Taming of a Shrew*, printed in 1594, which is likely to be some sort of adaptation or reconstruction of Shakespeare's original version. The text of *The Shrew* published in the First Folio may omit the later Sly passages because the play had to be adapted to a smaller acting company after 1594, when it would no longer have been practicable to retain actors playing Sly and others as 'presenters' in the gallery above the stage— they would have been needed to double up and take part in the play within.[3] If this theory is correct, then the original play presented four versions of courtship and/or marriage: Sly and his off-stage wife, Petruchio and Kate, Bianca and Lucentio, Hortensio and his widow.

Two of these four relationships are introduced at the very end. Hortensio marries the widow for her money. She shows signs of frowardness and has to be lectured by Kate. The first half of the famous submission speech is spoken in the singular, it is addressed specifically to the widow and not to woman in general:

> Thy husband is thy lord, thy life, thy keeper,
> Thy head, thy sovereign, one that cares for thee,
> And for thy maintenance commits his body
> To painful labour both by sea and land . . .
>
> (*Shrew*, v. ii. 151 ff.)

The contextual irony of this is not always appreciated: in contradistinction to Kate's prescriptions, in this marriage it will be the wife, the wealthy widow, who provides the 'maintenance'; Hortensio will be spared the labours of a breadwinner. According to Kate, all a husband

---

[3] The introd. to Brian Morris's 1981 Arden edn. gives a full exposition of the arguments and makes an expert statement of the case that I summarize here. Especially compelling evidence that there were originally Christopher Sly interludes throughout is that without them the so-called 'law of re-entry' would have been broken, with Katherine and Petruchio going off at the end of v. i and instantly re-entering for v. ii, something that tends only to happen in Shakespeare when there is textual corruption or revision (as with the inserted fly-killing scene in *Titus Andronicus*).

asks is love, good looks, and obedience; these are said to be 'Too little payment for so great a debt' (159). But the audience knows that the debt is all Hortensio's. Besides, he has said earlier that he is no longer interested in woman's 'kindness' or 'beauteous looks' (IV. ii. 41)—all he wants is the money. Kate's vision of obedience is made to look oddly irrelevant to the reality of marriage.

Sly's marriage provides a further contextual irony for the submission speech. If *The Shrew* originally ended as *A Shrew* does, the tinker will go home claiming that the play has taught him how to tame a shrew and so he will now be able to tame his own wife. But the tapster knows better: 'your wife will course you for dreaming here tonight'.[4] The hungover Sly is in no position to tame anybody; he will return home and be soundly beaten. Kate's speech propounds the patriarchal ideal of marriage, but the Slys' is another union which reveals the distance of that ideal from reality. For all the fine words that are spoken, what we see is that ambitious gentlemen marry rich widows for money and artisans stay out late at the tavern and are beaten by their wives when they eventually get home. The Sly frame stands for the reality known to the audience; its implied resolution, with the woman on top, intimates that in reality wives are not silent and obedient, and plays can't teach husbands to tame them into submission. Since Sly is so manifestly incapable of doing a Petruchio, the play sidesteps the uglier reality of men returning from the tavern and beating up their wives.

'But,' it will be maintained, 'Hortensio and Sly are negative examples—the supposedly positive image of marriage that is offered is the patriarchal one of shrew metamorphosed into obedient wife.' But is the play's most positive image of marriage that in which the wife offers to put her hand beneath her husband's foot? Might there not be alternative models?

The key scene for the transformation of Kate is that on the road to Padua, when she accepts that if Petruchio calls the sun the moon it is the moon. At this point Vincentio passes by, and Petruchio addresses him as a woman. Kate, having learnt to play Petruchio's game, addresses the old man as follows:

> Young budding virgin, fair, and fresh, and sweet,
> Whither away, or where is thy abode?
> Happy the parents of so fair a child,

---

[4] Conclusion to *A Shrew*, Additional passage E, l. 14, Complete Oxford Shakespeare text of *The Shrew*, 53.

> Happier the man whom favourable stars
> Allots thee for his lovely bedfellow.
>
> (IV. vi. 37–42)

The second half of this speech, with its careful rhetorical structure, is a compressed *imitatio* of a passage in the story which follows shortly after that of Pyramus and Thisbe in the fourth book of the *Metamorphoses*:

> right happie folke are they,
> By whome thou camste into this worlde, right happy is (I say)
> Thy mother and thy sister too (if any bee:) good hap
> That woman had that was thy Nurce and gave thy mouth hir pap.
> But farre above all other, far more blist than these is shee
> Whom thou vouchsafest for thy wife and bedfellow for too bee.
>
> (Golding, iv. 392–7)

This is Salmacis addressing the beautiful but reluctant Hermaphroditus. Shakespeare's use of the comparative adjective follows the Latin original: '*Happy* the parents . . . *Happier* the man' replicates 'qui te genuere, *beati* . . . *beatior* illa, | si qua tibi sponsa est' (iv. 322–6, 'happy are they who gave thee birth . . . happier she, whoever is your bride').[5]

It may be that Shakespeare is merely borrowing the rhetorical effect. But *imitatio* so often brings the matter with the trope, *res* with *verba*, that we should at least consider the possibility of contextual relevance. Ovid and Shakespeare are playing the same kind of joke with the gender of the addressee. As I pointed out in Chapter 2, Salmacis' wooing of Hermaphroditus is the classic source of sexual role-reversal: the female speaks the language of praise that is conventionally the prerogative of male courtship. Kate switches the gender back to that of convention, changing the lucky wife into a lucky husband, but the switch is ironically turned again when one remembers that, like Salmacis, she is in fact addressing a man. In a sense, she goes one up on Petruchio: she appears to be addressing Vincentio as a woman, in accordance with the demand of her husband, but the language in which she does so was in its original

---

[5] A. B. Taylor provides supporting evidence that Salmacis and Hermaphroditus was in Shakespeare's mind in this scene by pointing to the word 'froward' (IV. vi. 79) and the phrase 'The field is won' (IV. vi. 24): in Golding, Salmacis calls Hermaphroditus a 'froward boy' (iv. 459) and when she leaps on him in the pool she cries 'The prize is won' (iv. 440), a translation of Ovid's 'vicimus' (iv. 356), which in the Tereus and Philomel story is translated 'The fielde is oures' (vi. 654)—'Shakespeare and Golding', *N&Q* NS xxxviii (1991), 492–9 (p. 495).

context addressed to a man. Hermaphroditus is a sort of male shrew, tamed by Salmacis; by bringing their relationship into play, Kate inverts the roles which Petruchio has so painstakingly set up. This small linguistic victory may be seen as a first sign that Kate can give as well as take a taming, that, as in the subtitle of Fletcher's sequel to the play, the tamer will be tamed. In my discussion of *Venus and Adonis*, I argued that the union of Salmacis and Hermaphroditus served in the Renaissance as a model for the idea of marriage as the union of spiritual equals.[6] Its presence beneath the surface of the text in this crucial scene perhaps suggests that there may be a Salmacian/ Hermaphroditic inflection to certain images of mutuality elsewhere in *The Taming of the Shrew*—'madly mated', with its suggestion of two becoming one; 'Petruchio is Kated', with its fusion of names (III. iii. 116–17).

I have phrased the foregoing argument tentatively, for it is based on slender evidence. A theatre audience could not be expected to move from the brief *imitatio* to a general sense of Salmacian/Hermaphroditic equality. But the fact that Shakespeare went to Salmacis for the image is enough to suggest that the idea of marriage as mutuality rather than subjugation was in his mind as he wrote the play. Furthermore, whilst the idea of reciprocity is at most beneath the surface in the Petruchio/Kate plot, it is clearly on the surface, and available to be read by a theatre audience, in the Bianca/Lucentio plot. It is their relationship which offers the play's most positive model of courtship and marriage.

In an allusion early in the play, Lucentio empties Jupiter's disguised wooing of Europa of its deceit and interprets it in terms of male humility:

> O yes, I saw sweet beauty in her face,
> Such as the daughter of Agenor had,
> That made great Jove to humble him to her hand
> When with his knees he kissed the Cretan strand.
>
> (I. i. 165–8)

Metamorphosis can mean lowering one's estate before ultimately raising it. Prince Hal progresses through *Henry IV* by sounding the very bass-string of humility, but then breaking through the clouds as

---

[6] On this idea and its relevance to *The Taming of the Shrew*, see J. A. Roberts's suggestive article, 'Horses and Hermaphrodites: Metamorphoses in *The Taming of the Shrew*', *SQ* xxxiv (1983), 159–71, which takes off from the passage discussed here.

he is transformed into a feathered Mercury upon a fiery Pegasus, witching the world with noble horsemanship.[7] He describes the first part of the process by alluding, as Lucentio does here, to Jupiter's descent through the chain of being for the sake of Europa, daughter of Agenor: 'from a god to a bull—a heavy declension—it was Jove's case. From a prince to a prentice, a low transformation—that shall be mine' (*2 Henry IV*, II. ii. 165–7). By changing places with his servant, Lucentio is able to gain access to Bianca and express his love. But where Jupiter and Hal remain manipulative, Lucentio's transformation is wholly creative because the love turns out to be mutual. Bianca shares in the wonder of love's metamorphosis:

BIANCA. Cambio is changed into Lucentio.
LUCENTIO. Love wrought these miracles. Bianca's love
　Made me exchange my state with Tranio
　While he did bear my countenance in the town,
　And happily I have arrived at the last
　Unto the wishèd haven of my bliss.
                    (v. i. 114–19)

Kate's submission speech accepts patriarchy's chain of being, in which god, king, and husband are heads. The Bianca/Lucentio plot proposes a different model, one in which the chain of being is disrupted—a god humbles himself to become a bull, a gentleman becomes a schoolmaster, a servant becomes a master—in the name of a shared love.

The reciprocity that is so vital to the relationship is rendered partly by a bold reworking of Ovid, but the Ovid of the amorous poetry, not the *Metamorphoses*. The multiple disguises in *The Taming of the Shrew*, and particularly those that relate to the wooing of Bianca, are adapted from those in George Gascoigne's *Supposes*, itself a prose adaptation of Ariosto's highly classical Renaissance comedy, *I Suppositi*. Gascoigne's explanation of his title is also a proleptic reading of Shakespeare's play: 'But understand, this our Suppose is nothing else

---

[7] Vernon's speech (*1 Henry IV*, IV. i. 105–11), which I paraphrase here, is an odd composite allusion. In *Met.* iv, it is Perseus, not Mercury, who springs from the ground 'as light as any feather' and who is associated with 'Swift *Pegasus* the winged horse' who comes into being from the blood of the slain Medusa (Golding, iv. 765, 958). It was Mercury who gave Perseus his winged feet. Perhaps the point of invoking the god of furtiveness and trickery here is that the play charts Hal's reinvention of himself as a Perseus, a warrior-hero skilled in horsemanship, by means of an art that is always mercurial.

but a mystaking or imagination of one thing for an other. For you shall see the master supposed for the servant, the servant for the master . . . the stranger for a well known friend, and the familiar for a stranger.'[8] But where Gascoigne's play is set in Ferrara, Shakespeare transposes it to Padua, the centre of Aristotelianism and possibly the most renowned university city in Europe. Lucentio has come there to study; he begins with the Aristotelian and humanist view that education is synonymous with the pursuit of virtue (I. i. 8–20). But his knowing servant persuades him to reject the philosophical syllabus associated with the city of Padua:

> *Mi perdonate*, gentle master mine.
> I am in all affected as yourself,
> Glad that you thus continue your resolve
> To suck the sweets of sweet philosophy.
> Only, good master, while we do admire
> This virtue and this moral discipline,
> Let's be no stoics nor no stocks, I pray,
> Or so devote to Aristotle's checks
> As Ovid be an outcast quite abjured.

> (I. i. 25–33)

Tranio not only makes the Horatian case that pleasure should be mingled with profit, he also makes Lucentio see that what he 'affects' is Ovid's art of love rather than Aristotle's philosophy of virtue.

Accordingly, when Lucentio disguises himself as a schoolmaster in order to gain access to Bianca, his textbooks are Ovid's books of love rather than Aristotle's *Ethics* or Seneca's *Epistulae Morales*. A Latin lesson becomes a courtship device. Lucentio speaks under the mask of the schoolroom technique whereby a text is construed word by word. He 'translates' a couplet from the first letter of the *Heroides*, '*Hic ibat Simois, hic est Sigeia tellus,* | *Hic steterat Priami regia celsa senis*' (III. i. 28–9, from *Her.* i. 33–4):

Hic ibat, as I told you before—*Simois*, I am Lucentio—*hic est*, son unto Vincentio of Padua—*Sigeia tellus*, disguised thus to get your love—*hic steterat*, and that Lucentio that comes a-wooing— *Priami*, is my man Tranio—*regia*, bearing my port—*celsa senis*, that we might beguile the old pantaloon. (III. i. 31–6)

There may be a contextual irony in that the letter in question is

---

[8] Gascoigne, *Supposes* (1566), 'The Prologue or Argument', Bullough, i. 112.

written by Penelope while she is surrounded by wooers whom she'd rather be without. There may also be a glancing allusion to the play's disruption of social roles when 'Priami', the king, is translated into the servant Tranio, whose temporary elevation to the gentry also parallels Sly's temporary metamorphosis into a lord. But the chief effect of this device is to take the Latin text out of the schoolroom and make it a means to the fulfilment of desire. Lucentio is following Tranio's advice and using his learning to pursue what he most affects. In *Titus Andronicus* we saw that the disciplines of the schoolroom did not teach virtue: a reading in the grammar did not lead Demetrius and Chiron to integrity of life. In *Love's Labour's Lost*, bookish philosophy—the kind of Aristotelian pursuit of virtue which Lucentio described in his opening speech—is abandoned and truth is read in women's eyes.[9] Similarly, though *A Midsummer Night's Dream* is, as will be seen, a play full of Ovidian matter, 'love's richest book' in which Lysander finds 'Love's stories' is not a written text to be studied at school like the *Metamorphoses*, but the eyes of Helena (II. ii. 121–2). In Lucentio's wooing, on the other hand, the schoolroom is not rejected but appropriated for creative purposes. And, crucially, the woman gives as good as she gets. She answers the amorous appropriation of the text word for word: '*Hic ibat Simois*, I know you not—*hic est Sigeia tellus*, I trust you not—*hic steterat Priami*, take heed he hear us not—*regia*, presume not—*celsa senis*, despair not' (III. i. 40–3). Bianca is beautifully poised here, wholly in control: she gives ('despair not') but she also withholds ('presume not').

The symmetrical parodic construings of the extract from the *Heroides* set the tone for the relationship between Bianca and Lucentio. Theirs will be a marriage between equals, built on mutual desire and consent—Bianca escapes her class of sixteenth-century woman's usual fate of being married to a partner of the father's choice, to Hortensio or Gremio. If anything, she is the dominant

---

[9] Biron's speech to this effect (*Love's Labour's*, IV. iii. 287–341) has a nexus of references to Ovid's Orpheus, reinforcing some of the connections that I established in the previous chapter: 'bright Apollo's lute strung with his hair' adapts the 'Orpheus' lute was strung with poets' sinews' of *Two Gentlemen*; 'Make heaven drowsy with the harmony' is a variation on Cerberus being sung to sleep; and 'O, then his lines would ravage savage ears, | And plant in tyrants mild humility' is especially close to Lodowick in *Edward III*. The pedant's representation of those humanist exemplars, the Nine Worthies, contributes further to *Love's Labour's Lost*'s witty critique of book-learning: in the show staged by schoolmaster and curate, the great Hercules becomes a mote of a boy and the noble Hector a braggart Spaniard.

partner at the end. She is not read a lecture by Kate, as the widow is, and she gets the better of her husband in their final on-stage exchange:

BIANCA. Fie, what a foolish duty call you this?
LUCENTIO. I would your duty were as foolish too.
    The wisdom of your duty, fair Bianca,
    Hath cost me a hundred crowns since supper-time.
BIANCA. The more fool you for laying on my duty.
                                                    (v. ii. 130–4)

Like Beatrice in *Much Ado About Nothing*, she more than matches her man in the art of word play:

LUCENTIO. Now, mistress, profit you in what you read?
BIANCA. What, master, read you? First resolve me that.
LUCENTIO. I read that I profess, *The Art to Love*.
BIANCA. And may you prove, sir, master of your art.
LUCENTIO. While you, sweet dear, prove mistress of my heart!
                                                    (IV. ii. 6–10)

As Hortensio recognizes in the next line, she has proved a 'quick proceeder', a clever scholar. She is no longer the pupil: in her 'resolve me that', she turns the language of the schoolroom back on the 'master'.

The Art to Love, Ovid's *Ars Amatoria*, was excluded from the Renaissance schoolroom for obvious reasons. In this exchange it is recovered as part of a practical education in love. And its nature is subtly transformed. Petruchio implicitly bases his taming on one precept within it: 'Vim licet appelles: grata est vis ista puellis'—'You may use what is termed force: girls like you to use it' (i. 673). But he makes a fatal misreading, for this precept is from Book One, on the art of winning a lover, not Book Two, on the art of keeping her. If the relationship is to last, Ovid argues, the method of the male must be subtler:

> Though at the first you find her but untoward,
> Bear it, and she in time will prove less froward.
> The crooked arm that from the tree is cut
> By gentle usage is made streight; but put
> Such violence to it as thy strength delivers,
> And thou wilt break the short wood into shivers.
>   (Heywood's trans. of ii. 177–80)

This only means all dangers will disperse:
Yield her her humour when she grows perverse:
When she in conference argues, argue thou,
What she approves, in self-same words allow.
Say what she says, deny what she denies,
If she laugh, laugh; if she weep, wet thine eyes.
And let her count'nance be to thine a law,
To keep thy actions and thy looks in awe.
> (Heywood's trans. of ii. 197–202)

Here the man remains the master by allowing the woman to appear to be dominant, whereas when the text of the *Ars* is appropriated by Bianca it no longer serves as a token of male manipulativeness, a repository of cynical seductive ploys. It becomes instead a symbol of reciprocal adult love. The woman wants her man to be master of the art of love. One might almost say that where the *Ars Amatoria* is masturbatory in its self-regarding erotic wit, the witty verbal coupling of Bianca and Lucentio, like that of Beatrice and Benedick, is a sign that they will have a good sex life. Their presence in the play is a guarantee that it is no uncomplicated apology for patriarchy. Kate's submission speech propounds a theory of degree that is ultimately Aristotelian; thanks to Bianca, the play as a whole has just as much time for a playful, joyful theory of love that is ultimately Ovidian. In Fletcher's sequel, *The Woman's Prize; or, The Tamer Tam'd*, Petruchio is corrected by his second wife. The epilogue of that play applies to his marriage, and to marriage generally, a moral that could previously have been drawn from Bianca and Lucentio: men 'should not raign as Tyrants o'er their wives',

> Nor can the women, from this precedent
>   Insult, or triumph: it being aptly meant,
> To teach both Sexes due equality;
>   And as they stand bound, to love mutually.[10]

II

The induction of *The Taming of the Shrew* moves from a description of Ovidian pictures to a stage performance; it thus summons up only to stave off the possibility that the Ovidian tales might be acted out for Sly's benefit, as Gaveston proposes to stage the Actaeon story for

[10] Epilogue, in *The Woman's Prize*, ed. Fredson Bowers, in *The Dramatic Works in the Beaumont and Fletcher Canon*, gen. ed. Fredson Bowers, vol. iv (Cambridge, 1979), 117.

:dward II. With this possibility in mind, we could imagine another play beginning with an induction that opens like this:

—Is all our company here?

—You were best to call them generally, man by man, according to the scrip.

—Here is the scroll of every man's name which is thought fit through all Athens to play in our interlude before the Duke and the Duchess on his wedding day at night.

—First, good Peter Quince, say what the play treats on; then read the names of the actors; and so grow to a point.

—Marry, our play is The Most Lamentable Comedy, and Most Cruel Death of Pyramus and Thisbe.

—A very good piece of work, I assure you, and a merry.

The company has assembled to play out their dramatization of one of the best-known stories from the *Metamorphoses*. As in *The Taming of the Shrew* and other plays of the period such as Kyd's *The Spanish Tragedy* and Peele's *The Old Wives' Tale*, the whole of the main action would then be a play-within-a-play; the duke and duchess would be an on-stage audience, reacting to the 'Lamentable Comedy' that is enacted in their honour.

But what I have quoted is not, of course, an induction. The characters who speak the dialogue, Quince and Bottom, are artisans of the city, not the duke's professional players. Shakespeare, as so often, transforms a convention, for this is a second scene, which occurs after the duke and duchess and other well-born characters have been introduced, after the unfolding of the first events in a plot akin to, but different from, the story of Pyramus and Thisbe. The play replays, but updates and alters, the classical tale of parental resistance to young love and the lovers' plan to meet outside the city. Instead of the whole play being a play-within-a-play in the manner of *The Taming of the Shrew*, the play-within is withheld until the main action has been resolved.

When it comes, it is preceded by another quasi-induction, which offers a choice of Ovidian performances: before 'Pyramus and Thisbe' is selected, 'The battle with the Centaurs' from Book Twelve of the *Metamorphoses* is rejected, as is a dramatization of 'The riot of the tipsy bacchanals | Tearing the Thracian singer in their rage', the final stage of the Orpheus myth from Book Eleven (*Dream*, v. i. 44–9). Everybody in Athens seems to have been rehearsing the matter of the *Metamorphoses* in preparation for the wedding festivities of Theseus and Hippolyta, themselves characters from ancient myth. And the matter rehearsed serves as a reminder to both on-stage and off-stage audiences that courtship does not always end in the comic resolution of marriage—Pyramus and Thisbe go to the tomb, not the wedding-bed—and that the relationship between the sexes has its discords as well as it concords: the battle between the Centaurs and the Lapiths took place at a wedding and the Orpheus myth was, as I argued in the last chapter, bound up with rape and revenge.

A Midsummer Night's Dream may, then, be described as a displaced dramatization of Ovid. Why did Shakespeare include a parodic staging of Pyramus and Thisbe, one in which Golding's 'Ninus Tumb' becomes 'Ninny's tomb',[11] in a play which as a whole is deeply but not directly Ovidian? If he wished to proclaim himself as an Ovidian dramatist, why did he not simply stage Pyramus and Thisbe? The answer, I would suggest, may be found in Renaissance conceptions of *translatio* and *imitatio*. *Trans-latio*: to translate is to bring across; it is to make a text from an alien culture speak in the distinctive language of the translator's culture. George Chapman claimed in the dedicatory epistle to his translation of Homer's *Iliad* that the character of Achilles 'did but prefigure' the Earl of Essex.[12] He considered it part of his function as a translator to alter the original text in order to make it more conformable to his vision of Essex as a chivalric hero (Chapman's project is another context for Shakespeare's Ovid-like destabilization of the epic idiom in *Troilus and Cressida*). Imitation goes even further than translation in reconstituting the source-text in contemporary terms: for Spenser in *The Shepheardes Calender*, imitation of Theocritus and Virgil was a proper medium for reflection upon sixteenth-century ecclesiastical politics. It is through such processes of rewriting and 'modernization' that the classics are kept alive; Renaissance humanism proposes that it is exactly this capacity to become 'modern' that makes Homer, Virgil, Ovid, and the rest classics.

Quince's impromptu theatrical troupe do not understand the true nature of translation. Their obsessive literalism renders their performance risible. For Golding, translation was also interpretation: Lion, Wall, and Moonshine are there to be moralized. For Snug,

---

[11] The more educated Quince cites Ninus correctly (Golding, iv. 117; *Dream*, III. i. 92, v. i. 137), but to the others he is a Ninny (III. i. 91, v. i. 201, v. i. 258).

[12] *Seaven Bookes of The Iliades* (1598), in *Chapman's Homer*, ed. Allardyce Nicoll, 2 vols. (London, 1957), i. 504.

Snout, and Starveling, Lion, Wall, and Moonshine are there to be impersonated in as literal a way as possible, and if necessary the fact of the impersonation must be pointed out. Quince knows a little better, but only a little, for he too is a literalist. That is to say, he wants to follow the source-text to the letter: 'we must have a wall in the great chamber; for Pyramus and Thisbe, *says the story*, did talk through the chink of a wall' (III. i. 57–9, my emphasis). He is bounded by the letter and accordingly fails to perceive the spirit: his script leaves out the point of the story. Ovid's narratives climax with symbolic metamorphosis; Golding makes it his business as a translator to include interpretations in the form of applications of the narratives to contemporary moral values. Quince's dramatization, on the other hand, ends with the death of the lovers: there is no Ovidian metamorphosis and no Goldingesque moralization. A translation without application is of little more use than a grammar-school boy's crib—even in the classroom, pupils learnt to proceed from literal translation to rhetorical improvisation.[13]

In the last chapter I argued that *Titus Andronicus* is a *translatio* from the classroom to the theatre of the humanist ideal of the educative value of the classics; *A Midsummer Night's Dream* goes a step further and draws a distinction between different kinds of theatrical imitation. By including Quince's literal and therefore deficient *translatio*, Shakespeare draws attention to the higher level of his own. It is elsewhere in the play, not in 'Pyramus and Thisbe', that we find all the marks of true Ovidianism: a philosophy of love and of change, the operation of the gods, animal transformation, and symbolic vegetation. It is the translation of these elements out of the play-within and into the play itself that transforms *A Midsummer Night's Dream* into Shakespeare's most luminous *imitatio* of Ovid. The dispersal of Ovid throughout the text is what makes Shakespeare, to use the terms of Renaissance imitation theory, a true son rather than an ape.[14] The son distinguishes himself from the ape by virtue of difference, the *dissimilitudo* discussed in the last chapter in relation to

---

[13] Quince's translation is also deficient at a more basic level: he makes a number of schoolboy howlers. As A. B. Taylor points out, the solecism 'Sweet *moon*, I thank thee for thy *sunny* beams' (v. i. 267) is an attempt to translate Ovid's 'lunae radios' (iv. 99), but 'the phrase presented [Quince] with a problem because he knew *radius* only by a stock definition he found in dictionaries like Cooper's *Thesaurus*, as "A beame of the sunne"'—'Golding's Ovid, Shakespeare's "Small Latin", and the Real Object of Mockery in "Pyramus and Thisbe"', *ShS* xlii (1990), 53–64 (pp. 61–2).

[14] For this distinction see the passage from Petrarch, *Le familiari*, quoted in Ch. 3.

Titus Andronicus and 'the tragic tale of Philomel'. Quince does what the story says, whereas the motto for the relationship between the play as a whole and the *Metamorphoses* is Helena's reversal of a typical Ovidian sexual pursuit: 'The story shall be changed: | Apollo flies, and Daphne holds the chase' (II. i. 230–1). Quince attempts a literal translation of 'Pyramus and Thisbe', but his rehearsal is thrown into chaos when 'sweet Pyramus [is] translated' in another way (III. ii. 32).

Like Golding's translation at its best, the play is both ancient and modern. The opening scene sets a contemporary problem—the will of a father against the desire of his daughter—in the ancient Athens where many of Ovid's mythic encounters are located. The play engages with substantive matters of law and custom which speak directly to a Renaissance audience, but at the same time infuses the atmosphere with the power of the classical gods. Hermia swears 'By the simplicity of Venus' doves' (I. i. 170), taking us back to the silver doves who drew the love-goddess away in the final stanza of Shakespeare's narrative poem based on the *Metamorphoses*. She also swears 'by Cupid's strongest bow, | By his best arrow with the golden head' (I. i. 169–70), an explicit allusion to the first book of the *Metamorphoses*, where Ovid distinguishes between the mischievous boy's golden and leaden shafts:

> T'one causeth Love, the tother doth it slake.
> That causeth love, is all of golde with point full sharpe and bright,
> That chaseth love is blunt, whose steele with leaden head is dight.
> (Golding, i. 566–8)

The context of this allusion is Apollo's love for Daphne, a love 'Which not blind chaunce but *Cupids* fierce and cruel wrath did move' (i. 546). Apollo, flushed with pride after slaying the monstrous Python with his mighty bow and arrows, mocks Cupid as a 'wanton baby' whose own bow and arrows are but toys. Cupid promptly punishes Apollo by showing him what his little golden dart can do: the Olympian god falls in love with the chaste Daphne and chases her, but his love is not consummated, for she is metamorphosed into a laurel (taken by some interpreters to be symbolic of the virtue of chastity). Hermia, then, is swearing her love for Lysander by Apollo's love for Daphne. Once in the wood, Helena, with 'The story shall be changed: Apollo flies, and Daphne holds the chase', transforms the story by imagining Demetrius/Apollo as chaste and herself/Daphne as

rapacious. For a time, under the influence of love-in-idleness, Helena
succeeds in her rewriting of myth by becoming a kind of double
Daphne, pursued by both Demetrius and Lysander.[15] But then the
story is changed again, as Ovid's narrative of metamorphosis
replacing consummation is itself replaced by resolution in multiple
marriage. Where Ovid typically ends with the hardness of Daphne as
tree or the grotesquerie of the bubbling blood of the suicides in
Pyramus and Thisbe, Shakespeare's play offers more benign trans-
formations: 'Things base and vile, holding no quantity, | Love can
transpose to form and dignity' (1. i. 232–3). For Golding, Daphne was
a 'myrror of virginitie' and the fate of Pyramus and Thisbe a warning
against the 'headie force of frentick love' (Epistle, 68, 110);
Shakespeare, in contrast, celebrates the frenzy of love and makes even
Daphne a mirror of desire.

The language of the opening scene is also used to establish an
etiological framework. It is interested in finding stories which explain
the origin of the condition in which lovers find themselves: 'Love
looks not with the eyes, but with the mind, | And therefore is winged
Cupid painted blind' (234–5). Ovid was of course the classic source for
the etiology of love, but here Shakespeare has undertaken a subtle
inversion. He has already moved on from *Venus and Adonis*, which
was etiological in the traditional Ovidian sense: Adonis dies, Venus is
sorrowful, and *therefore* sorrow will always attend on love. But in
Helena's image it is the other way round: she begins with the nature
of love and moves the mythological figuration back to the sequential
clause. At one level she is merely giving the reason for the traditional
representation of Cupid as blind, but to explain that blindness as the
result of love's contrariness rather than make it into the active cause
of it is to shift the balance of power away from the gods.

This shift is important because the world of *A Midsummer Night's
Dream* is more anthropocentric than myth traditionally is. If the
distinction may be allowed, one might say that the mortals are the
playthings of the gods, *but only playfully so*. Take Cupid's bow and his
blindness literally and human beings are arbitrary victims of love.
Ovid does not take Cupid and the other love-gods quite so seriously: he
uses them to show his reader something about the capriciousness of

---

[15] Love's changes are rendered in a crisp rhetoric that is in part learnt from Ovid:
compare Demetrius' 'Not Hermia but Helena I love' with a line in the *Ars Amatoria*,
'Scilicet Hermionem Helenae praeponere posses?' (ii. 699, 'So you would be able to
prefer Hermione to Helena?').

love, but the writer of the erotic poems is always on hand to remind us
that love is also an art, something that we can control. The
Shakespeare of *A Midsummer Night's Dream* goes even further than
Ovid: he invites us to consider the possibility that the love-gods are no
more than a dream, something we invent to help us understand erotic
love, which comes wholly from within. The fiction of an external
form—call it Cupid, call it Puck—makes a complex condition easier to
comprehend. This is Theseus' view of the matter. He doesn't believe
the sort of things one reads in books like the *Metamorphoses*: 'I never
may believe | These antique fables, nor these fairy toys' (v. i. 2–3). In
his diagnosis, the art of a poet like Ovid who incarnates abstract forces
such as love and war in humanoid forms such as Venus and Mars is
an embodying and turning to shape of things unknown, a giving 'to
airy nothing | A local habitation and a name'. This, he says, is a
'trick' of the strong imagination (v. i. 14–18).

But, as critics have often noted, the play as a whole does not
endorse Theseus' reading.[16] We are not instructed to consider
everything that happens in the forest as no more than a dream.
Rather, we are invited to see double as Hermia does (IV. i. 189): to
believe and not believe. How can we believe in the fairy-world when
the play-within-the-play is then put on to remind us that the players
of the *Dream* are all just actors ('The best in this kind are but
shadows'—v. i. 210)? How can we not believe when the forest-gods
return and have the play's last words? A Renaissance humanist like
Golding would say that the stories of the pagan gods are worth
reading because they can be given a contemporary moral application.
Hippolyta is closer to this position than that of Theseus: she sees that
the story of the night, the story of love's metamorphosis in the forest,
has transfigured the minds of the lovers. Demetrius has come to see
that his deeper love is for Helena; 'Something of great constancy' has
grown from all the changes (v. i. 26). This pattern accords with the
kind of humanist revision of Ovid's book of changes—Spenser's in the
final stanzas of 'Mutabilitie', say—which proposes that they ultimately teach of the transience of all earthly things and the unique
constancy of God. So too with Hippolyta's response to the line about
the actors of 'Pyramus and Thisbe' as shadows: the audience's
imagination can 'amend them', rather as the imagination of the
reader can amend Ovid's narratives of the pagan gods into sources of

---

[16] See e.g. David P. Young, *Something of Great Constancy: The Art of 'A Midsummer Night's Dream'* (New Haven, Conn., 1966), 139–40.

moral (if you read with Golding) or psychological (if you read with Shakespeare) wisdom.

Shakespeare's humanistic amendment of Ovid is primarily achieved by a form of emendation in which the ancient is made modern. Puck stands in for Cupid, Titania and Oberon for others in the classical pantheon. Oberon sometimes seems to be Neptune transported to a wood or the lusting Jove, with the changeling boy as his Ganymede. The name 'Titania' is derived from Ovid, where it refers to a range of goddesses of the night—Diana, Latona, Circe, Pyrrha (in Golding, these are always 'Titan's daughter[s]', never 'Titania', so this is another small piece of evidence that Shakespeare remembered Ovid's Latin original).[17] Puck does Cupid's work throughout the night; one could almost say that in Oberon's etiology of love-in-idleness Puck could not see Cupid because he *was* Cupid ('That very time I saw, but thou couldst not . . .'). The wood outside Athens thus becomes an English wood peopled by fairies from the vernacular tradition. The Robin Goodfellow takes over the shape-changing art of the classical Proteus: 'Sometime a horse I'll be, sometime a hound, | A hog, a headless bear, sometime a fire'.[18] It is a more comprehensive *translatio* than that of Lyly in *Gallathea*, where the classical gods disport themselves slightly uneasily in the countryside around Hull. As Golding does with his rural vocabulary, Shakespeare translates Ovid into the native culture. It is a translation which at one and the same time reaffirms the original poet's classic status and elevates the native element to the status of high culture. Folklore becomes myth.

Shakespeare, as so often, seems to stand between high culture and popular tradition. One side of him looks down on what is represented by 'Pyramus and Thisbe', using it as a means to stake his own claim as a higher imitator, a true humanist. But another side of him shows solidarity with the artisans by putting the criticism of them in the mouth of a character such as Theseus who, as any half-way educated person in the Renaissance could tell you, was a notorious rapist. The play reminds the audience of what some of them would have read in Plutarch's *Life of Theseus*, that he ravished Perigouna and broke his faith with fair Aegles, with Ariadne and Antiopa (ii. i. 78–80). The

---

[17] Given Shakespeare's particular interest in the Actaeon story, it may be from there that the name 'Titania' for Diana struck him (*Met.* iii. 173).

[18] *Dream*, iii. i. 103–4. The *locus classicus* for the changes of Proteus—who of course gives his name to the fickle lover in *Two Gentlemen of Verona*—is *Met.* viii. 730–7.

well-known tenth letter of the *Heroides*, Ariadne's lament, would have predisposed many a listener against any claim made by Theseus. Partly because of the delinquencies of Theseus and partly because characters like Bottom have a kind of grace, the theatre audience is not encouraged to patronize the performers of 'Pyramus and Thisbe' quite so much as the well-born characters on stage do: as artisans they are in a sense representatives of both the professional actors of Shakespeare's companies and the groundlings who formed the bulk of the audience. To put a celebrated tragic tale from antiquity in their hands is to begin to bring high culture to the people, home-spun though the representation of it may be.

For Shakespeare to give the voice of scepticism with regard to antique fables to Theseus, himself an antique fable, further complicates the question of exactly what the play is or is not asking us to believe. Shakespeare resembles Ovid in that his attitude to the gods cannot be pinned down: we can never be sure whether or not they are anything more than external projections of human desires and predicaments. The gods and creatures of Ovidian myth are everywhere in the language of the forest. The beach is 'Neptune's yellow sands' (II. i. 126) and the sea itself is transformed by 'Aurora's harbinger' from 'salt green' to 'yellow gold' (III. ii. 381, 394), night is drawn by 'swift dragons' (III. ii. 380), the fairies sing of Philomel, and Oberon imitates Jupiter in his way of metamorphosing himself for the purposes of seduction: 'And in the shape of Corin sat all day, | Playing on pipes of corn, and versing love | To amorous Phillida' (II. i. 66–8). Hippolyta's forest memory is of being 'with Hercules and Cadmus once | When in a wood of Crete they bayed the bear | With hounds of Sparta' (IV. i. 111–13): this is not a direct memory of Ovid, but an elegant variation on him, for her image of herself, a beautiful huntress, in the company of the legendary heroes in pursuit of the bear seems to be adapted from Meleager's hunting of the Calydonian boar in the company of other legendary heroes, including Theseus, and a different beautiful huntress, Atalanta (*Met.* viii. 260–546). The transformation of Ovidian boar into Shakespearian bear is *imitatio* at its quickest.[19] So it is that the world of the *Metamorphoses* is revitalized in the imaginary wood. Whether or not we believe in the figures of Ovidian myth and whether or not we believe in the figures of the Shakespearian forest become one and the same question.

---

[19] It reverts to a boar when the image is replayed at *Two Noble Kinsmen*, I. i. 79.

That we should suspend our disbelief in them is perhaps forced
upon us by the fact that we are asked to believe that the
metamorphosis of Demetrius is permanent, not a temporary illusion
of the night. Since the agency which effects it is figured in an *imitatio*
of the *Metamorphoses*, we may infer that the Ovidian language of the
play is not mere embroidery: it is something of paradoxical constancy
rather than a trick of the strong imagination. If we look for the
symbolic vegetation which Quince forgets about in his dramatization,
we find that it is the chief instrument of the plot in Acts II to IV. As
Leonard Barkan has observed, the blood-coloured mulberry into
which Pyramus and Thisbe are metamorphosed is replaced by the
flower named love-in-idleness which works metamorphic magic
when squeezed upon a sleeper's eyes.[20] Each plant is 'Before,
milk-white; now, purple with love's wound'.

Oberon's account of the origins of the flower's power is *imitatio* at its
most complex. In contrast to the literalizing Quince, Shakespeare
catches the spirit of Ovid's god-infused nature by improvising on the
master's themes without overtly translating him.[21]

> Thou rememb'rest
> Since once I sat upon a promontory
> And heard a mermaid on a dolphin's back
> Uttering such dulcet and harmonious breath
> That the rude sea grew civil at her song
> And certain stars shot madly from their spheres
> To hear the sea-maid's music?
>
> (II. i. 148–54)

The mermaid on the dolphin's back is sitting in for Arion, who in the
Fasti (ii. 79–118) played on his lyre, charming the waves and paying
his fare in song to a dolphin who carried him to safety. Shakespeare
will put Arion back on the dolphin when he replays the image in
Twelfth Night, and in *The Tempest* Prospero's agent Ariel, whose name
may be a variant on Arion, will also affect the temper of the sea.
Indeed, a central process of Shakespeare's last solo performance is an
application to human characters of the metamorphosis of nature
described by Oberon here: after the rude sea of the tempest comes the

---

[20] *The Gods Made Flesh*, 257, an analysis to which I am much indebted.

[21] At this point Shakespeare may be fusing Ovid with the Seneca of *Hippolytus*: see
Harold F. Brooks's Arden edn. (London, 1979), pp. lxiii, 36–7, 142, though I think the
Senecan connections are overplayed.

growth to civility of the men of sin. What is distinctive about the image in *A Midsummer Night's Dream* is the absence of the directly Ovidian figures: Neptune has given way to the fairy king, Oberon, and Arion to the mermaid. The image is also an overgoing of Ovid in its conjunction of the sea and the stars. Ovid often metamorphoses his characters into creatures of the sea or astral formations, but never both simultaneously; the mermaid's music is an agent bringing transformation to diverse elements.

These changes signal to the careful listener that Shakespeare is varying his great original, as a good imitator should. We are thus prepared for a more startling variation when in Oberon's next speech an Ovidian figure, Cupid, *is* introduced:

> That very time I saw, but thou couldst not,
> Flying between the cold moon and the earth
> Cupid, all armed. A certain aim he took
> At a fair vestal thronèd by the west,
> And loosed his love-shaft smartly from his bow
> As it should pierce a hundred thousand hearts.
> But I might see young Cupid's fiery shaft
> Quenched in the chaste beams of the wat'ry moon,
> And the imperial vot'ress passèd on,
> In maiden meditation, fancy-free,
> Yet marked I where the bolt of Cupid fell.
> It fell upon a little western flower—
> Before, milk-white; now, purple with love's wound—
> And maidens call it love-in-idleness.
> Fetch me that flower; the herb I showed thee once.
> The juice of it on sleeping eyelids laid
> Will make or man or woman madly dote
> Upon the next live creature that it sees.
> (II. i. 155–72)

Having begun with Cupid, thus echoing the language in which Hermia established the Ovidian nexus in the opening scene, Oberon seems to stray from the *Metamorphoses* to modern high politics. There is a long tradition of reading the 'imperial vot'ress' passage as a compliment to Queen Elizabeth.[22] The combination of chastity and an imperial figure throned in the west makes such a reading hard to resist (the point of 'in the west' is that Elizabethan England was claimed as a

---

[22] See the extraordinary range of allegorical interpretations in the relevant note to H. H. Furness's New Variorum edn. of the play (Philadelphia and London, 1895), 75–91.

descendant from Troy and Rome by virtue of the westward shift of empire). The virgin Queen is the one human strong enough to withstand 'Cupid's fiery shaft', but the knock-on effect of her chastity is the wounding of the flower and the uncontrollable loves that are born with its juice. Where *Venus and Adonis* proposes that sorrow attends on love because of Venus' sorrow at the loss of Adonis, this image proposes that irrationality attends on love because of Elizabeth's strong chastity. Shakespeare seems to be saying: Cupid won't be gainsaid, so if you want a chaste Queen walking imperially on 'In maiden meditation, fancy-free', her subjects will have to bear mad doting in their love-lives. This seems a curious claim until you turn it upside-down, which is what you usually have to do to understand an etiology: Shakespeare observes that ordinary people do seem to spend much of their time 'madly doting'; his task as an etiologist is to invent a story to explain the cause of this phenomenon; where Ovid found causes in gods and ancient stories, Shakespeare finds it in contemporary history. This has the effect of 'updating' Ovid and, crucially, giving the Queen the kind of power that is usually given to the gods. It is at once a humanist move whereby the present is read with the apparatus of the classics (quasi-Ovidian etiology), and a politic one whereby the Queen is elevated into a mythic figure, as she is in Spenser's *Faerie Queene*.

The Ovidianism of Oberon's speech is comparable to that of Spenser, who so frequently demands to be read simultaneously in mythical and historical terms, as for example when in 'Mutabilitie' he rewrites the Actaeon myth in the landscape of the Ireland where he held a government post. It is very unusual for Shakespeare to 'politicize' Ovid in this way—it will be shown in a later section of this chapter that he did not take the opportunity to make Actaeon into the Earl of Essex, as Ben Jonson did. And in Chapter 6, I shall argue that Ovidian resonances are deployed in *The Tempest* to make the play transcend the polity of early Jacobean England; it is only with another passing compliment to Queen Elizabeth at the very end of *Henry VIII* that we get another historical allusion of this sort.[23] Why, then, did Shakespeare introduce this glancing figuration of the throned virgin?

I suspect that it may have been an attempt to forestall a dangerous

---

[23] The only other incontestable contemporary political allusion in Shakespeare is that to Essex's return from Ireland in the prologue to the fifth act of *Henry V*, but being a choric interjection it is not written into the play's narrative line as the two compliments to Queen Elizabeth are.

identification elsewhere in the text of *Dream*. In a pageant performed during the royal visit to Sudeley in 1592 Elizabeth herself was incorporated into an Ovidian dramatization in the role of Queen of Chastity: a tree is riven, Daphne issues out, Apollo pursues her, and she, 'running to her Majestie, uttered this: "I stay, for whither should Chastety fly for succour, but to the Queene of Chastety?"' [24] Gloriana, Spenser's fairy queen, is the chaste Elizabeth: doesn't that raise the possibility that all fairy queens are the chaste Elizabeth? Titania is of course frequently referred to as the fairy queen, so does this not invite the identification of her with Elizabeth? But the consequences of such a reading are alarming. Titania is anything but chaste: she fawns on her changeling boy [25] and she is the one who will be the chief victim of love-in-idleness. Oberon plans a bestial coupling for her:

> Be it on lion, bear, or wolf, or bull,
> On meddling monkey, or on busy ape—
> She shall pursue it with the soul of love.
>
> (II. i. 180–2)

What she ends up pursuing is, of course, an ass/weaver. Shakespeare cannot afford to license the interpretation of this as an image of the Queen in a perverse encounter which upsets both the natural and the social order; if such an interpretation were at all prominent, the Master of the Revels would not have licensed the play. By identifying the Queen with the imperial votaress, Shakespeare denies the transgressive identification of her with Titania. The historical reading is restricted to the etiology of love-in-idleness; we are accordingly asked to read the encounter with Bottom in other terms. Interpretation cannot of course be policed in the way that this implies, so there is nothing to stop an ingenious reader such as Louis Adrian Montrose relating the courtship of Bottom to the astrologer Simon Forman's dream of a sexual encounter with the Queen. [26] Montrose's reading

[24] *The Progresses and Public Processions of Queen Elizabeth*, ed. John Nichols, new edn., 3 vols. (London, 1823), iii. 139. Accidentals emended in my quotation.

[25] Provoking the jealous wrath of Oberon, which manifests itself in disruptions of nature imitated from those that occur when Ceres is angry after Dis abducts Proserpina (compare *Dream*, II. i. 88 ff. and Golding, v. 591–604). As with other aspects of the play's Ovidianism, the *imitatio* is marked by copiousness—thus Golding's 'the corne was killed in the blade' is embroidered into 'the green corn | Hath rotted ere his youth attained a beard'—and by *translatio* into the vernacular, as when Shakespeare adds in such distinctively English elements as the nine men's morris filled up with mud.

[26] Montrose, ' "Shaping Fantasies": Figurations of Gender and Power in Elizabethan Culture', *Representations*, ii (Spring 1983), 61–94.

might be said to be licensed by a mythographic way of approaching a text which sees multiple interconnectedness between different levels of figuration, but it does seem to me to run counter to Shakespeare's attempt to confine the figuration of Elizabeth to the etiological passage which is carefully placed in the play-world's past, not its present.

The business of Bottom and the ass's head is not a subversive historical allusion; rather, it is the play's most remarkable 'higher imitation' of Ovid. Quince is preparing an Ovidian play without a metamorphosis in it, but magically in the midst of rehearsals a metamorphosis does take place: Bottom is 'changed', as Snout puts it, 'translated', as Quince puts it in his slightly more learned vocabulary (III. i. 109, 113), and with him the story is changed or translated from that of 'Pyramus and Thisbe' into a combination of Ovid's Midas myth and a piece of vernacular folklore, probably derived from Reginald Scot's *Discoverie of Witchcraft*,[27] about the power of witchcraft to give a man an ass's head. This combination of classical and native elements is another mark that the play is a translation in the higher Renaissance sense, not a literalistic dramatization like Quince's. Two textual markers indicate the presence of Midas: Bottom's foolishness and Titania's emphasis on his 'fair large ears, my gentle joy' (IV. i. 4). Renaissance interpreters tended to elide the two parts of the Midas story into one. In Ovid he is first punished for his greedy desire that everything he touches should turn to gold, then punished again with the ass's ears when he misjudges the song contest between Apollo and Pan; but for Abraham Fraunce, he can be wrapped up in one line as '*Mydas* the golden asse, and miserlike foole'.[28] In the collapsed reading of the Midas story, the rich fool is punished with ass's ears; in the metamorphosis of Bottom, the poor man with his ass's ears is rewarded with the love of the fairy queen, but in his beautiful naïvety, his folly which is true wisdom, he does not want it—he only wants his ass's means of subsistence, some good dry oats, a bottle of hay, a handful or two of dried peas, and the blessing of sleep.

[27] See Scot, *Discoverie of Witchcraft* (1584), ed. Brinsley Nicholson (London, 1886), 94, 315. Scot cites a story from Bodin and also the *Golden Ass* of Apuleius, which Shakespeare may have known directly (the difference between Bottom's translation and that in *The Golden Ass* is that it is of the head only; the similarity is that the ass is desired by a female character whom the audience/reader is supposed to perceive as desirable herself).

[28] Fraunce, *The Third part of the Countesse of Pembrokes Yvychurch* (1592), p. 11ʳ. The ears apparently sprout on stage in Lyly's *Midas*, IV. i. 142.

The language of Bottom changes astonishingly between his first reappearance wearing the head, when he still speaks as Nick Bottom (III. i. 114 ff.), and the scene on Titania's flowery bed, when he requests an ass's food and thus really seems to be becoming an ass. This is one of the few moments in Shakespeare at which Ovidian metamorphosis actually seems to be taking place on stage. But of course the stage has certain limits. Supernatural interventions which lead to the transformation of human beings into animals, birds, trees, flowers, streams, and stars cannot be staged as they can be described in narrative poetry. And the characteristically Ovidian form of violent sexual activity, in which Jupiter becomes a bull, a swan, or a shower of gold in order to gain access to some hapless girl, would most definitely have been out of order on the Renaissance stage. When Thomas Heywood staged a whole sequence of stories from the *Metamorphoses* in his *Age* plays, he frequently had to resort to choric narrative rather than direct action. Titania with Bottom is the nearest Shakespeare comes to a god making violent love to a mortal: by inverting the customary gender roles—the rapacious divinity is female, as in *Venus and Adonis*—and by making the mortal into a wise fool, Shakespeare defuses the encounter into comedy. Johann Heinrich Fuseli's extraordinary paintings of the scene have exactly the grotesque quality of the more perverse couplings in Ovid, but in the theatre it is a tryst which provokes more mirth than discomfort.

So too with the metamorphosis itself. A man becoming an ass and a woman making sexual advances to the creature: if it were credible, it would be very unpleasant indeed. Shakespeare hints at its credibility just enough to give a keen edge to the drama, but the audience knows perfectly well that the ass's head is nothing more than a stage prop. My remark above to the effect that Bottom 'really seems to be becoming an ass' is at one level ludicrous: there is no Bottom, there is only an actor. Indeed, the dramatist goes out of his way to remind us of this by staging the metamorphosis in the middle of a play-rehearsal. It is as if he is saying, 'I will not insult you by pretending that a real metamorphosis has taken place; we all know that can't happen in the theatre; let us agree instead to enjoy the illusion together'. But at the same time, we begin to realize that a kind of metamorphosis *has* taken place: in the instant that we think 'Bottom is playing the ass', we stop thinking 'Will Kempe [or whoever] is playing Bottom'. It might be said, then, that a displacement of the illusion occurs, whereby when the character becomes an actor, the actor becomes the character. The comic deficiency of 'Pyramus and Thisbe' is that the actors keep telling us that they *haven't* become their characters. An assumption of disguise—Rosalind becoming Ganymede or Viola Cesario—does similar work to the translation of Bottom. Shakespeare's often-observed self-conscious theatricality, what has become known as his 'metadrama', simultaneously reminds us that we are in the theatre and helps us to forget where we are. In that forgetting, we come as near as is humanly possible to a witnessing of metamorphosis. With Bottom himself, we in the audience may say, 'I have had a most rare vision' (IV. i. 202). The medium of metamorphosis in Ovid is myth; in Shakespeare, it is drama. Shakespeare's capacity to metamorphose Ovid into a different medium is what makes his art *imitatio* of the highest form. As will be seen in Chapter 6, the climax of *The Winter's Tale* offers the supreme example of what I mean. There the art of 'that rare Italian master, Giulio Romano' replaces that of Ovid and is in turn replaced by that of Shakespeare.

III

As must by now be apparent, one of the books of the *Metamorphoses* on which Shakespeare drew most extensively during the 1590s was the fourth, with its stories of Pyramus and Thisbe and Salmacis and Hermaphroditus. Ovid's third and fourth books are unified by the figure of Cadmus. At the beginning of the third, he wanders the world in search of his lost sister, Europa, after her abduction by Jupiter as bull; but before Cadmus' story is resolved, there are narratives concerning a number of his relatives, including Actaeon, his grandson,[29] Semele, his daughter, who is burnt to a cinder when visited by Jupiter in the form of lightning, and Ino, her sister, who brings up Bacchus, the offspring of this union, is persecuted by Juno—ever jealous of her husband's infidelities—and is eventually driven into the sea, where Neptune transforms her into a goddess. At this point, Cadmus' own story is continued: 'And fleeting long like pilgrims, at the last | Upon the coast of Illirie his wife and he were cast' (iv. 700–1). Such tales as Pyramus and Thisbe, Salmacis and Hermaphroditus, and Actaeon are thus contained within a pattern of severings, wanderings, and sea-changes. The works in which these

[29] 'Nepos' (iii. 138): 'nephew' in Golding (iii. 161).

stories are recast, such as *A Midsummer Night's Dream, Venus and Adonis,* and *The Merry Wives of Windsor,* are themselves contained within a definable part of Shakespeare's career which begins with the supposes of *The Taming of the Shrew,* the Protean interchanges of *The Two Gentlemen of Verona,* and the confusions, separations, and reunions of *The Comedy of Errors.* Dromio of Syracuse's baffled cry, so obviously anticipatory of Bottom, might be the motto for all these plays: 'I am transformèd, master, am not I?' (*Errors,* II. ii. 198). The cry is the same for all those fictional selves who are destabilized by love: 'how farre Metamorphozed I am from my selfe, since I last saw thee'.[30] Shakespeare's last play in which this mode is dominant was *Twelfth Night.*

These connections may begin to explain why that play, so full of shifting watery images, should be set in an imaginary land called Illyria. Cadmus and his wife are washed up on the coast of Illyria, not knowing that their daughter and her child have been saved from drowning by being metamorphosed; Viola and Sebastian are washed up separately on the coast of Illyria, neither knowing that the other has been saved, though Viola is given hope by the captain saying that he saw her brother bind himself to a mast, 'Where, like Arion on the dolphin's back, | I saw him hold acquaintance with the waves' (I. ii. 14–15). The choice of simile here is telling. Drowning is averted not by external agency, as it is when Neptune comes to the aid of Ino and her son, but by the strength and imagination of the character himself: Sebastian is compared not to a victim of love in the *Metamorphoses,* but to Arion in the *Fasti,* who, as noted above with regard to the dolphin image in *A Midsummer Night's Dream,* saves himself through his own musical art. In *Twelfth Night,* too, the power of music—as embodied in the name Viola—calms emotional storms and restores harmony. It is noteworthy in this respect that the name of Cadmus' wife, though not mentioned by Ovid, is Harmonia.

Twelfth Night is pervaded by a sense of mutability; constancy and inconstancy in love shape both the twists of the plot and the preoccupations of the characters. The tone is set by Orsino's opening speech in which he changes his mind about whether or not he wants more music, and compares the spirit of love to the ebb and flow of the sea. 'So full of shapes is fancy, | That it alone is high fantastical' (I. i. 14–15): the language signals entry into that world of the

---

[30] Nashe's projection of the Earl of Surrey, in love with his Geraldine in *The Unfortunate Traveller* (*Works,* ed. McKerrow, ii. 243).

imagination and its inconstant shapes which Shakespeare explored most fully in *A Midsummer Night's Dream*. So it is that certain myths from the Cadmean section of the *Metamorphoses*, in particular those of Actaeon and of Narcissus and Echo (another watery story in Book Three) are among the controlling structures of the play.[31]

The image of metamorphosis is introduced openly when Orsino speaks of the effect of his seeing Olivia:

> That instant was I turned into a hart,
> And my desires, like fell and cruel hounds,
> E'er since pursue me.
>
> (I. i. 20–2)

The figure of Actaeon is so embedded in this trope that he is not mentioned by name. In reading the hounds as an image of Actaeon's own desires, Shakespeare is following the traditional interpretation of the myth: in Golding's Epistle it is a warning that we will be hunted by the dogs of our sensual excesses; according to Abraham Fraunce, 'Actaeon was devoured of his owne doggs, so he be distracted and torne to peeces with his owne affections, and perturbations';[32] and in the fifth sonnet of Samuel Daniel's *Delia* cycle, 'My thoughts like houndes, pursue me to my death'. Shakespeare's allusion economically suggests the exact sense of self-consuming passion that will recur throughout the play. And it is made in the expectation that the audience are capable of reading into it not only the name of Actaeon, but also the received interpretation.

In comparing himself to Actaeon, Orsino implicitly compares Olivia to Diana; thus, when he explicitly compares Cesario to Diana (I. iv. 31), we know that (s)he is replacing Olivia as the Duke's idealized object of desire. Diana is above all the goddess of chastity: it is because of Olivia's pose of chastity that Orsino's suit is unsuccessful and the pursuit of love turns self-destructively inward. Orsino is in love with the idea of being in love, and that is a state approaching the self-love of Narcissus. The abundant desire which surfeits on itself and so dies is that of Narcissus. Not only do many of the play's dilemmas

---

[31] My account here is in some respects anticipated by D. J. Palmer in 'Twelfth Night and the Myth of Echo and Narcissus', *ShS* xxxii (1979), 73–8. See also M. E. Lamb, 'Ovid's *Metamorphoses* and Shakespeare's *Twelfth Night*', in *Shakespearean Comedy*, ed. Maurice Charney, New York Literary Forum Special Issue (1980), 63–77, though the theory of names expounded there (e.g. Orsino as 'ursus', bear, and therefore Callisto, who becomes a bear) is tenuous.

[32] Fraunce, *The Third part of the Countesse of Pembrokes Yvychurch*, p. 43^r.

and potential disasters arise from the narcissism of Olivia and Orsino: the comic plot reiterates and emphasizes the motif. Malvolio is 'sick of self-love' (I. v. 86) and 'practis[es] behaviour to his own shadow' (II. v. 16) in the manner of Ovid's Narcissus, who is to be seen 'gazing on his shadow still with fixed staring eyes' (Golding, iii. 524). He is gulled into wearing yellow, the colour of the flower into which Narcissus is transformed.

Malvolio also presents a different angle on the Actaeon pattern. If the noble Orsino is to be read as Actaeon in that he is hunted by the dogs of his own desires, the steward may be viewed in terms of the myth's implication that it is dangerous to lift one's eyes above one's rank. In the box-tree scene, instead of seeing Actaeon spying on Diana, we watch an Actaeon figure being spied on himself as he fantasizes about his Diana's desire for him. As Malvolio interprets the meaning of the 'I' in the letter, Fabian remarks, 'Ay, an you had any eye behind you you might see more detraction at your heels than fortunes before you' (II. v. 132–4). The pun concentrates the double identity of Malvolio as Narcissus (the self-obsessed 'I') and Actaeon (the desiring 'eye'). The dogs are watching him—even Sir Andrew is 'dog at a catch' and, as Feste says, 'some dogs will catch well' (II. iii. 60–1)—and already snapping at his heels. The 'detraction' which comes to him is the play's version of the fate of Actaeon. Given this, it is tempting to read his final cry of vengeance as an image of Actaeon turning the story around and beating off the pursuing hounds: 'I'll be revenged on the whole *pack* of you'.[33] Malvolio is also a bear, baited by dogs.[34] It may therefore be that Shakespeare is making one of his characteristic fusions of high and low culture: the educated audience reads Malvolio as Actaeon and simultaneously the illiterate spectator—who does not view the theatre so differently from the bear-pit—sees him as a bear.

The hounding of Malvolio has reached its height in the Sir Topas scene, where, as in the main plot during the fourth act, identities and reality itself shift bewilderingly amid images of madness, darkness, and dream. Feste, in the guise of Sir Topas, alerts the audience to the Ovidian, metamorphic nature of this world when he asks Malvolio,

---

[33] v. i. 374, my italics. *OED*'s first usage of 'pack' for a company of hounds kept for hunting is 1648, but Shakespeare does sometimes use the word in contexts suggesting violent collective pursuit: 'God bless the Prince from all the pack of you! | A knot you are of damnèd bloodsuckers' (*Richard III*, III. iii. 4–5); 'Hence; pack! . . . Out, rascal dogs!' (*Timon of Athens*, v. i. 111, 114).

[34] See Stephen Dickey, 'Shakespeare's Mastiff Comedy', *SQ* xlii (1991), 255–75.

'What is the opinion of Pythagoras concerning wildfowl?' (IV. ii. 51). As in the Sonnets, mutability is suggested by means of allusion to the fifteenth book of the *Metamorphoses*. Malvolio has asked for his sanity to be tested 'in any constant question' (IV. ii. 49–50), by which he means any formal rational discourse, but Feste replies with a question that leads to the inconstancies of Pythagorean metempsychosis.

If all the characters in *Twelfth Night* were perpetually self-centred, it would be no comedy. It is above all Viola who effects a release from narcissism. When she first appears as Cesario, she too seems to be a Narcissus: the ambivalence suggested by ''Tis with him in standing water, between boy and man' (I. v. 153–4) associates Cesario with the sixteen-year-old Narcissus, who 'seemde to stande beetwene the state of man and Lad' (Golding, iii. 438). As Cesario attracts both Orsino and Olivia, so with Narcissus, 'The hearts of divers trim yong men his beautie gan to move, | And many a Ladie fresh and faire was taken in his love' (iii. 439–40). But Viola redeems the play because she proves to be selfless, not selfish, in love. She becomes Echo instead of Narcissus.

When Olivia asks Cesario what he would do if he were in love with her, the boy departs from the script which Orsino has given him, with its enumeration of the conventional courtly lover's groans and sighs, and speaks instead with an authenticity and intensity that immediately strike a chord in Olivia ('You might do much', she murmurs approvingly in reply):

> Make me a willow cabin at your gate
> And call upon my soul within the house,
> Write loyal cantons of contemnèd love,
> And sing them loud even in the dead of night;
> Halloo your name to the reverberate hills,
> And make the babbling gossip of the air
> Cry out 'Olivia!' O, you should not rest
> Between the elements of air and earth,
> But you should pity me.
>
> (I. v. 257–65)

The 'babbling gossip of the air' is an explicit allusion to Echo, prepared for by the images of the reverberating hills and of hopeless love—Echo's love is condemned because Narcissus loves only himself. Shakespeare's adjective was probably determined by Golding's 'A babling Nymph that *Echo* hight' (iii. 443). Cesario seems to speak authentically because it is really Viola speaking of her own secret love for Orsino; her plight, which requires silence and concealment of her feelings, appears to be like Echo's. So it is that when she is with Orsino, Viola implicitly compares herself to Echo by speaking of an imaginary sister, really herself, whose history is a 'blank',

> she never told her love,
> But let concealment, like a worm i'th' bud,
> Feed on her damask cheek. She pined in thought,
> And with a green and yellow melancholy
> She sat like patience on a monument,
> Smiling at grief. Was not this love indeed?
>
> (II. iv. 110–15)

This is a typically Shakespearian fusion of images. The motif of concealing love, pining, and eventually becoming a blank evokes Echo, but the similes of the canker and the funerary monument come from native traditions—Shakespeare and his audience would have read of Echo, but seen the worm in the bud and the figure of Patience on a monument. The latter may also have an Ovidian bearing in that the archetypal image of a female figure in stone, representing stoical endurance, is Niobe.

But not all the associations of Echo are melancholy. She functions in Ovid as an alternative to self-love: had Narcissus responded to her love, neither of them would have been destroyed. Viola's function is to enable characters to respond, to see that love requires echoing instead of narcissism. Here the mythological pattern is transformed into a metaphorical one. This process is at work earlier in the scene with Orsino. After speaking of the instability of lovers, 'Save in the constant image of the creature | That is beloved', Orsino asks Cesario how he likes the music that is playing:

VIOLA. It gives a very *echo* to the seat
    Where love is throned.
DUKE. Thou dost speak masterly.
        (II. iv. 20–1, my italics)

Viola has given words to Orsino's own thoughts: they echo each other in the belief that music echoes love. Viola harmonizes Illyria by teaching its inhabitants to echo and thus to love. Cesario, through being two natures in one, shows the others that their true selves are to be found by looking at others instead of contemplating their own images in the manner of Narcissus. The moment of greatest harmony occurs in the visual echo when Viola faces Sebastian, love is doubled, and the plot resolved.

Yet the resolution is by no means complete. Malvolio is still a Narcissus or an Actaeon, and Viola must be split from Cesario. *Twelfth Night* recognizes the fragility of Echo and the pervasiveness of Narcissus. It is no coincidence that the play stands on the threshold of the tragedies: narcissism is a characteristic not only of Feste's enemy, Malvolio, but also of King Lear, who, as his Fool recognizes, becomes his own shadow. *Twelfth Night* is and is not a benign rewriting of the myth, in which Narcissus recants of his narcissism, Echo is re-embodied and wins his love, and they live happily ever after. Quite apart from the little local problem of Malvolio's detention of the captain who holds the symbolic key to Viola's reassumption of feminine identity, the tonality of the final song is not that of living happily ever after: it is of the wind and the rain, it is to be reiterated in the storm by Lear's Fool.

Narcissus clearly functions in the play, as he does in the marriage-group of the Sonnets, as a negative *exemplum* which warns against introspective self-absorption. But the Echo who teaches Orsino and Olivia to look outside themselves is Cesario, and if we are to believe imaginatively in the union of Viola and Orsino, Cesario must be killed off—though it is clear from his final speech that Orsino rather hopes that they can go on acting out a relationship that bears some resemblance to that between Jove and Ganymede. It is important to remember that in Ovid, although the pining away to disembodiment is a consequence of unrequited love for the selfish boy, Echo is deprived of the power to initiate speech *before* she meets Narcissus: in punishment for her complicity in one of Jove's philandering sprees, Juno has ruled that all the girl can do is double the last word of what other people say. This, of course, gave Ovid the opportunity to use his virtuoso echo topos, which was so frequently imitated in the Renaissance. By becoming Cesario, Viola gains freedom of speech. When she becomes Viola again, she will revert to silence, not speaking unless spoken to, and when spoken to expected merely to echo her assent. She will, that is to say, become Echo in all her passivity and pathos. So it is that the character who has driven the plot for most of the play does not say a single word in the final one hundred and twenty-five lines of it.

Golding called Echo a 'babling Nymph'. The point is that she blabs, she talks too much: her skill in speech was such that she succeeded in detaining Juno in conversation, giving her fellow-nymphs the time to finish making love to Jove and then run away before the angry goddess could get them. That is why her tongue is curbed. In the moralizing tradition, the figure thus becomes a type for the woman of active tongue who must be silenced—in short, the shrew who must be tamed. As usual, and in accordance with the skilful rhetorician's capacity to present opposing arguments with equal force, Shakespeare leaves the question open. It remains for the judicious spectator to choose between a reading in which Viola empties Illyria of narcissism (Malvolio apart) and is rewarded with love—a Lucentio and Bianca reading, if you will—and a darker interpretation—a Petruchio and Kate one—in which woman is reduced to the status of man's echo.

The capacity of Ovidian allusion to destabilize comedy's march towards harmony is further demonstrable from *The Merchant of Venice*. At the end of the first scene of that play, Bassanio comes up with a plan to gain money in order to help Antonio: 'In Belmont is a lady richly left', he begins. His stressing of wealth before beauty and virtue has the effect that his subsequent term 'worth' comes to mean cash-value more than moral excellence:

> Nor is the wide world ignorant of her worth,
> For the four winds blow in from every coast
> Renownèd suitors, and her sunny locks
> Hang on her temples like a golden fleece,
> Which makes her seat of Belmont Colchis' strand,
> And many Jasons come in quest of her.
>
> (I. i. 167–72)

This is a fine example of the Renaissance habit of thinking in terms of parallels between present experience and mythological precedent. That Portia is like the golden fleece makes Belmont into Colchis' strand. The latter image is probably derived from the line describing Jason's success at the climax of the golden fleece story in Book Seven of the *Metamorphoses*: 'And so with conquest and a wife he loosde from *Colchos* strond' (Golding, vii. 218), a turn of phrase that applies very well to Bassanio on his departure from Belmont in Act III. Golding interpreted 'The good successe of Jason in the land of Colchos' as a sign 'That nothing is so hard but peyne and travell doo it win, | For fortune ever favoreth such as boldly doo begin' (Epistle, 143–6), and this positive reading could be applied to Bassanio: his travail on behalf of Antonio leads him to travel to Belmont, where he makes a bold choice of casket and is rewarded with good fortune.

But the terms of the allusion do not support this reading. Where the love of a woman, Medea, assists Jason in his winning of the fleece, Bassanio views the woman, Portia, as the fleece itself. She is a valuable treasure to be won, not a human being to be loved. When he comes to make his choice in Belmont, Bassanio knows his mythology sufficiently well to disdain the gold casket: it is 'food for Midas' (III. ii. 102) and thus brings disaster to those who choose it. He must not give the appearance of being in pursuit of gold; only by making the apparently unmercenary choice of lead will he gain the treasure. On opening the leaden casket he finds an image of his fleece in the form of the 'golden mesh' of Portia's hair (III. ii. 122). Once Bassanio's quest is fulfilled, his friend Graziano rounds off the comparison that was introduced in the first scene: 'We are the Jasons, we have won the fleece'.[35] Just to make it absolutely clear that in the minds of these men, coming as they do from the mercantile world of Venice, 'the fleece' denotes treasure more than beauty or virtue, Salerio replies, 'I would you had won the fleece that he hath lost', a reference to the wealth contained in Antonio's ships. The success of Bassanio and his friend as Argonauts is nothing more than a means of compensation for the loss of Antonio's argosies.

Portia, meanwhile, has read Bassanio as Hercules:

> Now he goes,
> With no less presence but with much more love
> Than young Alcides when he did redeem
> The virgin tribute paid by howling Troy
> To the sea-monster. I stand for sacrifice.
> The rest aloof are the Dardanian wives,
> With blearèd visages come forth to view
> The issue of th'exploit. Go, Hercules.
>
> (III. ii. 53–60)

She is romantically construing the moment of Bassanio's choice as the heroic one in which Hercules rescued Hesione from the sea-

---

[35] III. ii. 239. This is a suggestive echo of Ithamore's 'I'll be thy Jason, thou my golden fleece' in Marlowe's *Jew of Malta*, to which '*The Merchant* or otherwise called *The Jew of Venice*', as it was called in the Stationers' Register, alludes in so many ways. Ithamore's speech is an extraordinary one in which the slave and the courtesan become parodies of both Ovidian ('I'll be Adonis, thou shalt be Love's Queen') and Marlovian ('Shalt live with me and be my love') lovers (IV. ii. 92–102).

monster to which she had been sacrificed in order to save Troy (Shakespeare would have known this story from Book Eleven of the *Metamorphoses*).

But Bassanio promptly distances himself from Hercules, remarking that many men are cowardly at heart yet wear 'upon their chins | The beards of Hercules and frowning Mars' (III. ii. 84–5). He'd rather rely on Jason's cunning than Hercules' strength. His detachment of himself from Hercules is part of the argument about not trusting external appearances which enables him to see that gold was 'Hard food for Midas' and that he should therefore not do the obvious thing and choose the golden casket. Bassanio is simply not the heroic figure whom Portia imagines. His chosen model was one of the least heroic heroes in the mythological pantheon: Jason's labours in obtaining the fleece, such as encountering bulls who are all bellow and no bite, are a poor, even a parodic, version of those of Hercules.

Jason is a troubling precedent in another respect. He has the dubious distinction of being the recipient of two letters from deserted lovers in the *Heroides*: number six is from Hypsipyle, whom he deserted for Medea, and twelve is from Medea, whom he deserted for Creusa.[36] As Helen of Troy says in her letter, 'False Jason promised all things to Medea—was she the less thrust forth from the house of Aeson?' (*Her.* xvii. 229–30, 'omnia Medeae fallax promisit Iason— | pulsa est Aesonia num minus illa domo?'). Jason is *fallax Iason*, an archetype of male deceit and infidelity. That he will later be unfaithful to Medea, as Bassanio is symbolically unfaithful to Portia in the act of giving away her ring, does not make one sanguine as to the husbands' future conduct in the imaginary afterlife of the play's characters. Graziano has the last words on stage, and in them he harps on the idea of 'keeping safe Nerissa's ring' (v. i. 307). 'Ring' puns on the slang for female genitals, thus implying the husbands' proprietorial guarding of their wives' chastity and their fear of female infidelity. But, like the business of the rings, the allusions to Jason, which Graziano shares with Bassanio, suggest that what is really open to question is the future conduct of the men.

Does Bassanio's self-identification as Jason implicitly make Portia into Medea as well as the fleece? Certain resemblances may be

---

[36] In the context of the *Heroides* as a whole, Jason's position is unique: the only other man to receive two letters is Paris, but the second of these, from Helen, is one of the paired letters towards the end—the relationships where there is a reply are of a different order from those in which the only speaker is the deserted woman.

adduced. The great interior monologue early in Book Seven of the *Metamorphoses*, in which Medea's reason battles with her passion, could be read as a precedent for the speech with which Portia begins the scene in which Bassanio has to make his choice of casket. Like Medea, she struggles to suppress her love in a fragmented syntax that is mimetic of her divided mind: 'There's something tells me—but it is not love— │ I would not lose you'.[37] It could possibly be argued that as Medea assists Jason to the fleece by giving him enchanted herbs to charm the bulls, so Portia assists Bassanio to the correct casket and hence the fleece by dropping him a hint in the words of the song that is sung while he is making his decision ('ding, dong, bell' meaning 'choose the thing that's made of lead'). In the trial scene Portia proves herself to be a verbal magician; she works a kind of magic to renew the life of Antonio, who perceives himself as 'a tainted wether of the flock, │ Meetest for death' (IV. i. 13–14) and might therefore be thought of as equivalent to the ageing Aeson whose life is renewed by Medea. But these connections are tenuous: the story of Aeson is not explicitly alluded to in connection with Portia. In fact it is displaced into the play's other plot.

Lorenzo and Jessica's exchanges at the beginning of the final act sound to innocent ears like lyrical evocations of great lovers past:

> —in such a night
> Troilus, methinks, mounted the Trojan walls,
> And sighed his soul toward the Grecian tents
> Where Cressid lay that night.
>   —In such a night
> Did Thisbe fearfully o'ertrip the dew
> And saw the lion's shadow ere himself,
> And ran dismayed away.
>   —In such a night
> Stood Dido with a willow in her hand
> Upon the wild sea banks, and waft her love
> To come again to Carthage.
>   —In such a night
> Medea gathered the enchanted herbs
> That did renew old Aeson.
>   (V. i. 3–14)

---

[37] *Merchant*, III. ii. 4–5. For a wide-ranging account of the influence of the interior monologues of the *Metamorphoses* on the Shakespearian soliloquy, see J. W. Velz, 'The Ovidian Soliloquy in Shakespeare', *Shakespeare Studies*, xviii (1986), 1–24, a fine article which is especially persuasive on Angelo in *Measure for Measure*.

But to the mythologically literate members of Shakespeare's audience, these allusions would have been shot through with irony every bit as sharp as that of the subsequent exchanges in which Lorenzo speaks of stealing Jessica, Jessica of Lorenzo's 'many vows of faith | And ne'er a true one', and Lorenzo of Jessica's slandering and shrewishness (17–22). It is hardly auspicious that at this moment of union and harmony the lovers compare themselves to Troilus and Cressida, Pyramus and Thisbe, and Dido and Aeneas. Cressida is probably lying with Diomede as Troilus mounts the walls; Pyramus and Thisbe will soon be dead; Aeneas will not return to Carthage. Furthermore, 'Dido with a willow in her hand', signalling to the departing ship in the vain hope that she will be remembered, closely echoes an image in the lament of another woman deserted by her lover, Ariadne left on Naxos by the promiscuous Theseus in the *Heroides*.[38]

But most sinister of all is 'In such a night | Medea gathered the enchanted herbs | That did renew old Aeson'. At first glance this might seem to be an image of regeneration, perhaps a suggestion that old Shylock will come to accept his daughter's marriage and be given a new life. But what was the consequence of Medea's rejuvenation of Aeson? In Book Seven of the *Metamorphoses*—and it is unquestionable that Shakespeare was thinking of the *Metamorphoses* here, for the words 'enchanted herbs' and 'renew' are lifted from Golding's translation of the passage[39]—we learn that it was prelude to a peculiarly violent act: having rejuvenated Aeson by boiling him in a cauldron with those magic herbs, she gave the daughters of Pelias the opportunity to submit their father to the same process, but this time left out the key ingredients and thus killed Pelias. By activating Medea's destructive magic here, Shakespeare is contaminating a superficially lyrical interlude with a precursor text which is marked by bodily dismemberment that perhaps reawakens Shylock's demand for his pound of flesh (Ovid has a clinical description of the bleeding of Pelias). What is more, the image of Medea gathering ingredients for

---

[38] 'iactatae late signa dedere manus; | candidaque imposui longae velamina virgae— | scilicet oblitos admonitura mei!' (*Her.* x. 40–2, 'I sent you signals with my hands; and upon a long tree-branch I fixed my shining veil—of course to bring me to the memory of those who had forgotten'). I do not see why Chaucer's *Legend of Good Women* is given special prominence in discussions of this scene (see e.g. the fnn. in John Russell Brown's 1955 Arden edn.)—Medea's rejuvenation of Aeson, for instance, is in Ovid but not Chaucer.

[39] 'chaunted herbes', 'renew': Golding, vii. 204,381.

her cauldron evokes a world of witchcraft akin to that of Shakespearian tragedy, not comedy—her nocturnal gatherings are also of
ingredients like those of the weird sisters. 'I would outnight you, did
nobody come', Jessica concludes the exchange: the outnightings
have by this time become associated not with love, but with
desertions, dark deeds, and death.

In his allusion to Ovid's Orpheus (Ovid having become 'the poet'),
Lorenzo seeks to distance the associations of darkness by appealing to
the harmonizing power of music:

> Therefore the poet
> Did feign that Orpheus drew trees, stones, and floods,
> Since naught so stockish, hard, and full of rage
> But music for the time doth change his nature.
> The man that hath no music in himself,
> Nor is not moved with concord of sweet sounds,
> Is fit for treasons, stratagems, and spoils.
> The motions of his spirit are dull as night,
> And his affections dark as Erebus.
>
> (v. i. 79–87)

Poetry and music are elided here and a creative metamorphic power is
claimed for them: they soften hard hearts, bring concord and
animation. One thinks forward to the drawing of stone to life when
music strikes in *The Winter's Tale*. Leonard Barkan writes that Ovid's
presence is signalled in Lorenzo's speech by the word *change*,

and in that change the matter of Ovid has been transformed into a complete
world-picture, from the sensual accidents of individual loves to the universals
of cosmic harmony. That is, of course, the range of the *Metamorphoses* itself.
But it is viewed through a special Renaissance rose-colored glass, like that of
Titian's *Bacchanale of the Andrians*. Antiquity is seen as a golden world, in
which beauty and sensuality are not subject to accident but contribute to a
universal harmony.[40]

This is beautiful and just. It is a way of saying that Ovid and
metamorphosis help to bring the golden world of Shakespearian
comedy to resolution in cosmic harmony. But what it leaves out is an
acknowledgement of the fictiveness of the golden world and a sense of
the precariousness of the resolution. The phrase of Lorenzo's which it
passes over is 'for the time': the harmony is only momentary. Time

---

[40] *The Gods Made Flesh*, 272.

then moves on, as it does in Rosalind/Ganymede's ungolden anatomy of its crawl and gallop in *As You Like It*. For a moment our ears will be touched by the sweet music of the 'In such a night' exchanges; but a moment later comes the dissonance, as we see that the lovers invoked are far from exemplary.

Lorenzo begins his speech with the concord, but he cannot altogether banish the treasons, stratagems, and affections dark as Erebus. They are there at the end of the speech, just as they are there with the off-stage malevolence of Shylock and in the implications of the comparison between Bassanio and Jason. And they are there in the very allusion to Orpheus, which brings not only his music but also his association with Erebus. It is to the gods of Erebus ('deos Erebi') that Orpheus complains after Eurydice's second death and immediately before he touches his strings and moves the trees (*Met*. x. 76). Shakespearian comedy supposes that Eurydice really can be led out of the underworld—one thinks of the supposed death and supposedly miraculous restoration of Hero, of Helena, of Thaisa, of Hermione—but it also recognizes that its resolutions are only a suppose.

IV

In the tradition of *A Midsummer Night's Dream* and Lyly's *Gallathea*, *As You Like It* is another comedy in which the wood is mediated through Ovid. The old Duke and his fellow-exiles in Arden 'fleet the time carelessly, as they did in the golden world' (1. i. 112–13). In his commentary on Book One of the *Metamorphoses*, George Sandys crystallizes the Renaissance interpretation of the Golden Age, which will also be of great significance in *The Tempest*:

Then was there neither Master nor Servant: names meerly brought in by ambition and injury. Unforced Nature gave sufficient to all; who securely possest her undivided bounty. A rich condition wherein no man was poore: Avarice after introduced indigency: who by coveting a propriety, alienated all; and lost what it had, by seeking to inlarge it. But this happy estate abounding with all felicities, assuredly represented that which man injoyed in his innocency: under the raigne of *Saturne*, more truly of *Adam*.[41]

As You Like It opens with the relationship between a master and a servant, who is named Adam as if to evoke Eden, the Christian

[41] Sandys, *Ovid's Metamorphosis Englished*, 25.

equivalent of the golden world; with the move into Arden, Adam ceases to play the role of a servant and is treated with civility, waited upon by nobles. In Arden, the Duke laughs off 'The penalty of Adam, | The seasons' difference' (II. i. 5–6)—Ovid describes in Book One how the varying seasons come with the end of the Golden Age in which it was perpetual spring 'and *Zephyr* with his milde | And gentle blast did cherish things that grew of owne accorde' (Golding, i. 122–3). But although the Duke claims that he and his fellows do not feel the harsher seasons, 'the icy fang | And churlish chiding of the winter's wind' (II. i. 6–7) does blow through Arden. The play does not suppose that the Golden Age, with its perpetual mild zephyrs and gentle blasts, can be restored. It is uncompromising in its confrontation of those twin phenomena from which the Golden Age was imagined to be free: property (linguistically synonymous with 'propriety') and alienation (legal exclusion from property). To be exiled from the court to the forest is to be alienated, as Celia recognizes: 'But what will you be called? | Something that hath a reference to my state. | No longer Celia, but Aliena' (I. iii. 125–7). Corin does not live in Golden Age idleness; he is denied the *otium* of soft pastoral and is sold and bought along with the property of which he is tenant.

But the Duke's point is that the pains of the forest are as nothing compared with the perils of the envious court. The adversities of Arden can be transformed for positive ends. Nature, like the book of Ovid, can be read morally: 'Find tongues in trees, books in the running brooks, | Sermons in stones, and good in everything' (II. i. 16–17). One of the lessons to be learnt is the need to empathize with nature: as Ovid shows what it might be like to be a hunted hart or bear and ends his book with Pythagoras making the case for vegetarianism, so the Duke laments the necessity of killing deer for food and Jaques anthropomorphizes the poor sequestered stag. The fact that this does not stop the exiled lords celebrating the slaughter of a deer in the fourth act is another mark that they remain of the court and that this is not really the Golden Age—if it were, they would be living 'by Raspis, heppes and hawes, by cornelles, plummes and cherries, | By sloes and apples, nuttes and peares, and lothsome bramble berries' (Golding, i. 119–20). The Golden Age is exposed as a fiction, but it is nevertheless morally and socially enabling, in that it serves as a critique of the values of the court.

To go to Arden is also to go to Ovid in his capacity as 'praeceptor amoris'. Erotic love is a form of opposition to the court, which depends on dynastic liaisons and parental control. As the character of Aliena points out in Lodge's *Rosalynde*, sexual love transcends the barriers of rank: 'Experience tells thee, that Peasaunts have theyr passions as well as Princes, that Swaynes, as they have their labours, so they have theyr amours, and Love lurkes assoone about a Sheepcoate, as a Pallaice' (Bullough, ii. 224). The celebration of sexuality is accordingly a risky matter. The writing of the *Ars Amatoria* was one of the reasons for Ovid's exile from Rome; Marlowe's translation of the *Amores* was among the books banned and burned by episcopal order at the time when Shakespeare was writing *As You Like It*. Tranio nails his colours to the mast of love in *The Taming of the Shrew* by saying that Ovid should not be made an 'outcast'. To allude to the *Ars Amatoria*, as Lucentio and Bianca do, is to throw in one's lot with transgression. In *As You Like It*, it is by becoming outcasts from the court that Rosalind and Orlando can refine the art of love. As Ganymede, Rosalind becomes a 'praeceptor amoris', her sexual pragmatism as down-to-earth and her wit as sharp as they are in Ovid himself ('men are April when they woo, December when they wed; maids are May when they are maids, but the sky changes when they are wives'—iv. i. 139–41). Here power is given over to those who do not usually have it: the character who dominates the discourse is imagined simultaneously as a woman and a Ganymede—the name which served as Elizabethan slang for a catamite like Gaveston, alluding to the lovely boy for whom Jove/Jupiter (by whose name Rosalind/Ganymede keeps on swearing) was fired with love in Book Ten of the *Metamorphoses*.[42]

Touchstone explicitly reads the characters' exile in relation to Ovid's: 'I am here with thee and thy goats, as the most capricious poet honest Ovid was among the Goths' (iii. iii. 5–6). There was some confusion in the Renaissance as to whether the barbaric tribe who inhabited Tomis on the Black Sea where Ovid was exiled were Getes or Goths, but whichever they were it was agreed that they would have been incapable of appreciating the poet's witty writings. Ovid makes that complaint himself and Touchstone echoes him in his reference to a man's verses not being understood.[43] In *Pierce Pennilesse*, Thomas

---

[42] x. 155–61. The word 'catamite' is in fact a corrupt form of 'Ganymede'; *OED*'s first usage is Drayton, 1593.

[43] *Tristia*, iii. xiv. 39–40, iv. i. 89–90, v. xii. 53–4; also *Ex Ponto*, iv. ii. 15–38, though I have found no evidence that Shakespeare knew this work.

Nashe makes the encounter between Ovid and the Getes into the equivalent of reasoning with a man who wants only to drink beer: '*Ovid* might as well have read his verses to the *Getes* that understood him not, as a man talk reason to them that have no eares, but their mouths, nor sense but of that which they swallowe downe their throates' (*Works*, i. 180). Touchstone puns on the 'goats' of Audrey and on 'capricious' ('caper/capri', the goat, aligned with the capriciousness of Ovid's verbal play) with a wit that makes him into the equivalent of the banished Ovid. His 'honest Ovid' displaces the epithet: the court fool and the Roman poet are cunning sophisticates among 'honest' or simple country folk. But Touchstone benignly rewrites Ovid's fate: where the exiled poet was reduced to penning his *Tristia*, sad letters home to his wife and the emperor whose favour he had lost, the banished fool makes the best of things and marries a native of the forest. The play's vision of multiple marriage is large enough to include the conjunction of a court figure whose very foolishness is a mark of his sophistication and a goatherd from the very bottom of the social scale. One can only assume at the end of the play that places will change, bringing the goatherd to court and leaving a courtier, Jaques, in the forest.

It is Jaques who recognizes that the handy-dandy affects the social order. His exasperated reply to Touchstone's punning allusion to Ovid is 'O knowledge ill-inhabited; worse than Jove in a thatched house!' (III. iii. 7–8). The comparison flips from Ovid's life to his work. Its significance becomes apparent if we recollect *Much Ado About Nothing*'s image of descent from high to low in the context of wooing: when Don Pedro courts Hero at the ball on behalf of Claudio, he says, 'My visor is Philemon's roof; within the house is Jove', to which Hero replies, 'Why, then, your visor should be thatched' (II. i. 88–9). The allusion is to the encounter of the supreme god and humble humans when the disguised Jove is entertained in what Golding called the cottage 'thatched all with straw and fennish reede' of Baucis and Philemon (viii. 806). The hospitality exercised by this aged couple in their poverty-stricken home indicates that true nobility is not a matter of good birth. The theory of degree carries with it the assumption that well-born people behave well, basely-born ones basely. The pastoral virtues of Baucis and Philemon, and of Corin in the play, overturn this assumption. When Orlando arrives in the forest he expects to find barbarity, but he is greeted with civility: in giving food to old Adam, the Duke and his courtiers mirror the hospitality of Baucis and

Philemon, and the audience sees that Arden has begun its healing work.

As You Like It makes the court learn from the country, those of high degree learn from those of low. But the ending is different from Ovid's characteristic one. Where Baucis and Philemon are rewarded by Jove granting them their wish, and the problem of gender in the Iphis and Ianthe story (discussed in my first chapter) is solved by divine intervention, love's metamorphosis in Shakespeare's play is wrought by human agency. It is Rosalind who grants the wishes. Hymen is invoked and appears, as at the wedding of Iphis and Ianthe (*Met.* ix. 762–97), but his descent in *As You Like It* is more performance than theophany: the god is meant to be seen as an actor, for Rosalind is orchestrating the script. The Iphis and Ianthe story ends with the setting up of a tablet inscribed with the text '*The vowes that Iphys vowd a wench, he hath performd a Lad*' (Golding, ix. 933); its purpose is to give thanks to Juno, Venus, and Hymen for the transformation which has allowed this to happen. In *As You Like It*, it is Rosalind herself who sets up the multiple marriage vows and brings them to fruition. In this shift whereby metamorphosis comes from within the human world, thus dispensing with the magic of myth, the play anticipates the late romances, notably *The Winter's Tale*, in which Ovidian myth is recast in the form of Shakespearian metadrama.

As in *The Winter's Tale*, the resolution to which the metadrama steers the action is one in which the social order is upheld. Shepherdesses are not finally allowed to marry well-born characters; Touchstone will ditch Audrey a few months after returning to the court. The virtues of Baucis and Philemon can be read as an affirmation of degree just as easily as an overturning of it: they are 'the patternes of chast and constant conjugall affections: as of content in poverty; who make it easy by bearing it chearfully. A condition as full of innocency, as security: and no meane blessing, if wee could but thinke so.'[44] The reversion from the licence of Arden to the reaffirmation of orthodoxy in Shakespeare's comic endings is perhaps one mark of his political cautiousness—he does seem to have been about the only major dramatist of his age never to have been imprisoned or censured for his work. That caution is also apparent in the way that the Ovidianism of the comedies is political in a broadly conceptual, not a narrowly topical, sense. Save possibly in the case of

---

[44] Sandys, *Ovid's Metamorphosis Englished*, 295.

the love-in-idleness passage of *A Midsummer Night's Dream*, discussed in the previous section, Shakespearian comedy eschews the sort of specific historical allegory which Spenser deployed. Belphoebe in *The Faerie Queene* is at once Ovid's Diana and Queen Elizabeth. Phoebe in *As You Like It* is neither.

That the *Metamorphoses* could be used as a vehicle for contemporary political comment in the drama around the time that Shakespeare was writing his mature comedies is apparent from Ben Jonson's play, *Cynthia's Revels; or, The Fountain of Self-Love*, which was performed at court on Twelfth Night in January 1601. Jonson, writing for the Children of the Royal Chapel and the sophisticated Blackfriars and court audiences, works in an overtly mythological and allegorical mode; like Lyly before him, he has Ovidian characters playing major parts on stage. Indeed, the play was entered in the Stationers' Register with the title 'Narcissus, or the fountaine of selfe love'. In the first act, Echo speaks a lament beside the fountain in which Narcissus drowned while trying to kiss his own reflection. But the location of the scene introduces another myth: it is set in the vale of *Gargaphie*, sacred to Diana, in which Actaeon was torn to pieces. The character of Cupid explains that it is in celebration of Actaeon's destruction that Cynthia ('Phoebe and Cynthia being both names of Diana', as Spenser reminds us)[45] has ordered the revels: 'The Huntresse, and Queene of these groves, DIANA (in regard of some black and envious slanders hourely breath'd against her, for her divine justice on ACTEON, as shee pretends) hath here in the vale of Gargaphy, proclaim'd a solemne revells' (I. i. 91–5). This demands to be read as a topical allegory: the Queen will reassert her power and benevolence in order to stem the tide of discontent in the wake of the Earl of Essex's fall from grace. The context of this is the fact that the play was performed in the tense period between Essex's banishment to his house in 1600 and his attempted *coup d'état* in 1601. Actaeon peeping at the naked Diana thus becomes a representation of the Essex who, on his return from Ireland in 1599, had burst into the Queen's chamber in his riding-habit (Actaeon's dress) while she had 'her hair about her face'. The moment was 'as near an approach as an Elizabethan mortal was likely to make to gazing on "Cynthia's naked loveliness"'.[46] In the fifth act, Cynthia becomes Elizabeth, justifying her severity in

---

[45] 'A letter of the Author[']s . . . to . . . Sir Walter Raleigh', prefixed to *The Faerie Queene*.
[46] Herford and Simpson, in *Ben Jonson*, i. 395.

banishing Essex from the court. His Actaeon-like peep into her chamber was no small matter:

> Seemes it no crime, to enter sacred bowers,
> And hallowed places, with impure aspect,
> Most lewdly to pollute? Seemes it no crime,
> To brave a *deitie*?
>
> (v. xi. 19–22)

The full political force of the Actaeon myth in the Renaissance may be discerned from Sandys's commentary on Book Three: 'But this fable was invented to shew us how dangerous a curiosity it is to search into the secrets of Princes, or by chance to discover their nakednesse: who thereby incurring their hatred, ever after live the life of a Hart, full of feare and suspicion.' [47] Sandys then makes a crucial move from the fate of Actaeon to that of Ovid himself: 'Some such unhappy discovery procured the banishment of our *Ovid*.' In making the link between the myth and the poet's own transgression—the scandal ('error'), whatever it was, impinging upon the royal household— Sandys is following the precedent of Ovid himself. Inserted in the commentary on the *Metamorphoses* at this point is a translation of a passage from the *Tristia* written during Ovid's exile. It is the same passage as that cited by Thomas Watson in the headnote to 'Actaeon lost in middle of his sport':

> Why had I sight to make mine eye my foe?
> Or why did I unsought-for secrets knowe?
> *Actaeon* naked *Dian* unaware
> So saw; and so his hounds their master tare.
> The Gods sure punish fortune for offence:
> Nor, when displeased, will with chance dispence.
>
> (*Trist.* ii. 103–8, trans. Sandys)

'Guard we therefore our eyes; nor desire to see, or knowe more then concernes us: or at least dissemble the discovery', Sandys concludes from this, citing the case of Julius Montanus, put to death after meeting the emperor Nero in the dark.

But the Renaissance mythologist is driven by a restless desire to adduce multiple interpretations: 'But why may not this fable receave a double construction? Those being the best that admit of most

---

[47] *Ovid's Metamorphosis Englished*, 100. Subsequent quotations from Sandys in this and next paragraphs are from the same page.

senses.' In the case of Actaeon, the text of the *Metamorphoses* itself invites double construction, since Ovid ends the tale with its audience arguing about how to interpret it:

> Much muttring was upon this fact. Some thought there was extended
> A great deale more extremitie than neded. Some commended
> *Dianas* doing: saying that it was but worthely
> For safegarde of hir womanhod. Eche partie did applie
> Good reasons to defende their case.
>
> (Golding, iii. 305–9)

Sandys accordingly reads the story of Actaeon in a variety of ways. '*Actaeon*, neglecting the pursuite of virtue and heroicall actions, puts off the minde of a man, and degenerates into a beast': this offers the traditional moralization to which so many of Ovid's stories were submitted. But then the hounds who destroy Actaeon are 'ravenous and riotous sycophants: who have often exhausted the Exchequors of opulent Princes, and reduced them to extreame necessity': here Sandys introduces a distinctive twist on the political reading. Read morally, Actaeon is a general representation of illicit sexual desire; read politically, he is a specific representation of both the over-ambitious courtier and the over-opulent Prince.

But Shakespeare does not politicize the Actaeon story in the manner of Jonson or Sandys. Consider the play to which the figure of Actaeon is especially relevant, *The Merry Wives of Windsor*. With its clear allusion to the ceremonies associated with the Order of the Garter, this, if any, is a Shakespearian comedy with opportunities for myth to be read topically. But the opportunity is not taken. When Falstaff wears the horns, Actaeon is made to coalesce not with the contemporary court but with folk culture, with the native tradition of Herne the Hunter and the ritual mockeries of the mummers' play.[48] And the primary reading demanded by the play's allusions to Actaeon, both verbal and visual, is the traditional moralization in terms of self-destructive male sexual desire. His hart's horns come to symbolize cuckoldry. Pistol proposes this reading as a way of stirring the obsessively jealous Ford:

---

[48] On the fusion of classical and folk motifs, see François Laroque, 'Ovidian Transformations and Folk Festivities in *A Midsummer Night's Dream*, *The Merry Wives of Windsor* and *As You Like It*', *Cahiers Elisabéthains*, xxv (1984), 23–36, and *Shakespeare's Festive World: Elizabethan Seasonal Entertainment and the Professional Stage*, trans. Janet Lloyd (Cambridge, 1991), 266–7, 382.

FORD. Love my wife?
PISTOL. With liver burning hot. Prevent,
  Or go thou like Sir Actaeon, he,
  With Ringwood at thy heels.
  O, odious is the name!
FORD. What name, sir.
PISTOL. The horn, I say. Farewell.
        (*Merry Wives*, II. i. 111–17)

The joke on Falstaff is that he is made to wear the horns of a cuckold without even having a wife in the first place. His entrance with a buck's head is the nearest Shakespeare comes to metamorphosing one of his characters into one of Ovid's. As John Steadman perceives in an excellent article, 'Except for one comic variation—Sir John's obesity—there is a point-by-point correspondence between his disguise as Herne the Hunter and the standard Renaissance picture of Actaeon as a composite figure with stag's head, human body, and hunter's clothing.'[49] Visually, Falstaff resembles Actaeon in the process of being metamorphosed; his pinching at the hands of the children dressed as fairies is a comic nemesis that playfully revises the savaging of Actaeon by his own hounds. The audience knows that Falstaff will not really suffer the fate of Actaeon: he has time to pull off his Windsor stag's head whilst a noise of hunting is heard within. The real hounds won't get him. In Shakespeare's most local comedy, it is sufficient for the sexual adventurer to be bruised and humiliated, for the myth of auto-destructive desire to be domesticated.

Falstaff does not, however, perceive himself as Actaeon. He has another precedent for his transformation into a stag, and this takes us back to the general, non-topical, sense in which the Ovidianism of Shakespeare's comedies is political.

The Windsor bell hath struck twelve; the minute draws on. Now the hot-blooded gods assist me! Remember, Jove, thou wast a bull for thy Europa; love set on thy horns. O powerful love, that in some respects makes a beast a man; in some other, a man a beast! You were also, Jupiter, a swan, for the love of Leda. O omnipotent love! How near the god drew to the complexion of a goose! A fault done first in the form of a beast—O Jove, a beastly fault!—and then another fault in the semblance of a fowl—think on't, Jove, a foul fault! When gods have hot backs, what shall poor men do?   (V. v. 1–13)

---

[49] John M. Steadman, 'Falstaff as Actaeon: A Dramatic Emblem', *SQ* xiv (1963), 230–44, repr. in his *Nature into Myth: Medieval and Renaissance Moral Symbols* (Pittsburgh, 1979), ch. 8 (p. 118).

Part of the joke is that the audience sees Falstaff's horns as Actaeon's, whereas he sees them as Jove's. But he is more like Jove than Actaeon in that the animal form is his chosen disguise, not a state he is forced into. As in Falstaff's monologues on honour and on sack at corresponding positions to this in the two parts of *Henry IV* (in each of three plays, he soliloquizes in the field before some sort of violent encounter), there is wisdom here as well as self-deception. Love disrupts degree: it may make a god or a man into a beast, but since in some respects it makes a beast a man, it may by implication make men godlike—consider Antony and Cleopatra's vision of their love. As the scene unfolds, Falstaff suffers indignity, but he is just in his claim that he is in venerable company: Jupiter, king of the gods, was drawn by his love for Leda to become a swan, and a swan is very nearly a goose. Dignity, the propriety of the great chain of being, could hardly be ruffled more comprehensively than that. Ovid, it may be noted, did in fact draw a goose to the complexion of a god, when the 'unicus anser' of Baucis and Philemon recognizes the divine presence before the humans do.[50]

'When gods have hot backs, what shall poor men do?' is one of Falstaff's great cries for human tolerance. It is comparable to 'If sack and sugar be a fault, God help the wicked! If to be old and merry be a sin, then many an old host that I know is damned' (*1 Henry IV*, II. v. 475–7). The context of the latter is the demand that plump Jack should not be banished, that room must be kept for the body, for misrule, for all that is in opposition to the values of the Lord Chief Justice. It is a deeply subversive demand, and one which Prince Hal knows he must reject if order is to be maintained in the state. But it is a demand which the spirit of comedy always makes. The Falstaffian voice coalesces here with the Ovidian. Hal's model is in a sense Virgil's *Aeneid*, which says that in the name of historical destiny and the establishment of a new imperial nation, love (Dido) must regretfully be rejected. Ovid replies to Virgil as Falstaff justifies himself in Windsor forest: how can you expect men to reject love when the gods do not? The comprehensive catalogue of divine promiscuity of which the *Metamorphoses* is comprised makes the philandering of Falstaff and even that of the *Ars Amatoria* look like chicken-feed—fowl matter not foul matter, as Falstaff would put it. 'When gods have hot backs, what

[50] Baucis and Philemon are about to kill their only goose and it flies to their visitors for protection; the latter then reveal themselves as Jupiter and Mercury (*Met.* viii. 684–90).

shall poor men do?': Authority has no answer to this question. So Ovid is banished, Falstaff is banished.

Banishment is a recurring motif in Shakespeare. Touchstone's association of exile with 'Ovid among the Goths' raises the question of whether other Shakespearian banishments are keyed to Ovid. The language of exile in the first act of *Richard II* seems to echo that of the *Tristia*, with its emphasis on 'frozen winters' spent in banishment and separation from the native tongue.[51] But, save for Falstaff's, the most celebrated banishment is Romeo's. And here the association with Ovid, at least in the mind of one contemporary, is decisive. In a scene in *Poetaster* (1601) which veers notoriously between lyricism and parody, Ben Jonson rewrote the parting of Romeo and Juliet in the form of the parting between Ovid and the emperor's daughter, Julia. The Renaissance tendency to read the *Amores* autobiographically reinforces the association: all the poems are assumed to be addressed to Corinna and Corinna is assumed to be Julia, so I. xiii, the prime source for the genre of aubade (the lover's complaint to the rising sun),[52] is read in the context of Ovid and Julia. It follows that, by entering into that genre, the dawn parting in *Romeo and Juliet* is asking to be read in the tradition of Ovid and Julia.

Jonson's Julia 'appeareth above, as at her chamber window'. She begins, 'Ovid? my love?', to which he replies, 'Here, heavenly Julia'. But he is below where she is above (as in the first balcony scene in *Romeo and Juliet*), a visualization of their separation in rank; she is thus led to the confusion of 'Here? and not here?'. A series of near-departures and returns climaxes in

> OVID. Yet Julia, if thou wilt,
> A little longer, stay. JULIA. I am content.
> OVID. O, mightie Ovid! what the sway of heaven
> Could not retire, my breath hath turned back.[53]

In *Richard II* it is the 'breath of kings' that banishes or revokes

---

[51] Compare, for instance, the 'Six frozen winters', 'frosty Caucasus', and 'December snow' of *Richard II*, I. iii. 204, 258, 261 with Ovid's 'longius hac nihil est, nisi tantum frigus et hostes, | et maris adstricto quae coit unda gelu' ('nothing is farther away than this land except only the cold and the enemy and the sea whose waters congeal with the frost'—*Tristia*, ii. 195–6). These associations are pursued by Jeremy Maule in an as yet unpublished paper, 'Banishing Ovid'.

[52] Donne's 'The Sunne Rising' is only the most famous of the many Renaissance imitations of this poem.

[53] Quotations from IV. ix.

banishment; here the breath of the poet momentarily transcends his political fate. But it is only a moment, for Ovid then goes into exile as punishment for the liaison with Julia and for staging a wanton mythological pageant before the eyes of Augustus Caesar.

Poetaster as a whole is a critique of what Jonson saw as two kinds of false poetry, and a defence of what he took to be the true moral and civic function of the art. Because of interest in the so-called 'war of the theatres' of the first years of the seventeenth century, criticism has attended primarily to the attack on the poetry of detraction associated with Marston and Dekker (represented as Crispinus and Demetrius).[54] The other sort of false poetry is that associated with Ovid. At the beginning of the play, the character of Ovid seems to represent true poetry. The action begins with him speaking the lines on immortality which conclude the first book of the *Amores*: 'Then, when this bodie falls in funerall fire, | My name shall live, and my best part aspire' (I. i. 1–2, translating I. xv. 41–2). A little later, he recites the whole of *Amores*, I. xv, in a translation which Jonson adapted from Marlowe's. Ovid defends the vocation of poetry against his father's desire that he should pursue a career in the law, and Jonson is clearly in sympathy with this defence, as he is with Lorenzo Junior's similar one in *Every Man in his Humour*. Unlike the lawyer, the poet is morally independent, seeking for fame not place: Ovid refuses to 'prostitute [his] voyce in everie cause' (I. i. 48). But the play argues that he goes wrong in following the path of love. A humanist education should lead to possession of the self, whereas Ovid loses himself in the labyrinth of love. He perverts the power of poetry by staging a sensual banquet which celebrates sexual desire instead of the *civis*—indeed, his show proposes that all hierarchies are overthrown by love and appears to conclude by advocating mass adultery. Poetry, says Augustus, should praise the gods and teach and eternize virtue, whereas Ovid, he proclaims, has profaned the gods and reduced virtue to something 'painted'. His kind of poetry is 'idle' and hence politically dangerous.

Jonson collapses the whole history of Augustan poetry into a single action. Once Ovid is exiled, Virgil is brought on as an example of the true poet who practises decorum and celebrates piety, honour, and the best traditions of Rome. A translation from the *Aeneid* pushes aside

---

[54] Though see Eugene M. Waith, 'The Poet's Morals in Jonson's *Poetaster*', *MLQ* xii (1951), 13–19, and James D. Mulvihill, 'Jonson's *Poetaster* and the Ovidian Debate', *SEL* xxii (1982), 239–55.

that from the *Amores* which began the play, replacing Ovid's assertion of the love-poet's immortality with an image of ill fame (many-tongued Rumour), a 'monster' who is as covetous 'of tales and lies' as she is 'prodigall of truth' (v. ii. 97–8, from *Aeneid*, iv. 188). The passage in question concerns Dido, the type of erotic love whom Virgil's Aeneas rejects in the name of his political destiny, but whom Ovid defended when he rewrote the most celebrated part of *The Aeneid* in *Heroides*, Letter 7. *Poetaster* as a whole thus follows the line of Sir Thomas Elyot in *The Governour*, that classic of political humanism: Virgil is the pre-eminent model, whereas Ovid is distinctly problematic, for there is little learning in him 'concerning either virtuous manners or policy', his *Amores* contain nothing 'but incitation to lechery', and time spent reading him would 'be better employed on such authors that do minister both eloquence, civil policy, and exhortation to virtue. Wherefore in his place let us bring in Horace, in whom is contained much variety of learning and quickness of sentence.'[55] For Jonson, the danger of Ovid and Catullus is that much of their work does not exhort to virtue in the manner of Horace and Virgil. It offers instead incitements to sexual vice—it is with the language of first Catullus and then the *Metamorphoses* that Volpone attempts to seduce and rape the chaste Celia.

Jonson's learned humanism assumes that ancient Rome provides *exempla* which are applicable to his own times. Given this, the attack on Ovid in *Poetaster* must also be an attack on 1590s Ovidianism, just as the arraignment of Crispinus is an indictment of Marston. Jonson's own position is clearly identified with the decorum of Horace and his ideal for the function of poetry is the Augustanism of Virgil. The latter has plausibly though not conclusively been identified with Chapman,[56] who was himself a notable critic of the erotic reading of Ovid which predominated in the 1590s. His continuation of Marlowe's *Hero and Leander* morally corrects the poem by introducing an allegory which argues that love must be sanctified by Ceremony.[57] And where most Ovidian poems indulge the senses—Shakespeare's Venus works through a banquet of seeing, hearing, touching,

---

[55] Elyot, *The Book named The Governor* (1531), ed. S. E. Lehmberg (London, 1962), 32, 47.

[56] See the discussion in Herford and Simpson, *Ben Jonson*, i. 433–5.

[57] For Chapman's continuation as a moralizing development, even a 'correction', of *Hero and Leander*, see D. J. Gordon's essay, 'The Renaissance Poet as Classicist', in his *The Renaissance Imagination*, ed. Stephen Orgel (Berkeley and Los Angeles, 1975), 102–33.

smelling, and tasting (433–45)—Chapman's *Ovids Banquet of Sence* demands to be read either as a transmutation of the Ovidian erotic into the higher mode of Neoplatonic spirituality or as an assault on Ovid and the 1590s Ovidians for not making such an ascent.[58] Jonson is in accord with Chapman, as his Horace is with his Virgil. The Ovid of *Poetaster* is initially identifiable as a poet like Marlowe, who rejected the career for which his Cambridge education had prepared him and gave himself over to erotic verse-making, beginning with a translation of the *Amores*. But relations between Jonson and Shakespeare's company were not good at this time, so, given the status of *Venus and Adonis* as a showpiece of erotic Ovidianism, the celebration of the Ovidian labyrinth of love in Shakespeare's comedies, and the clear correspondence between Ovid and Julia and *Romeo and Juliet*, there is a strong case for reading the character of Ovid as Jonson's composite representation of Marlowe and Shakespeare.

Even if absolute identifications are resisted, there can be no doubt that Shakespeare was a prime mover in the 1590s Ovidian tradition which *Poetaster* is rejecting. That rejection is at once moral, political, and aesthetic. The banquet of senses in the fourth act, devised by Ovid with Mercury as his master of the revels, destabilizes both the political and the moral order as both gods and royals are made fools of love. It offers a poetics of play, not of edification. Shakespearian comedy does the same. Traditional orders are re-established in the endings, but for the duration of the action a space has been opened up in which there is a free countenancing of the licentious apophthegm with which Ovid departs from the action of *Poetaster* at the end of the balcony scene: 'The truest wisdom silly men can have, | Is dotage, on the follies of their flesh.'

---

[58] See Frank Kermode, 'The Banquet of Sense', in his *Shakespeare, Spenser, Donne: Renaissance Essays* (London, 1971), and Raymond B. Waddington, *The Mind's Empire: Myth and Form in George Chapman's Narrative Poems* (Baltimore, 1974). Waddington sees the poem as a development of *The Shadow of Night*, in which 'Chapman publicly takes sides against the vogue for the erotic Ovidian poem, seemingly epitomized for him by *Venus and Adonis* [the reference here is to what seems to be a slighting allusion to that poem's epigraph in 'Hymnus in Cynthiam'], and darkly proclaims his allegiance to the Ovid of the allegorized *Metamorphoses*' (p. 113).

5

Tragedy and Metamorphosis

Only then, when passion or suffering become too big for utterance, the wisdom of ancient art has borrowed a feature from tranquillity, though not its air. For every being seized by an enormous passion, be it joy or grief, or fear sunk to despair, loses the character of its own individual expression, and is absorbed by the power of the feature that attracts it. Niobe and her family are assimilated by extreme anguish . . . Clytia, Biblis, Salmacis, Narcissus, tell only the resistless power of sympathetic attraction.[1]

I

Save in the case of *Titus Andronicus*, modern criticism has attended more to the Ovidianism of Shakespeare's comedies than that of his tragedies. One reason for this is the particular association, discussed in the last chapter, between the *Metamorphoses* and the Golden Age, with its primal examples of many of Shakespearian comedy's key materials—the forest, the springtime, leisure, youth, and love. But Ovid described the Age of Iron too, and the language in which he did so opens on to the world of Shakespeare's tragedies. In the words of Golding's translation, in lines that are immediately preceded by a Timon-like reference to the divisive power of 'yellow golde' dug from the ground:

Men live by ravine and by stelth: the wandring guest doth stand
In daunger of his host: the host in daunger of his guest:
And fathers of their sonne in laws: yea seldome time doth rest
Betweene borne brothers such accord and love as ought to bee,
The goodman seekes the goodwives death, and his againe seekes shee.
The stepdames fell their husbands sonnes with poyson do assayle.

[1] Johann Heinrich Fuseli, lecture 5 of 1805, in *Lectures on Painting, by the Royal Academicians. Barry, Opie, and Fuseli* (London, 1848), 470.

To see their fathers live so long the children doe bewayle.
All godlynesse lyes under foote. And Ladie *Astrey* last
Of heavenly vertues from this earth in slaughter drownèd past.
(Golding, i. 162–70)

This famous passage is the source of the tag 'Terras Astraea reliquit', quoted in *Titus Andronicus* in the original Latin (IV. iii. 4). The tag is cited without any suggestion of allusion to Queen Elizabeth as the returned Astraea: as with his non-topical use of Actaeon, Shakespeare eschews the kind of direct contemporary political allegory that was practised by so many of his contemporaries, most notably Spenser.[2] The Age of Iron is made instead into the archetype of the time of tragedy, that in which justice has fled the earth. It is characterized by the breaking of sacred bonds—the bonds between host and guest, as in *Macbeth*, and above all those within the family. The divisions between kin described here are analogous to those of which Gloucester complains in the second scene of *Lear*; children tiring of seeing their fathers live so long are especially relevant to that play (as in Edmund's 'I begin to find an idle and fond bondage in the oppression of aged tyranny' in his forged letter—I. ii. 50–1). The correspondence is made explicit in *The True Chronicle Historie of King Leir*: 'Oh yron age! O times! O monstrous, vilde, | When parents are contemned of the child!'[3]

A sense of the relation between tragedy and the latter two of Ovid's four ages is reinforced by Heywood's *Age* plays: the *Golden* and *Silver* ages are concerned with the loves of the gods, while the *Brazen Age* includes such stories as 'The Tragedy of Meleager' and 'The Tragedy of Jason and Medea', and the two parts of *The Iron Age* tell the tragic story of Troy. The movement from comedy to tragedy may be conceived as a decline from the Golden Age through the Brazen to the Iron. All Shakespeare's works are to varying degrees tragicomedies, and his Ovidianism is complicit with this generic instability. The Ovidian tragedy of Pyramus and Thisbe is not only a play within the comedy of *A Midsummer Night's Dream*, it is also a precedent for the tragedy of Romeo and Juliet, as George Pettie saw in 1576, some twenty years before the play was written: 'such presiness [oppressiveness] of parents brought Pyramus and Thisbe to a woful end, Romeo

---

[2] On Elizabeth as Astraea, see Frances A. Yates, *Astraea: The Imperial Theme in the Sixteenth Century* (1975; repr. Harmondsworth, 1977), 29–87.

[3] ll. 761–2, Bullough, vii. 355–6. The exclamation combines the Iron Age with Cicero's much-cited tag, 'O tempora! O mores!'.

and Julietta to untimely death'.[4] Shakespeare may have been attracted to Arthur Brooke's *Tragicall Historye of Romeus and Juliet* partly because it translated into a modern setting the Pyramus and Thisbe plot in which lovers are divided by parental resistance to their union, the male partner makes the tragic mistake of thinking his beloved is dead and consequently takes his own life, and the woman is left to return or awake only to take her own life. Like Ovid's tales, Shakespeare's comedies never lose sight of the painfulness and the potential for the grotesque or for disaster wrought by love's changes; so it is that what Heywood called 'The Tragedy of Jason and Medea' is, as I have shown, a darkening point of reference in *The Merchant of Venice*. If part of the Ovidianism of the comedies is their potential for violence and tragedy, it would seem logical to expect that Ovidianism to be developed in the tragedies.

If *Titus* is recognized as one of Shakespeare's most characteristic plays, rather than dismissed as a juvenile aberration, it becomes much easier to see the tragedies as well as the comedies as metamorphic. This chapter will argue that the technique used so extensively in *Titus* of invoking mythological precedents as patterns for tragic structures is sustained throughout Shakespeare's career, with the difference that what was a prominently flaunted mode of composition in the early play became a more inwoven practice in the later ones.

In Chapter 1 I argued that the Phaëthon story provided a pattern for the falls of both Gaveston and Edward II in Marlowe's history play. Shakespeare's *Tragedy of King Richard the Second* closely resembles *Edward II*, with its weak king and his favourites, its deposition, imprisonment, and regicide, its sense of the king's struggle to find an identity once he has been stripped of his crown. It was perhaps from Marlowe, then, that Shakespeare saw the value of an allusion to Phaëthon in such a play. At the centre of the tragedy, in the scene set at Flint Castle, Richard stands on the walls (in the theatrical 'above' space) and accepts the inevitability of his fall from the throne:

> What must the King do now? Must he submit?
> The King shall do it. Must he be deposed?
> The King shall be contented. Must he lose
> The name of King? A God's name, let it go.
>
> (III. iii. 142–5)

---

[4] *A Petite Pallace of Pettie his Pleasure* (1576), quoted from Bullough, i. 374.

Northumberland summons him down with the words, 'My lord, in the base court he doth attend | To speak with you. May it please you to come down?' (175–6). The King replies,

> Down, down, I come like glist'ring Phaethon,
> Wanting the manage of unruly jades.
> In the base court: base court where kings grown base
> To come at traitors' calls, and do them grace.
>
> (III. iii. 177–80)

He exits, reappears below, and symbolically hands power over to Bolingbroke, anticipating the formal deposition two scenes later. The fall of Phaëthon thus serves as a mythological precedent for the *abase*ment of Richard, which is visually enacted in his move from the above space to below.

For the theatregoer or reader who knows the Phaëthon story and its standard sixteenth-century interpretations, a number of associations suggest themselves. Golding moralized the fable in terms of 'ambition blynd, and youthfull wilfulnesse': in his prison cell, Richard is led to reflect upon 'Thoughts tending to ambition' (v. v. 18) and their ultimate vanity; as for youth and wilfulness, lack of maturity is apparent in the king's choice of follower. Golding's moralization continues, 'The end whereof is miserie, and bringeth at the last | Repentance when it is to late that all redresse is past' (Epistle, 73–4): Shakespeare's play replicates the pattern of a movement towards misery, but has a characteristic shift of emphasis from moral judgement to psychological insight—it is not so much repentance to which Richard comes too late as knowledge of the restlessness of his own and all men's condition,

> But whate'er I be,
> Nor I, nor any man that but man is,
> With nothing shall be pleased till he be eased
> With being nothing.
>
> (v. v. 38–41)

Both Richard's language and the appeal to a mythological archetype invite the audience to universalize his tragedy, to read it in terms of what Vives called 'the essential nature of human beings'. Such a pull towards the universal has, of course, been a source of the endurance of Shakespearian tragedy.

But the Phaëthon myth was also given a more grounded and

political interpretation in the sixteenth century, and this is equally applicable to the play. According to Golding, the story shows 'how the weaknesse and the want of wit in magistrate | Confoundeth both his common weale and eeke his owne estate' (Epistle, 75–6). In the moralization of Sabinus, Phaëthon is the rash and ambitious young prince ('ambitiosi & temerarii Principis') and the horses are the common people ('per equos ipsum vulgus') who, when they are given a free rein or promoted into high office ('in officio'), go out of control and bring chaos to the body politic. As Sandys puts it, in a sentence translated from Sabinus: 'The Horses of the Sun are the common people; unruly, fierce, and prone to innovation: who finding the weaknesse of their Prince, fly out into all exorbitancies to a generall confusion.'[5] In the scene immediately after the one in which Richard makes himself into Phaëthon, the confounding into chaos of the commonwealth as a result of the king's weakness and his unwise choice of deputy (those 'caterpillars of the commonwealth' Bushy, Bagot, and Green) is emblematized in the image of the overgrown garden. One effect of the allusion to Phaëthon may therefore have been to contribute to the process whereby the play became more politically dangerous than Shakespeare intended it to be. It could be that he made the reference in order to universalize the fall of Richard, but the availability of an interpretation of it in terms of the government of the commonweal facilitated a contemporary application: Richard/Phaëthon thus becomes Queen Elizabeth, with her reputation for vacillation, and the deposition is seized upon by the Essex faction, who commission a performance of the play on the eve of their attempted *coup d'état*.

The Renaissance tradition of multiple interpretation means that the two readings of the allusion to Phaëthon—what would then have been called the moral and the historical, what we might now call the universalizing and the political—are not mutually exclusive. Phaëthon's inability to manage his 'unruly jades', as Richard describes them in language that is also Golding's, is at one and the same time a universally applicable emblem for loss of control of the passions and a politically specific figuration of the reins of power, in so far as the horses drive the chariot of the sun and the sun is an emblem of the monarch. Even within the historical interpretation there are several different strands: if we follow Golding's reading of Phaëthon,

---

[5] Sandys, *Ovid's Metamorphosis Englished*, 67. Georgius Sabinus, *Metamorphosis seu Fabulae Poeticae* (Wittenburg, 1555, quoted from edn. of Frankfurt, 1589), 55–7.

the play becomes an apology for strong government, but if we follow Sandys's, it becomes an appeal for rulers not to be arbitrary but to attend to wise counsellors: 'In that [he is] rash and unexperienced, he is said to be a boy, and refractory to counsell (with out which, Power is her owne destruction) and therefore altogether unfit for government, which requires mature advice.'[6] The allusion does not pin Shakespeare down, rather it opens up multiple possibilities.[7] Doubtless the Essex faction would have gone with the reading in terms of strong government, but according to Golding the most important thing about the fall of Phaëthon was that it was a negative example which 'dooth commende the meane' (Epistle, 79). Ironically, Essex himself became a Phaëthon by aspiring too high—here it may be recalled that it is not only Richard II and Edward II but also Gaveston who is figured as the ill-fated charioteer. Shakespeare himself seems to push the play in the direction of commending the mean by critiquing both the ineffectual rule of Richard and the Machiavellian drive of Bolingbroke.

The problem with the mean is that it is not very exciting dramatically. The play is most interested in exploring and seeking to make its audience feel what it would be like to be Richard, to be Phaëthon, tumbling in free fall. As so often, Shakespeare bypasses the moralizing tradition and returns to Ovid himself, who drives the original narrative with Phaëthon's energy and recklessness. The tale is a pattern for early Shakespearian tragedy because it shows how quick bright things come to confusion.

Ovid's classical horses of the sun run wild with the same abandon as those of the vernacular Queen Mab who, according to Mercutio in *Romeo and Juliet*, 'gallops night by night | Through lovers' brains'.[8] They cannot be stopped. When Friar Laurence enters at dawn (or is it when Romeo exits at dawn?), 'fleckled darkness like a drunkard reels | From forth day's path and Titan's fiery wheels' (II. ii. 3–4): one senses that the driver is not to be trusted here, for the drunkard only

[6] Sandys, *Ovid's Metamorphosis Englished*, 67.

[7] It thus leaves room for both my reading here and the rather different interpretation of Robert P. Merrix, who reads Richard's search for identity in relation to Phaëthon's search for his father: 'The Phaëton Allusion in *Richard II*: The Search for Identity', *ELR* xvii (1987), 277–87. On Richard's narcissistic identity in relation to Ovid's Narcissus, see A. D. Nuttall's elegant 'Ovid's Narcissus and Shakespeare's Richard II: The Reflected Self', in *Ovid Renewed: Ovidian Influences on Literature and Art from the Middle Ages to the Twentieth Century*, ed. Charles Martindale (Cambridge, 1988), 137–50.

[8] *Romeo and Juliet*, I. iv. 71–2. Mab's driver is a 'waggoner' (I. iv.65), Golding's word for Phaëthon.

narrowly escapes being run over. It seems to be Phaëthon at the wheel, streaking headlong to disaster. A few hours later, at nine in the morning, Juliet observes 'the sun upon the highmost hill of this day's journey' (II. iv. 9–10): from this point on, its motion—and with it that of the play—can only be downward like Phaëthon's.[9] By midday the temperature is fiercely hot, as if in repetition of the conflagration which occurs when the horses of the sun finally hit the earth. By evening, Juliet is willing the horses to run faster, the language learnt from Marlowe's *Edward II*:

> Gallop apace, you fiery-footed steeds,
> Towards Phoebus' lodging. Such a waggoner
> As Phaëton would whip you to the west
> And bring in cloudy night immediately.
>
> (III. ii. 1–4)

(Both 'fiery-footed' for the steeds and 'waggoner' for Phaëthon are taken from Golding.)[10] The dramatic irony of the allusion is intense. Juliet invokes Phaëthon because she thinks that he could quicken the pace of the sun and thus hurry time on to 'love-performing night'. The irony is that in willing on the night, she is willing on the tragedy, the moment of separation, Romeo's exile, and ultimately the confusion and mistiming which bring the death of both lovers. The audience sees, as the character does not, that to put Phaëthon in charge is to precipitate the catastrophe. The network of secondary allusions supporting Juliet's apostrophe is brought to completion at the very end of the play when the Prince begins the final speech, 'A glooming peace this morning with it brings: | The sun for sorrow will not show his head' (v. iii. 304–5), an image paralleling the aftermath of the fall of Phaëthon: 'And if it be to be beleved, as bruted is by fame, | A day did passe without the Sunne' (Golding, ii. 418–19).

But there is an important difference in the endings: where Phaëthon falls like a shooting star (as does Richard),[11] Juliet, in the soliloquy which begins 'Gallop apace', imagines raising Romeo to the

---

[9] In the note on these lines in his 1980 Arden edn., Brian Gibbons aptly cites Golding's translation of the equivalent moment in the Phaëthon story: 'the morning way | Lyes steepe upright, so that the steedes . . . have much adoe to climbe against the Hyll' (ii. 84–6).

[10] Golding, ii. 491, 394.

[11] 'But *Phaeton* . . . Shot headlong downe . . . Like to [a] Starre in Winter nightes' (Golding, ii. 404–6); 'Ah Richard! . . . I see thy glory, like a shooting star, | Fall to the base earth from the firmament' (*Richard II*, II. iv. 18–20, 'base' anticipating the language of the speech in which the king alludes to Phaëthon).

stars, in the manner of the apotheosis of Julius Caesar in Book Fifteen
of the *Metamorphoses*: 'Give me my Romeo, and when I shall
die | Take him and cut him out in little stars' (III. ii. 21–2). And
where Phaëthon is memorialized only in an epitaph inscribed upon
the stone which covers his smouldering body, Romeo and Juliet are to
be immortalized in the form of golden statues. In this symbolic
transformation, which secures the reunion of the divided households,
they are granted the sort of metamorphic release which Ovid usually
gives his characters but, exceptionally, denies to Phaëthon.

Shakespeare thus reverses the metamorphic Ovid. *Romeo and Juliet*
is also notable for a revision of the amorous Ovid. Whilst *The Taming of
the Shrew* shows how the *Ars Amatoria* may be a textual end to sexual
conquest, *Romeo and Juliet* turns one of that poem's precepts to
troubled account in Juliet's recognition of the perils inherent in the
articulation of love:

> Dost thou love me? I know thou wilt say 'Ay',
> And I will take thy word. Yet if thou swear'st
> Thou mayst prove false. At lovers' perjuries,
> They say, Jove laughs. O gentle Romeo,
> If thou dost love, pronounce it faithfully;
> Or if thou think'st I am too quickly won,
> I'll frown, and be perverse, and say thee nay,
> So thou wilt woo; but else, not for the world.
>
> (II. i. 132–9)

'At lovers' perjuries, | They say, Jove laughs.' In his translation of the
Ars Amatoria Thomas Heywood rendered the relevant image in
language very close to, possibly even borrowed from, that of *Romeo
and Juliet*: 'For *Jove* himself sits in the azure skies, | And laughs below
at Lovers perjuries'.[12] But the distance between the Ovidian and the
Shakespearian contexts of the laughing Jupiter is considerable. The
poet of the *Ars* is at his most cynical:

> Nec timide promitte: trahunt promissa puellas;
>   Pollicito testes quoslibet adde deos.
> Iuppiter ex alto periuria ridet amantum,
>   Et iubet Aeolios inrita ferre notos.

---

[12] *Ovid De Arte Amandi*, trans. Heywood (1682 edn.), 27. The translation is a fairly
obvious one and the line was well known, so the similarity of phrasing may be
coincidental, but it is noteworthy that where Ovid has 'Iuppiter' both Shakespeare and
Heywood choose 'Jove'. Heywood's trans. was probably made a few years after *Romeo
and Juliet*.

Per Styga Iunoni falsum iurare solebat
Iuppiter; exemplo nunc favet ipse suo.
Expedit esse deos, et, ut expedit, esse putemus.
                                    (*Ars Am.* i. 631–7)

Nor be timid in your promises; by promises girls are caught; call as witnesses
to your promise what gods you please. Jupiter from on high laughs at the
perjuries of lovers, and bids the winds of Aeolus carry them unfulfilled away.
Jupiter would swear falsely by Styx to Juno; now he favours his own example.
It is expedient that there should be gods, and, since it is expedient, we do deem
that gods exist.

The last line—to Renaissance eyes a Machiavellian proposition—is
the sort of startling claim which makes it comprehensible that the
writing of the *Ars* was one reason for Ovid's exile. The passage as a
whole has no interest in honesty in human relations ('deceive
women, for they're mostly deceivers themselves', Ovid continues) and
is as irreverent as the *Metamorphoses* in its acknowledgement of
Jupiter's perjuries and infidelities. Jupiter laughs because he knows
that he and everyone else are deceivers ever. Stylish, even jokey, as
the mode of expression may be, the reader is left with a distinctly sour
after-taste. Roman sexual mores are made to seem as self-serving as
imperial political strategies become in the *Annals* of Tacitus.

In Juliet's speech, on the other hand, the laugh is alluded to as part
of an attempt to elicit a 'true-love' language that is not dependent on
the formalization of an oath. Jove knows, she is saying, that human
beings are frail, and so to swear an oath is to court the breaking of it. It
is not a laugh of complicity, as in Ovid, but one of superiority. 'Do not
swear', Juliet says three times; especially do not swear 'by the moon,
th'inconstant moon | That monthly changes in her circled orb, | Lest
that thy love prove likewise variable' (II. i. 151–3). But love still has
to be mediated through language and thus remains painfully prone to
misinterpretation: hence 'Or if thou think'st I am too quickly
won, | I'll frown, and be perverse, and say thee nay'. For the speaker
of the *Ars*, language is an instrument of power; like Jupiter, he can get
what he wants by means of perjury. For Juliet, language is a trap.
Earlier in the scene she has been overheard pouring out her 'true-love
passion' (II. i. 146). Now she is in a bind: having acknowledged her
desire she cannot return to the reserved ('strange') and ultimately
false language of 'form' and 'compliment',[13] but by not doing so she

---

[13] 'Fain would I dwell on form . . . but farewell, compliment. . . . I'll prove more
true | Than those that have more cunning to be strange' (II. i. 130–1, 142–3).

runs the risk of seeming fast, 'too quickly won'. The Ovidian voice is supremely in control—to such an extent that it can produce the line about believing in the gods because it is expedient to do so (they are there to be invoked as precedents for one's own betrayals)—whereas Juliet is supremely out of control, because she is in love for the first time and because she is a woman who is culturally deprived of the right to give voice to her passion, on pain of being considered a whore. She is confused, her syntax stops and starts, whereas the speaker of the *Ars* is urbane and self-confident, free to play with words ('fallite fallentes': 'deceive the deceivers', i. 645). The reanimation of the Ovidian phrase in a context so antithetic to that of its source is an extreme example of what Thomas Greene calls 'dialectical' imitation. To hold the two contexts together is to be confronted with cultural difference: in form, the difference between the register of mock-didactic Augustan elegiacs and that of Elizabethan tragedy; in tenor, the difference between unashamed male desire and a recognition that women have traditionally been denied the language of desire because they have been constructed as the desired.

Juliet is trapped not only by woman's traditional passivity in love, but also by her father's will. She alludes to her concomitant linguistic imprisonment at the end of the first balcony scene:

> Bondage is hoarse, and may not speak aloud,
> Else would I tear the cave where Echo lies,
> And make her airy tongue more hoarse than mine
> With repetition of my Romeo's name. Romeo!
>
> (II. i. 205–8)

But in the very act of speaking thus, she overcomes her bondage. Unlike the conventionally silent woman, she speaks aloud; and, as Echo cannot, she initiates a further dialogue with her beloved. In a wonderful touch, she speaks her Romeo's name and the echo comes back, 'Romeo!'. She has become her own Echo, symbolically liberating both herself and her mythical antetype. Her liberation is short-lived, but the play's final couplet gives endurance to the transference by which she possesses rather than is possessed by her lover, as '*my* Romeo's name' is reiterated in 'For never was a story of more woe | Than this of Juliet and *her* Romeo'.[14]

---

[14] v. iii. 308–9. The closing line should not be dismissed as a convenient rhyme: the rhyme with 'woe' would still have been possible with, say, 'loved by Romeo'. Throughout the play, Juliet takes possession of Romeo's name far more often than vice versa.

II

Lavinia's nephew learns from his study of Ovid that 'Hecuba of Troy | Ran mad for sorrow' (*Titus*, IV. i. 20–1). His grandfather, who has a choice library, has said 'full oft' that 'Extremity of griefs would make men mad' (IV. i. 19). The *Metamorphoses* offered a vast repertory of tales in which extremity of suffering or desire brings about transformation. As was seen in Chapter 1, Shakespeare and his audience inherited a tradition centuries long in which Ovid's literal transformations were interpreted as metaphors for the internal changes effected by emotional and behavioural extremity. In the words of Georgius Sabinus in the prefatory material to his widely used 1555 edition,

Titulus inscribitur Metamorphosis, hoc est, transformatio. Finguntur enim hic conuerti ex hominibus in belluas, qui in hominis figura belluae immanitatem gerunt: quales sunt ebriosi, libidinosi, violenti & similes, quorum appetitus rectae rationi minime obtemperat.

The title is Metamorphosis, that is, transformation. For here are represented those who have changed from men into beasts, who bear the barbarity of the beast in the figure of man: such are the drunken, the libidinous, the violent and similar, whose appetite submits minimally to right reason.[15]

'Extremity of griefs would make men mad': the idea is relevant not only to Hecuba in the *Metamorphoses*, to Titus and Lavinia, but also to the various kinds of madness suffered by Hamlet, Othello, and Lear. Although direct allusions to Ovidian mythological material became less frequent in Shakespeare's Jacobean tragedies, perhaps because he no longer felt it necessary to display his literacy as he had done in *Titus*, and to a lesser extent *Richard II* and *Romeo and Juliet*, the notion of internal metamorphosis remained pivotal.

Othello hinges on the metamorphosis of the hero at the hands of Iago. 'These Moors are changeable', Iago informs Roderigo early on (I. iii. 346); 'The Moor already changes with my poison', he says in the interlude between the two central encounters in the great temptation scene (III. iii. 329). The deceitful language with which he convinces Othello that Desdemona has been unfaithful acts as a verbal equivalent to the poisonous shirt of Nessus with which Deianira is deceived into destroying another great martial hero, Hercules, after he has been unfaithful. I make this connection—an

---

[15] *Metamorphosis seu fabulae poeticae*, sig.) (8ᵛ (my translation).

affinity, not an allusion—because the shirt of Nessus has similar properties to the handkerchief: it is a charmed object that is supposed to subdue the partner entirely to the love of the person who gives it (cf. *Othello*, III. iv. 58–60) but in fact becomes the mechanism through which the lovers are destroyed.

The play's recurring images of monstrous birth and bestial transformation are also Ovidian. Sabinus read the *Metamorphoses* in terms of the animal in man; the play uses a sustained language of bestiality. In Sabinus' list of destructively metamorphic vices ('ebriosi, libidinosi, violenti'), drunkenness may seem the mildest, but Cassio knows that after he has been inveigled into drunkenness 'what remains is bestial', and that in getting drunk we 'with joy, pleasance, revel, and applause transform ourselves into beasts' (II. iii. 258, 285–6). He becomes the ass which is concealed in the middle of his name.[16] Iago's devilish skill is to transform the civilized Cassio into one of the 'ebriosi', and the noble Othello into one of the 'violenti' by persuading him that his wife is among the 'libidinosi'. His success in doing so owes much to the way in which he plays perniciously on the prejudice that merely through being a Moor Othello is already close to being a beast: 'you'll have your daughter covered with a Barbary horse, you'll have your nephews neigh to you, you'll have coursers for cousins and jennets for germans' (I. i. 113–15). In the temptation scene he infects Othello with the same kind of language: 'Exchange me for a goat', 'I had rather be a toad' (III. iii. 184, 274). By the end of the scene, the transformation has been effected and Othello is threatening to behave like a beast: 'I'll tear her all to pieces' (III. iii. 436). When he blows away his love and calls for vengeance to rise, he is dramatizing his internal metamorphosis.

Shakespearian tragedy makes universal claims for the personal and social transformations it stages. For Ovid, the primary universal metamorphosis was that from chaos into order with which the world— and his poem—began. In the beginning there was 'a huge rude heape' ('rudis indigestaque moles')[17] named Chaos and all things were 'at strife among themselves for want of order due' (Golding, i. 7–9). God and Nature then create order, separating heaven and earth, land

---

[16] See Anne Barton, *The Names of Comedy* (Oxford and Toronto, 1990), 124.

[17] *Met.* i. 7, applied by Shakespeare to Crookback Richard: 'foul indigested lump', 'an indigested and deformed lump' (2 *Henry VI*, v. i. 155, 3 *Henry VI*, v. vi. 51). Salisbury's lines to Prince Henry at the end of *King John*, 'you are born | To set a form upon that indigest | Which he hath left so shapeless and so rude' (v. vii. 25–7), give a political inflexion to Ovid's originary image: the young Henry III will bring order out of

and sea. Tragedy is universalized by being imagined as a breakdown of this order, a return to primal chaos. So it is that immediately before Iago begins his work of destructive change in the temptation scene Othello speaks after the parting Desdemona, 'But I do love thee, and when I love thee not, | Chaos is come again' (III. iii. 91–2). This becomes a terrible prophecy, for when he is turned to a monster within, it is as if Chaos has come again.

Shakespeare, then, works intensively with the Ovidian idea of raw emotion, engendered chiefly by sexual desires and fears, reducing man to the level of the beast. When Othello demands that Iago give him 'ocular proof' of Desdemona's infidelity, he says that if he does not, Iago 'hadst been better have been born a dog | Than answer my waked wrath' (III. iii. 367–8). This is based on a passage in the play's source, 'If you do not make me see with my own eyes what you have told me, be assured, I shall make you realize that it would have been better for you had you been born dumb',[18] but the change from the vague 'been born dumb' to the specific 'born a dog' produces one of a number of associations between Iago and a dog which may have an Ovidian provenance. The pattern of images culminates in Lodovico's 'O Spartan dog' (v. ii. 371). Why 'Spartan'? The New Cambridge editor notes that 'Spartan dogs were, according to Seneca's *Hippolytus* (trans. J. Studley, 1581), "eager of prey"',[19] an association that would tie in with Lodovico's ensuing line, 'More fell than anguish, hunger, or the sea'. But Iago is not merely eager of prey; he is treacherous. When Shakespeare had wanted a dog a few years earlier in *The Merry Wives of Windsor*, he had remembered Actaeon 'With Ringwood at [his] heels' in Golding's Ovid.[20] At the head of the list of Actaeon's dogs was Melampus, described by Ovid as 'Spartana gente'—'Blackfoote of Spart', as Golding has it.[21] Contemporaneously with *Othello*, Ben Jonson assumed that Spartan dogs were Actaeon's: 'Better not ACTAEON had . . . The dog of *Sparta* breed, and good, | As

the Chaos of John's troublesome reign. The juxtaposition of 'monsters and things indigest' in Sonnet 114 supports the association between Chaos and Ovidian monstrosity in the mind of Othello.

[18] Cinthio, *Gli Hecatommithi*, in Bullough, vii. 246.

[19] *Othello*, ed. Norman Sanders (Cambridge, 1984), 186.

[20] *Merry Wives*, II. i. 114; cf. Golding, iii. 270.

[21] *Met.* iii. 206–8; Golding, iii. 245–7. Ovid's Actaeon is almost certainly the source for Theseus' 'My hounds are bred out of the Spartan kind' (*Midsummer Night's Dream*, IV. i. 118), *pace* Harold Brooks's claims for Seneca's *Hippolytus* in his Arden edn., p. 94. John Harington linked Melampus and Ringwood in *The Metamorphosis of Ajax* (1596; ed. Elizabeth Story Donno, London, 1962), 110: 'in comes Melampus, or Ringwood'.

can ring within a wood'.[22] I do not want to overstretch the idea of Iago as Blackfoot, but I do think that 'Spartan dog' is supposed to suggest the foremost of Actaeon's dogs who destroy their own master— George Sandys referred in his commentary on Book Three of the *Metamorphoses* to servants who become traitors and 'inflict on their masters the fate of *Actaeon*'.[23]

Actaeon stands for all who are destroyed by sexuality. As was seen in *The Merry Wives*, his horns may easily stand for those of the cuckold. The identification is readily made even in a consciously unclassical, 'lowbrow' piece of writing like Thomas Deloney's *Jack of Newbury*: 'A maiden faire I dare not wed, | For feare to have *Acteons* head'.[24] Othello's 'A hornèd man's a monster and a beast' (IV. i. 60) is thus not only a conventional reference to cuckoldry, but also another figure of bestial metamorphosis. Characters in the *Metamorphoses* feel an intensely physical process at work when their arms begin to become the branches of trees or they start growing animal appendages; correspondingly, there is a highly tactile quality to Othello's 'I have a pain upon my forehead here' (III. iii. 288). But Othello is not exactly Actaeon, for where the latter is torn apart by his own dogs, the Moor is led to imagine himself tearing apart the body of Desdemona.

If the dog Iago is one of Othello's own stray desires, is the chaste, the divine Desdemona a Diana? Othello might think so, in that he takes himself to be as unworthy of her as Actaeon is of the Diana upon whom he gazes. But the parallel collapses with Desdemona's love; far from holding herself disdainfully aloof in the manner of Diana, she gives herself to Othello with trust and abandon. If we are looking for an Ovidian myth that has more tonal affinity with the relationship, we would do better to turn to an exemplary tale of love, such as Ceyx and Alcyone in Book Eleven of the *Metamorphoses*. Arthur Golding makes them into the ideal married couple: 'In Ceyx and Alcyone appeeres most constant love, | Such as betweene the man and wyfe too bee it dooth behove' (Epistle, 232–3). David Armitage has pointed out that the marine language of this tale was important for Shakespeare's late romances.[25] In particular, he singles out the image

[22] 'A Satyr', in *The Entertainment at Althorp* (1603)—*Ben Jonson*, vii. 128.

[23] *Ovid's Metamorphosis Englished*, 100.

[24] *The Works of Thomas Deloney*, ed. Francis Oscar Mann (Oxford, 1912), 7.

[25] Armitage, 'The Dismemberment of Orpheus: Mythic Elements in Shakespeare's Romances', *ShS* xxxix (1987), 123–33 (p. 128).

of the waves seeming to mount as high as the clouds: 'fluctibus erigitur caelumque aequare videtur | pontus et inductas aspergine tangere nubes' (xi. 497–8), 'The surges mounting up aloft did seeme too mate the skye, | And with theyr sprinckling for too wet the clowdes that hang on hye' (Golding, xi. 573–4). Shakespeare's use of this image is not confined to Armitage's instances, for one of the most memorable is in *Othello*, when the Second Gentleman describes the storm which caused the segregation of the Turkish fleet:

> The chidden billow seems to pelt the clouds,
> The wind-shaked surge, with high and monstrous mane
> Seems to cast water on the burning Bear
> And quench the guards of th' ever-fixèd Pole.
>
> (II. i. 12–15)

The image itself is a conventional one, which Shakespeare probably first encountered not in Ovid, but in the rhetorical handbook of Susenbrotus, used in schools, where 'ad sidera fluctus' ('the waves to the stars') is illustrative of hyperbole.[26] But the elaboration of it is Ovidian in its specificity: the water is made to seem truly wet, which it is not in the conventional figure. And the context is Ovidian too, with the motifs of lovers' separation, of sea-voyage and storm—Shakespeare departs from his source here, for in Cinthio the Moor and Disdemona go in the same ship and the sea is 'of the utmost tranquillity'.[27]

The affinity with Ceyx and Alcyone is strengthened by the ensuing image of Desdemona's beauty restoring the sea to calmness:

> Tempests themselves, high seas, and howling winds
>
> .   .   .   .
>
> As having sense of beauty do omit
> Their mortal natures, letting go safely by
> The divine Desdemona.
>
> (II. i. 69–74)

Here she is like Alcyone, who becomes the Halcyon during whose days 'the sea is calme and still, | And every man may too and fro sayle saufly at his will' (Golding, xi. 859–60). Given this identification, Golding's characterization of Alcyone's husband becomes suggestive, for the following could as well have been written of Othello as of Ceyx:

[26] See Baldwin, *William Shakspere's Small Latine and Lesse Greeke*, ii. 148.
[27] Bullough, vii. 243.

'His viage also dooth declare how vainly men are led | Too utter perill through fond toyes and fansies in their head' (Epistle, 236–7). The difference is that Othello puts too much faith in Iago, whereas for Golding Ceyx puts too much faith in an oracle. Similarly, Othello's metamorphosis is wrought by Iago whereas Ceyx's is by the gods. Ovid's psychological realism is retained while his supernatural agencies are removed. Ceyx and Alcyone are drowned, while Othello and Desdemona survive the storm only to be destroyed by human agency when they reach dry land. Equally, the story of Ceyx and Alcyone does not end with tragedy; the lovers' transformation into birds effects release and reunion. Yet, for all the variations of plot, there is a fundamental affinity in terms of emotional effect.

An argument in terms of plot parallels might be developed with respect to Cephalus and Procris. One of the most uncompromisingly tragic tales in the *Metamorphoses*, this story turns on the way in which jealousy, fear of infidelity, credulity, and misinterpretation precipitate the destruction of an initially joyous marriage. But if there is an influence on the plot of *Othello*, it is probably indirect, mediated through an updated version of the Cephalus and Procris story in George Pettie's *A Petite Pallace of Pettie his Pleasure*.[28]

Ovid has a memorable way of fixing the moment of death. The final words in Cephalus' narration of his wife's tragic end are

> labitur, et parvae fugiunt cum sanguine vires,
> dumque aliquid spectare potest, me spectat et in me
> infelicem animam nostroque exhalat in ore;
> sed vultu meliore mori secura videtur.
>
> (vii. 859–62)

> and with hir bloud
> Hir little strength did fade. Howbeit as long as that she coud
> See ought, she stared in my face, and gasping still on me,
> Even in my mouth she breathed forth hir wretched ghost. But she
> Did seeme with better cheare to die for that hir conscience was
> Discharged quight and cleare of doubtes.
>
> (Golding, vii. 1112–17)

Golding's cumbersome fourteeners lose much of Ovid's simplicity and concentration, and, as so often, introduce a moralizing tone that is

---

[28] Bullough (vii. 205–6) cites Pettie as a possible source, but does not explore the Ovidian connection. It is revealing that for Pettie the story is exemplary of 'that hatefull helhounde Jealousy'—*A Petite Pallace of Pettie his Pleasure* (1576), ed. Herbert Hartman (London, 1938), 186.

absent from the original. It is the original Latin, with its clear focus on a pale figure, a kiss and a look, that makes us think of the death of Desdemona or Cordelia.

From here it becomes apparent that it is in certain touches in the final scene, in the approach to death, that *Othello* is most profoundly Ovidian. When Othello addresses the sleeping Desdemona at the beginning of the scene, he speaks as if she is already dead. His images suggest that she has been metamorphosed into an object. Her skin is 'smooth as monumental alabaster': it is not that she is in her tomb, but that in Ovidian fashion she has become her tomb, her own monument. After the explicitly mythological, though not Ovidian, image of Prometheus, Othello continues,

> When I have plucked thy rose
> I cannot give it vital growth again.
> It needs must wither. I'll smell it on the tree.
> (v. ii. 13–15)

It is again as if she is no longer a person but an object in nature; the arresting of 'vital growth' is the process which takes place at moments of Ovidian petrification.

Having metaphorically addressed Desdemona as both stone and tree in his elegy to her, Othello introduces a further arboreal simile in his elegy on himself:

> of one whose subdued eyes,
> Albeit unusèd to the melting mood,
> Drops tears as fast as the Arabian trees
> Their medicinable gum.
> (v. ii. 357–60)

The New Cambridge editor says that 'The reference is to the myrrh tree and probably comes from a conflation of two passages in Pliny's *Naturalis Historia*'.[29] I do not see why it is necessary to go to two sources in Pliny when in Book Ten of the *Metamorphoses*, the primary source for Shakespeare's first narrative poem, we find the following description of the demise of Myrrha:

> Her bones did intoo timber turne, whereof the marie was
> The pith, and into watrish sappe the blood of her did passe.
> Her armes were turnd too greater boughes, her fingars into twig,
> Her skin was hardned into bark. . . .

---

[29] *Othello*, ed. Sanders, 186.

. . . .
Although that shee
Toogither with her former shape her senses all did loose,
Yit weepeth shee, and from her tree warme droppes doo softly woose:
The which her teares are had in pryce and honour. And the Myrrhe
That issueth from her gummy bark dooth beare the name of her,
And shall doo whyle the world dooth last.

(Golding, x. 565–77)

According to my argument in Chapter 2 it is of considerable
significance for Shakespeare's poem that Adonis was born from that
tree. The collocation in this passage of 'tears', 'gum', and the verb
'drop' suggests that Golding shaped Othello's image, especially as a
few lines earlier Myrrha has been described 'straying in the
broade | Datebearing feeldes of *Arabye*' (x. 547–8). Sandys's later
commentary also notes the tradition that the myrrh tree grew only in
Arabia.[30]

But the source is less important than the effect. What would
Shakespeare's original audience have made of Othello's image? I
believe that the more educated among them would have remembered
Ovid's etiological explanation of the oozing of the myrrh tree: the gum
represents the repentant tears of Myrrha. It does not necessarily
follow from this that Othello would have been seen as Myrrha, the
exemplar of incest; but it does, I think, follow that the image would
have been interpreted in terms of repentance and release from past
error. After the shifts and changes of the passions, the tree finally
offers something fixed and solid.

The difference between the last moments of Myrrha and those of
Othello is that she is released by the gods while he releases himself
through suicide. An Ovidian reading of Othello's last public speech
must now take a sideways step: the richest classical source of last
words and suicides is not the *Metamorphoses* but the *Heroides*, in
which there was particular interest around the time of the
composition of *Othello*, following the great success of Michael
Drayton's imitations of them, *England's Heroicall Epistles* (first
published in 1597, augmented and reprinted in 1598, 1599, 1602,
and 1605). Let us suppose, then, that Shakespeare reread or
recollected the *Heroides* at this time. Their relevance to Othello's
penultimate speech lies not only in their elegiac content, but also in
their epistolary form:

[30] Sandys, *Ovid's Metamorphosis Englished*, 364.

I pray you, in your letters,
When you shall these unlucky deeds relate,
Speak of me as I am. Nothing extenuate,
Nor set down aught in malice.

(v. ii. 349–52)

The *Heroides* are a pattern for letters concerning 'unlucky deeds'; like Othello, Ovid's deserted heroines claim to speak of themselves as they are, nothing extenuate, nor set down aught in malice. What Shakespeare learnt above all from these elegies was a way of writing about grief, a language that he could give to 'heroic' figures on the point of death, and an art of double revelation in which persuasive rhetoric reveals a character's strength yet also—unwittingly on the character's part—discloses her insecurities.

Consider, for example, the second letter, 'Phyllis to Demophoon'. Phyllis asks, 'Dic mihi, quid feci, nisi non sapienter amavi?' (ii. 27), 'Tell me, what have I done, except not wisely love?' (translated by George Turbervile as 'Denounce to me what I have doone, | But lovde thee all to well?'). Whether or not we see this as the actual source of Othello's 'one that loved not wisely', the two characters share a desperate desire to justify themselves. The more they protest that they 'nothing extenuate', the more it becomes apparent that extenuation is a prime purpose of their speeches. Phyllis and Othello both lament at how they have been beguiled by the words of others; both her letter and his speech try to assuage present catastrophic love by remembering past martial deeds (Othello his own, Phyllis her lover's father's).

They end with a similar self-dramatization. Phyllis closes with the words that she wishes to be inscribed on her tomb: 'PHYLLIDA DEMOPHOON LETO DEDIT HOSPES AMANTEM; | ILLE NECIS CAUSAM PRAEBUIT, IPSA MANUM'. The language here is extraordinarily compressed—to render it in English, Turbervile had to expand twelve words into twenty-three,

> Demophoon that guilefull guest,
> made Phyllis stoppe her breath:
> His was the cause, and hers the hande
> that brought her to the death.[31]

[31] George Turbervile, *The Heroycall Epistles of the Learned Poet Publius Ovidius Naso, in Englishe Verse* (1567), from *Heroides*, ii. 147–8. I attach no special significance to 'the cause', since I have found no evidence that Shakespeare used Turbervile as he did Golding (he would have had little trouble understanding the *Heroides* in their original Latin).

The translation loses not only Ovid's compression, but also the drama in the way that 'ipsa manum', 'her own the hand', is held back to the very end. Ovid's original offers a rhetorical stroke exactly analogous to Othello's dramatic 'And smote him thus'. Phyllis articulates, Othello articulates and dramatizes, the image by which they wish to be remembered. She composes her own epitaph, he his own funeral oration. They create their own myths: the confidence of their rhetorical performances serves to cover up their self-delusions and raise them to exemplary status.

III

In the foregoing account, I have frequently used the term 'affinity'. Allusion and affinity may, but do not necessarily, coexist: an allusion may signal a more far-reaching correspondence, but it may be merely incidental or ornamental; an affinity may be made apparent on the surface of the text, but it may operate at the level of the imagination. The terms broadly correspond to *paradigma* and *aemulatio*. Paradoxically, the most profound affinities may be the least demonstrable precisely because they go deeper than the explicit local parallel. The problem with affinities is that if you're looking for them they're easy to find, but if you're not they cease to exist. They don't have the solidity of overt mythological allusions. The search for them may be defended on historical grounds: as I suggested in the opening chapter, there is no more typical Renaissance intellectual activity than the quest for parallels between the present and the past, the moderns and the ancients. As Plutarch wrote his parallel lives of the most noble Grecians and Romans, so that inveterate reader of the classics, Shakespeare's Fluellen, searches for parallels between Harry of Monmouth and Alexander the Great. 'For there is figures in all things', he reminds Gower (*Henry V*, IV. vii. 32): it is accordingly by no means far-fetched to imagine a Renaissance reader finding Ovidian figures in Shakespearian things.

But some of Fluellen's grounds for comparison are flimsy: he 'proves' that Henry V is another Alexander the Great because the former was born in Monmouth, the latter in Macedon, there is a river in each place, 'and there is salmons in both' (IV. vii. 30). Richard Levin has shown how Fluellenism is open to ready abuse by literary critics since it 'can be used to equate any two objects in the universe, by searching through all the facts about them and seizing upon those that represent similarities, regardless of their importance, while ignoring all the rest'.[32] It would be a simple matter for the Fluellenist to 'prove', say, the influence of the *Metamorphoses* on *King Lear*.

If it is accepted that Shakespeare converts literal Ovidian metamorphoses into metaphors, the play's recurrent canine imagery, its sense of people being reduced to the level of dogs, could be derived from Ovid's story of Hecuba (which, as we know from *Hamlet*, is an archetypal tragic set-piece). A representative passage could be singled out:

> But shee was dumb for sorrow.
> The anguish of her hart forclosde as well her speech as eeke
> Her teares devowring them within. Shee stood astonyed leeke
> As if shee had beene stone. One whyle the ground shee staard uppon.
> Another whyle a gastly looke shee kest too heaven. Anon
> Shee looked on the face of him that lay before her killd.
>
> (Golding, xiii. 645–50)

The power of silence, the notion of extremity of emotion impeding utterance, the stress upon the heart, the corrosive quality of tears, the image of being turned to stone, the look to the heavens, the final concentration on the face of the dead child (her youngest-born): each element may be referred to *Lear*.

Alternatively, Lear holding the body of his child and cursing the heavens may be related to Niobe in Book Six of the *Metamorphoses*; after all, it is Niobe who most famously literalizes the image implicit in Lear's 'O, you are men of stones' (v. iii. 232). Or again, Lear's character could be illuminated by means of reference to Narcissus. 'So great a blindnesse in my heart through doting love doth raigne' (Golding, iii. 561): does not Lear's blindness arise from Narcissus-like self-love? As the Fool recognizes, Lear becomes his own shadow—a fate for which Narcissus offers the archetype. More locally, when Lear swears by 'The mysteries of Hecate and the night' (i. i. 110), it might be recalled that in Golding Jason swears to Medea 'By triple *Hecates* holie rites' (vii. 136). And so one could go on. The problem with this approach is that such topoi are common in the Renaissance. Many of them may have been learnt by Renaissance writers from Ovid more than from any other source; many of them are used by Shakespeare

[32] Levin, *New Readings vs. Old Plays: Recent Trends in the Reinterpretation of English Renaissance Drama* (Chicago, 1979), 97.

with a freshness, a precision, and a dramatic power that seem closer to Ovid than any other source. But none of them can be identified as uniquely or definitively Ovidian.

Consider, for example, the moment when Lear identifies with the elements because the storm is less unkind to him than his daughters. I know of no passage closer to this in manner and tone than the following in the *Heroides*:

> hiemis mihi gratia prosit!
> adspice, ut eversas concitet Eurus aquas!
> quod tibi malueram, sine me debere procellis;
> iustior est animo ventus et unda tuo.
>
> .   .   .   .
>
> duritia robora vincis . . .
>
> (vii. 41–4, 52)

Let the storm be my grace! Look, how Eurus tosses the rolling waters! What I had preferred to owe to you, let me owe to the stormy blasts; wind and wave are juster than your heart. . . . in hardness you exceed the oak . . .

But I cannot prove that the image in *Lear* is actually learnt from Ovid or that a Renaissance audience would have associated it specifically with Ovid. All one can say is that the spirit of the Roman poet has been caught in a way that licenses our applying Meres's remark about the soul of Ovid living in Shakespeare to works other than 'his Venus and Adonis, his Lucrece, his sugred Sonnets'.

Yet there is some harder evidence in the text of *Lear*. Fluellenism consists of the ingenious critic perceiving connections that others have not perceived (he is always likely to perceive them because once he has found one he hunts hard for others in order to support his case). It is a different matter if we make connections that the text asks us to make. Metamorphosis takes place when identity breaks down; it is the process we see Lear undergoing from Act III, scene iv onwards. In that scene, he begins to lose a sense of his own self ('Does any here know me? This is not Lear'—I. iv. 208), then by the time he exits the image of metamorphosis is explicit:

> Thou shalt find
> That I'll resume the shape which thou dost think
> I have cast off for ever.
>
> (I. iv. 288–90)

To the educated Elizabethan, Ovid's book of changes was the central point of reference for the notion of transformation—witness Spenser's use of the *Metamorphoses* in his cantos on 'Mutabilitie' and Shakespeare's borrowings of Pythagoras' discourse in his sonnets on time and change. Given this centrality, I do not see how audiences could have avoided calling the *Metamorphoses* to mind in response to Lear's image of shape-shifting. And, given the Renaissance reading of Ovidian metamorphosis as metaphor for monstrous human behaviour, Albany's castigations of Goneril, such as 'Thou changèd and self-covered thing, for shame | Bemonster not thy feature' (Q: xvi. 61–2), would have evoked a similar response.

Lear's involuntary psychological metamorphosis is accompanied by Edgar's controlled, if forced, transformation into Poor Tom through disguise:

> I will preserve myself, and am bethought
> To take the basest and most poorest shape
> That ever penury in contempt of man
> Brought near to beast.
>
> (II. ii. 169–72)

With Gloucester, Edgar works through a series of roles or metamorphoses, including an imaginary one that transforms him into a fiend with eyes like full moons, a thousand noses, 'Horns whelked and waved like the enridgèd sea' (IV. vi. 71). Although the idea of a fiend tempting one to commit suicide is Christian, the description is more mythological. This is Shakespeare's only use of the word 'whelked'; given the context, it is likely that he remembered it from Golding's translation of some lines in the *Metamorphoses* concerning the Libyan god Ammon: '*Joves* ymage which the Lybian folke by name of *Hammon* serve, | Is made with crooked welked hornes that inward still doe terve' (v. 416–17). The verbal parallel suggests the association in Shakespeare's mind; the finished image does not overtly allude to Ammon, but does summon up a monstrous pagan creature of supernatural power like Ammon. Ovid is much preoccupied with monsters in Books Four and Five of the *Metamorphoses*: the reference to Ammon comes shortly after the story of Perseus, which may itself lie behind another image of monstrousness in Lear,

> Ingratitude, thou marble-hearted fiend,
> More hideous when thou show'st thee in a child
> Than the sea-monster.
>
> (I. iv. 238–40)

Critics have had some difficulty identifying this sea-monster.[33] I would say that the image conflates two of the monsters slain by Perseus: 'marble-hearted' and 'hideous' come from the grotesque Gorgon's head which turns to stone, and the sea-monster itself is that from which Perseus saves Andromeda.

Such mythological allusions create an Ovidian context for the play's imagery of people becoming as beasts or behaving like monsters. Probably the most telling allusion of this sort is Lear's powerful and painful comparison of women to centaurs: Ovid was the *locus classicus* for centaurs. Their 'duplex natura' (*Metamorphoses*, xii. 503) was the perfect image for humankind's double nature as both beast and rational creature; as 'semihomines' (xii. 536) and 'biformis' (ix. 121), they are arrested in a perpetual state of semi-metamorphosis, an emblem of the process which is Ovid's theme.[34] All this also makes them an ideal emblem in *King Lear*, Shakespeare's fullest exploration of dual nature, of humanity's approximation to the bestial.

Lear obviously has his daughters in mind when he makes his comparison: does this implicitly make him into the father of the centaurs? The mythologically literate Elizabethan would have known that the centaurs were begotten by Ixion and a cloud-form sent by Jupiter in the shape of Juno, whom Ixion aspired to love. As a punishment for his presumption, Ixion was bound on an ever-turning wheel in the underworld. When Lear contrasts the heavenly state of Cordelia ('Thou art a soul in bliss') with a sense of his own punishment ('I am bound | Upon a wheel of fire'), the fate of Ixion is evoked. This moment is a characteristically Renaissance combination of the Christian and the classical: the fire suggests medieval images of Hell and Purgatory, the idea of being bound on a wheel the figure of Ixion.[35] What was Ixion's punishment taken to symbolize? Sabinus

[33] H. H. Furness's Variorum edn. (1880, p. 86) proposes the hippopotamus, the whale, a monster at Troy, and a picture said to be portrayed in the porch of the temple of Minerva at Sais. The most convincing of these possibilities is the monster from which Hercules rescues Hesione at Troy, alluded to as 'the sea-monster' in a passage of *The Merchant of Venice* discussed in my previous chapter—here again, the source is Ovid (*Metamorphoses*, xi: 'a monster of the Sea'; Golding, xi. 237).

[34] For a characteristic Renaissance view of the centaur embodying man's dual nature (from the wisdom of Chiron to the destructive drunkenness of the battle with the Lapithae), see Natalis Comes, *Mythologiae* (1551; repr. Venice, 1567), p. 215ʳ.

[35] Who is, incidentally, alluded to in Harsnett's Declaration of *Egregious Popish Impostures*, to which the vocabulary of Lear owes much (see Kenneth Muir's New Arden edn. (1952), 255).

refers it 'ad homines in Republica irrequietos', 'to men restless in matters of state':[36] Lear is thus paying the price for tampering with the running of the state by dividing his kingdom. Sabinus also offers a psychological reading of the punishments in Ovid's underworld: 'Genera suppliciorum allegorice ad animi perturbationes relata' (p. 137). Sandys expands upon this: 'all these forementioned punishments are allegorically referred to the perturbations of the minde. . . . *Ixions* wheele, to the desperate remembrance of perpetrated crimes, which circularly pursue, and afflict the guilty.'[37]

Not only is the 'perturbation of the minde' a fitting phrase for Lear's state at this point, but the specific interpretation of Ixion's punishment is appropriate to both the awakening scene, where so much turns on Cordelia's forgiving response to Lear's 'desperate remembrance' of his own errors, and the last part of the play in general, where we see perpetrated crimes circularly pursuing and afflicting the guilty. Ixion's wheel is a powerful symbol for this process of crime catching up on the perpetrator: Edmund recognizes at the end that 'The wheel is come full circle' (v. iii. 165). The image picks up on the Fool's 'Let go thy hold when a great wheel runs down a hill, lest it break thy neck with following; but the great one that goes upward, let him draw thee after' (ii. ii. 245–8). There is an interesting variant here in that this is an image of going up and down rather than round in a circle: the wheel has perhaps been displaced from Ixion and applied to the figure who is adjacent to him in Ovid's underworld, Sisyphus 'that drave against the hill | A rolling stone that from the top came tumbling downeward still' (Golding, iv. 569–70).

O. B. Hardison argued in a learned article that the myth of Ixion is actually an important source for *King Lear*.[38] He established a considerable number of correspondences between the play and Renaissance interpretations of the myth: Ixion was read as a symbol of the desire for pomp without responsibilities and as a type of ingratitude, the thunderbolt that hurls him to hell was interpreted as a symbol of both sudden disillusionment and providential justice, the centaurs were seen in some interpretations as both Ixion's offspring, representative of lust, and his hundred unruly retainers (this reading derives from the false etymology *centum armati*; it is an especially

---

[36] Sabinus, *Metamorphosis seu Fabulae Poeticae*, 137.
[37] Sandys, *Ovid's Metamorphosis Englished*, 163.
[38] Hardison, 'Myth and History in *King Lear*', *SQ* xxvi (1975), 227–42.

striking correspondence given that Lear's followers are not numbered one hundred in any of the play's direct sources).

Hardison's argument is attractive—it would make the myth of Ixion into the 'pattern' for *King Lear* as that of Philomel is the pattern for *Titus Andronicus*—but it depends on the synthesis of several mythographic sources. Even if it is accepted that Shakespeare made this synthesis, it seems unlikely that he would have expected his audience to do so. I think it is more probable that the allusive pattern is focused on Ovid, as it is in *Titus*, where the references to Philomel are accompanied by allusions to other metamorphoses, such as those of Hecuba and Io. The centaur and Ixion allusions come too late in Lear for the audience to read the whole play in terms of a sustained correspondence. I believe that, rather than impose a retrospective pattern of single analogy, they combine with the language of transformation, bestiality, and monstrousness to release the potential that is already there for the *Metamorphoses* to be brought to bear upon the play. They perhaps offer confirmation of earlier glancing intuitions that Lear might be a Narcissus or a Niobe. They certainly validate the claim that Ovid presides over not only the magical changes wrought by love in Shakespearian comedy, but also the dehumanization wrought by extremity of emotion in the mature tragedies.

This is a good point at which to pause and reflect more generally on the consequences of these mythological figurations for our conception of the kind of artist that Shakespeare was.[39] A. W. Schlegel and S. T. Coleridge in the early nineteenth century, then A. C. Bradley in the early twentieth, invented an idea which is still held by many theatregoers and students: that Shakespeare's most monumental achievement was in tragedy and that four tragedies in particular—*Hamlet*, *Lear*, *Macbeth*, and *Othello*—are his greatest plays. Their greatness was supposed to reside primarily in their unique depth of characterization; in the nineteenth century, Hamlet became the most famous character in world literature. In more recent times, *King Lear* has taken the palm and is lauded as Shakespeare's supreme achievement, on grounds less of characterization and more of its overall vision of how the world goes.[40] But whether the emphasis is on

[39] In the following reflections I have been helped obliquely by Marion Trousdale's informative *Shakespeare and the Rhetoricians* (Chapel Hill, NC, 1982).

[40] See R. A. Foakes, *Hamlet vs. Lear: Cultural Politics and Shakespeare's Art* (Cambridge, 1993).

character or total conception, what is made paramount is the *singularity* of these works. They are praised for their uniqueness, their incomparability—or their comparability only to a few other massively canonical texts, such as the masterworks of Tolstoy. The sublimation of influence is conventionally seen as a mark of this singularity. *Lear* is a greater tragedy than *Titus* because it does not depend on precedent as the earlier play does, it triumphantly casts off the skin of the old chronicle play of *Leir*—so the argument might go (and everyone would agree with at least the last part of it: everyone, that is, except Tolstoy, who, perhaps due to some anxiety of his own, claimed to prefer the old chronicle play).

At first sight, the development from *paradigma* to *aemulatio*, from allusion to affinity, which I have proposed in my readings of two of the 'four great tragedies' would seem to support views of this kind. Shakespeare has reached the highest form of imitation, where the classic exemplars have been fully *digested*. Petrarch's famous letter is so apt that it may be quoted again: 'Thus we writers must look to it that with a basis of similarity there should be many dissimilarities. And the similarity should be planted so deep that it can only be extricated by quiet meditation. The quality is to be felt rather than defined.' But, on further reflection, an enormous gulf between the Petrarchan and the modern position becomes apparent. It is best perceived at the level of metaphor: the Renaissance ideal is of consumption and transmutation, while the Romantic and post-Romantic one is of creation or generation. Of course *ingenium* is there in the Renaissance, as it is there in classical rhetoric, but it is always the sister of *imitatio*. In post-Enlightenment aesthetics, on the other hand, *genius* (the new word for extreme artistic creativity) is characterized above all by originality, the mark of which is the uniqueness, the singularity, of the artwork. 'Originality' originally suggested a return to a source; by the late eighteenth century, it implied newness, sourcelessness.[41] That is why students are nearly always puzzled when they discover that Shakespeare, whom they have been told is the essential artistic genius, based nearly all his plays

[41] For the shift from Renaissance quests for origins in an authoritative, ultimately a divine, 'source' to the Enlightenment desire for originality, and Milton's pivotal position in this development, see David Quint, *Origin and Originality in Renaissance Literature: Versions of the Source* (New Haven, Conn., 1983). On genius, see my chapter, 'Shakespeare and Original Genius', in *Genius: The History of an Idea*, ed. Penelope Murray (Oxford, 1989), 76–97.

on prose romances, plays and poems by other people, and history books. Fortunately for our cherished idea of Shakespeare's genius, even once this painful discovery has been made it is still possible to find all sorts of singularities in the character of Lear which are not there in Leir and in Othello which are absent from Cinthio's Moor (and, conveniently, the old *Hamlet* play is lost).

The normative way of watching and reading the 'four great tragedies' in our culture remains that of Coleridge and Bradley: we seek to build up a rich, unified conception of, say, Othello as a character; we proceed from the parts to the whole, according to the Schlegelian–Coleridgean model of the organic artwork. But the way of reading I have been proposing *fragments* the characters. It seeks not to build them up as unified consciousnesses, but to break them down into constituent parts. My concern is with the Ovidian constituents— there are of course many others. One can easily imagine a hostile response to such a procedure: 'we are interested in what makes Othello Othello, not in how here he is like Actaeon and there he is like Phyllis, how he resembles Ceyx one moment and Myrrha the next'. Such hostility would, however, be historically naïve. In Shakespeare's own time the pleasures of discovering singularity in the plays would have been outweighed by those of recognizing exemplarity. Novelty is viewed with suspicion; it is the appeal to experience that is valued. And experience, as Puttenham wrote, 'is no more than a masse of memories assembled'.[42]

Rhetoric is an art of memory which is a means of ordering experience and guiding the audience. The formal arrangement of verbal and visual languages has a suasive effect upon the viewer and listener. How do the viewer and listener know the 'right' response to a particular stage action or passion? By the force of example. That is to say, we would have been shown at school the example of Hecuba and told, 'This is how a person would speak and act in extremity of grief'. The boy in *Titus* has been taught this very lesson. Our education in tropes and figures would have given us a vast repertoire of categories which would enable us to classify the language we heard in the theatre. Thus, for example, we would have learnt that the effect of emotional stress on language is persuasively expressed by *aposiopesis*, which would have been exemplified in certain lines from Virgil and Ovid, such as Medea's 'ausus es—o, iusto desunt sua verba

[42] *The Arte of English Poesie*, bk. 1, ch. xix, p. 239.

dolori!— | auses es. . .' ('you have dared—but I cannot find the words which are adequate to my just grief—you have dared. . .').[43] This knowledge would have given us a category into which to fit Lear's 'I will do such things— | What they are, yet I know not; but they shall be | The terrors of the earth' (II. ii. 454–6).

Character and play are, then, constituted through the artful combination of pre-existent patterns or figures—not just the figures of rhetoric narrowly conceived as a patterning of syntax, but also the exemplary figures of history and myth, for, as Erasmus said, 'Most powerful for proof, and therefore for *copia*, is the force of *exempla*'. *Exemplum*, or, to use the Greek term as Puttenham did, *paradigma*, is a master-trope in the history of rhetoric. According to Aristotle, 'all orators produce belief by employing as proofs either examples [*paradeigmata*] or enthymemes and nothing else'. *Paradigma* is nothing less than the rhetorical equivalent of logical induction: 'the proof from a number of particular cases that such is the rule, is called in Dialectic induction, in Rhetoric example [*paradeigma*]'.[44] The 'proof' of Othello's passion is his resemblance to his exemplars; he becomes paradigmatic partly by virtue of his recognizability in terms of previous paradigms. The Renaissance mind took a particular pleasure in such recognitions. That pleasure is as old as ancient Greek culture, yet perpetually renewable:

> And I like the way of weaving:
> The shuttle runs, the spindle hums,
> And—flying to meet us like swan's down—
> Look, barefooted Delia!
> Oh how meagre life's weft,
> How threadbare the language of happiness!
> Everything existed of old, everything happens again,
> And only the moment of recognition is sweet.[45]

Thus Osip Mandelstam, remembering Ovid in 1918 (did he somehow

[43] *Heroides*, xii. 133–4. The most frequently cited example of *aposiopesis* was Virgil's 'Quos ego—sed motos praestat componere fluctus', 'Whom I—but it is better to calm the troubled waves' (*Aen*. i. 135).

[44] Aristotle, *Rhetoric*, I. ii. 8–9. See further, the introductory ch. of John D. Lyons, *Exemplum: The Rhetoric of Example in Early Modern France and Italy* (Princeton, NJ, 1989).

[45] 'Tristia', trans. James Greene, in the collection *The Eyesight of Wasps* (London, 1989), 55.

know that twenty years later he would follow his master into frozen exile and die in a transit camp in Siberia?).

Like all Renaissance artists, Shakespeare liked the way of weaving. Even plays superficially far distant from classical precedents offer moments of recognition. Lady Macbeth summons the spirits of darkness and is subliminally linked not only to Hecate and the weird sisters within the play, but also to Ovid's Medea, the great classical exemplar of the woman who unsexes herself in an appeal to night and to Hecate.[46] The willingness of the 'fiend-like queen' to dash out her baby's brains thus becomes recognizable as Medea's infanticide, whilst at the same time the recognition of the sisterhood of the two reveals that they are not mere fiends because they tell the truth about what they want in ways that their equivocating husbands, Macbeth and Jason, do not. Othello's sexual imagination is stirred and he loses control: he is Actaeon. He is torn to pieces within, as Actaeon is dismembered in the exemplary text. Everything existed of old, everything happens again: the recognition of the paradigm is itself a type of constancy in a world of mutability.

This last point is of great importance, for it ensures that we do not make the mistake of supposing that the fragmentation of character denotes the 'decentering' of 'man'. To acknowledge the role of rhetoric in the creation of Othello is not to lock him in the prison-house of language. Problematic as Renaissance theoreticians took the relationship between *verba* and *res* to be, they did not share the radical scepticism about *res* which is the characteristic of postmodern literary theory. The functioning of those master-narratives which we call 'myths' is of the essence here. The story (Actaeon, Narcissus, Hecuba, Niobe) translates into *verba* the *res* of desire and grief; it may be more or less successful in doing so (that will depend on the art of the translator), but no one questioned the existence of desire and grief as constituent parts of human nature. The modern theoretical disappearance of the *res*, the supposition that desire and grief are solely linguistic constructs, would have been incomprehensible in both classical and Renaissance culture.

This is not to say that nothing changes—everything changes, says

---

[46] For possible links between *Macbeth* and Seneca's, as opposed to Ovid's, Medea, see Inga-Stina Ewbank, 'The Fiend-like Queen: A Note on *Macbeth* and Seneca's *Medea*', *ShS* xix (1966), 82–94. As usual, Shakespeare synthesizes a range of sources: another of Ovid's witches, Tisiphone, may provide the weird sisters with an infernal brew including a filleted snake from the fens and a hemlock stalk (Golding, iv. 617–23); then

Ovid. In particular, modes of rhetoric change. Thus the Player's speech in *Hamlet* is not the play's characteristic pattern of grief. Hamlet is impressed by the Player's capacity to move himself and his audience, but Shakespeare is also parodying the overblown rhetoric of the previous decade's drama; he is implicitly suggesting that what really moves an audience is his own more supple, less showily formal, poetic language—this language is, however, still a supremely rhetorical language, full of doublets and amplifications. *Lucrece* finds a rhetoric in Hecuba which advances on that of the *Mirror for Magistrates*; *Hamlet* finds a still newer rhetoric which advances on that of Hecuba. Stylistic development of this sort is a form of Darwinian evolution: the fitter elements of the old style are adapted to a new environment and the species is able to mutate. *Hamlet* mocks the inflated epic idiom of 'The rugged Pyrrhus, like the Hyrcanian beast' and the hoary mythological display of 'Full thirty times hath Phoebus' cart gone round | Neptune's salt wash and Tellus orbèd ground', but when Hamlet, looking 'As if he had been loosed out of hell', turns 'his head over his shoulder' to gaze one last time at Ophelia before he sunders his love from her, the audience is given the pleasure of a recognition of Orpheus' glance back at Eurydice and in that recognition a confirmation of the truth of the old stories.[47] This Orphic glance occurs in a scene which Shakespeare does not dramatize: it is narrated by Ophelia. The allusion is possibly more readily recognizable as narrative than it would have been as stage image. Where in the late plays Shakespeare seems to move towards the dramatization of myth, here he detaches himself from the Player's crude enactment of Trojan matter and gives Hamlet's parting a quality that is rendered mythic by virtue of its very distance from immediate performance.

IV

As befits their subject-matter, the Roman plays revert to more explicit mythological allusiveness. Mars, the god of war, is written into the name of the warrior Caius Martius, later known as

a few lines later in bk. 4 of the *Metamorphoses* there is a murdered infant which serves Lady Macbeth: 'he snatched from betweene | The mothers armes his little babe . . . and dasht his tender head | Against a hard and rugged stone' (iv. 636–40).

[47] *Hamlet*, II. ii. 453, III. ii. 148–9, II. i. 84, 98.

Coriolanus. When the third Volscian servingman says that Caius Martius is 'so made on here within as if he were son and heir to Mars' (IV. V. 196–7), an audience member would have to be obtuse indeed not to make the connection. The end of Coriolanus' martial career is signalled by the moment when Aufidius denies him his right to appeal to Mars as his god:

CORIOLANUS. Hear'st thou, Mars?
AUFIDIUS. Name not the god, thou boy of tears.
CORIOLANUS. Ha?
AUFIDIUS. No more.
CORIOLANUS. Measureless liar, thou hast made my heart
  Too great for what contains it. 'Boy'? O slave!
                              (V. vi. 102–5)

For Coriolanus, to be deprived of the name 'Mars' and given that of 'Boy' instead is the ultimate insult. But of course Aufidius is not being a measureless liar in performing this switch of names, for when Volumnia persuaded Coriolanus not to attack Rome his response was signally that of a boy, a son, not a Mars.[48]

At his moment of capitulation outside the gates of Rome, Coriolanus says 'Behold, the heavens do ope, | The gods look down, and this unnatural scene | They laugh at' (V. iii. 184–6). A Jacobean audience would have been more likely than we are to recollect the most celebrated moment in classical mythology when the gods collectively look down and laugh. When Mars is caught *in flagrante delicto* with Venus, the other gods' reaction is to laugh at the indignity of the scene ('superi risere'—*Met.* iv. 188). In Thomas Heywood's *The Brazen Age*, the scene is staged in a way that makes the parallel with *Coriolanus* easy to see:

> *All the Gods appeare above, and laugh,*
> *Jupiter, Juno, Phoebus, Mercury, Neptune.*

MARS. The Gods are all spectators of our shame,
  And laugh at us.[49]

---

[48] In a strange half-echo during the battle in which he gains the name Coriolanus, the overreaching *Martius* seems to become not Mars but a different kind of overreacher, the Ovidian *Marsyas*, flayed for his misjudgement in challenging Apollo to a singing contest (vi. 382 ff.): 'Who's yonder, | That does appear as he were *flayed*?' (I. vii. 21–2, my emphasis).

[49] *The Brazen Age*, Act IV, *Dramatic Works of Heywood*, iii. 237.

Of all Shakespeare's plays, *Coriolanus* is the one in which Venus, erotic love, is least present. Sexual desire only seems to impinge at the charged moment when Aufidius embraces Coriolanus. Caius Martius himself seems immune to it: to perceive his humiliation at the hands of his mother as the play's equivalent of Mars' humiliation in the toils of passion is to see how the erotic is displaced into the filial.

Though Martius is manifestly under Mars, and Volumnia could conceivably be identified with Venus in her role as *genetrix, mother* of all things, the play does not invite us to imagine mother and son lying together like Venus and Mars in Vulcan's net. For the image of the gods of love and war in each other's arms, we must turn to *Antony and Cleopatra*. In the very first speech of the play, Antony is compared to 'plated Mars' (i. i. 4). The audience is then informed that he has been trapped by desire, transformed from warrior to lover. The idea immediately evokes the entanglement of Venus and Mars, for which there are many classical sources, among them the *Ars Amatoria*, where it is introduced as follows:

> Fabula narratur toto notissima caelo,
> Mulciberis capti Marsque Venusque dolis.
> Mars pater, insano Veneris turbatus amore,
> De duce terribili factus amator erat.
> *(Ars Am.* ii. 561–4)

There is a story, most famous over all the world, of Mars and Venus caught by Mulciber's [Vulcan's] guile. Father Mars, plagued by frenzied love of Venus, from a terrible captain became a lover.

Philo's opening image of Antony establishes the same movement from great military leader ('His captain's heart, | Which in the scuffles of great fights . . .') to slave of sexual desire ('To cool a gipsy's lust'). The play as a whole, down to its closing speech ('No grave upon the earth shall clip in it | A pair so famous'—v. ii. 353–4), celebrates the fame of the lovers, seeks to make their story 'toto notissima caelo'. Lest the connection with the gods of love and war should be missed, there is a reminder of it towards the end of the first act, in the playful context of the eunuch Mardian who can 'do nothing' sexually himself, but who has 'fierce affections' and can 'think | What Venus did with Mars' (i. v. 18–19, 'do' is of course slang for 'copulate with'). Cleopatra responds by thinking what she would like Antony to do with her, namely mount her as he does his horse ('O happy horse, to bear the weight of Antony'—i. v. 21). If this image of Antony and

Cleopatra lying together is conjoined with Mardian's imagining, it becomes proleptic of the lovers' downfall, for to think of what Venus did with Mars is also to think of what Vulcan did to the two of them, namely snare them in his net and make them the laughing-stock of the other gods. The love of Cleopatra and Antony is symbolic of cosmic harmony, as that of Venus and Mars was sometimes interpreted to be, but it is also undignified to the point of risibility.

In Golding's moralization, 'The snares of Mars and Venus shew that tyme will bring too lyght | The secret sinnes that folk commit in corners or by nyght' (Epistle, 111–12), and for Sandys, 'adulteries are taxed by this fable: which how potent soever the offenders, though with never so much art contrived, and secrecy concealed, are at length discovered by the eye of the Sun, and exposed to shame and dishonour' (Sandys, p. 157). But Antony and Cleopatra make no efforts to conceal their affair, and although Maecenas refers to the 'adulterous Antony' in the context of the dishonouring of Octavia (III. vi. 93), Octavius and his fellow-Romans disapprove of the liaison with Cleopatra primarily because they believe that Antony is wasting his martial powers and abnegating his duty to Rome. *Antony and Cleopatra* is anything but a fable taxing adultery. The allusions to Venus and Mars need to be read in other ways: first of all, they assert the god-like status of Antony and Cleopatra, and secondly they suggest some of the terms cited by Sandys elsewhere in his synthesis of Renaissance interpretations of the story: '*Mars* exciteth greatnesse of spirit and wrath in those in whose nativity he predominates; *Venus* ruling infuseth the effects of love; and *Mars* conjoyning, makes the force of that love more ardent.'[50] Antony, then, is Mars-like in his combination of greatness of spirit—his magnanimity is repeatedly stressed—and wrath, the latter manifested most vigorously in his treatment of Thidias.

His anger has two faces, for when wielded in battle it brings him glory, yet when indulged arbitrarily it debases him. This is Cleopatra's point when she describes him as a perspective painting, 'Though he be painted one way like a Gorgon, | The other way's a Mars' (II. v. 117–18). The Gorgon embodies the negative aspect of anger, as described by Ovid in the *Ars Amatoria*:

---

[50] Sandys, *Ovid's Metamorphosis Englished*, 157. Compare Abraham Fraunce's interpretation in *The Third part of the Countesse of Pembrokes Yvychurch* (1592), where Venus is 'Wantonnes' and Mars is 'hoate and furious rage' (p. 32ʳ).

Pertinet ad faciem rabidos compescere mores:
Candida pax homines, trux decet ira feras.
Ora tument ira: nigrescunt sanguine venae:
Lumina Gorgoneo saevius igne micant.
(*Ars Am.* iii. 501–4)

It is becoming to the appearance to hold wild moods in check; fair peace suits men, fierce anger beasts. The face becomes swollen with anger: the veins grow black with blood, the eyes flash more savagely than Gorgon fire.

The juxtaposition with Mars, representative of wrath in its positive aspect, suggests that Shakespeare expected his audience to read the allusion to the Gorgon in terms of rage, to interpret it along the lines of Thomas Elyot's gloss on the passage in the *Ars Amatoria*, 'This Gorgon that Ovid speaketh of is supposed of poets to be a fury or infernal monster, whose hairs were all in the figure of adders, signifying the abundance of mischief that is contained in wrath.'[51] According to Elyot, the man who aspires to be a governor should be without ire: Antony's implacability is thus revealed as the source of both his military strength and his failure as a ruler.

While Mars is Antony's divine type, his semi-divine one is Hercules. In Plutarch's 'Life of Marcus Antonius', Antony claims descent from Anton, son of Hercules; to Shakespeare's Cleopatra he is a 'Herculean Roman' (I. iii. 84). His allegiance to the greatest of the mythical heroes is strengthened by the strange scene in the fourth act, when music of hautboys is heard under the stage and the second soldier offers the interpretation that 'the god Hercules, whom Antony loved, | Now leaves him' (IV. iii. 13–14; in Plutarch, the music and the Antonine allegiance belong to Bacchus, to wine and revelry). The image of Antony and Cleopatra wearing each other's clothes, the 'sword Phillipan' exchanged for the woman's 'tires and mantles' (II. v. 22–3), may suggest not only the cross-dressing of Mars and Venus, a topos in Renaissance painting, but also that of Hercules and Omphale, as described in the *Heroides*:

nec te Maeonia lascivae more puellae
incingi zona dedecuisse putas?

. . . . . .

Haec te Sidonio potes insignitus amictu

---

[51] Elyot, *The Governor*, ed. Lehmberg, p. 112, cited by Waller B. Wiggington, ' "One way like a Gorgon": An Explication of *Antony and Cleopatra*, II. v. 116–17', *Papers on Language and Literature*, xvi (1980), 366–75, to which my paragraph is indebted.

>   dicere? non cultu lingua retenta silet?
>   se quoque nympha tuis ornavit Iardanis armis
>   et tulit a capto nota tropaea viro.
>   ('Deianira to Hercules', *Her.* ix. 65–6, 101–4)

And do you not think that you brought disgrace upon yourself by wearing the Maeonian girdle like a wanton girl? . . . These deeds can you recount, gaily arrayed in a Sidonian gown? Does not your dress rob from your tongue all utterance? The nymph-daughter of Iardanus [Omphale] has even tricked herself out in your arms, and won famous triumphs from the vanquished hero.

David Bevington notes that the story of Omphale and Hercules, in which the hero is subdued and put to work spinning among the maids of the Lydian queens, 'was widely used in the Renaissance as a cautionary tale of male rationality overthrown by female will'.[52] Thomas Heywood's dramatization of the story in *The Brazen Age* makes the parallel with *Antony and Cleopatra* easy to see: the hero who dominates the 'triple world', the bearer of the 'pillars' of Atlas, is brought under the spell of a 'Strumpet' and 'attired like a woman'. 'Hence with these womanish tyres, | And let me once more be my selfe againe', he cries out: the play dramatizes Hercules' ultimately doomed attempt to break free from the female will, just as Antony struggles to break free from his strong Egyptian fetters.[53]

Shakespeare's Antony explicitly compares himself to Hercules shortly before his attempted suicide. Rage is again the key emotion:

>   The shirt of Nessus is upon me. Teach me,
>   Alcides, thou mine ancestor, thy rage.
>   Let me lodge Lichas on the horns o'th' moon,
>   And with those hands that grasped the heaviest club
>   Subdue my worthiest self. The witch shall die.
>   (IV. xiii. 43–7)

('Alcides' is, of course, another name for Hercules.) Although the Hercules plays of Seneca provide a possible confirmatory source,

---

[52] New Cambridge edn. of *Antony and Cleopatra* (1990), 9. Bevington does not, however, cite the *Heroides*, which I take to be the likeliest source for Shakespeare's knowledge of the story. In 'The Comparison of Demetrius with Antonius', Plutarch notes that 'Cleopatra oftentimes unarmed Antonius' and compares this with 'painted tables, where Omphale secretlie stealeth away Hercules clubbe, and tooke his Lyons skinne from him' (Bullough, v. 319): this is a precedent for the linking of the two pairs of lovers, but the idea of mutual cross-dressing is not introduced.

[53] *The Brazen Age*, Act V, *Dramatic Works of Heywood*, iii. 242–7.

Shakespeare would have derived his knowledge of the hero's madness primarily from Ovid's accounts in the ninth book of the *Metamorphoses* and Deianira's letter in the *Heroides*.

Several parallels between Hercules and Antony are suggested by Deianira's letter. The idea of the warrior finally destroyed by love is expressed with great economy: Venus is his nemesis ('nocuit Venus'); he whom no military enemy could overcome is overcome by love ('vincit amor'). Hercules is seen as a superhuman figure, who once held up the earth on behalf of Atlas; Antony is 'The triple pillar of the world' and in Cleopatra's dream of him in the final act 'his reared arm | Crested the world'. The hero's death is precipitated by a mistake on the part of the woman: Deianira sends the shirt of Nessus under the impression that it is impregnated with a potion that will rekindle Hercules' love, whereas in fact it is poisoned; Cleopatra sends a false report of her own death with the same intention of reawakening love, but it has the effect of making Antony take his own life. Once her beloved is gone, the woman makes a series of farewells and takes her own life. But there are also certain variations: Hercules for a time brought universal peace ('se tibi pax terrae'), an idea which the play displaces on to Octavius ('The time of universal peace is near'); Deianira imagines with disgust the captive Iole, who has herself captured Hercules' heart, being paraded through the streets, while Cleopatra imagines with disgust herself being paraded in Rome as the captive of Octavius.[54] These changes are bound up with a shift of the balance of power to Octavius, who at the end of the play becomes Augustus, seen by Rome as another incarnation of Hercules.

More significant than any association of content between Deianira's letter and the play is the way that the voice which Ovid gives to the woman provides a model for Shakespeare in his giving of a voice to Cleopatra: although she is ultimately a character of pathos who lacks Cleopatra's power, Deianira serves as a precedent in terms of emotional range, as she veers between tenderness and scorn, anger at her lover for leaving her and pride in his achievements. The *Heroides* are important for *Antony and Cleopatra* because they see the male hero from the woman's point of view. More generally, they provide Shakespeare with examples of female characters who are witty as well as amorous, not merely moody but also full of vitality, linguistically

---

[54] Parenthetic quotations in this paragraph: *Heroides*, ix. 11, 26, 15; *Antony and Cleopatra*, I. i. 12, V. ii. 81–2, IV. vi. 4.

adept and good at arguing. Plutarch's interest is firmly in the life of Marcus Antonius; Ovid's letters of Deianira and Dido are female 'lives'. History is restructured, with the death of the woman, not that of the warrior, becoming the climax of the story. In each text the female character is made to define herself in relation to the man whom she loves and admires; once she has pushed him to his death, there is nothing left in life for her. But despite this, the female perspective stands in opposition to the male epic voice which orders the march of history.

Antony's direct allusion to Hercules and the shirt of Nessus looks as if it is based on the *Metamorphoses*, and its version of the story would certainly have been the one most familiar to those members of Shakespeare's audience who understood the reference. Lichas is the messenger who bears to Hercules the poisoned shirt which Deianira mistakenly believes is a love-token. Like Antony with Thidias and Cleopatra with the messenger who brings news of the marriage to Octavia, Hercules vents his wrath on the hapless go-between:

> Behold, as *Lychas* trembling in a hollow rock did lurk,
> He spyed him. And as his greef did all in furie woork,
> He sayd. Art thou syr *Lychas* he that broughtest untoo mee
> This plagye present? of my death must thou the woorker bee?
> Hee quaakt and shaakt, and looked pale, and fearfully gan make
> Excuse. But as with humbled hands hee kneeling too him spake,
> The furious *Hercule* caught him up, and swindging him about
> His head a halfe a doozen tymes or more, he floong him out
> Into th'*Euboyan* sea with force surmounting any sling.
> He hardened intoo peble stone as in the ayre he hing.
>
> (Golding, ix. 259–67)

In the blindness of his anger, Antony does not see the irony of his allusion. Hercules' fury at Lichas is a sublimation of his fury at Deianira, for she is the one who is the worker of his death; Antony, too, blames the woman, stigmatizing her as a witch and condemning her to death. He forgets that Deianira was innocent, that she was motivated only by love for Hercules, just as Cleopatra is innocent of the charge of deliberately selling Antony in battle to 'the young Roman boy' (IV. xiii. 48).

In appealing to Hercules to teach him anger, Antony is also preparing for his own suicide. The context of the allusion is decisive: immediately after flinging Lichas into the air, Hercules sets about preparing his own funeral pyre. He goes to his death rehearsing his own past glories, in the style of the stoic hero; in Antony's phrase, he 'subdues his worthiest self'.[55] But the manner of Antony's death is profoundly messy: he does not manage the deed with the style of Hercules or Othello. Cleopatra's assurance to him that he has not been vanquished by Caesar, that 'none but Antony should conquer Antony' (IV. xvi. 17), rings not a little hollow, for the botched suicide is hardly a mode of conquest to be proud about. It may not be a coincidence that the phrase echoes the suicide words of Ovid's Ajax: 'That none may *Ajax* overcome save *Ajax*'.[56] Ajax is another hero who is reduced in stature and comes to an ignominious end, in his case killing himself in a fit of pique after he has been routed by Ulysses in the argument about who deserves the arms of Achilles. He is also another figure with whom Antony claims affinity ('The seven-fold shield of Ajax cannot keep | The battery from my heart')[57] in terms of martial greatness, but this is yet one more affinity which rebounds unfavourably, in so far that Ovid, followed by Shakespeare in *Troilus and Cressida*, had reinvented Ajax as a blustering figure outwitted by the crafty Ulysses. So too is Antony outmanœuvred by the pragmatic Caesar.

Antony construes his own end as a dissolution, a watery metamorphosis: like a cloud, he 'cannot hold this visible shape' (IV. xv. 14). But in her dream of him as emperor bestriding the ocean, his body metamorphosed into cosmic forms, Cleopatra transforms his decease into an apotheosis. She reinvests Antony with Herculean qualities; her dream is the equivalent of the climax of the Hercules narrative in Book Nine of the *Metamorphoses*:

> so *Hercules* as soone as that his spryght
> Had left his mortall limbes, gan in his better part too thryve,
> And for too seeme a greater thing than when he was alyve,
> And with a stately majestie ryght reverend too appeere.
> His myghty father tooke him up above the cloudy spheere.
>
> (Golding, ix. 323-7)

This is one of Ovid's grandest transformations, but it is also one of his more particular allusions, for it has a political sub-text which is not

---

[55] IV. xii. 47, adapted to third person. For a fine account of the stoic subjugation of the self in Shakespeare and his contemporaries, see Gordon Braden, *Renaissance Tragedy and the Senecan Tradition* (New Haven, Conn., 1985).

[56] Golding, xiii. 472. Heywood's Hercules in *The Brazen Age* kills himself with the same vain assertion: '*Alcides* dies by no hand but his owne' (*Dramatic Works*, iii. 254).

[57] IV. xv. 38-9, probably derived from Ovid's description of Ajax as 'The owner of the sevenfold sheeld' (Golding, xiii. 3).

caught by Golding. The Elizabethan translator read Hercules as a type of virtue rewarded with heavenly glory, but Ovid also had a specific figure in mind: the original of Golding's line 'And with a stately majestie ryght reverend too appeere' is 'coepit et augusta fieri gravitate verendus' (ix. 270), in which 'augusta' is clearly meant to suggest Augustus and 'gravitate' the *gravitas* which Ovid's Caesar espoused. An association is thus being drawn between the universal peace brought by Hercules and the *pax Romana* under Augustus: the line anticipates the close of the poem, in which Ovid imagines Augustus himself ascending to the heavens.

Ovid is finally more interested in his own art than in praising Augustus. The imagined immortality of the latter is the penultimate, not the last, of the metamorphoses, for the poem ends with the apotheosis of the poet, not the *princeps*. The phrase that was applied to Hercules in Book Nine, 'parte sui meliore' (Golding's 'his better parts'), is reiterated in the envoi to Book Fifteen with the pronoun now in the first person: 'parte tamen meliore mei super alta perennis | astra ferar', 'Yit shall the better part of mee assured bee too clyme | Aloft above the starry skye' (*Met.* xv. 875–6; Golding, xv. 989–90).

That said, the *Metamorphoses* were the product of a literary culture in which the patronage of the Emperor was all-important (consider what happened to Ovid when he lost it), so in this sense George Sandys may be said to have been following Ovid's example when he dedicated his translation of the *Metamorphoses* to King Charles, and prefaced it with a panegyric in which he imagined the king holding 'Augustus' Scepter'. Sandys's summary account of Hercules' greatness also serves as praise of the Augustan aspirations of the Stuart monarchy: '*Hercules* better deserved a Deity then all the rest of the *Heroes*: who conquered nothing for himselfe: who ranged all over the world, not to oppresse it, but to free it from oppressors and by killing of Tyrants and Monsters preserved it in tranquillity' (Sandys, p. 329). This is the sort of thing that Renaissance monarchs and empire-builders liked to hear.

Given King James's well-known propensity to think of himself as another Augustus, it has been tempting to read *Antony and Cleopatra*, which ends with the establishment of the Augustan empire, as a play written in praise of the Stuart court.[58] If Cleopatra's apotheosis of

---

[58] See e.g. H. Neville Davies, 'Jacobean *Antony and Cleopatra*', *Shakespeare Studies*, xvii (1985), 123–58.

Antony is read as a *translatio* of Ovid's apotheosis of Hercules, this reading is complicated interestingly. As Ovid locates Augustan greatness in the dead Hercules, so Shakespeare finds it in the dead Antony more than in the Octavius who will become Augustus. The Augustan myth is thus held open to question. Shakespeare performs a destabilization which is quintessentially Ovidian: *Antony and Cleopatra* moves bewilderingly between a panegyric and an ironic tone, just as Ovid does in the Hercules narrative. Book Nine of the *Metamorphoses* at one moment has Hercules transformed into a god and into Augustus, then within a few lines moves on to the metamorphosis of Galanthis into a weasel. It is, to say the least, a bathetic juxtaposition. The bathos accords with the larger sense in which the *Metamorphoses* is ambivalent in its relationship to Augustus: the Emperor is specifically compared to Jove in the first book,[59] yet the rapacious Jove is hardly a role-model for the Augustus who sought to return Rome to moral austerity. And if there is a Jove in *Antony and Cleopatra*, it is the sexually active Antony, not the calculating Octavius—'Your Emperor | Continues still a Jove', says a soldier to Enobarbus, in recognition of Antony's magnanimity (IV. vi. 28–9). Later, Cleopatra wishes she had 'great Juno's power' so that Antony could be raised and set 'by Jove's side' (IV. xvi. 35–7). Like Jove and Juno, Antony and Cleopatra are supreme in everything including their bickering.

Ovid also destabilized another of the founding myths of the Roman empire, that of 'pius Aeneas'. In Virgil's *Aeneid*, the exemplary Augustan poem, Aeneas has to leave Dido in order to fulfil his destiny and establish Rome; the seventh letter of the *Heroides* questions this necessity by telling the story from Dido's point of view. 'Certus es, Aeneas, cum foedere solvere naves, | quaeque ubi sint nescis, Itala regna sequi?' (vii. 7–8, 'are you resolved, Aeneas, to break at the same time from your moorings and your pledge, and to follow the realms of Italy, which lie you know not where?'): here Aeneas is made to seem anything but 'pius' in his desertion of Dido. The pursuit of empire, rather than the pursuit of love, is made to seem wayward and unpredictable. Ovid appropriates Virgil's ruling adjective, *pius*, and gives it to Dido, associating it with her love instead of Aeneas' duty: 'Uror, ut inducto ceratae sulpure taedae, | ut *pia* fumosis addita tura focis' (my italics, vii. 23–4, 'I am all ablaze with love, like torches of

[59] 'nec tibi grata minus pietas, Auguste, tuorum | quam fuit illa Iovi' (i. 204–5)—'Nor is the loyalty of your subjects less pleasing to you, Augustus, than that was to Jove'.

wax tipped with sulphur, like pious incense placed on smoking altar-fires').[60] This Dido has a Cleopatra-like ability to blaze with love one moment and to be manipulative the next: her claim that she may be pregnant and that Aeneas is thus destroying his son as well as her is a clever means of making him feel guilty (vii. 133–8). It is also a clever revision of Virgil, for in the *Aeneid* Dido merely wishes that she had a baby to remind her of Aeneas and thus give her comfort (*Aen.* iv. 327–30). Where Virgil's Dido elicits pathos, Ovid's is admirable for her wit and inventiveness. Cleopatra is manifestly closer to the Ovidian version—indeed, her feigning of sickness in Act I, scene 3 might even suggest a pretence that she is pregnant.

Dido and Aeneas are mythico-historical precedents for the North African queen who distracts the Roman general from his imperial duty in Shakespeare's play. But Shakespeare, like Chaucer,[61] follows Ovid in revising the official version of the story by giving the dominant voice to the woman and to love. His Cleopatra echoes the language of Ovid's Dido: her scorn at Antony's enslavement to Fulvia, 'What, says the married woman you may go? | Would she had never given you leave to come!' (I. iii. 20–1), is a witty reduction of Dido's scorn at Aeneas' enslavement to Jupiter, ' "Sed iubet ire deus." vellem, vetuisset adire'—' "But," [you tell me], "the god says you must go." Ah, would he had forbidden you to come' (vii. 139). At least Aeneas could claim he was obeying the will of a god; with Antony it is just another woman.

The final scenes of the play seem to take the revision further than Ovid and to endorse the un-Roman love of Antony and Cleopatra to such an extent that they are allowed to believe that they will be reunited after death. When Antony imagines himself in the Elysian fields with Cleopatra he says, 'Dido and her Aeneas shall want troops, | And all the haunt be ours' (IV. xv. 53–4). But Dido and Aeneas did not end up together in the Elysian fields: in the underworld sequence of Book Six of *The Aeneid*, the dead queen turns away from the visiting Aeneas and rejoins her husband Sychaeus (*Aen.*

[60] For a good account of *Heroides*, vii, as a revision of Virgil, see Howard Jacobson, *Ovid's 'Heroides'* (Princeton, NJ, 1974), 76–93.

[61] The *House of Fame* includes a Dido-centred, Ovidian reading of Aeneas' desertion (i. 239–432). See the fine analysis by Jill Mann in her *Geoffrey Chaucer* (Hemel Hempstead, 1991), 8–13: 'When Dido reappears in the *House of Fame*, however, this Ovidian mode uncompromisingly reasserts itself—and it does so all the more powerfully in that it grows with a quasi-spontaneous momentum out of a Vergilian narrative.'

vi. 469–74). Ovid's Dido (a.k.a. Elissa) in the *Heroides* also turns back to Sychaeus:

> hinc ego me sensi noto quater ore citari;
> ipse sono tenui dixit 'Elissa, veni!'
> Nulla mora est, venio, venio tibi debita coniunx.
>
> (*Her.* vii. 101–3)

From [the shrine to Sychaeus] four times have I heard myself called by a voice well known; he himself calling in faint tones, 'Elissa, come!' I delay no longer, I come, I come thy bride, thine own by right.

Shakespeare replicates the reciprocal call between husband and wife ('veni! . . . venio, venio') but gives it over to the adulterous lovers in Antony's 'I come, my queen' (IV. xv. 50) and Cleopatra's 'methinks I hear | Antony call. . . . Husband, I come. | Now to that name my courage prove my title' (V. ii. 278–9, 282–3). Dido is Sychaeus' wife by legal right ('debita') and in her suicide she returns to him, whereas Cleopatra aims to prove her spiritual right to be Antony's wife by virtue of her courage in committing suicide.

These revisions of the received story might be seen to reflect ironically on the characters of Antony and Cleopatra. Perhaps the point is that Antony is deluded in his hope that he and Cleopatra will end up hand in hand where souls do couch on flowers: the audience members who know their *Aeneid* will know that Dido and Aeneas do not provide a precedent for reunion after death. The same goes for Cleopatra: the audience members who know their *Heroides* will know that the husband who calls Dido to her suicide is Sychaeus, not Aeneas. There is much in the play to support a reading that would make Antony and Cleopatra into self-deluding dotards. But such a reading is deaf to the language of the suicide speeches, which seeks to give the lovers the transcendence they imagine for themselves and each other. Through the power of metaphor to work metamorphically upon the imagination, the theatre audience may come for a moment to believe that Cleopatra is leaving her baser elements, that she undergoes the most refined of transformations, not into a bird or a flower but into 'fire and air'. To read the allusions to Dido and Aeneas as purposeful remakings is to read with the grain of the text. For Shakespeare, as for Ovid, myth is a creative resource, not a set of prescriptions: to believe Antony's 'Dido and her Aeneas shall want troops' and Cleopatra's 'Husband, I come' is to believe in the possibility that history, which these myths encode in archetypal form, can be rewritten. To make Aeneas not Rome's but Dido's—'*her* Aeneas'—is to question the primacy of empire.

So too with the play's final revision of the image of Venus and Mars. Octavius says that the dead Cleopatra looks 'As she would catch another Antony | In her strong toil of grace' (v. ii. 341–2). The image of being caught in a net ('toil') reintroduces the memory of 'What Venus did with Mars'. But this time the net belongs to Venus, not to Vulcan, and the sexual toil does not make the lovers a laughing-stock. Instead, it elevates them to a state of grace. Such revisions of received myth proclaim, as Helena does in *A Midsummer Night's Dream* with her 'Apollo flies, and Daphne holds the chase', that 'The story shall be changed'.

6

From Myth to Drama

But, to return from whence I have digressed to the consideration of the Ancients' writing and their wit . . . he of them who had genius most proper for the stage was Ovid.

(John Dryden, *Of Dramatic Poesy*)

I

Shakespeare refined his skills in the writing of narrative and his mastery of verbal wit in his early anatomy of sexuality, the overtly mythic and metamorphic *Venus and Adonis*; he wrote a formal imitation of Ovid in *The Rape of Lucrece* and used the tale of Philomel as a structural model for *Titus Andronicus*. And in *A Midsummer Night's Dream* he mingled direct and indirect dramatization of Ovid, whilst simultaneously following and outdoing the example of John Lyly in bringing to the stage a world of desire and change bathed in an aura of classical mythology. Though these early works bear the most obvious marks of Shakespeare's Ovidian education, the *Metamorphoses* and to some extent also the lesser works such as the *Heroides* remained, as I have shown, an underpresence in the mature plays, both comedies and tragedies. In the last plays, as Shakespeare tried out a more mythic mode of composition, Ovid returned to the surface of the drama.

Cymbeline is best regarded as Shakespeare's most experimental play: tragical-comical-historical-pastoral, it would have been Polonius' favourite work in the canon. One aspect of its experimentation is its way of reinvoking Ovid but dramatizing his myths at one remove. As in *Titus Andronicus*, a copy of the *Metamorphoses* is actually brought on to the stage as a prop. It is Imogen's bedtime reading:

> She hath been reading late,
> The tale of Tereus. Here the leaf's turned down
> Where Philomel gave up.
>
> (II. ii. 44–6)

The allusion marks the moment at which Imogen is 'given up'. But where in *Titus* Lavinia's quoting of Philomel's tragic tale is a revelation of her own rape, here the rape is metaphorical. The text that is opened out in *Titus* is folded back in *Cymbeline*. Iachimo completes the line 'Where Philomel gave up' with 'I have enough': the sight is all he needs. His removal of the bracelet from Imogen's arm is a symbolic violation of her chastity, but where Ovid's Tarquin pressed violently down on Lucrece's breasts, Iachimo merely observes Imogen's:

> On her left breast
> A mole, cinque-spotted, like the crimson drops
> I'th' bottom of a cowslip.
>
> (II. ii. 37–9)

It is the eyes of a spectator that do the undressing here, not the tearing hands of a Tarquin. When Iachimo himself alludes to Tarquin—'Our' Tarquin, a fellow-Roman—he rewrites the night-scene of *Lucrece* as something gentle:

> Our Tarquin thus
> Did softly press the rushes ere he wakened
> The chastity he wounded.
>
> (II. ii. 12–14)

The sibilance seems tender rather than sinister: 'Softly press' suggests not only stealth, but also a lover's touch. And 'wounded' grossly understates the severity of Tarquin's deed. This has the effect of sublimating the image of rape—Philomel gives up as in a dream, not in brutal reality as on the stage of *Titus*—and thus making it easier for the theatre audience to put itself in the position of Iachimo. To note and to wonder at the beauty of the sleeping Imogen does not seem to do any harm. But of course Iachimo does work harm, and it takes all the play's twists and turns, including an apparent death and an actual physical violation when Posthumus strikes Fidele/Imogen, to undo that harm.

The audience, then, is forced to confront its own complicity in Iachimo's deed. His gaze is ours. Shakespeare makes the point by means of the chimney-piece in the bedroom. At the time, Iachimo records 'the contents o'th' story' (II. ii .27), and in his subsequent narration to Posthumus he reveals those contents:

> The chimney
> Is south the chamber, and the chimney-piece
> Chaste Dian bathing. Never saw I figures
> So likely to report themselves; the cutter
> Was as another nature; dumb, outwent her,
> Motion and breath left out.
>
> (ii. iv. 80–4)

The gaze is fixed on the naked Diana bathing: Iachimo and with him the audience stand in the position occupied by Actaeon. The motif of auto-destructive desire is activated. But the chimney-piece was never seen by the audience: what we remember instead is the sight of Imogen, as mediated through the language of Iachimo's gorgeous but prurient soliloquy, a language so sexually evocative that the youth playing the part of Imogen seems to become, in the words of Marlowe's Gaveston, 'A lovely boy in Dian's shape'.

The slide from the imagined representation of Diana to the dramatically realized figure of Imogen is a mental *trompe l'œil*. The art of the chimney-piece, like that of Hermione's statue in *The Winter's Tale*, is said to have outdone nature. A few lines earlier, Iachimo has reported that the tapestry in Imogen's chamber told the story of Mark Antony meeting Cleopatra at Cydnus; here Shakespeare echoes back his own recent play in which Enobarbus describes Cleopatra at Cydnus as being so desirable that 'but for vacancy' the air would have joined the people of the city in going to gaze on her. The fictive chimney-piece recapitulates and goes beyond this: the artist's figures seem on the verge of speech and movement, they are 'likely to report themselves' and though they are 'dumb' they seem to make nature seem dumber. The air has vacated nature and entered the artwork. When we associate Diana with Imogen, the goddess seems to step down from the chimney-piece and on to the stage. The image effects in the audience's mind what *The Winter's Tale* feigns to deliver in performance: the metamorphosis of art into life.

In one sense, this is what Ovid constantly offers his readers. The *Metamorphoses* works so well as poetry because when its characters undergo transformations, the language takes the reader along too— we are deluded by Ovid's art into thinking that we can feel what it would be like to be, say, a hunted hart or a tree under the axe. It is no coincidence that near the climax of the poem Ovid includes the discourse of Pythagoras, who speaks in favour of vegetarianism and against blood-sports: metamorphosis anthropomorphizes nature—

each animal, each tree, each stream has a human history—and thus demands an empathy between humankind and nature. Pythagoras' theories are the intellectual equivalent of what the poem has achieved imagistically. Shakespeare alludes playfully to the opinions of Pythagoras in *Twelfth Night* and more seriously to his theory of universal flux in the Sonnets, but in *Cymbeline* he is most Ovidian in his sustained use of a language which fuses the characters with the natural world. In Iachimo's soliloquy, Imogen becomes a 'fresh lily' (II. ii. 15) and her breath perfumes the air of the room, while the 'flame o'th' taper | Bows toward her' (II. ii. 19–20) as wind or water, warm with desire, would playfully touch a nymph in Ovid; the mole on her breast takes its identity from the marking on a cowslip; even Tarquin seems to respect the rushes on the floor. Earlier in the play an image adapted from Ovid half-evinces sympathy for a gnat;[1] later, Arviragus establishes a sustained correspondence between the parts of Fidele's apparently dead body and a selection of flowers:

> Thou shalt not lack
> The flower that's like thy face, pale primrose, nor
> The azured harebell, like thy veins; no, nor
> The leaf of eglantine, whom not to slander
> Outsweetened not thy breath.
>
> (IV. ii. 221–5)

Here Shakespeare is writing in the same key as the Ovid who turns his golden lads and girls into flowers which all too quickly come to dust.

But Shakespeare also works actively to transform his audience in a way that Ovid does not. For all our empathy in reading the *Metamorphoses*, its narratives remain myths—stories that evoke wonder by virtue of their strangeness and their distance from the reader's own experience. What Shakespeare does when he makes us into the peeping Actaeon is bring the significance of these stories closer to home. He interprets and dramatizes myth. It is as if he says: of course you're never really going to see the naked Diana bathing, but what the story of Actaeon tells you is something about how it is a form of violation to gaze with desire on a woman when she is in a vulnerable state. But he doesn't say this in the form of a sermon, he

---

[1] The diminution and disappearance of Posthumus' ship—'till the diminution | Of space had pointed him sharp as my needle; | Nay, followed him till he had melted from | The smallness of a gnat to air' (I. iii. 18–21)—is an *imitatio* of that of Ceyx's ship in Book Eleven (Golding, xi. 537–47), but the gnat is Shakespeare's, not Ovid's.

dramatizes it so that it occurs in the very process of watching the play. The audience's complicity with Iachimo's notings is a reinvention of the Actaeon myth which disturbingly internalizes what was comically external in *The Merry Wives of Windsor*. Nor is the point made in the traditional language of patriarchy: the sub-text is more complicated than 'thou shalt not covet thy neighbour's wife', for the prying gaze is the direct consequence of Posthumus' own proprietorial display of his wife's chastity when he brags about it in the wager scene. In his way, he is an Actaeon too, which is why the play has to punish him.

II

The long and complex history of mythography, manifested in commentators as varied as Erasmus and Bacon in the Renaissance,[2] Frazer and Lévi-Strauss in more recent times, is testimony to the variety of interpretations which may be drawn from ancient stories in which mankind encounters divinities or the origins of natural phenomena are configured into narrative. As was shown in Chapter 4, the Actaeon myth was interpreted politically as well as sexually. A political interpretation is likely to be sparked by a particular historical moment—that of Ovid's exile or the Earl of Essex's intrusion—whereas other ways of reading seek to be transhistorical. Perhaps the most pervasive of these is that which reads myth in relation to the rebirth of natural things within the recurring cycle of the seasons—in Frazer's term, the 'vegetation' myth. Spenser's placing of Adonis in 'the first seminarie | Of all things' at the centre of Book Three of *The Faerie Queene* provides strong support for a Frazerian reading of the death and rebirth of that beautiful young man. But, for the Renaissance, the fundamental myth of spring's return was that of Proserpina. She has all the right qualifications: the daughter of Ceres, goddess of growing vegetation, she is young and fertile; when abducted by Dis (Pluto), she is carrying flowers; the contract by which she resides six months with him in the underworld and returns to earth for the other six is a perfect figure of winter and summer. Long

---

[2] I cite these two as 'various' because of Erasmus' desire to 'strip classical myth of allegorical accretions' (Terence Cave's phrase, *The Cornucopian Text*, 96–7) and Bacon's attempt to return to full-blooded allegorical reading (in his *De sapientia veterum* of 1609 and the ch. on poesy [ii. 13] in his *De augmentis scientiarum* of 1623). For the latter, see Charles W. Lemmi, *The Classic Deities in Bacon: A Study in Mythological Symbolism* (Baltimore, 1933).

before Ovid told her story, Proserpina (previously Persephone, in some versions Kore, the Virgin) symbolized the seed that had to lie in darkness beneath the earth for the six (in some versions four) months of winter before being reborn in the next spring's corn. Ovid's version of the familiar story states explicitly that prior to the abduction by Dis, 'continuall spring is all the yeare there founde' in the garden where Proserpine gathers flowers, and that the story is resolved when Jove divides the girl between her mother and her husband and thus 'parteth equally the yeare betweene them both' (Golding, v. 490, 700).

The Winter's Tale is Shakespeare's most overtly mythic play title. It announces a link between characters and their emotions on the one hand, and the seasons on the other. Since it locates itself within the economy of the seasons, the tale of winter cannot avoid gesturing towards the eventual return of spring. The unstated alternative title of the play may therefore be said to be *Waiting for Proserpina*. If this were a tragedy, as for much of the first half it seems to be, we would go on waiting for her indefinitely; like Godot, she would never come. But this is a play which moves from the winter of tragedy to the spring of romance, so she does come—although not before Leontes has to wait for her some sixteen years.

Shakespeare had already experimented with a Proserpina on stage. The virgin, the teenage daughter, is the key to the redemptive movement of the romance of *Pericles, Prince of Tyre*. She first appears with a basket of flowers, among them 'purple violets' which are shared with Ovid's Proserpina. Her first words place her in the arena of vegetation-myth: 'No, I will rob Tellus of her weed | To strew thy grave with flow'rs' (xv. 65–6). Tellus is a female personification of the earth, also invoked by Ovid's Medea in the prayer which Shakespeare freely translated in the mouth of Prospero.[3] Marina, the girl from the sea, begins by setting herself in opposition to Tellus, the girl of the earth. The character is thus established in terms of a quasi-mythic contest, a battle between the powers of the sea and the land. Shakespeare signals that he is moving into the same sort of mythic territory as that of Spenser in his tale of Florimell and Marinell, the flower-girl and the man on the seashore, who eventually fuse in marriage, though not before the girl has been held prisoner in the realm of Proteus, god of sea-changes.

[3] 'quaeque magos, Tellus, pollentibus instruis herbis' (*Met.* vii. 196).

Marina's pun on 'weed', implying both vegetation and clothing, is an anticipation of her own rape—by picking flowers, she is violating nature, as she herself will be violated. The weeds that will soon be torn are her own. When the flower-girl is abducted, the correspondence with Proserpina becomes apparent to any audience member with the slightest mythological literacy. If she were to drop her flowers, an obvious bit of stage business, which actually occurs in the dramatization of the rape of Proserpina in Heywood's *The Silver Age*,[4] she would be re-enacting one of Ovid's most tender details:

> And, as she'd torn the shoulder of her dress,
> The folds slipped down and out the flowers fell,
> And she, in innocent simplicity,
> Grieved in her girlish heart for their loss too.[5]

The girl's distress over the loss of her flowers is typical of the enchanting psychological details which are shared by Ovid and Shakespeare's last plays.

But, in accordance with the demands of the theatre, Shakespeare naturalizes the myth. Marina is seized by pirates instead of by Dis and the underworld to which she is consigned is a brothel. Mythic resonances are retained at the level of language: the epitaph written for the girl speaks of how she 'withered in her spring of year' and, echoing the opposition with Tellus, redescribes her death in terms of a battle between earth and sea.[6] When she emerges from the sexual underworld, she fulfils Proserpina's function as a bringer of new life, regenerating her father and eliciting a language of fertility: 'Thou that begett'st him that did thee beget' (xxi. 183). In this line, the parallel is slightly and suggestively skewed, for although Proserpina the daughter of the goddess of agriculture reanimates the nature that bore her, she cannot strictly be said to have 'begotten' her own

[4] When Ceres re-enters after the abduction of her daughter, she says, 'Her scattered flowers, | And garland halfe made up, I have light upon, | But her I cannot spy' (Act III, in *The Dramatic Works of Thomas Heywood*, iii. 137).

[5] A. D. Melville's trans. of *Met*. v. 398–401; Golding is wooden in his quaintness here ('a sillie simplenesse hir childish age yet beares'—v. 501). The detail of Proserpina dropping her flowers certainly caught Shakespeare's eye, for Perdita alludes to it (*Winter's Tale*, IV. iv. 117–18).

[6] The Oxford text prints the full epitaph as an additional passage, and includes in the text of its sc. xviii a shorter version, taken from Wilkins's novella, *The Painful Adventures of Pericles Prince of Tyre*, which explicitly reads Marina as the equivalent of Proserpina, the fairest flower of nature: 'In nature's garden, though by growth a bud, | She was the chiefest flower: she was good' (xviii. 36–7).

parent, since begetting is a male prerogative. By implicitly making
Marina into Pericles' father while at the same time retaining the
image of her as Proserpina, Shakespeare replaces the unnatural,
incestuous relationship between Antiochus and his daughter with
which his collaborator began the play with a regenerative parent–
child bond which answers to the order of nature.

The first act of *The Winter's Tale* does not include a single
mythological reference. Everything seems to come from within
Leontes' brittle psyche, nothing from the gods. The only image that is
a possible exception is Polixenes' 'Make me not sighted like the
basilisk' (I. ii. 388); this figure serves, however, not to make that
fabulous monster present, but to highlight the sense of the look that
can kill—the point is that Polixenes is no basilisk, rather it is Leontes'
vision which is grotesquely distorted.

The other-world beyond the febrile court is present for the first time
in Act III, scene i, when Cleomenes and Dion report from Delphos.[7]
Suddenly we are in the light and warmth of the ancient world. There
is ceremony and awe in the face of the power of divinity:

CLEOMENES. The climate's delicate, the air most sweet;
  Fertile the isle, the temple much surpassing
  The common praise it bears.
DION. I shall report,
  For most it caught me, the celestial habits—
  Methinks I so should term them—and the reverence
  Of the grave wearers. O, the sacrifice—
  How ceremonious, solemn, and unearthly
  It was i'th' off'ring!
CLEOMENES. But of all, the burst
  And the ear-deaf'ning voice o'th' oracle,
  Kin to Jove's thunder, so surprised my sense
  That I was nothing.
                              (III. i. 1–11)

But this brief interlude is cut short as the trial scene begins, and its

---

[7] Shakespeare takes over the conflation of Delos (Apollo's island birthplace) and
Delphi (site of the oracle) from Greene's *Pandosto*. Terence Spencer notes that in the
Renaissance the island was frequently known as Delphos; he suggests Virgil's *Aeneid*,
iii. 73–101, as a possible source for Cleomenes' and Dion's descriptive vocabulary
('Shakespeare's Isle of Delphos', *MLR* xlvii (1952), 199–202). Shakespeare might have
noticed Ovid's play on Apollo's presidency over the two like-sounding places, 'vimque
dei passam Delphos Delumque tenentis' (*Met.* ix. 332), 'For why the God of Delos and of
Delphos had hir frayd' (Golding, ix. 401).

values are rejected when Leontes denies the oracle of Apollo. The denial, however, is the turning point in the action: instantly the gods seem to intervene. Leontes begins thinking in the language of the world of classical myth, where thunderbolts are hurled with abandon: 'Apollo's angry, and the heavens themselves | Do strike at my injustice' (III. ii. 145–6). Cleomenes' association of Apollo's oracle and Jove's thunder has been borne out. Where with the abduction of Marina Shakespeare naturalized myth, here the nature of the events is left ambiguous: the precise cause of Mamillius' death is not given and the nature of Hermione's collapse is not explained. We cannot be sure whether or not the gods have acted directly. Since Hermione falls to the ground at the instant Leontes speaks of divine anger at his own injustice, he may imagine for a moment ('How now there?') that a thunderbolt has been thrown but that by some terrible mistake it has missed him and struck his wife instead, but very soon he reverts to a naturalistic language, expressing the hope that she has merely fainted ('Her heart is but o'ercharged'—III. ii. 149).

Eventually we discover that her removal from the action has been effected by the agency not of a god but of Paulina; at the time, however, the latter's performance is so convincing that the audience shares Leontes' belief that the queen really is dead. And anyone in the audience who had read Shakespeare's source, Robert Greene's novella *Pandosto*, would have been utterly sure of this, for there the queen is gone indeed, never to return. There is nothing in the first half of the play to indicate that the final scene will move away from Greene's 'tragicall discourse' (Bullough, viii. 173) and towards a rare metamorphosis into, rather than out of, life.

When the action shifts to Bohemia, the movement away from interiority quickens apace. External agencies of storm and bear see to Antigonus and the mariners who have been commissioned to dispose of Hermione's baby girl. The clown's description of the storm uses the Ovidian figure of a disruption of the elements so extreme that the sea cannot be distinguished from the sky: 'But I am not to say it is a sea, for it is now the sky. Betwixt the firmament and it you cannot thrust a bodkin's point' (III. iii. 82–4). As for the bear, its presence is usually attributed to the popularity of such episodes in the drama at this time—the version of the romance *Mucedorus* performed at court early in 1610 had a clown tumbling over a bear, and Jonson's *Masque of Oberon*, which may be the source for the satyr's dance in Act IV of *The Winter's Tale*, included a chariot drawn by two white bears. But the

Mariner has begun the scene by interpreting the storm in the same way that Leontes interpreted Mamillius' death:

> In my conscience,
> The heavens with that we have in hand are angry,
> And frown upon's.

(III. iii. 4–6)

It would therefore be only reasonable to interpret the bear as a mark of divine displeasure towards Antigonus. To interpret an animal in relation to transgression and supernatural punishment is to begin to read the phenomena of nature as they are read in the *Metamorphoses*.[8] Could this then be an Ovidian bear?

It is not always noticed that there is a good reason for both the entrance of the bear and its violent behaviour. It chases Antigonus because it is being chased itself. The Old Shepherd is understandably annoyed because the local youth are out hunting, despite the dreadful weather, and they have scared away two of his best sheep. It is only because the bear is frightened that it kills Antigonus: the hunted becomes the hunter, inverting the Actaeon story where the hunter becomes the hunted. The Old Shepherd's other cause for complaint about young men is that they go about 'getting wenches with child' (III. iii. 60); the discovery of the baby on stage seems to him to be further evidence of this. There is, then, a kind of symmetry between the bear and the child. Given this, is it coincidental that in the *Metamorphoses* there is a bear who *is* a wench got with child? Jove's roving eye is caught by Callisto, one of Diana's virgin huntresses; he disguises himself as Diana in order to approach her and is soon kissing her in an immoderate and unmaidenly fashion ('nec moderata satis nec sic a virgine danda'—ii. 431); she resists, but he rapes her and gets her pregnant. A significant length of time passes—'Nine times the Moone full too the worlde had shewde hir horned face' (Golding, ii. 564)—before Diana and her troop strip off to bathe, at which point Callisto's heavy pregnancy is revealed. She is immediately banished for her uncleanness; she bears a son, and then Juno takes her usual revenge on her husband for his infidelity by punishing the rape victim—Callisto is metamorphosed into a bear. Having once been one of Diana's hunters, she is now the hunted:

---

[8] Mouse, the Clown in *Mucedorus*, wonders whether the bear he meets is a supernatural agency: 'Nay, sure it cannot be a bear, but some devil in the bear's doublet; for a bear could never have had that agility to have frighted me' (I. ii. 2–4). 'Doublet' suggests a bear-costume and consequently an actor rather than a live animal.

How oft oh did she in the hilles the barking houndes beguile?
And in the lawndes where she hir selfe had chased erst hir game,
Now flie hirselfe to save hir lyfe when hunters sought the same?

(Golding, ii. 607–9)

The story ends with a second metamorphosis and a release: Callisto's son, Arcas (who gives his name to Arcadia), now 16, is out hunting and encounters his bear-mother; in a typically Ovidian moment, they both freeze for an instant—a glimmer of recognition in her case, a nameless fear in his—and in that instant Jove sweeps them into the sky in the form of neighbouring stars, the Great and Little Bears. Once one has read the story one cannot look at those constellations in the night without remembering Callisto.

The detail that will strike readers of *The Winter's Tale* is the passing of nine cycles of the moon as a mark revealing pregnancy. Polixenes' first words in the play are 'Nine changes of the wat'ry star hath been | The shepherd's note since we have left our throne | Without a burden' (i. ii. 1–3). The image comes to suggest more and more as the action unfolds: when Leontes makes his accusation, we remember it and see that it is physically possible that there are grounds for his suspicion (especially given the presence of the word 'burden', which can mean 'that which is borne in the womb'); when the action moves to Bohemia and a shepherd actually appears, we realize that the King of Bohemia has always spoken the language of pastoral ('We were as twinned lambs that did frisk i'th' sun'—i. ii. 69). The link between Polixenes' opening speech and the Old Shepherd's establishes the idea that whilst Perdita is not really the daughter of Bohemia, she will have a Bohemian surrogate father. It is conventional to measure the months by the moon, but the trick of making the measure serve also to reveal a pregnancy may have been learnt by Shakespeare from the Callisto story.[9]

Either just before or just after Shakespeare wrote *The Winter's Tale*, Thomas Heywood's *The Golden Age* was performed at the Red Bull.[10]

[9] Neither the bear nor the 'nine changes' are present in Greene's *Pandosto*: given the close dependence of *The Winter's Tale* on this one literary text for many of its details, it is logical to look to other literary texts for the origination of the details that are added to the events and the language.

[10] *The Winter's Tale* was written some time between 1609 and May 1611; *The Golden Age* was staged some time between 1609 and summer 1611 (it was entered in the Stationers' Register on 14 Oct. 1611, but must have been performed some considerable time earlier, since, according to its preface, its two sequels, *The Silver Age* and *The Brazen Age*, had by then 'adventured the Stage'; it dramatizes elements of Heywood's *Troia*

That play has at least two scenes which resemble parts of *The Winter's Tale*: Saturn intends to have his baby put to death, but Vesta goes to him in the manner of Paulina and persuades him to let it live; also, an enquiry is made of Apollo's oracle at 'Delphos', and a Lord reports how 'After our Ceremonious Rites perform'd, | And Sacrifice ended with reverence, | A murmuring thunder hurried through the Temple'.[11] *The Golden Age* also tells the story of Callisto. Its dramatization of Jupiter, dressed as a virago, attempting to seduce the hapless nymph is possibly the sauciest sexual tease in Jacobean drama—'nay let your skirt be raised . . . You are too wanton, and your hand too free . . . Oh God you tickle me'.[12] But Heywood's dramatization of the Callisto myth has one startling omission: when Arcas hunts her, she is in her original form. Presumably because of the difficulty of staging them, Heywood eschews actual animal metamorphoses; he accordingly follows a version of the story in which there is no bear. A London playgoer of 1610–11 would thus have had the curious experience of not seeing a bear where one would have been expected, in *The Golden Age*, and seeing one where it is quite unexpected in *The Winter's Tale*. Shakespeare reveals himself to be the bolder theatrical innovator: it is as if he shows Heywood that it would have been possible to bring Callisto on to the stage in her metamorphosed form.

To say 'the bear evokes Callisto' opens up some fascinating readings. Callisto and Hermione are both wrongfully accused of conceiving a child out of their own wantonness. The night before the ship lands on the coast of Bohemia, Antigonus dreams that the spirit of the dead Hermione comes to him—it would be ironic indeed if that spirit really did then come to him the next day in the form of a bear. The knowledge that Callisto would eventually become a star and achieve some sort of reunion with her child would open up the same

Britanica, which was entered on 5 Dec. 1608). The theatres were closed for much of 1609, due to plague; I suspect that both plays belong to 1610. Ernest Schanzer is, to my knowledge, the only critic to have considered the links between Heywood's and Shakespeare's romances: see his article, 'Heywood's *Ages* and Shakespeare', *RES* NS xi (1960), 18–28. I agree with Schanzer's view that the use of Gower in *Pericles* provided the structural model for the first three *Age* plays, which are narrated by Homer with supporting dumbshows in the choruses, and that the two parts of *The Iron Age*, Heywood's Trojan plays, borrow from the 1609 quarto of *Troilus and Cressida*, but I am not as convinced as he is that *The Winter's Tale* preceded *The Golden Age*—if there is an influence, it could go either way.

[11] Heywood, *Dramatic Works*, iii. 13.
[12] Ibid. 34.

kind of possibility for Hermione. But even if the identification of the bear with Callisto is dismissed as fanciful, I still believe that for Shakespeare and those members of his audience who knew their Ovid, a bear would have been more than just a bear—it would have brought with it a narrative that is characterized by destructive sexuality, disguise, abuse of an innocent woman, wrongful accusation, jealousy, and revenge. The story of Callisto shows that you shouldn't treat bears at face value: they may appear to be savage beasts, but they may be victims too. So often in Ovid, as in Shakespeare, you can never be quite sure who is the hunter and who is the hunted. If we put the blame for the death of Antigonus on the bear, rather than the youths who are hunting it, we may be making a misjudgement based on superficial appearances—the very kind of misjudgement that Leontes makes at the beginning of the play.

The story of Callisto also shows that bears may be a means through which the gods work out their arguments with each other and intervene in human affairs. To read mythically is to put every phenomenon *sub specie aeternitatis*. A stage bear, however, owes more to human than divine agency. Either it is a human in a bear skin—an actor who, in the fashion of Bottom as ass or Falstaff wearing the horns in *The Merry Wives of Windsor*, has undergone a comic metamorphosis into an animal—or it is a tame bear, from the local pit or wherever, which will inevitably make us reflect upon the art of the tamer, the skill of the keeper. The tame bear thus signifies not the intervention of the gods in human affairs, but the mastery of man's art over nature. Myth ultimately says something about human powerlessness—the archetypal pattern will repeat itself *ad infinitum*—whereas the artistry of actor and trainer says something about human power. In this sense, what is most significant about the bear is that it is *not* given a mythic interpretation. As when Paulina's agency replaces that of the gods, so with the bear Shakespeare replaces Ovid's *species aeternitatis* with a *species humanitatis*.

We may say the same about Time. In Ovid, as in Shakespeare's sonnets, it is uncontrollable, remorseless, the devourer of all things ('tempus edax rerum'), whereas in *The Winter's Tale* Time is a Chorus chatting to the audience and playfully breaking the rules of dramatic illusion. Customarily, the grains in his hour-glass trickle slowly but inexorably away; here, the actor takes control and turns his glass. Shakespeare does not pretend, as a neo-classical dramatist like Jonson would, that time in the theatre corresponds to time outside it. He establishes an alternative order in which the dramatist is free to lay down his own rules; without compunction he leaps over sixteen years, proving that this world is controlled by his art, not the gods. And he does it with a smile, saying to the audience something along the lines of 'I hope you're having a good time'.

Time moves in a circle even as it moves forward. His intervention marks not only the passing of sixteen years but also the movement from winter to a warmer season. Autolycus enters singing a song that begins with the daffodil of spring and proceeds to the 'summer songs' of lark, thrush, and jay (IV. iii. 1–12). In identifying himself, Autolycus confirms that the play is shifting into the register of myth: 'My father named me Autolycus, who being, as I am, littered under Mercury, was likewise a snapper-up of unconsidered trifles' (IV. iii. 24–6). The littering of Autolycus under Mercury is narrated by Ceyx in Book Eleven of the *Metamorphoses*. Chione, a nubile fourteen-year-old, is desired by both Apollo and Mercury (interestingly, the former sees her while on the way back from Delphos). Apollo disguises himself as an old woman and takes her at night, but before this Mercury has had her, having entranced her with his wand. She bears twin boys, one to each god. By Mercury she has

A sonne that hyght *Autolychus*, who provde a wyly pye,
And such a fellow as in theft and filching had no peere.
He was his fathers owne sonne right: he could mennes eyes so bleere,
As for to make ye black things whyght, and whyght things black appeere.
(Golding, xi. 359–63)

Shakespeare's Autolycus has learnt from Ovid's this art of making black seem white and vice versa: he can convince Mopsa and Dorcas that there is truth in a ballad of a fish that appeared on the fourscore of April forty thousand fathoms above water.

The twin borne of Chione by Apollo is Philammon, a renowned singer. To Chione, it proves a curse to have been loved by two gods, but in Shakespeare Autolycus has a benign metamorphic power. He represents the two boys rolled into one, bringing not only the filching of Mercury's son, after whom he has been named, but also Philammon's gift of song. He is in fact littered by both Apollo and Mercury; as such, he is a kind of agent of the dramatist who is himself both singer and thief (the plot is snapped-up from Greene). The words of Mercury and the songs of Apollo, divided at the end of *Love's Labour's Lost*, are united. At the end of the fourth act, Autolycus'

Mercurial actions unintentionally serve the Apollonian oracle: because he comes on to gloat over his thieving during the festival he is there to provide garments for Florizel's escape, and because he lives by the principle of knavery he conceals his knowledge of the escape from the king and diverts the shepherd and clown from Polixenes to Florizel.

Perdita first appears after Autolycus' first exit. She is garlanded with flowers and Florizel gives the first description of her: 'no shepherdess, but Flora | Peering in April's front' (IV. iv. 2–3). Shakespeare took this image from Greene's *Pandosto*, where, so to speak, the fauna became the flora: 'Fawnia . . . with a garland made of bowes and flowers; which attire became her so gallantly, as shee seemed to bee the Goddesse Flora her selfe for beauty' (Bullough, viii. 176). Perdita, Shakespeare's version of Greene's Fawnia, replies that of course she is not really Flora, goddess of spring and fertility, that she is only dressed ('pranked up') like her. For the audience it is a typically complex moment: we know as Florizel does not that Perdita really is of royal blood, that in being dressed as queen of the feast she is symbolically taking on her true identity, but we also know that (s)he is ultimately a boy actor who is merely dressed up for the duration of the play. Then again, if we can suppose that the boy actor is really a shepherdess acting the part of a princess, who is really a princess but doesn't know it, then we can also suppose that she is also an embodiment of a goddess.

But is the goddess necessarily Flora? We also know that Time has taken it upon himself to name Bohemia's son *Flori*zel, so for the latter to call Perdita Flora is to stake a claim for her by grafting his own name to her. This possessiveness is of a piece with Florizel's next mythological allusion, a justification of his own assumption of disguise as a shepherd on the grounds that the gods too have used disguise for the purposes of wooing:

> The gods themselves,
> Humbling their deities to love, have taken
> The shapes of beasts upon them. Jupiter
> Became a bull, and bellowed; the green Neptune
> A ram, and bleated; and the fire-robed god,
> Golden Apollo, a poor humble swain,
> As I seem now.
>
> (IV. iv. 25–31)

In terms of the play as a whole, Florizel's assumption of the same disguise as Apollo suggests that his wooing of Perdita is part of the pattern that will eventually lead to the fulfilment of Apollo's oracle. But, more locally, the allusions are troubling. Golding's preface to his translation of the *Metamorphoses* reminds the reader that Jupiter became a bull 'too winne his foule desyre'. And the ultimate source for the list of the gods' transformations is Arachne's tapestry in Book Six—her weaving shows how '*Europe* was by royall *Jove* beguilde in shape of Bull', Neptunus 'in the shape of Ram | Begetting one *Theophane Bisalties* ympe with Lam', and Apollo 'in a shepeherdes shape was practising a wile | The daughter of one *Macarie* dame *Issa* to beguile'.[13] The tapestry so annoys Minerva, 'Bicause the lewdnesse of the Gods was blased so in it' (vi. 164), that she rends the cloth in pieces and turns Arachne into a spider. Florizel seems to realize that it is not exactly tactful to allude at this moment to a series of stories of lewdness, but the language in which he tries to differentiate himself from the rapacious divinities is not entirely convincing: 'my desires | Run not before mine honour, nor my lusts | Burn hotter than my faith' (IV. iv. 33–5). The faith is all very well, but the lusts still burn hot. Shakespeare shares with Ovid the conviction that, whether or not it comes with honour, male desire always speaks the language of sexual conquest. In the final act we see that even after sixteen years' penance, Leontes is still capable of casting a lascivious eye on the fresh young Perdita.[14]

Shakespeare's decision to call Greene's Dorastus 'Florizel' and have *him* re-create Perdita as Flora displaces the identification and leaves room for an alternative mythological figuration that is not in Greene: Perdita herself appeals not to Flora but to Proserpina.[15] Where *Pandosto* includes an unspecified 'meeting of all the Farmers Daughters' (Bullough, viii. 177), Shakespeare locates his pastoral scene at a particular moment within the rhythm of the rural year. Perdita cannot be 'Flora | Peering in April's front', as Florizel has it, because it isn't April. Sheep-shearing festivals traditionally took place

[13] Golding, Pref. 34; vi. 127, 144–5, 154–5.

[14] V. i. 222–4, probably a vestige from *Pandosto*, where the motif of a potential incestuous relationship between Pandosto (Leontes) and Fawnia (Perdita) is much stronger—so strong, indeed, that when Pandosto discovers how close he has been to committing the unnatural deed, he commits suicide, thus 'clos[ing] up the Comedie with a Tragicall stratageme' (Bullough, viii. 199).

[15] In Peele's mythological play, *The Arraignment of Paris*, Flora herself delivers a flower-catalogue that is similar to Perdita's (I. i. 50–71); Shakespeare's departure from this precedent makes the identification with Proserpina all the more striking.

in late June; at this one, the queen of the feast hands out 'flowers | Of middle summer' (IV. iv. 106–7). The mood is further removed from that of April, indeed it becomes positively autumnal, when the girl addresses the two strangers and alludes to the liminal moment between summer and winter: 'the year growing ancient, | Not yet on summer's death, nor on the birth | Of trembling winter' (IV. iv. 79–81). Perdita has two problems in the sequence when she hands out flowers (a scene not in Greene): the first is that the fairest flowers of the late summer season appropriate to the ageing guests are carnations and streaked gillyflowers, which she lacks because of her distaste for grafting, a process she sees as interference with nature, and the second is the absence of spring flowers to give to the youthful characters who are in the springtime of their lives:

> O Proserpina,
> For the flowers now that, frighted, thou letst fall
> From Dis's wagon!—daffodils,
> That come before the swallow dares, and take
> The winds of March with beauty; violets, dim,
> But sweeter than the lids of Juno's eyes
> Or Cytherea's breath; pale primroses,
> That die unmarried ere they can behold
> Bright Phoebus in his strength—a malady
> Most incident to maids; bold oxlips, and
> The crown imperial; lilies of all kinds,
> The flower-de-luce being one, O, these I lack,
> To make you garlands of.
>
> (IV. iv. 116–28)

The undertow of allusion to the classical gods forces us to read this speech mythologically as well as naturally. Flowers here have a metamorphic power—daffodils can charm the wild winds of March and yellow fritillaries can signify royalty ('The crown imperial'), thus further anticipating Perdita's true royal identity. And the language itself is metamorphic: 'O, these I lack' comes as a shock because in the mind's eye the flowers have been present. For nearly everyone who sees the play, these spring flowers are more 'real', more memorable, than the rosemary, rue, and flowers of middle summer which Perdita has handed to Polixenes and Camillo. Something similar happens with the apostrophe to Proserpina: Perdita is saying that she is not like Proserpina, because she lacks the flowers, but in realizing the flowers linguistically she becomes Proserpina. She has picked up what her predecessor dropped when whisked away by Dis.[16]

At what moment in her story is Proserpina being reincarnated? In answering this question one sees why Florizel was wrong to mention April. The play does not have the bipartite structure that Time's division of it would seem to imply. To read the first three acts as winter (Leontes' frosty emotions and Hermione's apparent death) and the latter two as spring (Perdita as Proserpina returning from the underworld) is to oversimplify. Through her linguistic art in the flower-catalogue, Perdita is able to bring back the spring, but she can only do so for the duration of the speech; as the scene unfolds, it darkens. Polixenes' exit line threatens the dispatch of Perdita *to* the underworld:

> if ever henceforth thou
> These rural latches to his entrance open,
> Or hoop his body more with thy embraces,
> I will devise a death as cruel for thee
> As thou art tender to't.
>
> (IV. iv. 437–41)

In accordance with the reference to the year growing old, reaching the threshold between summer's death and the birth of trembling winter, this is the autumnal moment when Dis makes his annual reclamation of Proserpina. Florizel's oath to the effect that if he should prove unfaithful nature should 'crush the sides o'th' earth together | And mar the seeds within' (IV. iv. 478–9) raises the terrible possibility of Proserpina, personification of the seed within the earth, not being allowed out of the underworld. There is a chill in the air at the breaking up of the feast; summer is at an end, the holiday is over, and winter will return.

But then there is a turn in the action, effected by the benign agency of Camillo. He saves Perdita from her threatened death, as Paulina had previously saved Hermione—that is why his marriage to Paulina at the end, though it always raises a laugh in the theatre, is symbolically fitting. Thanks to Camillo, instead of going to her death

---

[16] E. A. J. Honigmann proposes further links between Perdita and Proserpina in his article, 'Secondary Sources of *The Winter's Tale*', *PQ* xxxiv (1955), 27–38: Leontes refers to Mamillius, the child whose loss is partially redeemed when Perdita is found, as his 'collop' (I. ii. 139), a word used by Golding's Ceres for Proserpina (v. 651); both girls are daughters of the Queen of Sicily (might this be why Shakespeare made Leontes Sicilian, whereas in his primary source Greene's *Pandosto* is Bohemian?).

Perdita goes to the winter kingdom of Leontes. Thus the play in fact has a tripartite structure: the first three acts are a sad tale signifying winter, the fourth traverses through the sheep-shearing festival to summer's end, and in the fifth we return to winter but this time Perdita enters it. She does so as Proserpina and we know that Proserpina's sojourn in the kingdom of death will be a temporary one, that she will soon emerge with the new life of spring. As Leontes turns to Perdita, early in the fifth act, he says to Florizel, 'Welcome hither, | As is the spring to th'earth!' (v. i. 150–1).

The Proserpina myth invites Shakespeare to enact the arrival of spring at the climax of the play in the form of a nature myth or fertility ritual. But he declines the invitation. In the fifth act, Perdita no longer wears her flowers. The reunion of father and child which gave the language of fertility to *Pericles* ('Thou that begett'st him that did thee beget') is removed from the centre, given only in reported speech. Nor, except fleetingly in Paulina's lines 'Do not shun her | Until you see her die again, for then | You kill her double' (v. iii. 105–7), does Shakespeare turn to the other great Ovidian ascent from the underworld, that of Eurydice, with its tragic end in the wife's 'double dying' (Golding, x. 69). What takes centre-stage instead is a myth that turns back Ovid's normal pattern, a metamorphosis that is driven by art not nature and that takes the form of depetrification rather than the usual petrification.[17]

[17] I am presupposing here that Shakespeare and his audience would have thought of the story of Pygmalion as the archetype for the animation of a statue. It was certainly much alluded to and illustrated in the 16th cent. It is possible, however, that there is an alternative or additional Ovidian archetype. When Polixenes threatens to disinherit Florizel he says that he will 'Not hold thee of our blood, no, not our kin, | Farre than Deucalion off' (IV. iv. 431–2). Why Deucalion? Is it simply to suggest distance (Deucalion lived a very long time ago)? Or is it to summon up the pattern of destruction and re-creation in bk. I of the *Metamorphoses*, where after the coming of death in universal flood, there is an advent of new life from the stones which Deucalion and Pyrrha throw over their shoulders at the command of the oracle of Themis?

> Even like to Marble ymages new drawne and roughly wrought,
> Before the Carver by his Arte to purpose hath them brought.
> Such partes of them where any juice or moysture did abound,
> Or else were earthie, turnd too flesh . . .
>
> . . . .
>
> Thus by the mightie powre of Gods ere longer time was past,
> The mankinde was restorde by stones the which a man did cast.
>   (Golding, i. 483–90)

If we link the animation of Hermione's stone to this moment, then the winter/spring pattern finds an antique parallel in that of flood/new life. The parallel is discussed in François Laroque, 'A New Ovidian Source for the Statue Scene in *The Winter's Tale*',

The myth in question is first signalled by an image used by the third gentleman in his account of Perdita's effect on the winter court: 'Who was most marble there changed colour' (v. ii. 89). This is not only in accordance with her spring-like capacity to bring warmth and colour; it also prepares the ground for the animation of 'her mother's statue', which is mentioned for the first time in the third gentleman's next speech. He describes it as 'newly performed by that rare Italian master Giulio Romano, who, had he himself eternity and could put breath into his work, would beguile nature of her custom, so perfectly he is her ape' (v. ii. 95–9). The figures of Perdita bringing colour to marble and the Italian master putting breath into his statue bring into proximity two key elements of Ovid's most celebrated story of artistic creation: Pygmalion and his ivory image of a beautiful girl. But Paulina's animation of Hermione's statue does not so much directly allude to the Pygmalion story as subtly metamorphose it; the relationship is more oblique than that of *Venus and Adonis* to its prototype story (which is told on the heels of that of Pygmalion). In contrast to his earlier practice, Shakespeare ignores the context in Book Ten of the *Metamorphoses*: it is not relevant that Pygmalion devotes himself to his statue because he is disgusted with women (he has witnessed the brazen behaviour of the Propoetides, the first prostitutes, who are turned to stone immediately before his story, with its inverse movement from stone); nor is it relevant that his sexual union with his artwork begets the tragic line Paphos, Cinyras, Myrrha, and Adonis. All these dark contours are removed. The mature dramatist concentrates instead on three positive aspects of the story: the power of imagination or wish-fulfilment, the magic of the awakening, and, crucially, the art that outdoes nature. In emphasizing art, Shakespeare is following Ovid, whose principal innovation in the myth was to make the man who desires the statue not a king but the sculptor himself.[18]

Pygmalion carves an ivory statue so realistic that it seems to be a real girl, so beautiful that he falls in love with it. He desperately wants to believe it is real and there are moments when the perfection of the art is such that the statue does seem to be struggling into life:

N&Q ns xxxi (1984), 215–17. The imagery of stones softening is striking, but ultimately the Pygmalion story is the more potent source because of its interest in the power of the *artist*.

[18] See Hermann Fraenkel, *Ovid: A Poet between Two Worlds* (Berkeley and Los Angeles, 1945), 96, and Barkan, *The Gods Made Flesh*, 303 n. 52. On Ovid's innovative handling of the story more generally, see Brooks Otis, *Ovid as an Epic Poet* (2nd edn.,

> With many a touch he tries it—is it flesh
> Or ivory? Not ivory still, he's sure!
> Kisses he gives and thinks they are returned;
> He speaks to it, caresses it, believes
> The firm new flesh beneath his fingers yields,
> And fears the limbs may darken with a bruise.[19]

(The image of a blue-black—'livor'—bruise on the snow-white ivory is quintessential Ovid.) Pygmalion acts out a fantasy of bringing gifts to and dressing his love; on the festival of Venus he prays for a bride who will be the living likeness of his ivory girl, when what he really means is that he wants the ivory girl itself. The idea that the 'living' being would be but an image of the statue is characteristic of the story's wholesale inversion of the normative relationship between life and art. When he returns from Venus' altar, his wish is fulfilled and a kiss brings the statue to softness, warmth, and colour:

> And he went home, home to his heart's delight,
> And kissed her as she lay, and she seemed warm;
> Again he kissed her and with marvelling touch
> Caressed her breast; beneath his touch the flesh
> Grew soft, its ivory hardness vanishing.
>
> .   .   .   .
>
> She was alive! The pulse beat in her veins!
> And then indeed in words that overflowed
> He poured his thanks to Venus, and at last
> His lips pressed real lips, and she, his girl,
> Felt every kiss, and blushed, and shyly raised
> Her eyes to his and saw the world and him.
>
> (x. 279–83, 291–6, trans. Melville)

This moment when the eyes are raised is one of the most theatrical in all Ovid. It is exactly the sort of detail that would have attracted Shakespeare to the story.

Shakespeare learnt from this sequence both an idea and a style. If you want something badly enough and you believe in it hard enough,

Cambridge, 1970): 'That it was Ovid himself who changed the indecent or pathological agalmatophily [sexual relation with a statue] . . . to the idealistic love of this episode is, it seems to me, overwhelmingly probable' (p. 389). The Pygmalion story, with its interest in the central Ovidian topoi of art, love, and stone, has been seen as a pivotal story in the *Metamorphoses* as a whole—Douglas T. Bauer, 'The Function of Pygmalion in the *Metamorphoses* of Ovid', *TAPA* xciii (1962), 1–21.

[19] *Metamorphoses*, x. 254–9, trans. Melville. Golding lacks the delicacy which the whole sequence in Ovid's original shares with the closing scene of *The Winter's Tale*.

From Myth to Drama

you will eventually get it. It is the idea which tragedy denies but comedy affirms. It is the illusion which theatre can foster, as Paulina insists through her challenge to her double audience, those on the stage and those looking at the stage:

> It is required
> You do awake your faith. Then, all stand still.
> Or those that think it is unlawful business
> I am about, let them depart.
>
> (v. iii. 94–7)

Linguistically, Ovid shows Shakespeare that the way to evoke this leap of faith is through pinpricks of sensation. The progression is both precise and sensuous: blood pulses through the veins, the lips respond, the ivory face flushes. Correspondingly, Leontes contrasts the warm life his queen once had with the coldness of the statue, but then he seems to see blood in the veins and warmth upon the lip. And when she descends and embraces him, she *is* warm.

I have shown that throughout his career Shakespeare transformed into metaphors the metamorphoses which Ovid played out at the level of mythic narrative. Malvolio speaks like a Narcissus without actually becoming a flower; it is Othello's language, not his body, that is reduced to bestiality; Lear's metaphor, 'O, you are men of stones', replaces the literal metamorphosis of Niobe into stone. Now near the end of his career, Shakespeare reverses the process, something he had previously done only in comedy (Bottom as ass, Falstaff as Actaeon). Initially, Leontes freezes Hermione out of his life. Her body-contact with Polixenes is 'Too hot, too hot' (I. ii. 110)—he wants her to be frigid. His jealous look is like that of the basilisk or the Medusa: he turns his wife to stone.[20] In the final act, this metaphor becomes a metamorphosis as Hermione is depetrified. The transformation is triumphantly realized on stage both linguistically and visually. 'Does not the stone rebuke me | For being more stone than it?', asks Leontes when confronted with the statue (v. iii. 37–8). The hardened image of his wife forces him at last to turn his gaze inward upon his own hard heart. The final act shows the melting of that heart and the rekindling of love, with its concordant release of Hermione back into warmth, softness, and life.

Although Venus gives Pygmalion a sign that she favours his

---

[20] 'The husband treats the wife lovelessly, and she becomes a stony lady', writes Leonard Barkan, linking the statue to the 'donna petrosa' figure in Petrarch. His discussion of the scene (*The Gods Made Flesh*, 283–7) is the best that I know.

request and he is appropriately grateful when the metamorphosis into life takes place, Ovid avoids actually saying that Venus quickened the statue. It is the force of Pygmalion's art, imagination, and will-power which seems to have done the trick. The girl becomes a reward for his skill and perseverance; the statue was made with an art that in concealing its own art ('ars adeo latet arte sua'—x. 252) surpassed nature, and the reward for this triumph is that it becomes life.

So too in *The Winter's Tale*. One life-bringing force is Perdita, but the other is Paulina's art, which stands in for Giulio Romano's, which stands in for Shakespeare's.[21] As every critic notices, a debate between art and nature pervades the play—it is there even in the opening dialogue as Camillo remarks that the two kings were 'train'd' together (I. i. 22), a verb suggesting on the one hand that the bond between the two kings is natural (tree-like), and on the other that it depends on the arts of educational nurture (analogous to horticultural artifice). When Perdita and Polixenes have their argument about art and nature in the pastoral scene, the choice is between unmediated nature and the art that shares with nature. But the final scene seems to offer an art like Pygmalion's, 'surpassing the perfection of Nature'.[22] Giulio Romano, it may be said, is at once Pygmalion and Shakespeare: he 'beguile[s] nature of her custom, so perfectly he is her ape'. Nature cannot bring Hermione back from the dead, but art does. In *The Tempest*, one will worry as to whether Prospero's magical art of opening graves is lawful, especially as it is imitated from Ovid's witch, Medea. But *The Winter's Tale* proclaims that Paulina's magic is 'an art | Lawful as eating' (v. iii. 110–11). Those who doubt it are politely told to depart.

It is lawful, of course, because this is not really an animation or a resurrection. Paulina is staging a theatrical coup. Shakespeare has triumphantly moved from Ovid's key of myth into his own of drama. The animation of a statue is a device by no means unique to this play—in Campion's *Lords' Masque*, performed, as *The Winter's Tale* was, in celebration of Princess Elizabeth's marriage in 1613, eight golden statues are 'new-transformed' into ladies[23]—but what is

[21] David Armitage ('The Dismemberment of Orpheus', 130) suggests that the art is also that of Orpheus: the Pygmalion story is in the Orphic section of the *Metamorphoses*, and a parallel is established by the combination of music and the animation of stone. As in *Titus Andronicus* and *Edward III*, Shakespeare implicitly makes an Orphic claim for himself.

[22] Sandys's commentary on bk. 10, *Ovid's Metamorphosis Englished*, p. 361.

[23] *A Book of Masques in Honour of Allardyce Nicoll* (Cambridge, 1967), 113.

exceptional in Shakespeare's effect is the perfect correspondence between the character's performance and the actor's. As the preserved Hermione pretends to be a statue coming to life, so does the boy actor. When we realize that Paulina and Hermione are staging a performance and when we see the correspondence between character and actor, we recognize that the magic which Paulina claims to be lawful is that of theatre. So we see that it is a magic which depends on our complicity: Paulina's demand that non-believers should depart is Shakespeare's demand that the theatre audience should suspend its disbelief, and Leontes' final request that each one should demand and answer to his part performed in the story is Shakespeare's request that we should go away and talk about the play and our role in it.

Although in these after-reflections we become aware of the contrivances of art, which of us can watch the moment of awakening in a good production and not believe for a moment that a statue is coming to life? In that moment, Shakespeare has achieved the seemingly impossible feat of staging an Ovidian metamorphosis. But in two crucial respects it is not a dramatization of the depetrification in the Pygmalion story. First, it is not a divine intervention but a human coup, a manifestation of creative female power: this is the distinctively Shakespearian *species humanitatis*. And secondly, where Pygmalion's statue becomes a beautiful woman in her prime, Giulio Romano's bears the marks of time. To Leontes' dismay, the face is wrinkled as his beloved Hermione's was not. 'So much the more our carver's excellence, | Which lets go by some sixteen years, and makes her | As she lived now' (v. iii. 30–2). Rosalie Colie saw the point and expressed it beautifully:

Beauty's perfection, exemplified in Perdita's smooth cheek, gives way before the meaning and pathos of those wrinkles—even the ideal beauty of a mode emphasizing aesthetic ideals retires before the values attributed to suffering and feeling, validated by being experienced over time. . . . Wrinkles are the anti-romantic attributes of mature life: if Hermione is to be restored to Leontes with any significance to that restoration, she must return at time's full cost, her loss made calculable and conscious. The wrinkles are signs that suffering really *means*.[24]

It is not enough to say of the statue scene that nowhere does Shakespeare's art substitute more brilliantly for myth, nowhere is there more powerful testimony to the creative, even redemptive,

---

[24] Colie, *Shakespeare's Living Art* (Princeton, NJ, 1974), 280, 282.

power of drama, nowhere is there a creative coup more *wonder*ful. For it must also be said that the redemption is only partial, it is neither a reversal of time nor a transcendence into eternity. Sixteen years was a very large proportion of an adult life in the seventeenth century; Leontes and Hermione have missed a lot and will not be together much longer. And Mamillius and Antigonus will not return. As a young man writing sonnets, Shakespeare could claim with Ovid that his art had the power to defeat time. Sonnets such as 19, 60, and 65 close with the same confidence as the *Metamorphoses*: 'Yet do thy worst, old time; despite thy wrong | My love shall in my verse ever live young'. As an older man, ending *The Winter's Tale*, Shakespeare does not wager on the future. He uses the drama not to articulate a mythic vision of the eternal nature of things, but to tell a story about how it is possible to love and to forgive. He asks only that we should have a certain faith in humankind, in its resilience and its capacity to start again.

III

Ovid told the story of Medea not only in the twelfth letter of his *Heroides* and the seventh book of his *Metamorphoses*, but also in a play. It was praised by Quintilian, but only two lines survive. Ovid's poems are so full of *coups de théâtre*, of supple insights into character, and of gestural precision that one longs for the *Medea* to be found. Euripides was doubtless its model, and it is highly probable that Ovid's tragedy would have been closer in spirit to its Greek original than to the surviving Roman dramatic version of the Medea story traditionally attributed to Seneca. Despite the resemblances between *The Winter's Tale* and *Alcestis*, *Titus Andronicus* and *Hecuba*, it cannot be proved that Shakespeare knew any of the plays of Euripides.[25] But there is no doubt that he derived a Euripidean spirit from Ovid. Euripides taught Ovid what Ovid taught Shakespeare: an art of tragicomedy, a way of writing about the mind under the stress of extreme passion, a sensitivity to female suffering. It is therefore fitting that *The Tempest* alludes crucially to the story that was the subject of Ovid's only play; Shakespeare ended his career by collaborating with Fletcher, but his last solo performance was a kind of collaboration with Ovid.

[25] The strongest, but by no means conclusive, arguments that he did are those of Emrys Jones in *The Origins of Shakespeare*.

The Tempest does not, however, have the kind of sustained relationship with the Medea story that *Titus Andronicus* had with the Philomel narrative. Rather, it moves among a bewildering array of mythic materials, echoing in its shifts of mood and tone the patterns of the *Metamorphoses*. *Titus* is Shakespeare's metamorphic tragedy, *A Midsummer Night's Dream* his metamorphic comedy, and *The Tempest* his metamorphic romance. All three plays apparently lack a direct source of the sort that Arthur Brooke's translation of Bandello was for *Romeo and Juliet*, Lodge's *Rosalynde* was for *As You Like It*, and Greene's *Pandosto* was for *The Winter's Tale*.[26] But all three are in profound ways shaped by Ovid: they represent progressively more distanced transformations of a matter and manner learnt from the *Metamorphoses*.

To describe *The Tempest* as a metamorphic romance is to beg the question of its generic classification. The compilers of the first folio placed it first among Shakespeare's comedies, while twentieth-century criticism has grouped it among the so-called late romances. Both generic terms would have been recognizable to a Jacobean audience, although the latter one was not usually applied to the drama. *The Tempest* shares with Shakespeare's earlier comedies a movement towards reconciliation and marriage, together with a sense of disaster averted. As Don John's conspiracy fails in *Much Ado About Nothing*, so the various conspiracies against Prospero fail in *The Tempest*; the play ends, in the traditional fashion of comedy, with the young lovers united, but also, like all Shakespearian comedies, with certain ends left untied—Antonio does not speak to Prospero when the elder brother offers him grudging forgiveness; the sense of exclusion recapitulates the way in which Shakespeare's earlier Antonios stand apart from the resolutions in marriage at the end of *The Merchant of Venice* and *Twelfth Night*. As for romance, *The Tempest* shares with *Pericles* sea-voyages and storm, lost children, magical transformations and revivals—all features of the romance form which may be traced back through medieval figures like Gower, the narrator of *Pericles*, to Hellenistic sources such as the tale of

[26] This is not the place to rehearse the relationship between *Titus*, the 1594 ballad on the subject, and the prose chapbook *History of Titus Andronicus*: as I intimated in Ch. 3, I agree with G. K. Hunter's argument that the order is play–ballad–chapbook, not chapbook–ballad–play, as most scholars have believed. *Titus* would then be Shakespeare's only 'sourceless' tragedy. My reasons for agreeing with Hunter, together with additional supporting evidence, will be laid out in the introduction to my forthcoming Arden edn. of the play.

Apollonius of Tyre, which lies distantly behind not only *Pericles* but also the romance element of *The Comedy of Errors*.

Recent critical readers have, however, described the play rather differently, proposing that it is an *imperial* drama. There have been attempts to link *The Tempest* to the Jacobean court: its two earliest recorded performances were at court, one of them during the celebrations for the marriage of the Princess Elizabeth and the Elector Palatine; furthermore, the play includes Shakespeare's most formal masque and may therefore be said to be his nearest approximation to a court drama. Prospero's show manifestly resembles such explicitly courtly and aristocratic works as Ben Jonson's wedding masque of 1606, *Hymenaei*. But Prospero's masque is not the whole play: indeed, it is not even completed and it is a symptom of the vain art that the play as a whole purports to reject. Nor is there any evidence that it was written as an allegory of the betrothal of the king's daughter, just as there is no evidence that *A Midsummer Night's Dream* was written for an aristocratic wedding. And the fact that the play was performed at court does not in any way mean that it was written for the court or about the court.

The external evidence for a reading of *The Tempest* as imperial drama is therefore flimsy. Two kinds of internal evidence have been adduced: first, the play's allusions to the establishment of empire, what may be described as its New World context; and, secondly, its apparent relationship with the exemplary poem about the establishment of empire, Virgil's *Aeneid*. Donna B. Hamilton has recently devoted an entire book to an imperial reading along Virgilian lines; she is of the view that *The Tempest* is 'a formal imitation of the first six books of the *Aeneid*, both in its larger patterns of theme and structure and in its smaller details of vocabulary and syntax'.[27]

The Virginia Company was established by royal charter in 1606, the Jamestown Colony set up in 1607. In 1609 several hundred potential new colonists ran into a storm near the Virginia coast; the ship of Sir Thomas Gates, the governor, was driven to Bermuda, where it landed safely and the voyagers were able to winter. It has long been recognized that William Strachey's eyewitness account of these events is a likely source for various details in the play, though Shakespeare would have had to see the 'Strachey letter' in

---

[27] Hamilton, *Virgil and 'The Tempest': The Politics of Imitation* (Columbus, Ohio, 1990), 4.

manuscript, since it was not published until 1625. Several allusions give the play a New World aura. Few audience members could have missed the resonance of Miranda's 'O brave new world', ironic as her wonder is in context. Ariel links the tempest to the New World with his reference to the 'still-vexed Bermudas'. Caliban's god Setebos is a Patagonian deity, mentioned in Magellan's voyages; the name Caliban itself inevitably suggests 'cannibal' and thus a certain image of New World savages. Prospero's enslavement of Caliban seems to be a stage-image of colonial oppression—in particular, his use of language as a method of control is, according to Stephen Greenblatt in his influential essay 'Learning to Curse', a classic strategy of colonialism.[28] Trinculo apprehends Caliban as a bizarre creature who may be exploited for financial gain: 'Were I in England now, as once I was, and had but this fish painted, not a holiday-fool there but would give a piece of silver. There would this monster make a man—any strange beast there makes a man. When they will not give a doit to relieve a lame beggar, they will lay out ten to see a dead Indian.' The idea is explained by Frank Kermode in a laconic footnote: 'Such exhibitions were a regular feature of colonial policy under James I. The exhibits rarely survived the experience.'[29]

The text also draws on more positive images of the New World: the island is rich in natural produce and may thus be read as a virgin land—a Virginia—ripe with Utopian possibilities. So it is that Gonzalo lifts from Montaigne's essay 'Of the Caniballes' a Utopian vision of what he would do if he had the 'plantation' (the word denotes the right to colonize) of the isle. Montaigne inverted the normative view of the relationship between 'civilized' and 'savage', arguing that the inhabitants of the 'new world' of the Americas were the truly civilized ones since they were closer to 'their originall naturalitie' and 'the lawes of nature' than are the Europeans. 'It is a nation', he wrote in a sentence closely imitated by Shakespeare,

that hath no kinde of traffike, no knowledge of Letters, no intelligence of numbers, no name of magistrate, nor of politike superioritie; no use of service, of riches or of povertie; no contracts, no successions, no partitions, no

---

[28] Greenblatt, 'Learning to Curse: Aspects of Linguistic Colonialism in the Sixteenth Century', in *First Images of America: The Impact of the New World on the Old*, ed. Fredi Chiappelli, 2 vols. (Berkeley and Los Angeles, 1976), ii. 561–80, repr. as the title-essay of Greenblatt's *Learning to Curse* (London, 1990).

[29] Note to Trinculo's speech at II. ii. 27–32, in Arden edn. (London, 1954).

occupation but idle; no respect of kinred, but common, no apparrell but naturall, no manuring of lands, no use of wine, corne, or mettle.[30]

That Shakespeare read Montaigne's wide-ranging critique of European assumptions about the inferiority of 'barbarians' prior to writing *The Tempest* is the most compelling piece of evidence in support of the view that the play is a troubled exploration of imperial and colonial strategies. Montaigne and Shakespeare have thus come to the assistance of post-colonial critics who for good reasons need to work through their own guilt about these matters.

But there are problems with a New World reading. Caliban's god may be of the New World, but his mother, a much more important figure, is from the old world: apparently Prospero considers it necessary to remind Ariel once a month that she was born in Algiers. Caliban himself is not a native inhabitant of the island: he is the child of the Algerian Sycorax who was herself an earlier exile to the island. Prospero is not establishing an empire, he is exiled to a place that is thought to be barren. The play is not at all interested in the things that colonization is primarily interested in: gold, spices, tobacco. And the location of the island is not the New World, but what was for the Elizabethans the centre of the old world, the Mediterranean; Shakespeare is careful to inform his audience that the shipwreck occurs *en route* from Tunis to Naples.

This is where the second imperial strand, Virgil's *Aeneid*, enters. In the first scene in which the victims of the storm appear on the island, there is a lengthy exchange about 'widow Dido', 'widower Aeneas', and the identity of Carthage with Tunis. One gets the impression of Shakespeare vigorously waving a flag marked *Aeneid*. 'This Tunis, sir, was Carthage' (II. i. 88). As in the Dido section of *The Aeneid*, there is a broad pattern of storm, shipwreck, and new love. Then again, Naples is close to Cumae, where Aeneas made landfall in Italy. Cumae was the entrance to the underworld: critics have therefore compared the adventures in the enchanted island of *The Tempest* to those of Aeneas in the underworld; in each strange place, both past and future are conjured up, a process of sacrifice and initiation is undergone, and the initiates emerge in some sense redeemed, ready for a fresh start.[31] A

---

[30] 'Of the Caniballes', *The Essayes of Montaigne*, bk. 1, ch. 30, Florio trans., quoted from 1933 edn., p. 164.

[31] This argument seems to have been first articulated by Colin Still in his mystically minded *The Timeless Theme* (London, 1936); more recent treatments include two essays by Jan Kott reprinted in his *The Bottom Translation* (Chicago, 1987), Robert Miola, 'Vergil in Shakespeare: From Allusion to Imitation', in *Vergil at 2000: Commemorative*

number of local borrowings have also been traced: for instance, the appearance of Ariel 'like a harpy' during the banquet (III. iii. 52sd) echoes an incident in the third book of *The Aeneid* when harpies befoul the Trojans' food on the Strophades; and Ferdinand's reaction to the sight of Miranda, 'most sure, the goddess | On whom these airs attend' (I. ii. 424–5), is also that of Aeneas to the sight of Venus after the Trojan shipwreck ('O dea certe'—*Aen.* i.32 8).

But it is extremely difficult to make the pattern fit. An alternative source for the harpy has been found in Sabinus' commentary on Ovid, where it is connected to King Alfonso of Naples.[32] And as for the broader parallel, is it with Dido's Carthage or the Sibyl's underworld? Claribel in Tunis is not a distraction from empire-building, as Dido Queen of Carthage was for Aeneas (or indeed as Cleopatra is for Antony). The dynastic marriage linking Milan with Naples at the end of the play is something very different from Aeneas' founding of a new empire in Rome. Nor is there a generic match: *epic* is the form of imperial narrative, not romance or comedy, the genres of *The Tempest*.

Shakespeare's play could, however, be described as a romance-style reworking of epic material. His precedent for such a reworking was Ovid's *Metamorphoses*, the later books of which cover some of the same ground as *The Aeneid*, but in a revisionary way. Robert Wiltenburg concludes his essay on 'The *Aeneid* in *The Tempest*' with the following claim:

> Just as Virgil subsumed the Homeric stories of men who fight primarily for themselves to the story of a man who fights primarily for his culture, his concept of civilization, so Shakespeare has subsumed the search for law, for justice, the story told so well by Virgil, into his own larger story of the search for 'kindness'.[33]

I do not find the comparison with Virgil's treatment of Homer at all illuminating. I would say rather that Shakespeare revises—which is

Essays on the Poet and his Influence, ed. J. D. Bernard (New York, 1986), 241–58, John Pitcher, 'A Theatre of the Future: *The Aeneid* and *The Tempest*', *Essays in Criticism*, xxxiv (1984), 193–215, Robert Wiltenburg, 'The *Aeneid* in *The Tempest*', *ShS* xxxix (1987), 159–68, and the book by Donna B. Hamilton cited above. Among the countless misrepresentations in Ted Hughes, *Shakespeare and the Goddess of Complete Being* (London, 1992), is the claim that 'The smouldering presence of that previous life, in which Miranda was Dido, seems to become more and more the secret, poignant, smothered tragedy of this play' (p. 423).

[32] See Anthony DiMattio, '"The Figure of this Harpy": Shakespeare and the Moralized Ovid', *N&Q* NS xxxviii (1991), 70–2.

[33] Wiltenburg, 'The *Aeneid* in *The Tempest*', 168.

to say incorporates but also in important ways sidesteps—Virgil's imperial theme in the same way that Ovid does.[34] In Ovid, Aeneas' journey is a *frame*: the real interest is in the metamorphic encounters along the way. So too in *The Tempest*, the voyage is a frame; the redemption of the three men of sin, Alonso, Antonio, and Sebastian, is not the absolute focal point, indeed it is questionable whether it fully occurs, given Antonio's apparent refusal to acknowledge Prospero at the moment of forgiveness. What the imperial theme is subsumed into is a demonstration of the pervasiveness of change, and in this sense *The Tempest* is Shakespeare's last revision of the *Metamorphoses*.

The earlier Shakespearian play which *The Tempest* comes closest to resembling is that other most Ovidian comedy, *A Midsummer Night's Dream*. Like Puck, the vernacular equivalent of Ovid's Cupid, Ariel both changes form himself and is an agent who brings about change in the mortals on whom he works. We see him as water-nymph, as Harpy, as actor playing Ceres. We hear of him dividing himself like fire aboard the king's ship and of him leading the conspirators a dance so that they prick their ears like unbacked colts and low like calves. Above all, we hear him sing the great song of metamorphosis:

> Full fathom five thy father lies.
>   Of his bones are coral made;
> Those are pearls that were his eyes;
>   Nothing of him that doth fade
> But doth suffer a sea-change
> Into something rich and strange.
>   (I. ii. 309–404)

The father is not literally changed into part of the sea, as would happen in Ovid or in Spenser's protean world; instead, the bodily changes are metaphors for the inner changes that Prospero seeks to work. When Alonso is brought to see his wickedness, he inwardly undergoes the voyage to the bottom of the sea that Ariel has evoked in the song to Ferdinand:

> It did bass my trespass.
> Therefore my son i'th' ooze is bedded, and
> I'll seek him deeper than e'er plummet sounded,
> And with him there lie mudded.
>   (III. iii. 99–102)

[34] Ariosto provides a parallel 'romance' reworking: as Daniel Javitch shows, Astolfo's adventures in hell and ascent to the moon in canto 34 of *Orlando Furioso* are a parodic rewriting of Dante's *Commedia*, inspired by Ovid's version of *The Aeneid* in

'Sea-change' is, as Reuben Brower pointed out in an analysis of the play's imagery,[35] this drama's principal motif. To see this is to apprehend Shakespeare's drift away from the stability of *The Aeneid* into the shifting world of the *Metamorphoses*, where nothing fades but everyone suffers water-change, land-change, or god-change into things rich and strange.

The comparison between Prospero's island and Virgil's underworld seems to me hard to sustain. Tonally, there is much more of a resemblance to the islands visited by Ovid's Aeneas and to the pastoral landscapes and language of the narratives framed by the voyage. A favourite Ovidian device was the representation of a landscape *in bono* or *in male* according to the state of mind of the describer. Shakespeare has a very formal imitation of the device in *Titus Andronicus*: when Tamora is making love to Aaron, the wood is a *locus amoenus*, but when she feigns that Bassianus and Lavinia mean to do her mischief the place suddenly becomes 'A barren detested vale'—in her first description 'The snakes lie rollèd in the cheerful sun', in the second the sun never shines and the snakes are hissing.[36] When Caliban is helping Trinculo and Stephano, the island is fertile and abundant with food:

> I prithee, let me bring thee where crabs grow,
> And I with my long nails will dig thee pig-nuts,
> Show thee a jay's nest, and instruct thee how
> To snare the nimble marmoset. I'll bring thee
> To clust'ring filberts, and sometimes I'll get thee
> Young scamels from the rock.
>
> (II. ii. 166–71)

But when he is cursing Prospero and Miranda, it is a barren and unhealthy place:

> As wicked dew as e'er my mother brushed
> With raven's feather from unwholesome fen
> Drop on you both! A south-west blow on ye
> And blister you all o'er!
>
> (I. ii. 323–6)

bks. 13 and 14 of the *Metamorphoses*—'The *Orlando Furioso* and Ovid's Revision of the *Aeneid*', *MLN* xcix (1984), 1023–36.

[35] Brower, 'The Mirror of Analogy: *The Tempest*', in his *The Fields of Light: An Experiment in Critical Reading* (London, 1951), 95–122.

[36] *Titus Andronicus*, II. iii. 12–29, 92–108.

and, again, 'All the infections that the sun sucks up | From bogs, fens, flats, on Prosper fall' (II. ii. 1–2).

Embedded within the Aeneas narrative in Book Thirteen of the *Metamorphoses* is the tale of Polyphemus the Cyclops. Like Caliban, the Cyclops is perceived as deformed, yet endowed with a vivid poetry of nature. In his courtship of Galatea, he holds out the promise of lush fruits:

> Gay Apples weying downe the boughes have I, and Grapes like gold,
> And purple Grapes on spreaded Vynes as many as can hold,
> Bothe which I doo reserve for thee. Thyself shalt with thy hand
> The soft sweete strawbryes gather, which in wooddy shadowe stand.
> The Cornell berryes also from the tree thy self shalt pull,
> And pleasant plommes, sum yellow lyke new wax, sum blew, sum full
> Of ruddy jewce. Of Chestnutts eeke (if my wyfe thou wilt bee)
> Thou shalt have store: and frutes all sortes.
>
> (Golding, xiii. 956–63)

This speech is heavy with wonder and sensuousness in its feel for the textures of the fruits of the earth; it adumbrates the rich natural language that is given first to Caliban and then to Ceres/Ariel as (s)he sings of 'Vines with clust'ring bunches growing, | Plants with goodly burden bowing'. But when Galatea refuses to yield to Polyphemus' love, nature is turned around and used as a way of describing her cruelty: she is said to be harder than aged oak, tougher than willow twigs, sharper than thorns, more pitiless than a trodden snake, and so on.[37]

Caliban is a deeply un-Virgilian creation. If we are to think in the characteristically Renaissance way and find a classical precedent for this figure created from more contemporary sources, such as travel literature, it is to Ovid that we must go. In the 'Names of the Actors' at the end of the folio text Caliban is described as a 'salvage and deformed slave': the *Metamorphoses* constitute classical literature's major depository of deformities; George Sandys, who actually began his translation whilst crossing the Atlantic to take up the post of treasurer of the Virginia Company, described the Cyclops in his commentary as a 'salvage people . . . more salvage than are the *West-Indians* at this day', treating them as exemplars of lawlessness and lack of civility.[38]

---

[37] *Met.* xiii. 789–97 and 798–807 represent a formally paired set of apostrophes, the first *in bono*, the second *in male*: they could well be the model for Tamora's pair of speeches in *Titus*.

[38] Sandys, *Ovid's Metamorphosis Englished* (1632), 477–8.

A second precedent for Caliban might be the semi-human Cercopes, who are encountered early in Ovid's version of Aeneas' travels. They are 'an evillfavored kynd of beast: that beeing none, | They myght yit still resemble men', their bodies clad all over with 'fallow coulourd' hair (Golding, xiv. 110–14). They swear and perjure themselves until in punishment they lose their speech and are turned into screeching monkeys; in Golding's translation, Jupiter 'did bereeve them of the use of speeche and toong, | Which they too cursed perjurye did use bothe old and yoong' (xiv. 116–17). Language raises man above the beasts; when it is debased, man returns to bestiality. Sandys's commentary on the 'Circopians' draws a parallel which is illuminating in the light of Coleridge's comparison of Caliban to the man of base language in *Troilus and Cressida*: 'From which consideration it was devised by *Plato* that the soule of *Thersites* (of all that came to *Ilium* the basest and most shamelesse) entred into an Ape; still intimating the actions of men, but retaining his old manners agreeable to that creature'.[39] By teaching Caliban language, Prospero tries to civilize him, but since the salvage and deformed creature is naturally bestial, since he has a devilish nature on whom nurture can never stick, all he learns is how to curse. Caliban expresses his own affinity with the Cercopes when he recognizes the risk that he and his fellow-conspirators may be turned by Prospero 'to apes | With foreheads villainous low' (IV. i. 247–8).

But the complexity of the play is such that this is not the whole truth about Caliban. He does not only curse, he also has his language of nature's fertility and his capacity to hear music. As the Cyclops aspires to become a lover and a poet, in a sequence of the *Metamorphoses* that holds the beautiful together with the grotesque, so the play demands that we see pathos, even beauty, in the deformed creature. Both Ovid and Shakespeare have some cruel comedy at the expense of their creations—Polyphemus sees himself reflected in a pool and, not realizing what a fool he is making of himself, tries to convince Galatea that hairy is beautiful—but their writing also expresses extraordinary pity for these articulate beings trapped in ugly bodies.

It is Jove who metamorphoses the Cercopes into apes, Prospero who has the power to do the same to Caliban. This is a crucial difference between *The Tempest* and the *Metamorphoses*. As the play's sea-

---

[39] Ibid. 476. For Coleridge on Thersites as 'the Caliban of demagogic life', see *The Romantics on Shakespeare*, 548.

changes herald inner transformations, so the poem intimates in its first line that it will be characterized by change and strangeness: 'In nova fert animus mutatas dicere formas | corpora' (*Met.* i. 1–2, translated by Golding as 'Of shapes transformde to bodies straunge, I purpose to entreate'). But the second line of the poem ascribes those changes to the gods: 'di . . . nam vos mutastis et illas' ('Ye gods . . . for you are they that wrought this wondrous feate'). It is a mark of Prospero's power that he can perform the transformations tradition-ally enacted by the gods: he can release Ariel from a tree and imprison him there again (there could be no more Ovidian idea than that of birth from and metamorphosis to a tree); he can restrict Caliban ('you sty me | In this hard rock'—i. ii. 344–5) and can freeze a group of mortals, imprisoning them in the lime-grove from which they cannot budge till he releases them. But might such actions also be indications that Prospero is usurping powers which should properly belong only to a god?

Mortals may perform transformations by means of magic; in the Renaissance, the changes wrought by witchcraft and alchemy would have been thought of as prime examples. Like language, magic is a mark of man's superiority over the beasts. In his *Magnalia Naturae*, Bacon proposed that the new philosophy would give man the power to raise storms, control the seasons, and hasten the harvest; by studying nature, one could come to understand it and take control of its forces. Sir Walter Ralegh, in his *History of the World*, associated magic with the wise man who connected different natural agents to bring about effects which seem wonderful to those who do not understand them.[40] But there is always the risk of going too far, transgressing upon divine prerogatives, and sliding from white magic to black. The classic case is that of Dr Faustus. Occasionally in Ovid, metamorphosis is carried out by someone other than the gods. But the characters responsible are viewed as transgressive and not to be admired, for they interfere with the natural order. The most notable of them is the witch Medea.

I do not think it can be mere chance that Prospero's lengthiest description of his magical powers constitutes Shakespeare's most sustained Ovidian borrowing and identifies the arts of the mage with those of Medea. The passages in question were discussed briefly in my

---

[40] The examples from Bacon and Ralegh are both cited by Stephen Orgel in the fine introduction to his edn. of *The Tempest* (Oxford, 1987), 20.

opening chapter, in order to demonstrate that Shakespeare knew both Ovid's original Latin and Golding's translation. The dramatic significance of the correspondence must now be addressed.

Medea concentrates especially on her power to overturn the normal processes of nature:

> Ye Charmes and Witchcrafts, and thou Earth which both with herbe
>   and weed
> Of mightie working furnishest the Wizardes at their neede:
> Ye Ayres and windes: ye Elves of Hilles, of Brookes, of Woods alone,
> Of standing Lakes, and of the Night approche ye everychone.
> Through helpe of whom (the crooked bankes much wondring at
>   the thing)
> I have compelled streames to run cleane backward to their spring.
> By charmes I make the calme Seas rough, and make the rough
>   Seas plaine
> And cover all the Skie with Cloudes, and chase them thence againe.
> By charmes I rayse and lay the windes, and burst the Vipers jaw,
> And from the bowels of the Earth both stones and trees doe drawe.
> Whole woods and Forestes I remove: I make the Mountaines shake,
> And even the Earth it selfe to grone and fearfully to quake.
> I call up dead men from their graves: and thee O lightsome Moone
> I darken oft, though beaten brasse abate thy perill soone
> Our Sorcerie dimmes the Morning faire, and darkes the Sun at Noone.
>   (Golding, vii. 263–77)

When she makes this appeal to Hecate and other spirits of the night, Medea is out gathering herbs by the light of the moon. She emphasizes inversion—streams running backward to their sources, darkness at noon—because what she is preparing herself for is a reversal of the ageing process: her herbs will be placed in a cauldron in which Aeson, her father-in-law, will be rejuvenated. But, as I pointed out in my discussion of *The Merchant of Venice*, a little later Medea uses her reputation as a restorer of youth to trick the daughters of old King Pelias into killing him (she pretends he's going to be rejuvenated too, but the magic herbs are left out of the pot). In the larger context of Book Seven of the *Metamorphoses*, the association between Medea and the powers of darkness serves to highlight her wickedness and unnaturalness. And yet when she is first introduced at the beginning of Book Seven, before we hear of her magical powers, Medea is portrayed as a victim of love: Ovid gives her one of the embattled soliloquies in which his characters struggle against the passion that is overcoming them. 'Aliudque cupido, | mens aliud suadet': 'desire draws me one way, reason another' (vii. 19–20). Hers is a divided self, as may be seen from her way of addressing herself, 'Medea', in the vocative. Like his master Euripides and his pupil Shakespeare, Ovid recognizes that people who torment others are usually suffering from inner torment themselves. By the end of her soliloquy, Medea seems to have staved off desire by summoning up rectitude, filial duty, and modesty ('rectum pietasque pudorque'—vii. 72). Whatever dark deeds she subsequently performs, the reader cannot forget her potential for *pietas* and *pudor*; like Shakespeare, Ovid finds some soul of goodness in things evil.

The question with regard to Prospero's magic is whether the opposite applies: is there some soul of darkness in his white magic? From a technical point of view, his speech is a typical, if extremely skilfully managed, piece of Renaissance imitation. That is to say, a number of details are selected from the original passage and improvised upon. Thus the opening invocation of spirits is full of additional colour:

> Ye elves of hills, brooks, standing lakes and groves,
> And ye that on the sands with printless foot
> Do chase the ebbing Neptune, and do fly him
> When he comes back; you demi-puppets that
> By moonshine do the green sour ringlets make
> Whereof the ewe not bites; and you whose pastime
> Is to make midnight mushrooms,[41] that rejoice
> To hear the solemn curfew; by whose aid . . .
> (v. i. 33–40)

After this seven-line improvisation, Shakespeare reverts to the source-text and freely translates a sequence of elements from it—darkening the sun and raising storms, uprooting trees and shaking the earth, waking the dead and releasing them from their graves. It is the last image that is most alarming. The earlier part of the speech seems to be a lightening of the original: the playful spirits chasing the tide as it ebbs and running from it as it comes back are like children on the beach, they are by no means sinister. But for Prospero, imagined as a virtuous ruler, to bring a pagan image of raising the dead into the

---

[41] The mushrooms may be picked from Medea's subsequent flight to Corinth, where men 'Did breede of deawie Mushroomes' (Golding, vii. 500).

Christian era, in which that power should belong uniquely to Christ and his Father, is deeply disturbing.

The capacity to raise the dead, mentioned here for the first time in the play, is the final mark of the potency of Prospero's art. It is also a sign of its roughness and a reason for its abjuration. Like Medea, Prospero has achieved renewals through his magic—the spiritual rejuvenation of Alonso substitutes for the physical rejuvenation of Aeson—but, also like Medea, he has used his magic to exercise power, to control other people. Prompted by Ariel's pity for the penitent mortals, and in particular Gonzalo, Prospero recognizes that 'The rarer action is | In virtue than in vengeance' (v. i. 27–8). Whereas Medea goes on using her magic to act out revenge plots, Prospero renounces his and in so doing marks a movement away from the pagan world towards Christian 'kindness'. Medea's powers are summoned up not so that they can be exercised, but so that they can be rejected.

This is what makes the allusion so purposeful. The logical place to have put it would have been at the very beginning of the play, before the storm; in the manner of Book Seven of the *Metamorphoses*, and indeed of *Dr Faustus*, we would then have first heard the magical incantation, then seen its effect. Instead, the audience is given its incantatory fix only when the necessity of withdrawal is apparent. Recognition of the source is absolutely crucial, for it puts the audience into the same position as Prospero: as he sees that his magic must be rejected because it may so readily be abused when driven by vengeance rather than virtue, so at exactly the same moment we see that it must be rejected because it is, for all its apparent whiteness, the selfsame black magic as that of Medea.

The speech in Ovid was viewed in the Renaissance as witchcraft's great set-piece: it was cited by Bodin in *De Magorum Demonomania*, by Cornelius Agrippa in *De Occulta Philosophia*, and by Reginald Scot in his debunking *Discoverie of Witchcraft*.[42] Jonson imitates it in the principal witch's invocation in *The Masque of Queens*.[43] Middleton, in

[42] See William Carroll, *The Metamorphoses of Shakespearean Comedy* (Princeton, NJ, 1985), 237–8, 284.

[43] This masque was performed at court in 1609. In a marginal note to the invocation, which includes the familiar catalogue of raising storms and darkening the noonday sun (ll. 218–47), Jonson indicates that he is combining the Medeas of Ovid and Seneca with the Erichtho of Lucan's *Pharsalia* (vi. 695 ff.): 'These Invocations are solemne with them; whereof we may see the formes in *Ovid. Meta. lib. vii. in Sen. Trag. Med. in Luc. lib. vi.* which of all is the boldest, and most horrid' (*Ben Jonson*, vii. 295).

his play *The Witch*, has Hecate quoting Ovid's lines in Latin, and then translating them for the benefit of the Latinless:

> Can you doubt me then, daughter?
> That can make mountains tremble, miles of woods walk,
> Whole earth's foundation bellow, and the spirits
> Of the entombed to burst out from their marbles,
> Nay, draw yond moon to my involved designs?[44]

Playgoers who frequented the Red Bull as well as the theatres for which Shakespeare wrote would have found it especially easy to make the connection. Thomas Heywood's *The Brazen Age* had been performed by 1611, the probable year of *The Tempest*.[45] The third act of that play contains 'The Tragedy of *Jason* and *Medea*': it is in all essentials a dramatization of Book Seven of the *Metamorphoses*. On her first appearance Medea says:

> I can by Art make rivers retrograde,
> Alter their channels, run backe to their heads,
> And hide them in the springs from whence they grew.
> The curled Ocean with a word Il'e smooth,
> (Or being calme) raise waves as high as hils,
> Threatning to swallow the vast continent.
> With powerfull charmes Il'e make the Sunne stand still,
> Or call the Moone downe from her arched sphaere.
> What cannot I by power of *Hecate*?
>
> (*Dramatic Works*, iii. 209)

A little later she gathers enchanted herbs, and begins her nocturnal soliloquy:

> The night growes on, and now to my black Arts,
> Goddesse of witchcraft and darke ceremony,
> To whom the elves of Hils, of Brookes, of Groves,
> Of standing lakes, and cavernes vaulted deepe
> Are ministers.
>
> (*Dramatic Works*, iii. 215)

Heywood, then, is imitating Ovid even more closely than Shakespeare

---

[44] Middleton, *The Witch*, v. ii. 25–9, in *Three Jacobean Witchcraft Plays*, ed. Peter Corbin and Douglas Sedge (Manchester, 1986).

[45] *The Brazen Age* was not printed until 1613, but, as noted earlier, the address to the reader prefixed to *The Golden Age*, printed in Oct. 1611, refers to that play as 'the eldest brother of three Ages, that hath adventured the Stage' (Heywood, *Dramatic Works*, iii. 3).

does. His particular emphasis is on the association between Medea and Hecate, 'Goddess of witchcraft'. Given that *The Brazen Age* was in the London theatrical repertory in 1611, it is almost certain that some theatregoers would have recognized Heywood's and Shakespeare's shared allusion to Ovid (via Golding);[46] in the wider context of the association between the speech and witchcraft, it would have been impossible for Shakespeare to empty it of its darker tones, as some critics have supposed he did.[47]

There is internal evidence as compelling as the external. Medea has a proxy in the play in the form of Sycorax, the witch on whom Prospero harps so persistently in his rehearsals of the past; Stephen Orgel has even suggested that her strange name may be derived from one of the epithets for Medea, 'Scythian raven' ('Sy-', as prefix, 'korax' meaning raven, a bird with which Sycorax is associated in Caliban's first speech, quoted above).[48] Sycorax, as modern criticism has recognized,[49] is a disturbing double of Prospero himself. She is his dark Other. Each of them is banished and finds new life on the island; each makes Ariel a servant and controls the spirits of the isle; Sycorax confined Ariel in a cloven pine, Prospero threatens to peg him in an oak. When Prospero confronts Caliban at the end of the play he remembers Sycorax one more time: 'His mother was a witch, and one so strong | That could control the moon, make flows and ebbs' (v. i. 272–3). The tidal image links her powers with Prospero's control of the spirits of the sand who go backwards and forwards with 'the ebbing Neptune'. Now that he has been unburdened of his magic, Prospero, who previously set himself up as the opposite of Sycorax, recognizes that his arts were as one with hers. And so it is that he can recognize that her progeny is also his: 'This thing of darkness I | Acknowledge mine' (v. i. 278–9). The subject hangs at the line-ending, split from its verb as a token of the split between darkness and light, the division within Prospero himself, a division that he shares

[46] The presence in both plays of Golding's phrases 'elves of hills' and 'standing lakes' must mean that both Heywood and Shakespeare used the English translation as a crib (there are other marks of Golding's vocabulary elsewhere in each play). It is intriguing, though it may be coincidental, that for Golding's 'woods' both Heywood and Shakespeare have 'groves': might there then be a direct influence between the two plays? If so, whichever way round it is (the chronology cannot be known for certain), the link between Prospero and Medea is reinforced.

[47] Most influentially, Frank Kermode: 'Only those elements . . . consistent with "white" magic are taken over for Prospero' (Arden edn., p. 149).

[48] Orgel's edn., p. 19 and n.

[49] See e.g. Carroll, *Metamorphoses*, 238 ff., Orgel's edn., p. 20.

with the Medea whose own self was racked across a line-ending early in Ovid's seventh book ('aliudque cupido, | mens aliud suadet').

Why is it that the darkness of Caliban is an inescapable part of Prospero? Why does the island have to contain this creature who must be subdued and controlled, who tries to rape Miranda and lead a rebellion against Prospero, who must eventually be humiliated so that he is led to seek for grace?

In answering this, we need to return to Gonzalo's Utopian vision. Though Shakespeare imitated it from Montaigne, his audience would have been more likely to identify it with Montaigne's source. As so often in the play, the 'discourse of colonialism' is summoned up only to be displaced into the discourse of myth. A signal in the text alerts the listener to the original source: 'I would with such perfection govern, sir, | T' excel the Golden Age' (II. i. 173–4). Montaigne's vision of peace and of the absence of law, labour, and agriculture aligns the New World with the oldest world; he says that life in the 'barbarian' nations exceeds 'all the pictures wherewith licentious Poesie hath proudly imbellished the golden age' (*Essayes*, p. 164). He is thinking in particular of the Golden Age as it is described in Book One of the *Metamorphoses*:

There was no feare of punishment, there was no threatning lawe
In brazen tables nayled up, to keepe the folke in awe.
There was no man would crouch or creepe to Judge with cap in hand,
They lived safe without a Judge in every Realme and lande.

. . . .

There was no towne enclosed yet, with walles and ditches deepe.
No horne nor trumpet was in use, no sword nor helmet worne.
The worlde was suche, that souldiers helpe might easly be forborne.
The fertile earth as yet was free, untoucht of spade or plough,
And yet it yeelded of it selfe of every things inough.

. . . .

The Springtime lasted all the yeare, and *Zephyr* with his milde
And gentle blast did cherish things that grew of owne accorde.
The ground untilde, all kinde of fruits did plenteously avorde.[50]

---

[50] Golding, i. 105–24. The phrase 'to keepe the folke in awe' is an insertion by Golding which suggests a distinctively 16th cent., quasi-machiavellian, view of the law; the image of creeping to the judge, cap in hand, is also a sharpening of Ovid's original text. Shakespeare has a similarly charged sense of the relationship between the Golden Age and justice, of the absence of justice in the Iron Age of the present, when he quotes the line 'terras Astraea reliquit' in the context of Titus Andronicus' discovery that there is no justice at Saturninus' court—the same idea is dramatized in the figure of the Clown in *Titus* who goes cap in hand for justice and is rewarded with hanging.

The Latin original of this passage would have been encountered early in a boy's grammar-school education; for many playgoers it would therefore have been Ovid, not Montaigne, who would have been evoked by Gonzalo's 'no name of magistrate', 'Bourn, bound of land, tilth, vineyard, none', and

> All things in common nature should produce
> Without sweat or endeavour. Treason, felony,
> Sword, pike, knife, gun, or need of any engine,
> Would I not have; but nature should bring forth
> Of its own kind all foison, all abundance,
> To feed my innocent people.
>
> (II. i. 165–70)

But man is fallen and the Golden Age is irrecoverable. The very presence of the characters on the island is a sign of this, for Ovid had pointed out that one feature of the Golden Age was the absence of travel. People remained contentedly in their own fertile land, 'The loftie Pynetree was not hewen from mountaines where it stood, | In seeking straunge and forren landes to rove upon the flood' (Golding, i. 109–10). It was in the Iron Age, according to Ovid, that the first sea-voyages took place. The first sea-voyagers were Jason and his Argonauts, so the encounter with Prospero's forebear Medea was a direct consequence of the decline of Ages.[51] The Iron Age also brought craft, treason, violence, envy, pride, lust, the parcelling out of land (Gonzalo's 'plantation') which was previously held in common, and family quarrels ('yea seldome time doth rest | Betweene borne brothers such accord and love as ought to bee'—Golding, i. 164–5). All the dark elements in *The Tempest* are of the Iron Age. Gonzalo gets into a tangle in his speech, and can be mocked by Sebastian and Antonio, precisely because of the incompatibility between the Golden Age ideal of no law, no property, no need to till the land, and his own Iron Age mentality which thinks in terms of the right to plant, of sovereignty and rule.

Shakespeare has therefore reversed Montaigne. The Frenchman idealized the New World and its inhabitants, seeing in them the Golden Age restored (or rather a realization of what poets feigned in

---

[51] For Jason as the first ship-builder, see e.g. *Met.* viii. 302 ('primaeque ratis molitor Iason') and *Amores*, II. xi. 1–6. I would like to thank A. D. Nuttall for reminding me of this connection when I presented a version of this reading of *The Tempest* to the Oxford Renaissance Seminar.

their licentious fictions of the Golden Age). The island in *The Tempest*, on the other hand, is shot through with Iron Age characteristics, many of them embodied in Caliban, but some of them brought by Prospero—Caliban is only provoked into a claim that he owns the land, 'this island's mine, by Sycorax my mother' (I. ii. 333), by Prospero's appropriation of it. The play leaves open the question as to whether Caliban's fallenness is innate, as Prospero's abuses imply ('a born devil'—IV. i. 188), or in some sense created by Prospero himself, as may be admitted in his acknowledgement of the darkness as his own. Either way, Shakespeare denies the myth of the Golden Age restored in a New World peopled by noble cannibals.

What positive myth is available, then? The answer comes in Prospero's masque, though the fact that its performance is inter-rupted by Caliban's conspiracy shows that it offers a precarious and vulnerable stasis. When the Golden Age ended, says Ovid, the Silver Age brought the seasons—as was noted in *As You Like It*, in the Golden Age it was always spring—and agriculture: 'Then first of all were furrowes drawne, and corne was cast in ground' (Golding, i. 139). The loss of the Golden Age, the fall of man, means that human society cannot escape the seasonal cycle and its dependence on agriculture. It becomes necessary to hope and pray for fertile land and a good harvest. Prospero's masque fuses this hope with a prayer for fertility in the marriage of Miranda and Ferdinand.

The land described in the masque is husbanded, not in a state of nature. It is under Ceres, patroness of agriculture: her 'rich leas' are sown with 'wheat, rye, barley, vetches, oats, and peas', her vineyards are 'pole-clipped' and her flat meads 'thatched with stover' (IV. i. 60 ff.). The language here is that of Ovid's Ceres: 'Dame *Ceres* first to breake the Earth with plough the maner found, | She first made corne and stover soft to grow upon the ground' (Golding, v. 434–5, 'stover' is winter forage for cattle). Where Caliban spoke of the island yielding up its own fruits in the ready abundance of the Golden Age, Prospero's actors acknowledge the need to work the land.

Agriculture is, as I have said, a Silver Age phenomenon; it was in his *Silver Age* play that Heywood placed Ceres and the story of the rape of her daughter Proserpina. It is because she presides over the period immediately after the Golden Age that Ceres also 'first made lawes' (Golding, v. 436, translating Ovid's 'prima dedit leges'). In the Golden Age, when there was no law and all things were held in common, there could be free love (Montaigne's cannibals share their women without jealousy); in the Silver Age, love must be bounded within the laws of marriage. So it is that the masque is part of Prospero's project to ensure that Ferdinand's motives are chaste and that he is not over-hasty in seeking sexual union; for fertility to be achieved, sexual desire must be controlled. The plot of the masque allegorizes this idea: Ceres is summoned to Juno, goddess of marriage, in order to ensure that Venus and Cupid, forces of sexual desire, are banished. There is an allusion to an Ovidian innovation in the Proserpine myth, namely a twist whereby Venus and Cupid are the agents who inspire in Dis the desire that prompts him to abduct Proserpina—the ambition of Venus and Cupid in this was to extend their domain from the sky, the sea, and the earth (where they already rule over the desires of Jupiter, Neptune, and all mortals) to the underworld (*Met.* v. 363–79). In the masque, Iris reassures Ceres that Venus has flown off to Paphos and Cupid's arrows are broken, so the 'wanton charm' they were to cast on Miranda and Ferdinand has been avoided, and accordingly 'no bed-right shall be paid | Till Hymen's torch be lighted' (iv. i.91–101).

The commonplace Renaissance theme of the dangers of lust is a key motif in both *The Tempest* and the age's reading of Ovid. In the interstices of the Aenean section of the *Metamorphoses* is the tale which Lodge retold in the first Elizabethan 'minor epic', that of Scylla, the nymph who is metamorphosed so that dogs and wolves encircle her loins; Prospero, who is capable of unleashing dogs himself, would have interpreted her fate as George Sandys did, as an allegory of the dual nature of human beings:

That the upper part of her body, is feigned to retaine a humane figure, and the lower to be bestiall, intimates how man, a divine creature, endued with wisdome and intelligence, in whose superiour parts, as in a high tower, that immortall spirit resideth, who only of all that hath life erects his lookes unto heaven, can never so degenerate into a beast, as when he giveth himselfe over to the lowe delights of those baser parts of the body, Dogs and Wolves, the blind and salvage fury of concupiscence.   (Sandys, p. 475)

Scylla's metamorphosis is performed by Circe, whom Frank Kermode sees as a model for Sycorax (Arden edn., p. 26). This is a suggestive link, since Prospero's obsession with Ferdinand's possible concupiscence seems to be provoked by the attempt of Sycorax's son to rape Miranda. Prospero thus unfairly associates Ferdinand with the bestial as opposed to the heaven-looking aspect of man: 'To th' most of men this is a Caliban | And they to him are angels' (i. ii. 483–4).

To ideologically minded critics, the theme of the need for desire to be tamed within the formal structure of marriage is political, and in this instance dynastic; to psychologically minded ones, it is connected with Prospero's possessiveness towards his daughter, his hang-ups about the idea of her having sex with another man. These readings may well be valid, but it seems to me that the play itself makes the point in terms of the decline of the Ages. Furthermore, the Ages are not politicized, as they easily could have been. As so often, Shakespeare eschews topical reference. One may see this by contrasting *The Tempest* with 'De Guiana', a poem by George Chapman, published in 1596 among the prefatory material of Lawrence Keymis's *A Relation of the Second Voyage to Guiana*. The poem is a plea to Queen Elizabeth to accept Guiana as a colony; because gold is to be found there, it can become a new golden world:

> Then most admired Soveraigne, let your breath
> Goe foorth upon the waters, and create
> A golden worlde in this our yron age.
>
> (lines 30–2)

The pursuit of gold also leads Chapman to Jason's quest for the golden fleece: Sir Walter Ralegh thus sails to Guiana with 'his *Argolian* Fleet'.[52] No such connections are made in Prospero's masque. It makes moral rather than imperial use of the Ages. Free love was all very well in the Golden Age, but with the Silver Age comes the law of marriage, and if that law is broken, one is on a slippery path to the lust that deforms the Iron Age. That sex must take place within marriage is standard Christian theology; here, in characteristically Renaissance fashion, it is smuggled into a pagan nature myth.

The masque is a manifestation of the art which Prospero renounces. Even before he puts it on, he refers to it dismissively as 'Some vanity of mine art' (IV. i. 41). By the time he speaks his epilogue he has ceased to use pagan myth as a vehicle, and he speaks instead the unalloyed language of Christianity (despair, prayer, mercy, faults, pardoned, indulgence). This is an implicit recognition on Shakespeare's part of the distance between Ovidian art and

[52] Line 159, quoted from Chapman's *Poems*, ed. Phyllis Brooks Bartlett (New York, 1941). The association between the Iron Age, shipping, trade, and the pursuit of gold is also apparent from the language of Barabas in Marlowe's *Jew of Malta* (see e.g. his image of 'Ripping the bowels of the earth', I. i. 107, which comes from Ovid's 'sed itum est in viscera terrae', i. 138, in the description of the Iron Age).

orthodox Christianity; to use Thomas Greene's term, cited in my first chapter, it renders his imitation of Ovid 'dialectical'. It could be described as his equivalent to the two stanzas of the 'unperfite' eighth canto of Spenser's 'Mutabilitie', which come to rest on 'the pillours of Eternity' that are 'contrayr to [Ovidian] Mutabilitie' (*Faerie Queene*, VII. viii. 2). In this sense, Leonard Barkan is both elegant and just when he describes Prospero's burial of his book as Shakespeare's magisterial closing of the book that Lavinia so clumsily opened in *Titus Andronicus*.[53] But although the masque belongs to Prospero's rejected art, for a Jacobean theatre audience it would have been the high point of the play, in terms of both spectacle and allegorical sophistication. And in this sense Shakespeare's art remains co-ordinate with, dependent upon, Ovid's.

For a theatre audience the most memorable thing about the masque is not the plot—it is only in a reading that we stop to think through the business about the threat of Venus and Cupid—but the sense of fruition, the harmony and the harvest. With our eyes, we wonder at certain nymphs and certain reapers, properly habited, joining together in a graceful dance. With our ears, we absorb the language of fruitfulness, the sense that the harshness of Proserpina's winter confinement in the underworld can be overstepped as spring returns in the very moment of autumn's harvest:

> Earth's increase, foison plenty,
> Barns and garners never empty,
> Vines with clust'ring bunches growing,
> Plants with goodly burden bowing;
> Spring come to you at the farthest,
> In the very end of harvest.
> Scarcity and want shall shun you,
> Ceres' blessing so is on you.
>
> (IV. i. 110–17)

As Prospero's incantation intersects with the Medea of Heywood's *Brazen Age*, so this celebration of agricultural plenty resonates with Heywood's *Silver Age*. In that play, which is contemporaneous with *The Tempest*, Mercury flames amazement like Ariel, Juno and Iris work in tandem, descending from the heavens on several occasions; there is also a *Cymbeline*-like moment in which to thunder and lightning

---

[53] Barkan, *The Gods Made Flesh*, 288.

'Jupiter descends in his majesty, his Thunderbolt burning'.[54] And at the centre of the play is a 'harvest home' which represents the closest analogue in all Jacobean drama to the agricultural benison of Prospero's masque of Ceres. Heywood's play remains little known, so I make no apology for quoting at length:

> *Enter* Ceres *and* Proserpine *attired like the Moone,*
> *with a company of Swaines, and country Wenches:*
>
> *They sing.*
>
> *With faire* Ceres *Queene of graine*
> *The reaped fields we rome, rome, rome,*
> *Each Countrey Peasant, Nimph and Swaine*
> *Sing their harvest home, home, home:*
>   *Whilst the Queene of plenty hallowes*
>   *Growing fields as well as fallowes.*
>
> *Eccho double all our Layes,*
> *Make the Champains sound, sound, sound*
> *To the Queene of harvest praise,*
> *That sowes and reapes our ground, ground, ground.*
>   *Ceres Queene of plenty hallowes*
>   *Growing fields as well as fallowes.*

CERES. As we are *Ceres*, Queene of all fertility,
The earthes sister, Aunt to highest *Jupiter*,
And mother to this beauteous childe the Moone,
So will we blesse your harvests, crowne your fields
With plenty and increase: your bearded eares
Shall make their golden stalkes of wheat to bend
Below their laden riches: with full sickles
You shall receive the usury of their seeds.
Your fallowes and your gleabes our selfe will till
From every furrow that your plow-shares raze
Upon the plenteous earth, our sisters breast,
You shall cast up aboundance for your gratitude
To *Ceres* and the chaste *Proserpina.*

>   .   .   .   .

Now that the heavens and earth are both appeas'd
And the huge Giants that assaulted *Jove*,
Are slaughtered by the hand of *Jupiter*;
We have leasure to attend our harmelesse swaines:
Set on then to our Rurall ceremonies.   *Exeunt singing.*

---

[54] Heywood, *Dramatic Works*, iii. 154.

> *Tempests hence, hence winds and hailes,*
> *Tares, cockle, rotten showers, showers, showers,*
> *Our song shall keep time with our flailes,*
> *When* Ceres *sings, none lowers, lowers, lowers.*
> *She it is whose God-hood hallowes*
> *Growing fields as well as fallowes.*
>
> (*Dramatic Works*, iii. 133–4)

'Tempests hence'; 'plenty and increase' come hither. The fruits of labour in the fields bend with 'their laden riches': the tonality and the rhythm are Shakespeare's. I am not proposing a 'source' here, since it is impossible to establish which play was written first.[55] The point of my collocation is that the two plays were in the repertory at the same time. Indeed, they were performed at court within a few weeks of each other in the winter of 1611–12; *The Silver Age* was played by the King's Men and Queen's Men together, so Shakespeare's company had direct contact with Heywood's song to Ceres. Both the court audience and any playgoers who kept up with the repertory of the two leading companies would have been presented with a striking parallel between Prospero's masque and the Silver Age, just as they would have been presented with a striking parallel between Prospero and the Medea of *The Brazen Age*. While one parallel darkens the character of Prospero, the other lightens him and warms the audience. When watching the masque at the Globe or Blackfriars, as when watching *The Silver Age* at the Red Bull, the city-dwellers in their leisure engage with an image of country-dwellers singing or dancing in their moment of leisure once the harvest is safely gathered in.

According to Sir Philip Sidney in his *Apology for Poetry*, the poet ranges freely within the zodiac of his own wit, bringing forth the wonderful forms of myth: the heroes, demigods, and Cyclops. Thus it is that where nature's world is brazen, 'the Poets only deliver a golden'.[56] Heywood and Shakespeare were not so idealistic: in *The Silver Age*, shortly after the passage quoted above, Proserpina is abducted by Pluto, 'his Chariot drawne in by Divels'; in *The Tempest*, the nymphs and reapers 'heavily vanish' as 'a strange, hollow, and confused noise' heralds the entrance of Caliban and his fellow-conspirators, the intrusion of the Iron Age of treason, violence, and

---

[55] Though the scene in Heywood must come first if, as has sometimes been supposed, the masque was an interpolation in *The Tempest* for the performance at court as part of the royal betrothal celebrations during the winter of 1612–13.

[56] Sidney, *Apology*, in *Elizabethan Critical Essays*, i. 156.

envy. Shakespeare was too much of a sceptic to suppose that he could deliver up the Golden World, but for a moment, through Prospero's theatrical arts, which are of course also his own, he provides some consolation by conjuring the Silver Age back to life. The drama itself becomes a harvest home.

IV

The temptation to end there is almost irresistible. By transforming Shakespeare into Prospero, we make him into a kind of magician and we end in wonder, awe-inspired by his art. A new myth is created, that of Shakespeare's transcendent, history-defying genius. The book is closed with a flourish, *The Tempest*'s privileged status being licensed by its prime position in the First Folio or by a romantic construction of Prospero's epilogue as Shakespeare's farewell to the stage. Many a reading concludes in some such manner.

But Shakespeare's career didn't end with *The Tempest*. He went on to write his three collaborations with John Fletcher, *Henry VIII*, *The Two Noble Kinsmen*, and the lost *Cardenio*. That Shakespeare had bequeathed some of his Ovidianism to Fletcher is apparent from the younger dramatist's earlier performances, in which characters are seen to rewrite Ovid as a way of dramatizing their own fates. *The Maid's Tragedy* (?1610) provides the finest example. Aspatia, having been forsaken by her lover, finds her maid working with a needle upon a picture of Ariadne. As in *Lucrece*, the picture becomes a means for the woman to express her emotion. The handling of the encounter is as boldly revisionary as anything in Shakespeare. Instead of the picture of the deserted Ariadne being a 'lively image' of Aspatia, the character makes herself into 'a miserable life' of the picture:

ASPATIA.   . . . but where's the Lady?
ANTIPHILA. There Madame.
ASPATIA. Fie, you have mist it here *Antiphila*,
You are much mistaken wench:
These colours are not dull and pale enough,
To show a soule so full of miserie
As this sad Ladies was, doe it by me,
Doe it againe, by me the lost *Aspatia*,
And you shall find all true but the wild Iland;
I stand upon the Sea-beach now, and thinke

Mine armes thus, and mine haire blowne with the wind,
Wilde as that desart . . .
                                   —looke, looke wenches,
A miserable life of this poore picture.[57]

The normative relationship between observer and observed is reversed, the maid required to refinger her design. Aspatia outpassions the passioning Ariadne. Even more poignant is her revision of the other character in the story. She asks what happened to Theseus, who is for her a representation of the philandering Amintor: 'Does not the story say', she asks, that he was shipwrecked on leaving Naxos, in punishment for his cruelty? 'Not as I remember', Antiphila the maid answers, to which Aspatia responds by rewriting the narrative: 'It should ha been so . . . in this place worke a quick-sand, | And over it a shallow smiling water, | And his ship plowing it'. Antiphila claims that such a revision would 'wrong the story', but for Aspatia 'Twill make the story, wrong'd by wanton Poets, | Live long and be beleev'd' (II. ii. 46–58). Antiphila has the literal-mindedness of Peter Quince: she sees herself as a remembrancer of the story. Aspatia, on the other hand, takes it upon herself to remake the story. She introduces a poetic justice that is not there in the original; indeed, she charges previous poets—Ovid is naturally the chief culprit—with Theseus' own wantonness. Aspatia alters the Ariadne story in ways that Julia in *The Two Gentlemen of Verona* does not: a rewriting which involves the imposition of poetic justice is not Shakespeare's usual kind of revision, but my point is that Shakespeare taught Fletcher an art of dramatic engagement with Ovid which he then developed in his own style.[58]

---

[57] *The Maid's Tragedy*, II. ii. 58–76, in *The Dramatic Works in the Beaumont and Fletcher Canon*, vol. ii (1970), 61–2. The scene is generally reckoned to be one of only four which Fletcher contributed to the play.

[58] *Philaster* provides another example when the character of Arathusa wilfully writes herself into Ovidian myth: instead of being overheard as Actaeon, like Falstaff or Malvolio, she asks to become a female Actaeon:

> *Diana* if thou canst rage with a maid,
> As with a man, let me discover thee
> Bathing, and turne me to a fearefull Hynde,
> That I may dye persued by cruell hounds,
> And have my story written in my wounds.

(III. ii. 169–74, in *The Dramatic Works in the Beaumont and Fletcher Canon*, vol. i (1966), 447; the attribution of this scene is uncertain.)

Collaboration with Ovid is one of the marks of Fletcher and Shakespeare's collaboration with each other. Among the many respects in which *The Two Noble Kinsmen* re-traverses the ground of *A Midsummer Night's Dream* is its use of 'low' figures who plan an entertainment for Duke Theseus. Gerald the Schoolmaster stands in for Peter Quince and with him Fletcher replicates the early Shakespearian technique of parodying a pedant's superficial knowledge of the classics. Gerald has all the tags, but cannot apply them to high civic matter in the manner of a true humanist. Bathetically, he intends the morris-dancers to break out of the thicket in front of the Duke 'As once did Meleager and the boar'; preposterously, *'Quousque tandem?'* ('How long then?'), Cicero's celebrated question at the beginning of his first oration against Catiline, is applied to the troupe's deficiency of female dancers; and, most ludicrously, the great climax in which Ovid proclaims the completion of the *Metamorphoses* is applied anti-climactically to the making up of the numbers for the dance by the arrival of the mad gaoler's daughter: *'Et opus exegi, quod nec Iovis, nec ignis—* | Strike up, and lead her in.'[59]

In Shakespeare's contribution to the play the *Metamorphoses* are once again metamorphosed in the arena of desire and identity. When Emilia remembers Flavina, whom she loved as a girl, she remakes Venus' plucking of Adonis' flower:

> The flower that I would pluck
> And put between my breasts—O then but beginning
> To swell about the blossom—she would long
> Till she had such another, and commit it
> To the like innocent cradle, where, phoenix-like,
> They died in perfume.
>
> (I. iii. 66–71)

The dying flower in *Venus and Adonis* is an emblem of unrequited love. The phoenix and the turtle in Shakespeare's marriage-poem published with Robert Chester's *Love's Martyr* are emblems of reciprocal love between male and female. In Emilia's image, the paired flowers become two phoenixes—a wonderful contradiction of the bird's defining uniqueness—and thus proclaim the perfection of same-sex love. The speech can therefore end with the claim that 'the true love

[59] *Two Noble Kinsmen*, III. v. 18, 38, 89–90.

'tween maid and maid may be | More than in sex dividual'
(i. iii. 81–2). *The Two Noble Kinsmen* is a tragedy because same-sex
love is disrupted by heterosexual desire and the conflicting demands of
different gods, demands enacted in the sacrifices before the altars of
Mars, Venus, and Diana in Act V. The momentary fusion of the two
pubescent girls remembered by Emilia cannot be replicated between
Palamon and Arcite. 'Were they metamorphosed | Both into one!',
exclaims Emilia as the two men fight over her (v. v. 84–5). But they
cannot be: Mars can only be joined with Venus by being stripped of his
armour, his martial identity.

Shakespeare's final representation of sexual relations is uncom-
promising. There is no idealized image of marriage conveyed through
a celebratory reading of the fusion of Salmacis and Hermaphroditus,
as at the end of the 1590 *Faerie Queene*. Where *A Midsummer Night's
Dream* moves towards a celebration of the nuptials of Theseus and
Hippolyta, *The Two Noble Kinsmen*, from the first disruptive entry of
the three widowed queens, moves rapidly away from that union. Nor
are the two men united: the play is centrally concerned with their
splitting apart as they grow into adulthood and one submits to Venus,
the other to Mars. The only achieved union is the remembered one
between Emilia and the Flavina who died when she was 11 years old.
That union is valued because it is 'innocent'—it is under Diana, not
the disruptive Venus. To view the budding breasts with Ovidian
prurience would be to misread the tone. Flavina is a version of the
dead votaress whom Titania loved, but one who dies before the fall
into sexuality which brings so much confusion even to Shakespeare's
comedies. She is the mark of a yearning in Shakespeare for a kind of
pre-sexual love, free from the quest for mastery. Ovid would have
been of the view that there can be no such thing: no encounter in his
world is innocent. In exile he writes less of sexual desire, but there is
still a far from innocent fascination with power as he tries to insinuate
his way back into the Emperor's favour. Shakespeare half-knows that
Ovid is probably right, but he refuses to relinquish the half-belief that
he might be wrong.

Where *The Two Noble Kinsmen* is Shakespeare's last word on
Ovidian desire, two key sequences in *Henry VIII* offer alternative
versions of the relationship between broadly Ovidian matter and
history. Either or both of the two scenes in question are likely to have
been written by Fletcher, but that is no reason to exclude them from a
study of Shakespeare: *Henry VIII* is a finely constructed play in which

the original audience would not have seen the joins,[60] so it may be considered as the product of a unified if double dramatic consciousness.

In the first of the scenes, metamorphic music represents a consolation for a victim of history. Art is something you turn to when all else is lost. The victim is Queen Katharine, rejected and arraigned because the king wishes to marry Anne Bullen. In private after her trial she asks her woman to sing in order to disperse her cares. In earlier work, most notably *Titus Andronicus* and *Lucrece*, the music of Orpheus had been alluded to in speech. Now it is heard in the form of a song:

> Orpheus with his lute made trees,
> And the mountain tops that freeze,
>   Bow themselves when he did sing.
> To his music plants and flowers
> Ever sprung, as sun and showers
>   There had made a lasting spring.
>
> Every thing that heard him play,
> Even the billows of the sea,
>   Hung their heads, and then lay by.
> In sweet music is such art,
> Killing care and grief of heart
>   Fall asleep, or hearing, die.
>
>   (III. i. 3–14)

If there were a lute accompaniment, it would be as if Orpheus himself were singing, as he does in Book Ten of the *Metamorphoses*. In *The Merchant of Venice*, Lorenzo said with regard to 'the sweet power of music' that 'the poet | Did feign that Orpheus drew trees, stones and floods'. In this song, the poet—Ovid—and Orpheus have become one. The music does not only charm trees, stones, and floods, it also evokes other benign Ovidian metamorphoses as it precipitates the return of the spring in the manner of Proserpina (or Perdita) and the calming of stormy seas in the manner of Arion (or Ariel acting for Prospero). Above all, the very sound of it kills care, just as metamorphosis brings freedom from care to Ovid's suffering characters and as Paulina's

---

[60] As in many Elizabethan plays, history is built on a pattern of rises and falls: Buckingham falls, Anne Bullen rises, Wolsey rises, Katharine falls, Wolsey falls, Cranmer rises.

music puts grief of heart to sleep by awakening Hermione. For
Katharine, the resolution is suspended as a gentleman comes on to
break off the song by announcing a delegation of power in the form of
the Cardinals Wolsey and Campeius. But in the following act the
Queen, now sick and in another chamber, orders more solemn music
and sees a vision of blessed spirits. They bring her spirit to rest: doing
the work of Orpheus, they kill her grief before granting her a release
into eternal peace.

But the play as a whole ends with a vision of blessedness that is
firmly rooted in this world, not the next. Where Katharine is taken via
Orphic music to the Christian heaven in a move redolent of the
allegorized Ovidianism of the Catholic Middle Ages, Archbishop
Cranmer prophesies that England will be taken via Queen Elizabeth to
a new Silver Age of agricultural plenty. Protestant nationalism
reawakens Ovidian myth in modern history:

> This royal infant—heaven still move about her—
> Though in her cradle, yet now promises
> Upon this land a thousand thousand blessings,
> Which time shall bring to ripeness . . .
>
> .   .   .   .
>
>   Good grows with her.
> In her days every man shall eat in safety
> Under his own vine what he plants, and sing
> The merry songs of peace to all his neighbours.
>
>   (v. iv. 17–20, 32–5)

Here linguistic art is an instrument of secular power. Ovidianism is
part of the fabric of history, not an escape from it. Cranmer's language
is the same as that of Prospero's masque, save that the source of a
good harvest and a peaceful commonwealth is located differently: it
comes not from Ceres, not from Ariel-as-Ceres, which is to say from
Prospero's magical arts, but from an idealized earthly queen. Astraea,
who fled the earth in the time of Iron, has returned in the form of
Elizabeth.

This vision of community and fruitfulness is a piece of Elizabethan
nostalgia typical of the period around 1610–13. The poor harvests of
the 1590s have been quietly forgotten. Like all nostalgia, the speech
carries with it an implicit critique of the turn history has taken.
Cranmer goes on to prophesy that a successor as blessed as Elizabeth
will rise, phoenix-like, from her ashes, but by invoking the language

of the Silver Age which Prospero's spirits had used, he inevitably introduces a model of historical decline. Ovid's Ages become a reading of recent history. *Henry VIII* dramatizes the issue over which England broke from Rome; the crux of the play is the fall of Wolsey, mediator between the King and the Pope. Cranmer speaks from the early Reformation, rather as Gonzalo, with his vision of a new Golden Age, speaks the language of early humanism (of More's *Utopia*). But Cranmer, more of a politician than Gonzalo, recognizes that the modern body politic, with its need for legal structures and agricultural production, can at best replicate the Silver Age, not the Golden. It is in Silver terms that he prophesies the Elizabethan settlement and the defeat of Catholic Spain: 'She shall be loved and feared: her own shall bless her; | Her foes shake like a field of beaten corn' (v. iv. 30–1— note the Ceres-influenced simile). For the play's audience the Elizabethan Age is now gone, so the moment at which the prophecy is heard is dangerously liable to be post-Silver. James's England could easily become a Brazen world. The praise of the King is also an implicit warning: without a revival of Elizabethan values, the country will go on a downward spiral towards the Age of Iron. It is significant that the play was written in close proximity to the death of Prince Henry, whose radical protestantism and chivalric aspirations made him a far better candidate than James himself for the role of Elizabeth's phoenix.[61]

All this is stated very subtly. Shakespeare,[62] elusive even when allusive, never took the political risks that Ovid, Marston, and Jonson did. He would never have got himself exiled for insulting his imperial ruler or imprisoned for writing a seditious play. But the nostalgia and the quiet critique which mark the late plays perhaps suggest that the death of Prince Henry was his cue to retire from the theatre. The last plays keep reaching back to the Elizabethan works, *Pericles* to *The Comedy of Errors*, *Cymbeline* to *Lucrece*, *The Winter's Tale* to *As You Like It*, *The Tempest* to *A Midsummer Night's Dream*, *The Two Noble Kinsmen* to both *Dream* and *The Two Gentlemen of Verona*. Their mythologizing is a leading strand of their nostalgic weave. It may be recalled that Thomas Carew praised John Donne as a 'modern' poet because he was supposed to have banished the train of heathen mythology which

---

[61] For the Prince's Elizabethan associations, see Roy Strong, *Henry, Prince of Wales and England's Lost Renaissance* (London, 1986), esp. 47 ff.

[62] Here more probably 'Fletcher in Shakespearian mode'.

had been so visible in the age of Spenser.[63] The triumphant renaissance of Ovidianism in Shakespeare's last plays contributes enormously to their art but also helps to keep them at a distance from Jacobean England—they constantly conjure up new worlds in order to dissolve them into the old ones of myth.

Shakespeare established his reputation with the Ovidian showpieces *Venus and Adonis* and *Titus Andronicus*, a play which Jonson in Jacobean times mocked for its outdatedness.[64] Throughout his career he experimented with a vast repertory of metamorphic Ovidian manœuvres. The nimbleness of the intertextual play was decisive proof of his mobility as a dramatist. 'Ovids Metamorphoses, nothing else, but Mercuries pageants, where Jupiter, and Apollo do everywhere Mercurize for lyfe; and sumtymes Martialize uppon occasion': thus Gabriel Harvey in some marginalia to Joannis Foorth's *Synopsis Politica*.[65] Harvey's word 'Mercurize' is not recorded in the *Oxford English Dictionary*, but the third sense of 'Mercurial', 'Of persons: Born under the planet Mercury; having the qualities supposed to proceed from such a nativity, as eloquence, ingenuity, aptitude for commerce', is first attributed to him.[66] For Harvey, the value of the *Metamorphoses* was that they could teach a politic art of social mobility; follow the metamorphic example of Jupiter and Apollo, and you will be able to 'Mercurize, or strategize at every occasion: may manage any exployte, or practise any fortune'. This is what Ovid enabled Shakespeare to do: not in the world of high politics to which Harvey aspired with such singular lack of success, but in his chosen sphere of the theatre. From impressive début to strategic withdrawal, the grammar-school boy managed every dramatic exploit and was able to retire having made his fortune. He left behind a body of work which everywhere Mercurizes for life.

[63] In his 'Elegie upon the Death of the Deane of Pauls', Carew wrote of how Donne had 'silenc'd' the 'tales o' th' Metamorphoses' (l. 66).

[64] Induction to *Bartholomew Fair*, Ben Jonson, vi. 16.

[65] *Gabriel Harvey's Marginalia*, ed. G. C. Moore Smith (Stratford-upon-Avon, 1913), 193. Subsequent quotation from the same page.

[66] Citation of *Pierces Supererogation*.

Bibliography

This bibliography aims to provide a reasonably comprehensive list of scholarly material on Shakespeare and Ovid, and some material on the Renaissance Ovid more generally. It omits sixteenth- and seventeenth-century material quoted in my text for comparative purposes and a few works of Shakespearian criticism which are cited in the book but do not have any direct bearing on the relationship with Ovid. It should be noted that many local parallels and other useful references are to be found in the introductions and notes to the Variorum, New Variorum, New Arden, Oxford, and New Cambridge editions of Shakespeare.

Place of publication is London, unless otherwise stated.

ALLEN, D. C., 'On Venus and Adonis', in *Elizabethan and Jacobean Studies Presented to F. P. Wilson*, ed. H. Davis and H. Gardner (Oxford, 1959), 100–11.

—— *Mysteriously Meant: The Rediscovery of Pagan Symbolism and Allegorical Interpretation in the Renaissance* (Baltimore, 1970).

ANDERS, H. R. D., *Shakespeare's Books* (Berlin, 1904).

ANTON, HERBERT, *Der Raub der Proserpina* (Heidelberg, 1967).

ARMITAGE, DAVID, 'The Dismemberment of Orpheus: Mythic Elements in Shakespeare's Romances', *ShS* xxxix (1987), 123–33.

ASHTON, J. W., 'The Fall of Icarus', in *Renaissance Studies in Honour of Hardin Craig* (Stanford, Calif., 1941), 153–9.

BAKER, HOWARD, *Induction to Tragedy* (Baton Rouge, La., 1939).

BALDWIN, T. W., 'Perseus Purloins Pegasus', in *Renaissance Studies in Honour of Hardin Craig* (Stanford, Calif., 1941), 169–78.

—— *William Shakspere's Petty School* (Urbana, Ill., 1943).

—— *William Shakspere's Small Latine and Lesse Greeke* (2 vols., Urbana, Ill., 1944).

—— *Shakspere's Five-Act Structure* (Urbana, Ill., 1947).

—— *On the Literary Genetics of Shakspere's Poems and Sonnets* (Urbana, Ill., 1950).

—— *On the Literary Genetics of Shakspere's Plays, 1592–94* (Urbana, Ill., 1959).

BARKAN, LEONARD, 'Diana and Actaeon: The Myth as Synthesis', *ELR* x (1980), 317–59.

BARKAN, LEONARD, ' "Living Sculptures": Ovid, Michelangelo and *The Winter's Tale*', *ELH* xlviii (1981), 639–67.

—— *The Gods Made Flesh: Metamorphosis and the Pursuit of Paganism* (New Haven, Conn., 1986).

BARNETT, LOUISE K., 'Ovid and *The Taming of the Shrew*', *Ball State University Forum*, xx, no. 3 (1979), 16–22.

BARROLL, J. L., 'Shakespeare's Other Ovid: A Reproduction of Commentary on Metamorphoses I–IV', *Shakespeare Studies*, iii (1967), 173–256.

BARTLETT, PHYLLIS, 'Ovid's "Banquet of Sense"?', *N&Q* cxcvii (1952), 46–7.

BATE, JONATHAN, 'Ovid and the Sonnets; or, Did Shakespeare Feel The Anxiety of Influence?', *ShS* xlii (1990), 65–76.

BAYNES, T. S., 'What Shakespeare Learnt at School', in his *Shakespeare Studies and other Essays* (1894), 147–249.

BERGGREN, PAULA, ' "From a God to a Bull": Shakespeare's Slumming Jove', *Classical and Modern Literature*, v (1985), 277–91.

BINNS, J. W. (ed.), *Ovid* (1973).

BOAS, F. S., *Aspects of Classical Legend and History in Shakespeare* (1944).

—— *Ovid and the Elizabethans* (1947).

BOLGAR, R. R., *The Classical Heritage and its Beneficiaries* (Cambridge, 1954).

BONO, BARBARA J., *Literary Transvaluation: From Vergilian Epic to Shakespearean Tragicomedy* (Berkeley, Calif., 1984).

BOOTH, STEPHEN, *An Essay on Shakespeare's Sonnets* (New Haven, Conn., 1969).

—— (ed.), *Shakespeare's Sonnets* (New Haven, Conn., 1977).

BRADBROOK, M. C., *Shakespeare and Elizabethan Poetry* (1951).

—— 'Beasts and Gods: Greene's *Groats-Worth of Witte* and the Social Purpose of *Venus and Adonis*', *ShS* xv (1962), 62–72.

BRADEN, GORDON, *The Classics and English Renaissance Poetry: Three Case Studies*, Yale Studies in English 187 (New Haven, Conn., 1978).

—— *Renaissance Tragedy and the Senecan Tradition* (New Haven, Conn., 1985).

BREWER, WILMON, *Ovid's Metamorphoses in European Culture* (3 vols., Francestown, NH, 1933–57).

BROOKS, HAROLD, '*Richard III*: Antecedents of Clarence's Dream', *ShS* xxxii (1979), 145–50.

BROWER, R. A., 'The Mirror of Analogy: *The Tempest*', in his *The Fields of Light: An Experiment in Critical Reading* (1951), 95–122.

—— *Hero and Saint: Shakespeare and the Graeco-Roman Heroic Tradition* (Oxford, 1971).

BULLOUGH, GEOFFREY (ed.), *Narrative and Dramatic Sources of Shakespeare* (8 vols., 1957–75).

BUSH, DOUGLAS, *Mythology and the Renaissance Tradition in English Poetry* (1932; rev. edn., New York, 1963).

—— 'Classical Myth in Shakespeare's Plays', in *Elizabethan and Jacobean*

Studies Presented to F. P. Wilson, ed. H. Davis and H. Gardner (Oxford, 1959), 65–85.

—— *Prefaces to Renaissance Literature* (New York, 1964).

CANTELUPE, E. B., 'An Iconographical Interpretation of *Venus and Adonis*, Shakespeare's Ovidian Comedy', *SQ* xiv (1963), 141–51.

CARLSEN, HANNE, '"What fools these mortals be!": Ovid in *A Midsummer Night's Dream*', in *A Literary Miscellany Presented to Eric Jacobsen*, ed. G. D. Caie and Holger Nørgaard (Copenhagen, 1988), 94–107.

CARROLL, WILLIAM C., *The Great Feast of Language in 'Love's Labour's Lost'* (Princeton, NJ, 1976).

—— *The Metamorphoses of Shakespearean Comedy* (Princeton, NJ, 1985).

CAVE, TERENCE, *The Cornucopian Text: Problems of Writing in the French Renaissance* (Oxford, 1979).

CHAMBERS, E. K., *William Shakespeare: A Study of Facts and Problems* (2 vols., Oxford, 1930).

CHARLTON, H. B., *The Senecan Tradition in Renaissance Tragedy* (1921; repr. Manchester, 1946).

COLIE, ROSALIE L., *Shakespeare's Living Art* (Princeton, NJ, 1974).

CONLEY, C. H., *The First English Translators of the Classics* (New Haven, Conn., 1927).

COOPER, C. B., *Some Elizabethan Opinions of the Poetry and Character of Ovid* (Menasha, Wis., 1914).

CREIZENACH, W., 'Shakespeare und Ovid', *Jahrbuch der Deutsche Shakespeare-Gesellschaft*, xli (1905), 211.

CURTIUS, E. R., *European Literature and the Latin Middle Ages*, trans. W. R. Trask (New York, 1953).

CUTTS, J. P. '"Till Birnam Forest come to Dunsinane"', *SQ* xxi (1970), 497–9.

DAVENPORT, ARNOLD, 'Weever, Ovid and Shakespeare', *N&Q* cxciv (1949), 524–5.

DAVIDSON, CLIFFORD, 'Timon of Athens: The Iconography of False Friendship', *HLQ* xliii (1980), 181–200.

DEAN, JOHN, *Restless Wanderers: Shakespeare and the Pattern of Romance* (Salzburg, 1979).

DEAN, PAUL, '*Antony and Cleopatra*: An Ovidian Tragedy?', *Cahiers Elisabéthains*, xl (1991), 73–7.

DICKENS, BRUCE, '"Pythagoras concerning Wild-Fowle": (*Twelfth Night*, IV. ii. 52–58)', *MLR* xx (1925), 186.

—— 'Two Queries on *Twelfth Night*', *MLR* xxix (1934), 67.

DiMATTIO, ANTHONY, '"The Figure of this Harpy": Shakespeare and the Moralized Ovid', *N&Q* ns xxxviii (1991), 70–2.

DONALDSON, IAN, *The Rapes of Lucretia: A Myth and its Transformations* (Oxford, 1982)

DONNO, ELIZABETH STORY (ed.), *Elizabethan Minor Epics* (1963).

DORAN, MADELAINE, *Endeavors of Art: A Study of Form in Elizabethan Drama* (Madison, Wis., 1954).

—— 'Some Renaissance "Ovids" ' ', in *Literature and Society*, ed. Bernice Slote (Lincoln, Nebr., 1964), 44–62.

DRAPER, R. P., 'Timon of Athens', *SQ* viii (1957), 195–200.

DREXLER, R. D., 'Ovid and *The Tempest*', *N&Q* NS xxviii (1981), 144–5.

DUBROW, HEATHER, *Captive Victors: Shakespeare's Narrative Poems and Sonnets* (Ithaca, NY, 1987).

DUNCAN-JONES, E. E., 'Hermione in Ovid and Shakespeare', *N&Q* NS xiii (1966), 138–9.

DUNCAN-JONES, KATHERINE, 'Pyramus and Thisbe: Shakespeare's Debt to Moffett Cancelled', *RES* xxxii (1981), 296–301.

DUNDAS, JUDITH, 'Wat the Hare, or Shakespearean Decorum', *Shakespeare Studies*, xix (1987), 1–15.

DUROCHER, RICHARD J., *Milton and Ovid* (Ithaca, NY, 1985).

EAGLE, R. L., 'Shakespeare's Learned Ladies', *N&Q* NS v (1958), 197.

FAIRCHILD, A. H. R., *Shakespeare and the Arts of Design* (Columbia, Mo., 1937).

FARMER, RICHARD, *An Essay on the Learning of Shakespeare* (Cambridge, 1767).

FEUILLERAT, A., *John Lyly: Contribution à l'histoire de la Renaissance en Angleterre* (Cambridge, 1910).

FINDLAY, L. M., 'Enriching Echoes: Hamlet and Orpheus', *MLN* xciii (1978), 982–9.

FORREST, J. F., ' "Blocks" and "Stones" in *Julius Caesar*', *N&Q* NS xx (1973), 134–5.

FRAENKEL, HERMANN, *Ovid: A Poet between Two Worlds* (Berkeley and Los Angeles, 1945).

FRIEDMANN, A. E., 'The Diana–Actaeon Episode in Ovid's *Metamorphoses* and the *Faerie Queene*', *CL* xviii (1966), 289–99.

FRIPP, E. I., 'Shakespeare—Boy and Man', *The Shakespeare Review*, i (1928), 239–48.

—— 'Shakespeare's Use of Ovid's *Metamorphoses*', in his *Shakespeare Studies, Biographical and Literary* (1930), 98–128.

—— 'His Ovid's *Metamorphoses*', in his *Shakespeare: Man and Artist* (2 vols., 1938), i. 102–14.

FRYE, NORTHROP, *A Natural Perspective* (New York, 1965).

FYLER, J. M., *Chaucer and Ovid* (New Haven, Conn., 1979).

GALINSKY, G. KARL, *Ovid's Metamorphoses* (Oxford, 1975).

GARBER, M. B., *Dream in Shakespeare: From Metaphor to Metamorphosis* (New Haven, Conn., 1974).

GARTON, CHARLES, 'Centaurs, the Sea, and *The Comedy of Errors*', *Arethusa*, xii (1979), 233–54.

GIBBONS, BRIAN, ' "Unstable Proteus": Marlowe's "The Tragedy of Dido

Queen of Carthage"', in *Christopher Marlowe*, ed. Brian Morris, Mermaid Critical Commentaries (1968), 25–46.

GILLIES, JOHN, 'Shakespeare's Virginian Masque', *ELH* liii (1986), 673–707.

GOLDING, L. T., *An Elizabethan Puritan: Arthur Golding the Translator of Ovid's Metamorphoses and also of John Calvin's Sermons* (New York, 1937).

GRAFTON, ANTHONY, and JARDINE, LISA, *From Humanism to the Humanities* (1986).

GRAS, HENK, '*Twelfth Night*, *Every Man out of his Humour*, and the Middle Temple Revels of 1597–98', *MLR* lxxxiv (1989), 545–64.

GREENE, THOMAS M., *The Light in Troy: Imitation and Discovery in Renaissance Poetry* (New Haven, Conn., 1982).

GUILLORY, JOHN, *Poetic Authority: Spenser, Milton, and Literary History* (New York, 1983).

HAMILTON, DONNA B., *Virgil and 'The Tempest': The Politics of Imitation* (Columbus, Ohio, 1990).

HANKINS, J. E., 'Suicide in Shakespeare', in his *The Character of Hamlet and other Essays* (Durham, NC, 1941), 222–39.

—— '"The Penalty of Adam"—*As You Like It*, II. i. 5', in *Shakespearean Essays*, ed. A. Thaler and N. Sanders, Tennessee Studies in Literature Special No. 2 (Knoxville, Tenn., 1964), 41–3.

HARDING, D. P., *Milton and the Renaissance Ovid* (Urbana, Ill., 1946).

HARDISON, O. B., 'Myth and History in *King Lear*', *SQ* xxvi (1975), 227–42.

HARRISON, T. P., Jr, 'Aspects of Primitivism in Shakespeare and Spenser', *University of Texas Studies in English*, xx (1940), 39–71.

HARVEY, GABRIEL, *Marginalia*, ed. G. C. Moore Smith (Stratford-upon-Avon, 1913).

HERBERT, T. W., *Oberon's Mazèd World* (Baton Rouge, La., 1977).

HERPICH, C. A., '"The Penalty of Adam": *As You Like It*, II. i. 10', *N&Q* ii (1904), 524.

HIGDON, D. L., 'Shakespeare's *King Richard III*, v. ii. 7–11', *Explicator*, xxxiii, no. 1 (1974), item 2.

HIGHET, GILBERT, *The Classical Tradition: Greek and Roman Influences on Western Literature* (Oxford, 1949).

HOLAHAN, M. N., '"Iamque opus exegi": Ovid's Changes and Spenser's Brief Epic of Mutability', *ELR* vi (1976), 244–70.

HOLMER, J. O., 'Othello's Threnos: "Arabian Trees" and "Indian" versus "Judean"', *Shakespeare Studies*, xiii (1980), 145–67.

HONIGMANN, E. A. J., 'Secondary Sources of *The Winter's Tale*', *PQ* xxxiv (1955), 27–38.

HUEBERT, RONALD, 'Levels of Parody in *The Merry Wives of Windsor*', *English Studies in Canada*, iii (1977), 136–52.

HULSE, CLARK, *Metamorphic Verse: The Elizabethan Minor Epic* (Princeton, NJ, 1981).

HUNT, MAURICE, 'Compelling Art in *Titus Andronicus*', *SEL* xxviii (1988), 197–218.

HUNTER, G. K., *John Lyly : The Humanist as Courtier* (Cambridge, Mass., 1962).

—— 'Seneca and the Elizabethans: A Case-Study in "Influence"', *ShS* xx (1967), 17–26.

—— 'Sources and Meanings in *Titus Andronicus*', in *The Mirror up to Shakespeare*, ed. J. C. Gray (Toronto, 1983), 171–88.

—— 'The "Sources" of *Titus Andronicus*—Once Again', *N&Q* ns xxx (1983), 114–16.

JAMES, HEATHER, 'Cultural Disintegration in *Titus Andronicus*: Mutilating Titus, Vergil and Rome', in *Violence in Drama, Themes in Drama*, xiii (1991), 123–40.

JAVITCH, DANIEL, 'The *Orlando Furioso* and Ovid's Revision of the *Aeneid*', *MLN* xcix (1984), 1023–36.

JED, STEPHANIE H., *Chaste Thinking : The Rape of Lucretia and the Birth of Humanism* (Bloomington, Ind., 1989).

JONES, EMRYS, *The Origins of Shakespeare* (Oxford, 1977).

JOSEPH, MIRIAM, *Shakespeare's Use of the Arts of Language* (New York, 1949).

KAUL, R. K., 'Lodge, Shakespeare, and the Olde Daunce', *Literary Criterion* (Mysore), vi, no. 1 (1963), 19–28.

KEACH, WILLIAM, *Elizabethan Erotic Narratives : Irony and Pathos in the Ovidian Poetry of Shakespeare, Marlowe and their Contemporaries* (New Brunswick, NJ, and Hassocks, 1977).

KERMODE, J. F., *Shakespeare, Spenser, Donne : Renaissance Essays* (1971).

KERRIGAN, JOHN (ed.), *Motives of Woe : Shakespeare and 'Female Complaint' : A Critical Anthology* (Oxford, 1991).

KLOSE, DIETRICH, 'Shakespeare und Ovid', *Deutsche Shakespeare-Gesellschaft West Jahrbuch* (Heidelberg, 1968), 72–93.

KNAPP, PEGGY ANN, 'The Orphic Vision of *Pericles*', *TSLL* xv (1974), 615–26.

KNOESPEL, KENNETH J., *Narcissus and the Invention of Personal History* (New York, 1985).

KOPPENFELS, WERNER VON, 'Lust in Action: ber einige Metamorphosen Ovids in der elisabethischen Literatur', *Shakespeare-Jahrbuch* (East), cxxv (1989), 242–65.

KOTT, JAN, *The Bottom Translation* (Chicago, 1987).

LAMB, M. E., '*A Midsummer Night's Dream*: The Myth of Theseus and Minotaur', *TSLL* xxi (1979), 478–91.

—— 'Ovid's *Metamorphoses* and Shakespeare's *Twelfth Night*', in *Shakespearean Comedy*, ed. Maurice Charney, New York Literary Forum Special Issue (1980), 63–77.

—— 'Ovid and *The Winter's Tale*: Conflicting Views Toward Art', in *Shakespeare and Dramatic Tradition : Essays in Honor of S. F. Johnson*, ed. W. R. Elton and W. B. Long (Newark, Del., 1989), 69–87.

LANHAM, R. A., *The Motives of Eloquence: Literary Rhetoric in the Renaissance* (New Haven, Conn., 1976).

LAROQUE, FRANÇOIS, 'A New Ovidian Source for the Statue Scene in *The Winter's Tale*', *N&Q* ns xxxi (1984), 215–17.

—— 'Ovidian Transformations and Folk Festivities in *A Midsummer Night's Dream*, *The Merry Wives of Windsor* and *As You Like It*', *Cahiers Elisabéthains*, xxv (1984), 23–36.

—— 'Métaphore et métamorphose dans *A Midsummer Night's Dream*, *The Merry Wives of Windsor* et *As You Like It*', in *Actes du Congrès d'Amiens, 1982*, Études Anglaises, xciv (Paris, 1987), 91–108.

LATHROP, H. B., *Translation from the Classics into English from Caxton to Chapman, 1477–1620* (Madison, Wis., 1933).

LEE, SIDNEY, 'Ovid and Shakespeare's Sonnets', in his *Elizabethan and other Essays* (Oxford, 1929), 116–39.

LEISHMAN, J. B. (ed.), *The Three Parnassus Plays* (1949).

—— *Themes and Variations in Shakespeare's Sonnets* (1961).

LEO, F. A., 'Shakespeares Ovid in der Bodleian Library zu Oxford', *Jahrbuch der Deutsche Shakespeare-Gesellschaft*, xvi (1881), 367–75.

LEVER, J. W., *The Elizabethan Love Sonnet* (1956).

LEVIN, HARRY, *The Myth of the Golden Age in the Renaissance* (New York, 1969).

LIM, C. S., 'An Ovidian Source for Othello's Success in Love (I. iii. 128–67)', *N&Q* ns xxxix (1983), 127.

LOEWENSTEIN, JOSEPH, *Responsive Readings: Versions of Echo in Pastoral, Epic, and the Jonsonian Masque* (New Haven, Conn., 1984).

LONGO, JOSEPH A., 'Myth in *A Midsummer Night's Dream*', *Cahiers Elisabéthains*, xviii (1980), 17–27.

LOTSPEICH, H. G., *Classical Mythology in the Poetry of Edmund Spenser* (Princeton, NJ, 1932).

LYONS, JOHN D., *Exemplum: The Rhetoric of Example in Early Modern France and Italy* (Princeton, NJ, 1989).

MAHON, JOHN W., 'Perdita's Reference to Proserpina in Act IV of *The Winter's Tale*', *N&Q* xxxi (1984), 214–15.

MARTINDALE, CHARLES (ed.), *Ovid Renewed: Ovidian Influences on Literature and Art from the Middle Ages to the Twentieth Century* (Cambridge, 1988).

—— and MICHELLE, *Shakespeare and the Uses of Antiquity: An Introductory Essay* (1990)

MEISSNER, PAUL, 'Das Goldene Zeitalter in der Englischen Renaissance', *Anglia*, lix (1935), 351–67.

MERRIX, ROBERT P., 'The Phaëton Allusion in *Richard II*: The Search for Identity', *ELR* xvii (1987), 277–87.

MILLER, PAUL ALLEN, 'Sidney, Petrarch, and Ovid, or Imitation as Subversion', *ELH* lviii (1991), 499–522.

MILLER, P. W., 'The Elizabethan Minor Epic', *SP* lv (1958), 31–8. But see also Walter Allen, Jr., 'The Non-Existent Classical Epyllion', ibid. 515–18.

MIOLA, ROBERT S., '*Titus Andronicus* and the Mythos of Shakespeare's Rome', *Shakespeare Studies*, xiv (1981), 85–98.

—— *Shakespeare's Rome* (Cambridge, 1983).

—— 'Vergil in Shakespeare: From Allusion to Imitation', in *Vergil at 2000: Commemorative Essays on the Poet and his Influence*, ed. John D. Bernard (New York, 1986), 241–58.

—— *Shakespeare and Classical Tragedy: The Influence of Seneca* (Oxford, 1992).

MOSS, ANN, *Ovid in Renaissance France: A Survey of the Latin Editions of Ovid and Commentaries printed in France before 1660* (1982).

—— *Poetry and Fable: Studies in Mythological Narrative in Sixteenth-Century France* (Cambridge, 1984).

MOWAT, BARBARA A., 'Lavinia's Message: Shakespeare and Myth', *Renaissance Papers 1981* (1982), 55–69.

MUELLER, MARTIN, 'Hermione's Wrinkles, or, Ovid Transformed: An Essay on *The Winter's Tale*', *Comparative Drama*, v (1971), 226–39.

MUIR, KENNETH, 'Pyramus and Thisbe: A Study in Shakespeare's Method', *SQ* v (1954), 141–53. But see also K. Duncan-Jones, above.

—— *The Sources of Shakespeare's Plays* (1977).

MULVIHILL, JAMES D., 'Jonson's *Poetaster* and the Ovidian Debate', *SEL* xxii (1982), 239–55.

NASS, BARRY, ' "Of one that loved not wisely, but too well": *Othello* and the *Heroides*', *ELN* xix (1981), 102–4.

NEVO, RUTH, *Comic Transformations in Shakespeare* (1980).

NIMS, J. F., Introduction to *Ovid's 'Metamorphoses': The Arthur Golding Translation* (New York, 1965).

NOHRNBERG, JAMES, *The Analogy of The Faerie Queene* (Princeton, NJ, 1976).

NOSWORTHY, J. M., 'Shakespeare's Pastoral *Metamorphoses*', in *The Elizabethan Theatre VIII*, ed. G. R. Hibbard (Port Credit, Ontario, 1982), 90–113.

ORGEL, STEPHEN, *The Illusion of Power* (Berkeley and Los Angeles, 1975).

OTIS, BROOKS, *Ovid as an Epic Poet* (2nd edn., Cambridge, 1970).

OWEN, S. G., 'Ovid and Romance', in *English Literature and the Classics*, ed. G. S. Gordon (Oxford, 1912), 167–95.

PALMATIER, M. A., 'A Suggested New Source in Ovid's *Metamorphoses* for Shakespeare's *Venus and Adonis*', *HLQ* xxiv (1961), 163–9.

PALMER, D. J., '*Twelfth Night* and the Myth of Echo and Narcissus', *ShS* xxxii (1979), 73–8.

PANOFSKY, ERWIN, *Studies in Iconology: Humanistic Themes in the Art of the Renaissance* (1939; repr. 1972).

PEARCY, LEE T., *The Mediated Muse: English Translations of Ovid 1560–1700* (Hamden, Conn., 1984).

PEYRÉ, YVES, 'Les "Masques" d'Ariel: Essai d'interprétation de leur symbolisme', *Cahiers Elisabéthains*, xix (1981), 53–71.

PIGMAN, G. W., III, 'Versions of Imitation in the Renaissance', *RenQ* xxxiii (1980), 1–32.

PITCHER, JOHN, 'A Theatre of the Future: *The Aeneid* and *The Tempest*', *Essays in Criticism*, xxxiv (1984), 193–215.

POISSON, RODNEY, '*Coriolanus* I. vi. 21–24', *SQ* xv (1964), 449–50.

PRESSON, R. K., *Shakespeare's Troilus and Cressida and the Legends of Troy* (Madison, Wis., 1953).

PUTNEY, RUFUS, '*Venus and Adonis*: Amour with Humor', *PQ* xx (1941), 533–48.

—— 'Venus Agonistes', *University of Colorado Studies*, iv (1953), 52–66.

RAND, E. K., *Ovid and his Influence* (Boston, 1925).

RICK, L., *Ovids Metamorphosen in der englischen Renaissance* (Münster, 1915).

—— 'Shakespeare und Ovid', *Jahrbuch der Deutsche Shakespeare-Gesellschaft*, lv (1919), 35–53.

RICO, B. R., 'From "Speechless Dialect" to "Prosperous Art": Shakespeare's Recasting of the Pygmalion Image', *HLQ* xlviii (1985), 285–95.

RIEHLE, WOLFGANG, *Shakespeare, Plautus and the Humanist Tradition* (Woodbridge, 1991).

RINGLER, RICHARD N., 'The Faunus Episode', *MP* lxiii (1965), 12–19.

ROBERTS, J. A., 'Animals as Agents of Revelation: The Horizontalizing of the Chain of Being in Shakespeare's Comedies', in *Shakespearean Comedy*, ed. Maurice Charney, New York Literary Forum Special Issue (1980), 79–96.

—— 'Horses and Hermaphrodites: Metamorphoses in *The Taming of the Shrew*', *SQ* xxxiv (1983), 159–71.

ROBERTSON, JEAN, 'Macbeth on Sleep: "Sore Labour's Bath" and Sidney's *Astrophil and Stella*, xxxix', *N&Q* NS xiv (1967), 139–41.

ROOT, R. K., *Classical Mythology in Shakespeare* (New York, 1903).

ROSENBERG, ELEANOR, *Leicester: Patron of Letters* (New York, 1955).

ROUSE, W. H. D., Introduction to *Shakespeare's Ovid being Arthur Golding's Translation of the Metamorphoses* (1904; repr. 1961).

RUDD, NIALL, 'Pyramus and Thisbe in Shakespeare and Ovid: *A Midsummer Night's Dream* and *Metamorphoses* 4.1–166', in *Creative Imitation and Latin Literature*, ed. David West and Tony Woodman (Cambridge, 1979), 173–93.

—— '*The Taming of the Shrew*: Notes on some Classical Allusions', *Hermathena*, cxxix (Winter 1980), 23–8.

RUEGG, AUGUST, 'Caliban und Miranda', *Shakespeare Jahrbuch*, lxxxix (1953), 128–31.

SALINGAR, LEO, *Shakespeare and the Traditions of Comedy* (Cambridge, 1974).

SCHANZER, ERNEST, 'Heywood's *Ages* and Shakespeare', *RES* NS xi (1960), 18–28.

SCHMITT-VON MUHLENFALS, FRANZ, *Pyramus und Thisbe: Rezeptionstypen eines Ovidischen Stoffes in Literatur, Kunst und Musik* (Heidelberg, 1972).

SCRAGG, LEAH, 'Shakespeare, Lyly and Ovid: The influence of *Gallathea* on *A Midsummer Night's Dream*', *ShS* xxx (1977), 125–34.

—— *The Metamorphoses of Gallathea: A Study in Creative Adaptation* (Washington, DC, 1982).

SEDGWICK, W. B., 'The Influence of Ovid', *The Nineteenth Century*, cxxii (1937), 483–94.

SHACKFORD, M. H., '*Julius Caesar* and Ovid', *MLN* xli (1926), 172–4.

SHULMAN, JEFF, 'At the Crossroads of Myth: The Hermeneutics of Hercules from Ovid to Shakespeare', *ELH* l (1983), 83–105.

—— 'Ovidian Myth in Lyly's Courtship Comedies', *SEL* xxv (1985), 249–69.

SIMPSON, PERCY, 'Shakespeare's Use of Latin Authors', in his *Studies in Elizabethan Drama* (Oxford, 1955), 1–63.

SLIGHTS, W. W. E., ' "Maid and Man" in *Twelfth Night*', *JEGP* lxxx (1981), 327–48.

SMITH, BRUCE, *Ancient Scripts and Modern Experience on the English Stage* (Princeton, NJ, 1988).

—— *Homosexual Desire in Shakespeare's England* (Chicago, 1991).

SMITH, G. GREGORY (ed.), *Elizabethan Critical Essays* (2 vols., Oxford, 1904).

SMITH, HALLETT, *Elizabethan Poetry: A Study in Conventions, Meaning, and Expression* (Cambridge, Mass., 1952).

SPENCER, HAZELTON, 'Shakespeare's Use of Golding in *Venus and Adonis*', *MLN* xliv (1929), 435–7.

SPENCER, TERENCE, 'Shakespeare's Isle of Delphos', *MLR*, xlvii (1952), 199–202.

SPINGARN, J. E. (ed.), *Critical Essays of the Seventeenth Century*, vol. i [1605–50] (Oxford, 1908).

STANTON, KAY, 'Shakespeare's Use of Marlowe in *As You Like It*', in *'A Poet and Filthy Play-Maker': New Essays on Christopher Marlowe*, ed. Kenneth Friedenreich, Roma Gill, and C. B. Kuriyama (New York, 1988), 23–35.

STARNES, D. T., 'Sonnet 60: Analogies', *N&Q* cxciv (1949), 454.

—— 'Actaeon's Dogs', *Names*, iii (1955), 19–25.

—— and TALBERT, E. W., *Classical Myth and Legend in Renaissance Dictionaries* (Chapel Hill, NC, 1955).

STATON, W. F., Jr., 'Ovidian Elements in *A Midsummer Night's Dream*', *HLQ* xxvi (1962–3), 165–76.

STEADMAN, J. M., ' "Perseus upon Pegasus" and Ovid Moralized', *RES* ix (1958), 407–10.

—— 'Falstaff as Actaeon: A Dramatic Emblem', *SQ* xiv (1963), 230–44.

—— *Nature into Myth: Medieval and Renaissance Moral Symbols* (Pittsburgh, 1979).

STEVENSON, D. L., *The Love-Game Comedy* (New York, 1946).

SUZUKI, MIHOKO, '"Truth tired with iteration": Myth and Fiction in Shakespeare's *Troilus and Cressida*', *PQ* lxvi (1987), 153–74.

TAYLOR, A. B., 'Shakespeare and the Apes', *N&Q* ns xvi (1969), 144–5.

—— 'Shakespeare's Ovid: Golding's *Metamorphoses* and Two Minor Elizabethan Writers', *N&Q* ns xxiv (1977), 133–4.

—— 'Shakespeare and Golding: Viola's Interview with Olivia and Echo and Narcissus', *ELN* xv (1977), 103–6.

—— 'Golding's *Metamorphoses* and *Titus Andronicus*', *N&Q* ns xxv (1978), 117–20.

—— 'The Non-Existent Carbuncles: Shakespeare, Golding, and Raphael Regius', *N&Q* ns xxxii (1985), 54–5.

—— '"O brave new world": Abraham Fraunce and *The Tempest*', *ELN* xxiii (1986), 18–23.

—— 'The Elizabethan Seneca and Two Notes on Shakespeare and Spenser', *N&Q* ns xxxiv (1987), 193–5.

—— '"The fellies, spokes, and knaves of Fortune's wheel": A Debt to Arthur Golding in *Hamlet*', *ELN* xxv (1987), 18–20.

—— '"Wash they his wounds with tears?": Shakespeare's Discriminate Reading of Golding', *N&Q* ns xxxv (1988), 52.

—— 'Shakespeare's Use of Golding's Ovid as Source for *Titus Andronicus*, *N&Q* ns xxxv (1988), 449–51.

—— 'Shakespeare, Studley, and Golding', *RES* xxxix (1988), 522–7.

—— 'Chaucer's Non-Involvement in "Pyramus and Thisbe"', *N&Q* ns xxxvi (1989), 317–20.

—— 'Golding's Ovid, Shakespeare's "Small Latin", and the Real Object of Mockery in "Pyramus and Thisbe"', *ShS* xlii (1990), 53–64.

—— 'Shakespeare and Golding', *N&Q* ns xxxviii (1991), 492–9.

—— 'Arthur Golding and the Elizabethan Progress of Actaeon's Dogs', *Connotations*, i (1991), 207–23.

THOMPSON, ANN, 'Philomel in *Titus Andronicus* and *Cymbeline*', *ShS* xxxi (1978), 23–32.

THOMSON, J. A. K., *Shakespeare and the Classics* (1952).

TILLEY, M. P., '*Euphues* and *Ovid's Heroical Epistles*', *MLN* xlv (1930), 301–8.

TOBIN, J. J. M., *Shakespeare's Favourite Novel: A Study of 'The Golden Asse' as Prime Source* (Lanham, Md., 1984).

TRICOMI, A. H., 'The Aesthetics of Mutilation in *Titus Andronicus*', *ShS* xxvii (1974), 11–19.

TROUSDALE, MARION, 'Recurrence and Renaissance: Rhetorical Imitation in Ascham and Sturm', *ELR* vi (1976), 156–79.

—— *Shakespeare and the Rhetoricians* (Chapel Hill, NC, 1982).

VAN EMDEM, WOLFGANG, 'Shakespeare and the French Pyramus and Thisbe Tradition, or Whatever Happened to Robin Starveling's Part', *Forum for Modern Language Studies*, xi (1975), 193–204.

VELZ, J. W., *Shakespeare and the Classical Tradition: A Critical Guide to Commentary 1660–1960* (Minneapolis, 1968).

—— 'The Ovidian Soliloquy in Shakespeare', *Shakespeare Studies*, xviii (1986), 1–24.

VICKERS, NANCY J., 'Diana Described: Scattered Woman and Scattered Rhyme', *Critical Inquiry*, viii (1981–2), 265–79.

—— ' "The blazon of sweet beauty's best": Shakespeare's *Lucrece*', in *Shakespeare and the Question of Theory*, ed. Patricia Parker and Geoffrey Hartman (New York, 1985), 95–115.

WADDINGTON, RAYMOND B., *The Mind's Empire: Myth and Form in George Chapman's Narrative Poems* (Baltimore, 1974).

WAITH, E. M., 'The Metamorphosis of Violence in Titus Andronicus', *ShS* x (1957), 39–49.

—— *The Herculean Hero in Marlowe, Chapman, Shakespeare and Dryden* (1962).

WARREN, ROGER, 'Prospero's Renunciation and Coriolanus's Capitulation', *N&Q* NS xxi (1974), 134–6.

—— 'Trembling Aspen Leaves in *Titus Andronicus* and Golding's Ovid', *N&Q* NS xxix (1982), 112.

—— *Shakespeare in Performance: Cymbeline* (Manchester, 1989).

WATKINS, W. B. C., *Shakespeare and Spenser* (Princeton, NJ, 1950).

WEST, G. S., 'Going by the Book: Classical Allusions in Shakespeare's *Titus Andronicus*', *SP* lxxix (1982), 62–77.

WHITAKER, V. K., *Shakespeare's Use of Learning* (San Marino, 1953).

WHITTIER, GAYLE, 'The Sublime Androgyne Motif in Three Shakespearian Works', *JMRS* xix (1989), 185–210.

WIGGINGTON, WALLER B., ' "One way like a Gorgon": An Explication of *Antony and Cleopatra*, II. v. 116–17', *Papers on Language and Literature*, xvi (1980), 366–75.

WILKINSON, L. P., *Ovid Recalled* (Cambridge, 1955).

WILLIAMS, GORDON, 'The Coming of Age of Shakespeare's Adonis', *MLR* lxxviii (1983), 769–76.

WILLIAMS, W. H., 'Shakespeare, *King Lear*, IV. vi. 70–2', *MLR* vi (1911), 88. But see also W. W. Skeat, ibid. 209–10.

WILLSON, R. F., Jr., 'Golding's *Metamorphoses* and Shakespeare's Burlesque Method in *A Midsummer Night's Dream*', *ELN* vii (1969), 18–25.

WILSON, J. DOVER, 'Shakespeare's "Small Latin"—How Much?', *ShS* x (1957), 12–26.

WILTENBURG, ROBERT, 'The Aeneid in *The Tempest*', *ShS* xxxix (1987), 159–68.

WIND, EDGAR, *Pagan Mysteries in the Renaissance* (1958).

WOOD, J. O., ' "Fillet of a Fenny Snake" ', *N&Q* NS xii (1965), 332–3.

—— 'Lady Macbeth's Suckling', *N&Q* NS xiii (1966), 138.

YATES, FRANCES A., *Shakespeare's Last Plays* (1975).

YOUNG, DAVID, *Something of Great Constancy : The Art of 'A Midsummer Night's Dream'* (New Haven, Conn., 1966).

—— *The Heart's Forest: A Study of Shakespeare's Pastoral Plays* (New Haven, Conn., 1972).

ZIELINSKI, T., 'Marginalien', *Philologicus*, lxiv (1905), 17–19.

ZITNER, S. P., 'Gosson, Ovid, and the Elizabethan Audience', *SQ* ix (1958), 206–8.

—— 'Iago as Melampus', *SQ* xxiii (1972), 263–4.

Index

Myths treated in the *Metamorphoses* and *Heroides* are listed under Ovid, with references to the Latin text.